Hermeneutics between
History and Philosophy

Also available from Bloomsbury

Ancient Sources, Modern Appropriations, Hans-Georg Gadamer
The Beginning of Knowledge, Hans-Georg Gadamer
Beginning of Philosophy, Hans-Georg Gadamer
A Century of Philosophy, Hans-Georg Gadamer
Hermeneutics between History and Philosophy, Hans-Georg Gadamer
Truth and Method, Hans-Georg Gadamer

Forthcoming from Bloomsbury

*Ethics and Aesthetics in History: The Selected Writings of
Hans-Georg Gadamer: Volume II*, Hans-Georg Gadamer

Hermeneutics between History and Philosophy

The Selected Writings of Hans-Georg Gadamer: Volume I

By Hans-Georg Gadamer

Edited and translated by
Pol Vandevelde and Arun Iyer

BLOOMSBURY ACADEMIC

LONDON • NEW YORK • OXFORD • NEW DELHI • SYDNEY

BLOOMSBURY ACADEMIC
Bloomsbury Publishing Plc
50 Bedford Square, London, WC1B 3DP, UK
1385 Broadway, New York, NY 10018, USA

BLOOMSBURY, BLOOMSBURY ACADEMIC and the Diana logo are trademarks of
Bloomsbury Publishing Plc

First published in Great Britain 2016
This edition published 2019

Copyright © Bloomsbury 2019

Pol Vandevelde and Arun Iyer have asserted their right under the Copyright,
Designs and Patents Act, 1988, to be identified as Translators of this work.

A catalogue record for this book is available from the British Library.

A catalog record for this book is available from the Library of Congress.

ISBN: HB: 978-1-4411-5844-4
       PB   978-1-3500-9140-5
       ePDF: 978-1-4742-7499-9
       ePub: 978-1-4742-7500-2

Typeset by Fakenham Prepress Solutions, Fakenham, Norfolk NR21 8NN
Printed and bound in Great Britain

To find out more about our authors and books visit www.bloomsbury.com
and sign up for our newsletters

Contents

Acknowledgements   vii

Translators' Preface   viii

Translators' Introduction: Hermeneutics at the Crossroads between
History and Philosophy   xvi

Part 1 History as a Problem: On Being Historically Affected

1   Is There a Causality in History? (1964)   3

2   Historicity and Truth (1991)   13

3   The History of the Universe and the Historicity of Human
   Beings (1988)   25

4   A World without History? (1972)   43

5   The Old and the New (1981)   51

6   Death as a Question (1975)   59

Part 2 The Impetus for Thinking Hermeneutically: On the Task of Dilthey

7   The Problem of Dilthey: Between Romanticism and Positivism (1984)   73

8   Dilthey and Ortega: The Philosophy of Life (1985)   91

9   Hermeneutics and the Diltheyan School (1991)   103

Part 3 Confronting Other Intellectual Movements and Disciplines

10   Subjectivity and Intersubjectivity, Subject and Person (1975)   125

11   On the Contemporary Relevance of Husserl's Phenomenology (1974)   139

12   'Being and Nothingness' (Jean-Paul Sartre) (1989)   151

13   Heidegger and Sociology: Bourdieu and Habermas (1979/1985)   167

14   Hermeneutics on the Trail (1994)   179

Part 4 Hermeneutics of Beginnings and Returns: The Case of Heidegger

15 Remembering Heidegger's Beginnings (1986)   209

16 The Turn in the Path (1985)   221

17 On the Beginning of Thought (1986)   227

18 On the Way Back to the Beginning (1986)   247

Appendix: Glossary of German Terms   271
Glossary of Latin and Greek Expressions   279
Notes   281
Works Cited by Gadamer   315
Index of Names   329
Index of Subjects   334

Acknowledgements

This edition and translation project started with discussions with David Avital, then editor at Continuum. We benefited from his suggestions and advice for finalizing the project. Sarah Campbell continued to support the project as editor and provided us with her ideas and encouragement. In the transition to Bloomsbury we worked very efficiently with Liza Thompson and her assistant, Frankie Mace.

We also benefited from the advice, suggestions and support of James Risser, Jeff Malpas, and Helmut Gander, to whom we express our gratitude.

Pol Vandevelde received a reduced teaching load during some part of this project thanks to the Way Klingler Humanities Fellowship from Marquette University.

We are grateful to the director and staff of the Deutsche Literatur-Archiv in Marbach where Pol Vandevelde spent several weeks collecting information on Gadamer's essays and where he was able to consult Gadamer's personal library.

We also want to thank Daniel Adsett for his excellent editorial skills, Peter Burgess for his work toward solving queries and bibliographical issues, and Sarah Kizuk for her help with the index. We benefited from the expertise of David Twetten for the Latin and Greek expressions.

Finally, we are also thankful to the Seattle University philosophy department for their material support of this project.

Translators' Preface

When it comes to a major philosopher like Gadamer a strong case can be made that scholars need to have all available essays in order to assess the different components of the philosopher's theses, to measure the evolution of his thought through time, and to grasp all the intricacies of his views in the different contexts of their application. This is the aim of this edition. The present volume is part of a series of three that will, under the title *The Selected Writings of Hans-Georg Gadamer*, complete the English translation of Gadamer's essays, included in his 'Complete Works'.[1]

To date about 130 articles from Gadamer's *Gesammelte Werke* have been translated in various anthologies, collected works and edited volumes. To these we will be adding another fifty essays. Short addresses and book reviews were omitted along with some essays that did not contain anything of philosophical import not already included in the other essays selected. We have organized these fifty articles in three main collections, each corresponding to a volume devoted to a single theme: philosophy of history, ethics, and aesthetics. This division allows us to accentuate the common threads that run across Gadamer's articles despite their covering disparate subjects.

These essays give us a wider range of Gadamer's views than some of his pronouncements in *Truth and Method* and other published books. They help consolidate how Gadamer is viewed in the English-speaking world where he, for the most part, has led a divided existence. We have the independent philosopher of *Truth and Method*. But we also have an original interpreter of ancient philosophy competing with other interpreters from the Anglo-American tradition. Apart from *Truth and Method* and some of his early works on Plato and Aristotle, the later texts of Gadamer have been sporadically translated. This may give the English-speaking reader the skewed impression of there being either nothing much of importance in these essays other than repetitions and reformulations, or of his views changing drastically in his later works. By showcasing Gadamer's works through the whole span of his intellectual life, encompassing his contributions as an independent thinker and an interpreter, this translation shows that his views did not change drastically in the 1980s and the 1990s, but the emphasis he puts on several topics and the nuances he introduces in them sometimes varied to a great extent. These essays collected in three volumes furnish readers with further evidence demonstrating the philosophical significance of his work beyond *Truth and Method* and integrate into a coherent whole the two aspects of Gadamer, as a philosopher and interpreter.

The present first volume, titled *Hermeneutics between History and Philosophy*, contains articles pertaining to reflections that emerge from Gadamer's hermeneutic studies on the problem of history as well as the history of philosophy. As Jean Grondin notes, Gadamer was born in 1900, which is technically the end of the nineteenth century, lived through the whole twentieth century, and died in 2002 in the twenty-first century, thus enjoying a life spread over three centuries.[2] He was an observer of his century and an active participant in it, taking part in all the major philosophical debates, commenting on many of the epoch-making events of his time. More importantly, Gadamer also influenced these new trends and forcefully engaged their proponents, showing how philosophical hermeneutics situates itself in relationship with the work of the Diltheyan School, the existential ontology of Jean-Paul Sartre, sociological critique of Heidegger by Bourdieu and Habermas, the deconstruction of Jacques Derrida, and the new interest in Heidegger's early years. These essays fill the gap in Gadamer's itinerary and indicate interesting twists in his views, changes of heart, significant nuances to views presented elsewhere.

The volume is organized into four sections: I. History as a Problem: On Being Historically Affected; II. The Impetus for Thinking Hermeneutically: On the Task of Dilthey; III. Confronting Other Intellectual Movements and Disciplines; and IV. Hermeneutics of Beginnings and Returns: The Case of Heidegger.

The first section 'History as a Problem: On Being Historically Affected' contains essays that provide a clear glimpse of Gadamer's own intellectual development and how the problem of history, the central motif of *Truth and Method*, assumed such a central place for him. The first essay 'Is There a Causality in History?', written in 1964, shortly after the publication of *Truth and Method*, is a welcome elucidation of what has already been taken up in *Truth and Method*, namely the way human beings experience history and are affected by it. It is the experience expressed by such words as 'destiny' and 'fate', however inchoately. In this essay Gadamer responds to the challenge posed by the natural sciences to any attempt at understanding history in its terms. He tries to salvage our experience of history, which he shows to be very different from the scientist's experience of a causally determined nature. The article is written in the spirit of an invitation for a dialogue with philosophers from the rival tradition of analytic philosophy, who embrace naturalism in some form or other. Many of the articles attempt to reconcile historicity and truth by showing how 'it should even be possible at all to raise claims to truth as thinkers, when we are conscious of our own historical conditioning in any of our attempts to think' (p. 13). The essay 'Historicity and Truth' is dedicated to such a reconciliation, as Gadamer engages with the views of Leo Strauss. The essays 'The History of the Universe and the Historicity of the Human Beings', written in 1988, and 'A World Without History', written in 1972 also take up the same problem of the conflict between scientific naturalism and the experience of history but from a different perspective. These essays are written in the same invitational style wherein a dialogue with philosophers from a rival tradition is not only expected but also welcomed.

Gadamer ends many of his essays with formulations that remind us of the paradox of human existence in its striving for fixed truths and being denied that very fixity by its transient nature. We have nice and touching illustrations of Gadamer's existential sense of paradox in his essays 'The Old and the New' and 'Death as a Question'. In the case of 'The Old and the New' Gadamer shows how the terms 'old' and 'new' have a different sense when applied to things as opposed to human beings, who are not new but young and grow old. The paradox is that old and the new are relative terms, with regard to each other, and provisional descriptions with regard to history: the new can quickly become obsolete or the old rejuvenated in new and fashionable ways. 'Death as a Question' is an article that brings out the intimate relationship between the experience of history and the experience of one's mortality. The notion of historicity always implies a transcendence of individual subjectivity toward an intersubjective community. Gadamer shows the paradox of death as an ending, thus a finality, but with the subsistence of death for those who cultivate the memory of the dead. He expresses the paradox by saying that death is indeed a question even if there is no question that we all will die.

Although indirectly hinted at in *Truth and Method,* all of these themes were never explicitly taken up for reflection. Gadamer's 'philosophical hermeneutics' as presented in *Truth and Method* was of itself a new discipline and a new way of doing philosophy. The essays in this volume add some significant nuances and sometimes corrections to the canonical presentation of 1960. Different from his predecessors, Friedrich Schleiermacher and Wilhelm Dilthey, Gadamer does not see hermeneutics simply as a method of understanding. In the present essays Gadamer brings out in the most clear and rigorous manner all the implications of his thesis that the human being is not just a natural organism, but is more essentially a historically affected consciousness. Given that these articles cover every decade from the 1960s to the 1990s, they also illustrate the development of Gadamer's views from the 1960s, when his magnum opus *Truth and Method* appeared, to the 1990s just before the time of his death, allowing readers to assess the development of Gadamer's views on this subject.

The second section is titled 'The Impetus for Thinking Hermeneutically: On the Task of Dilthey'. It contains three essays on the work of Dilthey, who was one of the earliest thinkers to reflect on the importance of hermeneutics as a method for the social sciences, articulating the difference between explanation, which is the aim of the natural sciences, and understanding, which is the aim of the social sciences. Gadamer shows the tensions and even the conflicts in Dilthey's lifework between the new imperative to focus on the human being's historical situatedness and the ideal of scientificity current at his time. Gadamer takes issue with the common developmental view of Dilthey as a steady advance from psychology toward hermeneutics. Instead, Gadamer argues that Dilthey never quite resolved the conflict between life and scientificity, and that this tension may be intrinsic to historical situatedness itself or what may be called our hermeneutic situation: this situation requires an ever evolving scientificity and can never be plumbed with some finality as a set of states of affairs.

In section III 'Confronting Other Intellectual Movements and Disciplines', we have essays discussing Husserl, Sartre, Bourdieu, Habermas and Derrida. In the two essays on Husserl, Gadamer shows the relevance of Husserl's phenomenology, highlighting its inability to never quite come to grips with the phenomenon of intersubjectivity. He discusses Sartre's magnum opus *Being and Nothingness*, re-evaluating the project of an existential ontology. Gadamer indicates how *Being and Nothingness* offers new insights for understanding negation. Using Heidegger's account of 'nothingness' as a foil, Gadamer shows how the Heideggerean perspective illuminates the originality of Sartre's position on negation and how Sartre's view can in turn make Heidegger's position clearer. The expanded review of both Pierre Bourdieu's book and Jürgen Habermas' chapter on Heidegger allows Gadamer to reformulate Heidegger's ontological views more forcefully and make them relevant against a sociological interpretation that either does not pay attention to the philosophical content of Heidegger's work (Bourdieu) or explains away the specific claims Heidegger makes by reducing them to the play of social and cultural forces in Heidegger's time (Habermas). In 'Hermeneutics on the Trail', Gadamer lays out the similarities and differences between hermeneutics and deconstruction by describing his different encounters with Derrida and trying to understand why Derrida and he never managed to have a true dialogue. He sees the reasons for this in their different deconstructive and hermeneutic projects. This is a remarkable and quite subtle essay that shows Gadamer's skills as an interpreter and debater.

In section IV 'Hermeneutics of Beginnings and Returns: The Case of Heidegger', Gadamer re-examines Heidegger's philosophy from the standpoint of his early work showing how it contains the keys to understanding his late philosophy. Gadamer is extremely well versed in the details, hesitancies, difficulties and breakthroughs that Heidegger went through when seeking his own path, away from his religious beginnings and his Catholic faith, toward a more and more historically minded notion of 'being'. Against the traditional readings of Heidegger as *Heidegger I* becoming *Heidegger II* or the existential Dasein becoming a history of being, Gadamer shows how ambivalent Heidegger's philosophy has always been and that the 'new' discoveries of the history of being were already contemplated by Heidegger himself in his early years. There is thus not just one beginning in Heidegger, but several, fulfilling Husserl's wish for the philosopher to be a constant beginner. There is also not just one single *Kehre*, but many turnings in Heidegger's thought that may not need to be isolated at specific points of his development. For Gadamer argues that his very thought is about turnings and turning is always a return to earlier forms of thought, Plato and Aristotle or the pre-Socratics. These turns, however, are not backward-looking, in an effort to retrieve what may have been occluded, but forward-looking. Instead of rescue operations, these turns in thinking aim at preparing a new way of thinking, the philosophy of the future as a mode of thinking that contributes to the shaping of the future.

Overall, the essays in the present volume confirm in complementary detail and nuances how Gadamer's work served as a transition between the phenomenology of Husserl and Heidegger, on the one hand, and French and Italian contemporary philosophy, on the other. Philosophical hermeneutics is an attempt to reformulate decisively what a human subject is and how it can arrive at an understanding of the world. This amounts to rejecting the view inaugurated by Descartes that the human subject is pure and timeless, thus devoid of tradition, history and world, and simply encounters the object, grasping it with the intellect and providing descriptions of it. It also means rejecting a transcendentally modified version of Descartes as presented by Husserl, for whom the life-world itself remains a feature of the transcendental ego and not a departure from it. Gadamer continues in the present essays to work out the question of what the subject is and what is involved in the very act of understanding. Instead of being a pure subject in the Cartesian sense or a transcendentally enhanced source of validity, the human being is a consciousness that is, as he famously formulated it, exposed to the effects of history (*wirkungsgeschichtliches Bewusstsein*), a new concept he now says he considered provisional, an *ad hoc* remedy, as it were. The subject is a part of history and shaped by it while also in turn shaping history in the very process.

Because the subject is historically situated, the subject's acts of understanding are always historical acts. This means that, instead of being timeless and unchangeable entities, objects are, first and foremost, revealed to the subject as objects only through history and tradition. As a consequence, it is not just the understanding that is historically mediated because of the subject's situatedness in history. The objects themselves are mediated by history and tradition. Understanding involves a stance or a specific position toward the object and it is only through such position-taking that one sees the object 'as' something. This position-taking involved in every attempt at understanding is what is called interpretation. As such, it underlies our most basic relationship to the world around us. As human subjects we are born into a place and time with a history and a tradition, and our understanding involves interpretation, namely starting from this tradition and taking a position toward it. This situation is irreducible for Gadamer in the sense that it is part of our horizon and cannot be eliminated, although it can be elucidated.

In addition, Gadamer's relentless discussion of historicism, through the works of Dilthey, Ortega y Gasset and Heidegger, as well as his discussion of the issues of world history make intelligible the kind of interest he elicited in some American philosophers. John McDowell and Donald Davidson, for example, have either acknowledged the influence of Gadamer's ideas on their work or have found an affinity between his philosophical hermeneutics and their respective programs. McDowell has openly acknowledged the influence of *Truth and Method* on his work *Mind and World*. He writes: 'In *Mind and World* I wrote of a conceptually mediated openness to reality, partly constituted by inheritance of a tradition. My invocation of tradition was inspired by Gadamer.'[3] Donald Davidson reveals the deep affinities between his own work and that of Gadamer when he writes: 'Where Gadamer sensed from the start the goal he would pursue, and pursued it with brilliant success, I by chance started in somewhat the same place (but without the clear goal) and have, by what seems to me a largely accidental but *commodius vicus* of recirculation, arrived in Gadamer's intellectual neighborhood.'[4]

What McDowell and Davidson acknowledge is Gadamer's role in bringing to philosophical prominence the constitutive role history and, by extension, tradition play in human understanding and engagement with the world. The recognition of these roles shows that understanding is not merely our ability to provide descriptions of the world, but that it already presupposes an interpretation of the world. Gadamer has indeed compelled some leading analytic philosophers to take seriously the role that tradition plays in the acquisition of knowledge, as we see in the case of McDowell, or the substantial role of interpretation and translation in human understanding, as we see in the case of Davidson. Gadamer has thus been indirectly responsible for fostering a dialogue in the Anglo-American world between the two rival traditions of analytic and continental philosophy on the nature of understanding and the role of language in arriving at an understanding.

Let us now have a word about Gadamer's style. Gadamer's language displays a tremendous range of vocabulary, sparkling metaphors and idioms, literary allusions, Latin and Greek phrases, and the use of conventional words in a non-conventional sense. We have tried to render the different levels of speech his writings exhibit from the more casual, informal use of language, to sophisticated idiomatic expressions, to the academic style employing highly technical language. For technical terms we have added the original German in square brackets both to indicate the provenance of our translation and to give scholars a consistent basis for following Gadamer's argument and understanding his different plays on words.

In contradistinction to deconstruction, Gadamer has emphasized the role of the speaking voice in the constitution of understanding. For Gadamer, it is not the text with its words on the page, whose meaning is constantly prone to dissemination and dispersion, that constitutes the fundamental site of understanding. Rather, in Gadamer's view, every text is animated by a speaking voice, which is articulated through punctuation and the tone authors render to the text that they set out to write. True to his thinking, Gadamer's articles are articulated in a variety of speaking voices. We have the voice of scholarly authority (in his exegesis of thinkers such as Dilthey, Husserl, Sartre and Heidegger), the voice of free reflection (in essays such as 'Death as a Question', 'Is there a Causality in History?', 'The History of the Universe and the Historicity of Human Beings'), the voice of a concerned citizen (in 'A World Without History?'), or the voice of a biographer (when reconstructing the social milieu in which a given thinker was active).

It is the liveliness of these speaking voices as they emanate from his writings that make him in our view one of the finest essayists of the twentieth century. If we take Montaigne as the standard bearer of the genre of the essay, we see that essays use the particular and the universal as two poles that are moved toward each other in different ratios. They are certainly meant for a universal audience. The essay does not presuppose scholarly erudition on the part of the reader, but at the same time it seeks to draw out from the readers their reflective side. Its goal is to make them think.

The peculiarity of Gadamer's scholarly works on thinkers, who were his contemporaries, consists in his ingenious uses of anecdotes to enliven a theoretical point. He possesses an unmatched skill to weave anecdotes into rigorous philosophical discussion, without compromising its rigour in any way. The anecdotes pertaining to Heidegger's quirks in the classroom, Gadamer's own reception of the correspondence between Count Yorck and Dilthey, his meeting with Jean-Paul Sartre illuminate for us the urgency that these thinkers felt in their work and the extent to which thought is embedded in the warp and woof of everyday expectation, economic turmoil, geo-political shifts, and other overarching phenomena.

Many of Gadamer's essays bear a resemblance to those of Schopenhauer in their style in their constant interweaving of foreign phrases, literary allusions, and the human concerns they deal with. If Schopenhauer's essays speak with a bitter, even mocking pessimism of someone hell-bent on opening the eyes of his reader to the harshest of truths, Gadamer's essays speak with the gentle, soothing voice of the wisdom accumulated over a life long lived. This voice does not refrain from speaking the truth but it is infused with hope and seeks to console and give us hope.

Conventions

We have inserted the pagination of the original German text of the *Gesammelte Werke* in square brackets in the body of the translation. The notes added by the translators are clearly designated as such. For technical terms or words with which Gadamer plays, we have inserted the German words in square brackets. We have provided the broader context to allusions or quotations that Gadamer makes. In order to give a systematic aspect to all the references that Gadamer makes, we have provided a list of works cited by Gadamer with the English translations added when available. Two glossaries follow, one of the most important German words and the other of Greek and Latin phrases. All these tools should provide readers with an easy way to follow the specific terms that Gadamer uses and to keep track of the allusions or direct references he makes.

Translators' Introduction:
Hermeneutics at the Crossroads between History and Philosophy

When we say that hermeneutics stands between history and philosophy we do not mean that it as an alternative to two well-established areas of knowledge, history and philosophy. What the title suggests is rather a proposal at the core of Gadamer's philosophical hermeneutics: to reformulate the very task of philosophy by reintroducing the active role of history. The way Gadamer makes a case for this active role of history is by showing that history in fact has an 'articulating' function. Consequently, history is not a bland character of some things, people or events that have fallen into history, as if history was a recipient or a label of things past. History is rather a way of describing things, events or people, but such that they neither are completely absorbed by history, as if they could be 'past' through and through, nor can they ever be taken out of their historical flesh, as if things, events and people could enjoy some 'in itself' before being taken up by history. 'Being historical' is thus neither accidental to being – we recognize here Heidegger's marking influence on Gadamer – nor a challenge to being and existence, as if being historical would decrease the very being of a thing, an event or a person. This articulating role of history is made possible by language in the form of dialogue. Let us examine briefly these two aspects, which are at the core of this volume: history as an articulating force and language as the engine of history. We will then show in the third section how Gadamer uses these two dimensions in order to re-describe the task of philosophy as a 'mediating discourse'. In the fourth section we sketch how philosophy as a mediating discourse leads to a new understanding of *praxis* as history or historical *praxis*.

1. The articulating role of history

As is clear in this volume, Dilthey occupies a central place for Gadamer both with regard to the concept, function and expanse of hermeneutics, and with regard to the dilemma with which Dilthey found himself confronted. As Gadamer convincingly shows, Dilthey was torn during his whole life between two goals: to bring to prominence and clarity the importance of life in its concretion in historical forms and to reach a level of scientificity that could rival the achievements of the empirical sciences. This tension that Dilthey felt and tried to resolve is already an indication that the simple opposition between understanding and explanation needs nuances or that the opposition between 'truth' and 'method' cannot be a mutually exclusive opposition. We also understand how much Gadamer himself was motivated by Dilthey's failure to resolve the tension and why he attempted to neutralize the allure of scientificity and liberate himself from the mesmerizing effects of empirical data, neat numbers and iron-clad protocols. Gadamer comes back again and again to this ideal and shows the massive presuppositions it must make and the hermeneutic decisions that go into this methodological dogma of analysing anything as a natural entity to be described in a static way. Gadamer thus shows that the human sciences are not about different objects than those of the natural sciences, but that the human sciences are even presupposed by the methodology of the natural sciences. For the latter can only function by bracketing everything that is human and historical, thereby ignoring the genesis of the very concepts they use: subject, object, nature, mind, as well as their 'operative' concepts: causality, inference, essence, substance, temporality, etc.

Instead of trying to resolve the tension between life and scientificity, Gadamer proceeds as a true hermeneuticist, and this means as a practitioner of interpretation. Throughout the essays of this volume and in different ways, with changing emphasis, he brings out the active role of history. This active role can be described, at least, at three levels: history pertains to the articulation of concepts, history pertains to the articulation of texts, and history pertains to the articulation of human beings. These three aspects of history represent in fact as many challenges for philosophy and it is Gadamer's originality to have formulated the problem that history represents for knowledge in a forceful manner. Each of these aspects corresponds to a question and Gadamer's position is precisely the hermeneutic effort to formulate the question in clear terms and, in so doing, to provide a way of solving the problem of history.

The first question is about what is added to the discussion when we take into consideration how a philosophical problem arose or when we examine the historical genesis of the concepts used to formulate the problem. This typically hermeneutic and highly Gadamerian question tests the strict divide between the history of philosophy and systematic philosophy. By challenging and rejecting this opposition between history as being about obsolete or dead ideas, no longer relevant for solving contemporary problems, and systematic philosophy as being an ahistorical technique for finding answers to what become puzzles, Gadamer forcefully makes a case for an articulating role of history. It is not just the *Problemgeschichte* as a kind of contextualization of the problem at hand. When discussing subjectivity, for example, Gadamer reminds us after Heidegger that the word 'subject' comes from the Greek *hupokeimenon* and the Latin *subiectum*. This allows us to have a feel for the kind of transformation that took place when Descartes turned the subject in the sense of 'what lies at the foundation' into a thinking that thinks itself and is as such a 'thinking thing'. In another remarkable conceptual analysis, again following Heidegger, Gadamer explains how *ousia* as landed property could become our philosophical term 'substance'. The landed property indicates the 'worth' of a farmer and allows the farmer to enjoy presence. When Plato and Aristotle apply this term to a thing, *ousia* is what makes the worth of the thing, what constitutes it as such, that without which the thing could not enjoy presence, could not present itself.

The second question is about the texts to be interpreted. How can a text that emerges contingently in history have a universal and enduring meaning that goes beyond history? More specifically, how can past authors, living and thinking in a different time period and dealing with issues and problems that were historically situated, manage to be our contemporaries so that we can have a dialogue with them? Gadamer wants to show how a text depends on a tradition while also contributing to this tradition. This is the issue of the fusion of horizons of the original and the interpretation, which renders fluid both the original text and the interpretation. Gadamer provides a model of the text that is neither a canonical well-delineated entity commanding respect by itself nor a place-holder for the free play of signifiers in Derrida's fashion, but is rather a negotiated product between the original and the interpretation within the constraints of a tradition. Gadamer clarifies further his position through an enlightening discussion of Derrida's deconstruction in the essay 'Hermeneutics on the Trail'.

The different encounters with Derrida were certainly frustrating for Derrida's discussion partners (Ricoeur confirmed this), but also for the readers of those exchanges. This prompted Gadamer to try to isolate what the problem was since these encounters took the form of a dialogue, which is quite familiar and dear to Gadamer. It was a dialogue that did not get traction. Gadamer revisits this notion of dialogue in light of Derrida's emphasis on the semiotic dimension of statements and sentences. Quite convincingly and even performatively, Gadamer is able to show that there is a 'dissemination' – Derrida's term of choice

– in the very structure and dynamics of the dialogue itself to the extent that the positions of speaker and addressee can very quickly and unexpectedly switch, the speaker being questioned and the addressee redirecting the discussion. There is also the disseminating effect of allusions, irony, metaphors, even intonations. All these disseminating factors unsettle any stable power speakers in a dialogue may believe they have. However, against Derrida's views, Gadamer powerfully shows that these disseminating factors are 'existential' and thus within the grasp of what subjects can do, even if individual subjects may be unsettled by them. Contrary to Derrida, it is not the signs themselves, words or metaphors, or the conceptual oppositions at play in all languages that actually speak or impose a subtext to what speakers say. What speaks – what speaks in actuality – is a person. Obviously, as Gadamer has shown in the case of Husserl, subjectivity is itself a communal enterprise or a corporate entity. We are thus not coming back to any traditional subjectivity. Rather, it is the very structure of the dialogue that animates subjectivity, as it were, breathing intersubjective life into it. Gadamer can thus reclaim for dialogue the disseminating effects of signs and language in general, while showing the implausibility of Derrida's hyperstructuralism in which a system of signs could constrain subjectivity and thought.

The third question that is at the core of this volume is: how can human beings who are born in a specific time and place, speak a particular language, transcend their own historical horizons, and speak as a voice bearing universal relevance? This is the issue of subjectivity. Constantly, Gadamer points out how fundamental Husserlian phenomenology was and how limited it is because of its focus on subjectivity, however pure and transcendental it is, for founding the ultimate repositories of knowledge. Clearly siding with Heidegger and against what he sees as the extremes of Derrida's postmodernism, he maintains that knowledge is more than just scientific knowledge and more than just cultural values embedded in the words and concepts we use. Gadamer offers a way to avoid an ahistorical and worldless pure subjectivity as well as a subject reduced to being the function of signs or the tool of cultural forces. His is a way of a concrete subject inhabiting a world with a thick history, showing how both transcendental subjectivity and a radically historical and culturally permeated subject are in fact both the same form of a bloodless subjectivity, the former because there is no blood in it and the latter because the bloodstream is not its own.

If, as Gadamer shows, history is not merely a qualification of ideas with regard to their chronology, but describes their conceptual life – how ideas were used – the subject cannot remain an unchangeable source of validity (as in Husserl) and certainly not a mere functional device of consciousness accompanying representations (as in Kant). The subject is not an anonymous machine of meaning churning up representations or cranking up judgements. As a lesson learned from Dilthey, but also from Ortega y Gasset, Gadamer sees the subject or subjectivity as life. It is a life that thinks, not a Cartesian 'thinking thing'.

This reformulates rather drastically the relationship between subjectivity and intersubjectivity away from the model of parts and wholes or members belonging to a group. Subjectivity and intersubjectivity are not two entities, but descriptions of how life takes its form in the case of human beings. We have the *logos*, which Gadamer understands after Heidegger as language, but, different from Heidegger, language is dialogue. It is in language in the form of a dialogue that subjectivity and intersubjectivity are intertwined as partners in an exchange. History itself is to be understood from within a dialogue so that past authors, such as Plato and Aristotle, become our discussion partners, beyond the distinction between past and present or old and new.

As Gadamer points out, dialogue takes the form of question and answer. Even if the answer is related to the question, because the question imposes the framework of the debate, the questioner can unexpectedly be put to the question and now it is the questioner that is left dangling, at the mercy of the dialogue. Plato's question about *ousia* is not Aristotle's question about the 'same' topic, just as Heidegger's question about *ousia* turns the question around and asks: what is the framework within which the very question of *ousia* arose? Furthermore, even if Plato and Aristotle had a good grasp of what they meant by *ousia*, when we read them, using their words, but transposing the sense of their views in a different linguistic, historical and cultural framework, we ask them questions they did not even intend to answer and we can interpret their answers in relation to issues and problems they had not anticipated.

The three questions mentioned above illustrate the extent to which nothing is really set in the sediments of history when it comes to matters of the mind. Dialogue takes the form of many undercurrents that unsettle the sediments of history, bringing to the surface forgotten connections – *ousia* and landed property – and give to what was past and old the allure of what is worth preserving or even rejuvenating. History works between old and new, as the always uncertain force that keeps the old and the new on the edge, unstable, challenging us and fascinating us.

The form that the articulating power of history takes is the dialogue. History gains its actuality through language. However, if history 'speaks', it is neither in the Heideggerean sense of a history of being nor in the Derridean sense of a system of signs that speakers have to pass through in order to 'think'. Against the oblivion in Heidegger's sense or Derrida's *différance*, Gadamer manages to recover in language a dimension that is neither merely linguistic – as a systematic order of differences – nor ontological – as another voice behind that of the speaker.

2. Language as the heart of the dialogue and the engine of history

In several essays Gadamer illustrates in a very illuminating manner how language works at the heart of a dialogue and how this role of language allows dialogue to be the engine of history, making communities move ahead, while constantly reinterpreting themselves, thereby reinventing their history in a creative way. Gadamer calls *Sprachlichkeit* this role of language engaging the movement of a dialogue. The term is usually translated as 'linguisticality'. However, given Gadamer's whole argument against any theoretical approach to language and against Derrida's deconstruction and his contention that language and writing should not be systematized as some form of means or medium that can be totalized, it may be better to say simply 'the dimension of language'. *Sprachlichkeit* names a dimension or an order that is not merely a mediation for concepts, but the soil out of which concepts arise. The verbal is inchoately conceptual or is, as Gadamer uses the expression, conceptual in its very exercise as verbal. There is thus an inscription in what is merely verbal, but this inscription, against deconstruction, has an existence only in the dialogue in which the verbal lives and unfolds.

In other words, Gadamer proceeds as a hermeneuticist. He does not just name or describe, but shows in practice, *in actu exercito*, as he says. The German expression that he uses, *im Vollzug*, is indeed an apt one for showing what *Sprachlichkeit* actually means in addition to the conceptual level at which Gadamer explains it. After Heidegger, but in a manner far more concrete and clearer, Gadamer argues that concepts originate in language as it is used. Although he does not mention it and does not broach this discussion, he would be in the camp of those opposed to the existence of a language of the brain, a 'mentalese' or whatever fancy term philosophers may invent. He would also not be in the camp of those who claim that perception, for example, has a conceptual content. Yet, he acknowledges in an essay that not all conceptual activity requires language. His approach is subtle and, if heeded, could force some reformulations in some contemporary discussions in philosophy of mind about what is meant by 'concept' or 'conceptual'.

Very often in current discussions about perception, 'conceptual content' in fact means 'object of perception', the argument being that, if there is an object in a perception, such as a dog, there must be a concept involved, namely 'dog'. We recall Heidegger's own views on the matter in *On the History of the Concept of Time*: 'It is not so much that we see the objects and things but rather that we first talk about them … We do not say what we see, but rather the reverse, we see what *one says* about the matter.'[1] This was arguably under Husserl's influence through the categorial intuition: we do not just perceive the piece of paper and the colour white, but the 'paper being white'. The category is in our perception, turning the content of perception into a categorial formation. Heidegger's formulation puts a strong emphasis on language as used: we see what we can say about the matter. Gadamer too constantly talks about the linguistic dimension of our experiences as what makes them 'hermeneutic'. Yet, he wants to limit the linguistic nature of those experiences against interpretations such as Derrida's, who was himself heavily influenced by Heidegger. Gadamer clearly wants to demarcate himself against such a radical move and, by the same token, save Husserl and Heidegger against the drift of the signifier. As he says about listening to the lectures of Husserl and Heidegger, 'we did not have the feeling of progressing from point to point, from argument to argument, but rather believed in the end to have circled around a single object and in such a way that this something finally stood before our eyes in its three dimensions'.[2]

In the case of Husserl, this is rather easy, given Husserl's clinging to a transcendental ego. In making a case for a form of mediation through language that is not what Derrida makes of it, Gadamer points to a quite original position that makes Heidegger's own views about language as 'speaking' far more intelligible than what Heidegger himself says. In fact, Gadamer charts a way between two caricatures of Husserl and Heidegger respectively. The caricatural Husserl is the philosopher who discovered the categorial intuition at the beginning of his career, the life-world at the end, but still maintained a transcendental stance, against all philosophical odds: Husserl the schizophrenic. The caricatural Heidegger is the philosopher of existence that transforms phenomenology as a science of essence into a hermeneutics of facticity and, later on, escapes philosophical discourse into poetic musings about the different spellings of being – Heidegger the *Hausmeister* of being.

Gadamer gives us a different tack or a different track to make sense of the role of language. Language neither expresses what would already be thought at some nonverbal – transcendental – level nor directly speaks through us, using us as channels or sound chambers. To Derrida's emphasis on the dissemination of signs and to Heidegger's stress on the original speaking of language, Gadamer reaffirms, after Plato and as a rejuvenated Plato, the articulating role of the dialogue. There is indeed a dissemination and there is indeed a first speaking before our actual personal speech, but the first initiative is neither by signs nor by language. The first impetus is the existential and historical situation of those who speak with the power that a dialogue partner has to initiate a discussion or redirect a debate. *Sprachlichkeit* is thus neither a semiotic instance nor a metaphysical one, even within the history of being, but is language in exercise, in performance, within which we, human beings, find our place – always historically situated – and our voice – always responsible and accountable. Dialogue as the primal existential and historical situation does not fall under the power of Derrida's deconstruction, because it is not made of signs or of differences. It also escapes Heidegger's 'destruction' of metaphysics, because it is not about a primal articulation by language, but an after-the-fact response by human beings.

Gadamer thus offers an alternative to the subject disseminated through the semiotic means of language – which is a function of language (Derrida) – and to the substantial subject of metaphysics that Heidegger replaced by a being-there or *Da-sein,* which is a clearing. Gadamer's alternative is a dialogical subject as an instance that responds and whose power of constitution – in the phenomenological sense – lies in 'interpreting' after the fact, allowing the 'object' of interpretation to bear upon us not as a causal force in the mode of empiricism, but rather through the way it opens itself to us and is there for us. Our position as subject is always responsive. Reality is of the nature of a trace. As he magnificently reflects on the notion of trace as used by Heidegger and Derrida in 'Hermeneutics on the Trail', we can still understand the trace in a non-sceptical, non-relativist, non-idealistic manner. It is a positive trace as what we construe through our interpretation, but also what we justify through our dialogical exchanges with other subjects. Reality is a trace in the positive sense of a transaction. Although construed, it is not a mere construct and although interpreted, it is not a fabrication. Dialogue offers the boundaries of the transaction as well as the framework for the vocabulary used in the transaction and the parameters agreed upon. Dialogue thus offers stability – the traditional notion of *ousia* as what subsists – and change – the import of the traditional *metabolē* as historical change and its power to make obsolete and rejuvenate.

The best illustration of what Gadamer means is in the manner Gadamer writes. His vocabulary is unbelievably rich and variegated. Translators may believe, as the present ones did, that after translating several essays by the same author, a recurrent glossary would become evident and a tentative algorithm would emerge for how to translate other essays by the same author. This is certainly the case with philosophers like Kant, about whom translators can give a fairly consistent glossary and continue to translate Kant sometimes mechanically by using the same English term any time Kant uses the same German term. In Gadamer's case, it is not possible. From essay to essay the vocabulary changes. He appeals to all sorts of levels of speech, technical expressions, idiomatic forms, old-fashioned usages. He thus resists what makes the translator's job easier, the direct passage to the conceptual level. For this is what a glossary is and what an algorithm can do. Instead, Gadamer lives and inhabits words. This is where translators have to meet him. This actually means that Gadamer by so doing is also reformulating in *actu exercito, im Vollzug,* in the very performance of thinking, what concepts are or how the conceptual level actually operates. Translating Gadamer – but this would hold for any real 'thinker' – means finding for a certain sequence of German words another sequence of words in English that would render the same effect. We say 'effect' instead of 'meaning' or 'conceptual content' precisely because the whole point is about what 'meaning' is or what a 'concept' is.

'Concepts', Gadamer says, are nurtured by language, grow out of language. They do not pre-exist language. Yet, language does not precede thinking as a pre-thinking and does not come before concepts as 'pre-conceptual'. What matters is to render 'passable again the path from the concept to the word so that thinking speaks to us again'.[3] Between Husserl, the logician, and Heidegger, the poetic thinker – these are the two caricatures – Gadamer forces us to think a third way for understanding the relation between words and concepts. Philosophy cannot be equated with concepts as it has been traditionally done. But philosophy at the same time cannot be equated with language either. Philosophy is a kind of mediating discourse between language and concepts. To speak with Gadamer:

> We only should not think of this as though philosophical concepts were available in some warehouse to be simply hauled out from there. When we are thinking in concepts the situation is rather not as different as when we are using language. When using language, it is also the case that no one can initiate a new use of language. Rather, the use of language initiates itself, constitutes itself in the life of the language, until it has acquired a fixed status. Conceptual thinking is always found with blurry edges, as Wittgenstein said. This is why we should follow the semantic life of language and this means: go back to the point where

the concept emerges out of speaking itself, out of the 'situatedness in life' [*Sitz im Leben*].[4]

And he does it performatively, by showing us what this means. In speaking we use words with the meanings that they have received and that we have learned. We then add nuances or use words in unusual contexts, like Aristotle using landed property, *ousia*, and applying it to a thing. It becomes what allows a thing to dwell by analogy with what allows a farmer to dwell. Just as we can speak then of the 'worth' of the farmer according to the landed property of the farmer, we can speak of the 'substance' of a thing according to what allows it to be present. We can then speak of 'substance' or 'essence' in an abstract sense and have 'concepts'. We can even claim that these concepts are different from words – they are what remain the same, for example, through translations among different languages. We can then claim for them a logical precedence in the order of thinking and speaking: what you say is what you mean and thus what you intended to say before you started saying it.

Yet, although this traditional view is by and large correct, it has erased its own genesis in asserting its power, just as Husserl criticizes Galileo for having absolutized the ideality of scientific representation that originated from the life-world. Arguably, the power of the traditional view, holding concepts in some absolute status, lies precisely in this erasure. We do not see where they come from and thus tend to believe that they were not born from somewhere and not borne by some predecessors. What Gadamer shows is the need to make a distinction in speaking between a synchronic and a diachronic perspective. Again, Husserl made this distinction when speaking of a constitutive and genetic phenomenology. In *Being and Time* Heidegger puts history at the central place of existence or what he calls 'Dasein'. Yet, neither of them managed to explain in a convincing manner how the two dimensions can work together. Gadamer manages this feat, to the dismay of new translators.

As Paul Ricoeur also remarks, when translating we do not have three parameters: the original German, the English target language, and the conceptual level of what Gadamer, for example, thought. We only have Gadamer's words concatenated in sentences, themselves organized in an 'essay', and our English language. The move by translators has no verticality. It does not migrate to some realm of thoughts or conceptual ether. The move is irremediably horizontal and Gadamer made this move famous as a fusion of horizons. This in fact comes from Goethe and Gadamer is certainly fond of Goethe, for whom the ideal translation is neither the one that assimilates the foreign text nor the one that overly accommodates the foreign so as to deny its own identity, but a fusion of the two, so that the target German text is 'anglicized' and the English translation is 'Germanized' just up to that point where it would no longer sound English.

This is what *Sprachlichkeit* means: Goethe's ideal of stretching and kneading a language so as to make it say what it was not able to say before the hard work of translation or, for that matter, before thinking took place. Thinking is a matter of stretching words, expanding their semantic field, making them fill out a space where they usually did not tread. *Sprachlichkeit* is thus no 'linguisticality', but the natural sphere of power of language where words, like in conversation, give traction to thought, leading to new associations or forcing us to backtrack: 'this is not what I wanted to say'. *Sprachlichkeit* is the dimension of speech or language that neither precedes thinking – against Heidegger's slogan that language speaks – nor disseminates it – against Derrida's pronouncement that the subject is a function of language. *Sprachlichkeit* is what goes along with thinking, providing building blocks, allowing a concrete meaning. It is the *hulē* – the wood or scaffolding – to graft onto what Aristotle meant as the scaffolding of a thing or its matter: the 'that out of which' it is made. *Sprachlichkeit* is also what allows a relativization of concepts by keeping them linked to their genesis, preventing them from solidifying in self-evident conceptuality. Concepts remain within the flux of language understood in its dialogical nature and are at the service of existence or at the service of this engine of social interaction, the dialogue. It is not a Habermasian dialogue as communication with its structural claims to validity, but something more primordial, an exchange that is a constant unsettling of the subject, occupying the position of speaker as the receiver of an address who is then always susceptible to be questioned and put in the position of a listener. *Sprachlichkeit* is the dimension of speech within which concepts live, are alive, and do their work in what is called thinking, but in the Heideggerean sense of what calls for thinking.

3. Philosophy as mediating discourse

Gadamer's effort to show how concepts are embedded in language assigns a new and rather specific role to philosophy. Philosophy loosens the grip that the concept has on our thinking. With great ingenuity Gadamer dissipates the idea of a simple correspondence between concept and reality. The concept is not a mere description of reality but more truly a human intervention into reality.

> In a concept something is put together [*zusammengegriffen*], combined together [*zusammengefasst*]. The word says that the concept seizes [*greifen*], grabs [*zugreifen*], and puts together [*zusammengreifen*] and, in this way, conceives [*begreift*] something. Thinking in concepts is thus an active thinking that is intrusive [*eingreifend*] and far-reaching [*ausgreifend*].[5]

Against the view that concepts are tools that we use in order to organize the world around us, Gadamer inverts the relationship. It is not so much the concept that organizes experience, as it is experience that gives rise to the concept, but of course not at the same time. Those concepts that organize our experiences grew out of other experiences and others' experiences. Concepts are laden with experiences and this sedimentation of experiences in the course of time represents a dimension of history at the heart of our concepts that is our blind spot.

> Concepts are not arbitrary tools of human understanding by which it organizes or controls experiences. Rather, concepts have always already grown out of experience; they articulate our understanding of the world and predelineate thereby the course of experience. Thus, with any concept through which we think, a pre-decision has already been made, whose legitimacy we no longer verify.[6]

When we use concepts, we forget about this 'pre-decision' and this oblivion in fact allows us to use concepts. However, philosophy has the power to trace the path from the concept to the fluid field of human experience and, thus, to examine the pre-decision at the heart of the concept. Philosophy is thus not merely a conceptual enterprise, but also a mediating discourse. Philosophy is hermeneutics in this mediating sense.

This mediating role of philosophy, as it always finds itself in the company of the hermeneutic and the historical, is particularly apt at dealing with our present situation. From the very beginning Gadamer's hermeneutics has been a sustained reflection on the place of philosophy in the age in which natural scientific mentality has become absolutely dominant. In his magnum opus *Truth and Method*, we find truth opposed to method: method, which defines the mentality of the natural sciences, and truth, which is his proposal for what has defined and ought to define the mentality of the human sciences. Gadamer's effort in that book is to invoke the realm of art to show what he means by truth and how it can be understood as a different but necessary paradigm of rationality that ought to be fostered in the age of the dominance of the natural sciences. Gadamer continues to develop this trajectory in his many essays that follow *Truth and Method*.

We can reformulate this concern about philosophy with the following question: can philosophy in the age of modern science be understood as something more than an '*ancilla scientiarum*, the handmaiden of the sciences … called to service with the ceremonious name of "theory of knowledge"'?[7] Gadamer's answer to the question is an emphatic 'yes' because scientific knowledge can tell us nothing about human *praxis* at the individual and social level. Indeed, for Gadamer *praxis* cannot be reduced to a simple application of scientific knowledge for the production of amenities and services for individual and social comfort.

Gadamer's understanding of practical philosophy goes back to Aristotle and the distinction between *epistēmē* and *praxis*. *Epistēmē*, Gadamer argues, is a mathematical knowledge that is pursued for its own sake. It is an autotelic activity, which has absolutely nothing to do with describing the real world. *Praxis* can thus not be a mere application of *epistēmē* to the real world and cannot be subordinated to *epistēmē*. In fact, Gadamer argues that science cannot really adjudicate how its own knowledge should be applied to the real world. Should we simply produce something just because it is technologically possible? Are the laws of production simply to be governed by the availability of the technological means to do so? For Gadamer these questions are themselves not scientific but rather praxiological, which go beyond anything that science can say or show.[8] It is clear that modern scientific knowledge allows us to utilize various laws of nature in order to intervene into the course of nature for our own benefit. In this sense modern scientific knowledge increases the space of human freedom. However, scientific knowledge cannot subsume that human freedom under any specific law of nature.[9] This is where philosophy comes in and has to play a role far more important than some kind of theory of knowledge. Philosophy has to be practical philosophy.

Practical philosophy does not mean the application of philosophical theory for solving practical problems. Practical philosophy, which, we must note, is not applied philosophy, is to be understood in its most literal sense as the practical nature of philosophizing itself. *Praxis* is philosophy and philosophy is a *praxis*. Thus, *praxis* is to be seen as an autonomous dimension of human existence. The natural sciences cannot have any jurisdiction over this *praxis* although they will have an influence on it. Indeed, for Gadamer *epistēmē* and *praxis* are two essential aspects of human existence and neither should be subsumed under the other. He sees the human sciences on the side of *praxis* and the natural sciences on the side of *epistēmē*. This is why he is critical of the human sciences when they imitate the methods of the natural sciences like the exclusive use of the survey questionnaire for collecting data. When they do this they fail to nurture the spirit of practical philosophy, which finds its rightful place, for Gadamer, in the human sciences.[10] When he speaks about how the human sciences cannot aspire to the same level of scientificity and objectivity of knowledge as the natural sciences, he is making a plea for the contemporary relevance of *praxis* against the exclusive power of *epistemē* and for the role of practical philosophy as it is embodied in the human sciences. This is how Gadamer may concede the truth of the mocking remark made by the Vienna Circle about the human sciences being at most ten percent science when it comes to their scientificity. But he emphasizes that it is the other ninety percent that is the most crucial from the standpoint of human existence as it concerns shared living and solidarity.[11]

We can also make sense of Gadamer's prolonged engagement with the work of Wilhelm Dilthey in this context of the idea of practical philosophy. Dilthey's quandary, described above, is in fact characteristic of the age of science and Gadamer shows us how Dilthey's works are indeed the battlefield for the soul of the human sciences and the place of philosophy in the age of modern science. As mentioned above, in Gadamer's eyes, Dilthey is caught between the twin impulses of positivism and romanticism. He is impressed by the empirical method of the modern natural science, which takes the facts accessed by empirical experience as their starting point, but at the same time finds it hard to let go of the legacy of the romanticism of which is he is an heir. In *Truth and Method*, Gadamer was critical of Dilthey for his inability to follow up on his intention to go beyond British empiricism and do justice to the historicity of human experience.[12] In his later essays on Dilthey, we find his stance toward Dilthey softened as he shows how Dilthey was partially successful in questioning the concept of experience prevalent in British empiricism and the natural sciences. He also broadened the concept of experience to include the experience of history, which is an inner experience giving us access to a factual realm, impervious to the view and methods of the natural sciences.[13] Gadamer details with great sympathy the Olympian struggles of Dilthey as he tries to provide an account of the new factual realm opened by inner experience in a manner that is as rigorous as the natural sciences and does not degenerate into some kind of historicism or relativism. Gadamer's final verdict on Dilthey is that he did not entirely succeed in his mission of making the human sciences the redeemers of humanity, as he is never quite able to escape the shadow of the empirical sciences in the way he saw and characterized the nature of the human sciences and, by extension, philosophy. As a result the human sciences remain tied to the ethos of detached observation rather than that of engaged *praxis*. It is in this respect that Gadamer believes himself to have gone past Dilthey by finding recourse to the Aristotelian concept of *phronēsis*, which, Gadamer argues, articulates itself in a dialogical manner, thus weaving it together with Plato's dialectic of question and answer.

Praxis is a collective action that includes in principle the whole of humanity and is based on the collective seeing of what is the right course of action resulting from a mutual understanding that we all collectively arrive at through the process of a dialogue.[14] Gadamer's understanding of *praxis* combines, as it were, Aristotle's concept of *phronēsis* as deliberation with the Platonic idea of dialogue with its dialectic of question and answer. Gadamer emphasizes that this mutual understanding does not imply agreement. In fact where there is already agreement, there may be no need for a common understanding.[15] Gadamer also emphasizes that the communal existence of human beings and their modes of life can be a fractious affair.[16] By fractious he means that we are always called upon to answer for our mode of living and justify it. We are challenged by questions and we come up with answers that redirect the questions or challenge the questioners.[17] Dialogue is thus not a cosy and risk-free conversation, but the very dynamics of what it means to be human and to live with others, always oneself and yet always already 'another'. It is in this continuous dialectical movement of challenged question and tested answers that *phronēsis* articulates itself, giving rise to collective action. But this *phronēsis* is intimately connected to philosophy's mediating role between language and concept.

We described above how Gadamer sees concepts as originating from language. Bringing concepts back to their original birthing place, in language, also has a praxiological impact. This tracing back from concept to language has a critical impetus toward science. 'What philosophical reflection discovers is that there are pre-decisions in concepts that are so fundamentally hidden that one is somehow entrapped within their interpretive horizon.'[18] By revealing to us a dimension that is below that of concepts and from which concepts emerge, philosophy brings to the fore the almost ideological nature of the blindness of science toward the genesis of its concepts and the tool to power that such an erasure of history represents.

Gadamer takes up, for example, the modern scientific concept of causality and shows us how this concept was developed by Aristotle in his physics but from a very specific human experience. The experience is that of production. From the standpoint of the experience of a human being making something, there are four factors that contribute to the making of the thing. There is the raw material, which is processed into the final product (the material cause). There is the specific form that our final product has, which the raw material receives in becoming the final product (formal cause). In the case of a potter it could be the form of a utensil or a figurine or some such thing. Then there is the activity of the maker, who actively manipulates the raw materials so that they receive their finished form (efficient cause). Finally, we have the purpose that the makers have in mind when going about the task of collecting the raw materials, fashioning them into a final product with its very specific form (final cause). It is the purpose that guides the makers so to speak into doing what they do. The fourfold concept of cause thus emerges from a very specific kind of human experience, the experience of producing something.

Gadamer argues that it is precisely this experience that acts as the starting point for Aristotle's investigation into nature. He sees nature analogously to the human producer with the fundamental difference that nature produces something from out of itself so to speak. From the standpoint of such an experience, of course, nature itself seems as if it were guided by a hidden purpose in its abundant workings. Nature thus comes to be viewed teleologically from the standpoint of Aristotelian physics, which is rooted in one fundamental experience, the experience of the human producer. Modern science, however, originates in opposition to this old Aristotelian way of conceiving nature. Modern science tries to understand nature from out of itself, as it were, by completely excluding the standpoint of human subjectivity. Nature is thus purged of all traces of human subjectivity and conceived purely in itself. From such a standpoint, the only conception of cause that matters is the efficient cause, namely the activity of one thing upon the other, and the fourfold concept of cause is undone at its seams.

While the Aristotelian model had no problems when accounting for the freedom of human activity in relationship to nature, this human freedom becomes a genuine problem for the modern scientific mentality. It is like a ghost from a past that lingers in the present but cannot quite be exorcised, no matter what conceptual tricks one tries to play. This shows that we cannot absolutize the modern scientific concept of cause. Thus, we can say that the modern scientific concept of causality emerges and pre-delineates a very specific human experience. But our humanity is not exhausted by this experience of nature. As a consequence, it should not be used as a paradigm to legislate or subjugate other experiences, which are experiences of a completely different kind. We experience art, we experience our freedom to act, we experience the shared nature of communal living; all of these experiences for Gadamer go on to constitute the rich tapestry of humanity and should be equally respected for what they are. The perspective we take when making these claims about the concept of causality is not subjugated to science, but on the other hand it is not an absolutizing perspective that seeks to swallow up everything in its wake, including science. It is an autonomous space and, for Gadamer, the space of philosophy as mediating discourse and historical *praxis*.

4. What kind of *praxis* is this historical *praxis*?

We can now finally see how Gadamer uses Dilthey in order to go beyond him. Dilthey was well aware of the inscrutable nature of life from which all acts of cognition emerged and was always troubled by the need to defend the objectivity and absoluteness of knowledge, even when he was forced to acknowledge the all-encompassing wildness of life from which all conceptuality emerged.[19] The superiority of Gadamer's position lies in the fact that he does not take sides here and does not absolutize life in relationship to knowledge or knowledge in relationship to life. Rather, he is interested in opening up the path from life to knowledge and knowledge back to life, and showing in the process the fluid interaction between these two realms. Philosophy as hermeneutics is a discourse that inhabits the middle ground between these two realms. Indeed we can see the original sense of hermeneutics shine through: like the god Hermes, hermeneutics plays the role of messenger going back and forth between these two realms.

It is in this respect that Gadamer believes he diverges from his master Heidegger, who according to Gadamer, was engaged throughout his life in an Ahab-like quest for his white whale: the original experience of being that lay at the basis of the ancient concept of metaphysics as onto-theology and the modern concept of science, but which we have somehow forgotten and from which we have moved away. This quest leads Heidegger back to the obscure origins of metaphysics and science in Miletus. It is a quest in which, according to Gadamer, Heidegger conceded he failed.[20] For Gadamer there is no beginning, no end, and no other beginning. Rather we are always in-between, always on the way. This is the fate of language and thinking in language, as we move from question to answer to question. To speak with Gadamer:

> The signs that we call words are *kata sunthēkēn*, which means: they are conventions. This does not mean agreements that were struck at a certain time. Yet,

signs are also not from nature. This is a singularity that includes us from the outset and which precedes all linguistic differentiation into this or that word, into this or that language. This is the beginning that has never begun, but is always already. It grounds the ineradicable proximity between thinking and speaking, and itself remains superior to the question of the beginning or the end of philosophy.[21]

We have seen the two ways in which Gadamer characterizes philosophy in the modern age of science tied ineluctably to hermeneutics and history. We can now make more explicit the inner connection between philosophy as practical philosophy and philosophy as a mediating discourse between language and concept. Philosophy exposes us to the living fact of language and shows us how language is not reducible to concepts. Yet, neither are concepts simply reducible to language. By manifesting the active role and living breath of history in our very *praxis,* philosophy as mediating discourse makes it clear that the conceptual language of the various sciences cannot by themselves govern every aspect of our lives. They cannot govern our social lives because our life in common concerns what we are going to do with science, how we are going to be responsible to the future, to nature, to our fellow human beings. As members of society we are not mere observers of nature, but participants in the process that we influence and for which only we are responsible. This is how *phronēsis* examines itself.

Gadamer reads the early Platonic dialogues as ones initiated by the definition[22] and not about defining a concept. The former is not an agonistic exercise on the basis of the ideals of logical rigour wherein the strongest arguments win and weaker arguments are vanquished. This is why Gadamer resolutely defends Heidegger against the criticisms raised by Carnap, for whom philosophy has to be ultimately reduced to symbolic logic. Siding with Heidegger's attempts to free philosophy from the straitjacket of symbolic logic, Gadamer even argues that Aristotle's work must not be read simply as a system of arguments and concepts to be used as and when necessary. Against such a scholastic interpretation of Aristotle, Gadamer emphasizes the non-systematic nature of Aristotle's thought and the constant interaction between Greek life, language and scientific conceptuality in his work. An exclusive focus on arguments and their formalization by the notations of symbolic logic would cut us off from the soil in which arguments emerge. This soil is language along with the life experience of the individuals who speak and share those experiences in speaking. It is in keeping alive this connection between language and concept, as we have seen above, that the two aspects of philosophy come together in Gadamer. This loosening of the hold of concepts and the praxiological nature of philosophizing as dialogue are both rooted in the ability of language to move us and in our attempts to move it.

Gadamer's characterization of the praxiolgical nature of philosophy compels us toward the consideration of another thinker who showed the remarkable influence of Aristotle and who too saw philosophy as *praxis* and a medium for shaking up the hold of a certain set of concepts. That was the early Marx, who in his 'Critique of Hegel's Philosophy of Right' sees philosophy as the head of emancipation, as the medium for social revolution and for the emancipation of mankind.[23] Marx is however remarkably missing from Gadamer's detailed histories of nineteenth century thought. When Gadamer gave what he thought was his last lecture at the University of Heidelberg in 1969, as Jean Grondin relates it, Heidegger was present and made some remarks, noting that Gadamer attended his, Heidegger's, first official lecture in Marburg in 1923 and forty-five years later he, Heidegger, attended Gadamer's last official lecture. On this occasion Heidegger noted and emphasized the link between thinking and praxis. He quoted the 11th thesis of Marx on Feuerbach: 'philosophers have only *interpreted* the world in various ways; the point is, to change it.'[24] As Heidegger remarked, the world needs to be interpreted if one wants to change it.[25] Interpretation is something unavoidable. In developing the notion of philosophy as interpretation into philosophy as dialogical *praxis*, Gadamer was indeed close to Marx.

In outlining his notion of dialogical praxis Gadamer states very clearly that he sought a very specific understanding of 'the other' and that he found such an account missing in Heidegger. This is the conception of the other as partner in a dialogue.

> Given the manner Heidegger developed his project in the preparation for the question of being and elaborated understanding as the most authentic existential structure of Dasein, the others could only manifest themselves in their own existence as a limitation. Eventually, as I claimed, it was only when the others are starkly held up against me that the authentic possibility of under-standing opened up to me. To let the other stand against oneself – and it is from there that all my hermeneutic works slowly arose – does not only mean to recognize in principle the limitation of one's own project. It also demands simply going beyond one's own possibilities in a dialogical, communicative, and hermeneutic process.[26]

Gadamer sees no genuine framework for dialogue in Heidegger. The other can only be 'the mere addressee, not the partner in a dialogue.'[27] It is only in his late work that he 'ventured some hints at what a dialogue really is and only by choosing the style of dialogical form in *On the Way to Language*.'[28]

In turn, we could ask Gadamer whether this characterization of the other can do full justice to it. Is the other always fundamentally a partner amenable to a dialogue? Why does Gadamer not even mention the Marxian alternative of a revolutionary *praxis*? Or why does he believe that his conception of a non-revolutionary dialogical *praxis* is the best or the only viable? It would be interesting to know how Gadamer would respond to an alternative to his rather equanimous and irenic coming to a mutual understanding even if not agreement, despite significant differences in social or cultural status? And what about ethnic and religious differences? How can there be a genuine dialogue between people who see others as enemies, even class enemies? If they come to an understanding without coming to an agreement, which Gadamer acknowledges as a possibility, what kind of disagreement is to be accepted or tolerated among those disagreements that are not amicable?

In contrasting Gadamer's discovery of the dialectic of language as it is founded on dialogue, in its movement from question to answer, to the history of discourse in Michel Foucault and Heidegger's history of being, all of which in some way attempt to overcome the hegemony of the modern subject, the *ego-cogito*, so to speak, we need to emphasize how, unlike the history of being and history of discourse, Gadamer's dialectic of language displays a remarkable continuity and is free from any upheavals, showing no propensity to ruptures, leaps, beginnings, ends, and 'other beginnings'. In short, the history that Gadamer's dialectic of language articulates is not a revolutionary history. This certainly has repercussions for Gadamer's characterization of philosophy as *praxis*.

Our societies are faced with this challenge where violence has become one of the arts of 'praxes' within traditional liberal democracies. This may be a challenge harder to face than the challenge of the sciences. Can Gadamer's reading of history deal with alternate 'readings' and respond to them or engage them? Here we can even add Heidegger and Foucault to the mix. What Heidegger, Foucault and Marx have in common is the understanding of the revolutionary nature of history, whether it is the transition from capitalism to communism, from contemporary age of human beings to an age without human beings, from the end of the first beginning to the other beginning. They also see philosophy as something revolutionary in nature. What is the nature of the revolution that hermeneutics, lying between philosophy and history can foment?

Part One

History as a Problem: On Being Historically Affected

1

Is There a Causality in History? (1964)[1]

[107] The modern concept of causality has its own right to a home in the circle of concepts that were originally coined for the natural sciences. This is because the mode of being of nature as it appears in our experience is constituted in such a way that it can only be conceived as a sequential connection of cause and effect. This is the reason why Kant counted causality among the originary concepts of our understanding, those that in fact make our very experience *a priori* possible. It is indeed true that experience and the natural sciences founded upon experience carry with them the following assumption about the being of nature: that which is without foundation, the accidental, the miraculous has no place in it. To speak with Kant, nature is nothing other than 'matter submitted to laws'. It is easy to see that the principle of causality in this sense belongs to the fabric of nature as such. For, a natural connection that would be interrupted by unforeseeable intrusions coming from another order would destroy the unity of experience, making it impossible thereby to anticipate the course of things. It would thus destroy the presupposition that underlies the management of the forces of nature in the service of human purposes, what we call technology.

It can be said, though, that experience teaches us precisely that the unpredictable arbitrariness of human beings constantly intervenes in the course of nature and that, nevertheless, it is possible to some extent to anticipate the course of things. Thus, for example, we make prognoses about economic and social developments, although we are undoubtedly dealing with the effects of free human decisions here. The fact that the social action of human beings – despite their inner consciousness of being free – allows for predictions to be made at least in general, seems to prove that human nature itself remains a member of the complex of nature into which everything fits nicely.

Yet, the experience of history is something completely different. To apply the concept of causality here is in fact to pose a problem. For, history is a course of things, a complex of events that is not primarily experienced in the mode of planning, expecting and anticipating – however uncertain this anticipation may be. Rather, history as a complex of events is always experienced fundamentally as something that has already happened. This is why such a complex of events belongs to a completely different [108] dimension. Here, the free decisions by individuals do not enter into a calculation the result of which is foreseeable. The free decision is rather experienced here as what was not to be predicted and made history precisely because it happened as it happened. These are Ranke's 'scenes of liberty'[2] out of which world history is made. This formulation makes history appear as a staged drama. In it, there are scenes, which initiate the affected spectators into a new direction taken by the course of things. It may be that the course of things is determined in general by the given circumstances in such a way that many possibilities are foreclosed and only a few open. Yet, the complex in which world history fits is anything but knowable or even foreseeable in its necessity. The complex does not have the character of a connection between cause and effect in the way it underlies our knowledge and calculation of the course of nature. If it is an old fundamental principle of the knowledge of nature that the cause must be equal to the effect, the opposite is true when it comes to the experience of history: small causes have huge consequences. It obviously belongs to the experience of those who stand within history that it surprises them. Never do they possess an adequate awareness of what is the case. For any situation in which they find themselves, there are already in fact infinitely many things that have been decided beforehand, of which they know nothing. The behaviour of individuals in an unrepeatable moment of their action is certainly not that of complete cluelessness or total blindness. They try to come to grips with the situation in which they find themselves and find the right course of action, do what is required and handle the situation in the desired sense. Yet, 'what are hopes, what are plans that human beings, in their transience, build on grounds so fleeting?'[3] Human beings have no solid ground. What truly is the case, nobody knows exactly. These are the unfathomable beginnings out of which ensues what will take hold of the future. These beginnings are not known, even to those, and perhaps least of all to those who occupy 'leading' positions in political or economic life. These people know what is planned, what is going on, what is expected. What they necessarily forget is what is to be expected, that is to say, what cannot be predicted, what was not planned, what is unforeseen. Naturally, people in political life need a special sense for opportunities and possibilities, a nose for what is coming. Salespeople too, let alone economic leaders and political leaders, must have something similar. Yet, how little is all of this a knowledge, how little is it a certainty, and how much is it an instantaneous adaptation to changing situations or the capacity always to wrestle something positive from any event? The opportunist is always far closer to the reality of history than the dogmatist.

In this situation, what can 'the causality in history' mean? **[109]** Obviously it is the question of something unknown that handicaps the consciousness of human freedom and responsibility in a specific way. We must only look for it in our own concrete attitudes [*Gestalten*], for example in the oppressive weight of guilt. The question of who and what was at fault for things turning out badly is not only a question that unavoidably imposes itself upon us. It is also and primarily a question that leaves us at a loss, even awakening in us an internal resistance. As if we can be at fault for something that we did not want and certainly did not intend in that way. What does historical responsibility mean? Is it not the dark unintelligibility of destiny that lets the wretched feel guilt?[4] What is historical experience if not a mixture of belated comprehension and regret?

What about the life of the individual? Indeed, historical experience is always also an experience of the individual. Anyone will be affected by what happens on a large scale even if this experience is, for the individual, that of a guiltless suffering – what we call destiny. Does this not mean that it is not just 'evil' deeds – what were meant and intended in an evil manner – that recoil upon us having their undeniable existence in comprehension and regret, guilt and punishment? Is it also the same in the life of individuals, namely that they also regret what they did not foresee, precisely because they did not foresee what resulted from their deeds? Even the moral problematic is not so simple as if it were just a matter of good or evil intent, the unforeseen consequences being of no weight. It is the merit of the great sociologist Max Weber to have pointed out the opposition between an ethics of intention [*Gesinnung*] and an ethics of responsibility and, through this distinction, to have elaborated the problem we are dealing with here in clear terms. He has shown that not having knowledge when one can know is itself blameworthy. This is an uncontestable truth, but it receives its full acuteness only in this: the limits of what one can know or could have known weigh heavily on the mind of someone with a sensitive conscience.

Thus, the question of causality in history is affected by a schism. On the one hand, causality appears as what limits and threatens human freedom and responsibility, leading to the experience of an impotence in the face of history and an attitude of a socio-political fatalism that drives headlong into the 'unpolitical'. On the other hand, causality in history is dictated by the wish and the will to penetrate with the light of understanding and the conscientiousness of knowledge even the enigmatic happening that produces history and to determine its course. This wish and this will even lead to the audacious hope of political utopianism that humanity having attained its emancipation will one day take its destiny into its own hands and make its way into the future with scientific exactitude. These are the two extremes that make visible to us the question of the causality in history. [110] Is there a true middle way here, which is neither the one nor the other, or is the whole alternative skewed? Perhaps the whole question starts from presuppositions that are not suited to the *condition humaine*, the fundamental human constitution in its greatness and misery.

One must ask these questions. For, it could very well be that the modern concept of causality, which finds its classical expression in seventeenth-century mechanics and receives its philosophical legitimacy in the eighteenth century through Hume and Kant, is a genuine constitutive category when it comes to natural events. However, it may affect what happens in human affairs, what we call history, in fact only at the margins and not in its essence. If one ventures to ask these questions, one has, first, to examine the very concept of causality itself.

Concepts are not arbitrary tools of human understanding by which it organizes or controls experiences. Rather, concepts have always already grown out of experience; they articulate our understanding of the world and predelineate thereby the course of experience. Thus, with any concept through which we think, a pre-decision has already been made, whose legitimacy we no longer verify. To become aware of this pre-decision is to acquire a new intellectual freedom; it means seeing new questions and opening new paths for solving old problems. When we question in this sense the provenance of the concept of causality and seek out the original conceptual context to which it belongs and out of which it acquires its precise determination, it means that we uncover pre-judgements, under which the question of causality in history already stands. It is indeed always so and it turns the business of philosophy into a genuine contribution toward bringing human beings to understand themselves. This is the case even in this age of unconditional faith in science, which no longer concedes to philosophy any real knowledge of its own. Were it the case that the answers to the questions that we raised lie under the jurisdiction of scientific methodology alone, then philosophy may not be able at all to compete with the sciences. In fact, philosophy starts earlier, there where no questions have been raised yet, with the concepts through which we think and which are in general unquestionably obvious.

What philosophical reflection discovers is that there are pre-decisions in concepts that are so fundamentally hidden that one is somehow entrapped within their interpretive horizon. It could be that the experience of history too can only be brought to its truth when we become aware of the obvious dominance that certain concepts, such as causality, exercise on our thinking.

To causality we connect the question of the lawfulness of what is happening. All of science seems to be unquestioningly captivated by this question. Already one thinker of antiquity, who is cited many times [111] as the chief witness for modern science, Democritus, the creator of Greek atomic theory, was known in antiquity as the *aitiologikos*, the one who looks for causes everywhere. A nice story, one of these anecdotes in which there is more truth than in a reliable report, tells us that he one day bought a piece of pumpkin from the market. As he began to eat from it at home, he was completely taken in by the uncommon honey-like sweetness of this pumpkin. Full of excitement, he jumped to his feet and hurried back to the market to inquire from the woman farmer about the field where and the conditions under which this sweet pumpkin had grown. To the general laughter of all those around, he learned there that the pumpkin was brought to the market on a bed of honey. As everyone laughed at him, he angrily and resolutely responded: 'And yet, I will not stop researching into the cause.'

Is the happening of history also the kind of happening into whose cause one must not stop researching? Are there laws here too, and does the knowledge of history mean the knowledge of the laws that govern history? Where the laws of nature are known there we have a new freedom from these laws that consists in using them to fulfil our own purposes – what we call 'technology'. Do we also have something similar in the knowledge of the laws of history, by means of which we can acquire a freedom from history, to steer history according to our own purposes? Or is it the opposite? Does causality in history mean the dissolution of human freedom exposing the human consciousness of freedom as an illusion? Does causality presuppose freedom or does it simply exclude freedom? These are all questions that make it impossible to circumvent a return to an original understanding of what we mean by causality.

The concept of causality refers back to one of the doctrines developed by Aristotle. Aristotle distinguished four senses of cause. What we call causality is what the scholastic reception of Aristotle calls *causa efficiens*.[5] It is only one of the four kinds of cause, with which Aristotle attempts to think the question of being. Matter, form, impetus to motion, end, all of these four causes are in play wherever one talks of being and, above all, where we are dealing with nature, that is to say, with that which has its being from itself. The world of human action and affairs may have been originally thought under these four causal aspects. These four fundamental concepts of cause that Aristotle analyses may in fact have been thought from the human perspective, on the basis of human experiences, with its possibilities to call something into being, which means knowing how to produce something. Yet, these four concepts must also grasp that which exists from itself. Already this point of departure makes it clear that cause is not only something that effects a change. In order to be able to effect a change [112] there must be something more original than such an origin of change. We must have there what is to be changed, and this obviously means two things: it must be there in such a way that, out of it, something else can come about and it must at the same time be there in a way that it endures through all the changes as it is in itself. This is indeed the insight that guides all our activities of production: that we produce something out of something.

To produce something means that through our action, through our labour something comes into being, which was not there before: generally, it is something useful, a device, a tool, and this means something that still exceeds the usefulness of nature for human purposes. These are the artificial products of the ingenuity of the human spirit. These products are determined by their purpose, and this means: by their use. Their form, shape, appearance must be suited to their use. Purpose and form thus determine what one produces. Yet, one produces them always out of something. There must always already exist that out of which one produces something purposeful and useful in the way described. We call this the material of our work. Even this must be there before one can begin to work. The thing consists of that out of which it is made. This thing *is* wood or bronze or other such things. However, it *is* also a statue or a bowl. Purpose, form, and matter thus represent the original conditions for the *being* of what is produced. The producing agent, the *causa efficiens*, that which ultimately gives the impetus to the beginning and the execution of the production, is not the only thing that must already be there.

It is with this model of human experience that Aristotle undertakes to think the being of nature and his particular achievement has become the foundation for all our concepts with which we articulate our cognition of nature. Aristotle sees nature as something that brings itself into being from out of itself, where there are no producing agents, no artists or craftsmen facing an already existing material, pursuing goals arisen from their mind, and impressing on the material the forms they invented. Aristotle sees that nature carries all that in itself: in it there is a becoming-other, even a constant becoming-other, which still is not an arbitrary flow of appearances, but always produces a permanent order and sustains it. The processes of natural occurrences thus seem as if, like the process of production, they are guided by a preexisting *purpose*, striving toward a pre-determined *form,* for example, the form of the developed living organism.

All this seems as if what already exists sets itself into motion toward its ultimate form. This material, which we prefer to call matter, appears to generate out of itself the process of becoming and change.

All this may sound very unscientific to modern ears and it [113] is absolutely true that what we have here are fundamentally merely descriptions of the course of nature as it presents itself to human experience and can be thought from the standpoint of human experience. It seems like a dangerous anthropomorphic construction when one sees purposes at work in nature and believes to be explaining what happens in nature through the idea of purpose. As a matter of fact, it was the resistance to such a teleological-dogmatic cognition of nature that allowed the modern science of the seventeenth century to think of the complex of nature only on the basis of the idea of the moving cause. The disentanglement of *causa efficiens* from out of the complex of the four causes and, in particular, out of the framework of the structural whole of the four causes, which is determined by the idea of purpose, is the birth of the concept of causality in modern thought.

However, with this change, freedom at the same time becomes a real problem. As long as a natural occurrence was thought within the same conceptuality as the purposeful action of human beings, human action and production were like a continuation, an imitation or a completion of the productivity of natural occurrence. Certainly, there belongs to such human action and production a space of free play. Ingenious craftspeople have a higher degree of freedom than nature. Within certain limits, they can almost produce anything out of any thing. Creative nature also has something of this. It fills out, as it were, a realm of the possible with its free productions. The former as well as the latter are 'freedom', but, as it were, included in what we call the course of things. As Stoic ethics did, one can even raise to the level of a principle of human morality the idea of living in harmony with nature: not setting oneself against what is inevitable in the order of natural events, steering one's will only toward what is possible, not making one's fortune dependent on the vicissitudes of human life, but grounding oneself in that which one controls. Therein lies a very precise concept of freedom, one can even say: the first concept of universal freedom. For, such a freedom is not, like the freedom proposed in Classical Greece, the freedom of action and freedom of choice of those who are their own masters, in contradistinction to the slaves, who have to follow the whims of their masters and not their own. Freedom in this sense was the property of a political status, precisely of the free. Now, in Stoic ethics freedom becomes an inner determination that is independent of all external conditions, as it is grounded in the interiority of human self-possession. According to Stoic doctrine, even the slave can be free and his master unfree by being addicted to vice.

Yet, freedom obviously becomes something completely different when one thinks of the course of nature not as a given and unchangeable order, in which one must find oneself and which limits human choice, but [114] rather as a connection that can be explained, as a network of processes that all have their cause. It is possible to disentangle this network until one can follow the individual threads and so recognize the isolated processes by the factors that cause them. Such a knowledge of nature makes it possible for human action itself to become a factor, a causal moment. The freedom implied here is not solely a freedom of self-determination, a freedom from nature, but rather also a freedom against nature, an ability to transform what happens in nature itself, to manage nature according to one's own purposes and to dominate it.

There exists an inner connection between the isolation of the efficient cause, thus the idea of cause, and the domination of nature by human beings. We have here a dialectical connection. On the one hand, we have the uninterrupted causality of events, under which we conceive of nature, and, on the other, the freedom of human beings, who control nature, to the extent that they know in advance, plan in advance, and subject the sequential connection of occurrences to their purposes. These two are not on the same level. The peculiar dialectic between freedom and natural necessity consists in this that the freedom, which makes natural occurrences susceptible to be manipulated in their inner necessity, is itself excluded at the same time by the idea of natural necessity. In the end, human beings are also natural entities. Yet, their intervention in the course of nature appears as a genuine causality, a 'causality of freedom', as Kant had called it. Its peculiarity is obviously the fact that the foreseen result of the action is, at the same time, its cause. Schopenhauer calls it a 'causality seen from the inside'. It is, in the truest sense of the word, a 'ground of motion', the motive. How is such a causality possible when nature is constituted by the uninterruptedness of the causal nexus? According to Kant, this is an irresolvable mystery for theoretical reason. Certainly, it cannot be the case that certain gaps in the chain of cause and effect make freedom possible; these would be, as it were, gaps of chance, at which points the human will could intervene. This is contradicted all too heavily by the unambiguous assertion human beings make of their awareness of being free.

For, what is at stake in the human awareness of freedom is not the fact that human beings can occasionally perceive accidental opportunities that allow them to steer the course of things. To the contrary, what is required is that the actual purposes that human beings pursue in their actions are chosen by them freely and pursued freely. Their consciousness of being free is in the end just as much their consciousness of being responsible. They feel responsible for their actions and they can feel that way only when they believe themselves to be free. Thus, it is a moral instance to which the consciousness of freedom appeals. As morally responsible beings, we cannot think of any world in which [115] our actions, that is to say, our free decisions, would not matter. The great achievement of Kantian philosophy consists not so much in the fact that it had put forth a theory for the possibility of freedom, as in the fact that, on the contrary, it proved the impossibility of a theory that would satisfactorily explain how the human will, how human freedom intervenes in natural events. Even our actions, which we perform in the consciousness of our responsibility, can most definitely result from natural determining factors when seen through the need for theoretical explanations. One only needs to think of the ungraspable difference that opens up between our conscious will and the fact that we are determined by the unconscious, even perhaps by our genes. The fateful course of life seems to exhibit two faces, depending upon whether one sees it from the inside, as the consequence of our actions and decisions, or from the outside, as the mere consequence of given factors (or even: the hand of providence). Both cases would be cases of 'causality'.

When applied to historical connections, this two-faced aspect changes its spots in surprising ways. This is because the connections of history are something other than the connections of planned actions or of the totality of our life when we confront it in the realization that it is our own destiny. These connections of history are also not simply the natural course of things. Does it even make sense here to speak of a (dual) 'causality'? It is true that history also seems to be governed by causes. Thus, certain historical laws single themselves out, such as the law that an extreme democracy usually turns into a tyranny. This is an observation on which Plato had already founded his doctrine of the cycle of state constitutions. One is tempted to say, accordingly, that these constitutions implement themselves like natural laws, whether or not the individual agents know these laws. Does this also mean that we recognize in them a causality and can use our knowledge of this causality for acting more justly? Or do only those kinds of law-like patterns become visible in history whose high formal generality hinders their practical utility? And above all: does the genuine experience of history not remain the fact that its progression is not foreseeable? It is another sense of 'cause', not the sense of the causality that determines the connection of history.

We all know the problematic that lies here from historical research. Since Thucydides, when faced with a momentous event, such as the breaking out of a war, we are used to inquiring into its causes. It is also clear to us that what immediately occasions a catastrophe does not also represent its true causes. Just as individuals cannot really feel guilty about the far-reaching historical consequences of their actions, so too the individual occasion that leads to the catastrophe cannot be its true reason. Investigating the deeper reasons for the historical course of things is absolutely not an attempt [116] at a 'causal' explanation, which would only ask for the *causa efficiens*. When we discern historical connections, we have not discovered a web of causal factors – of nature and freedom – whose threads we isolate only to be able to get our hands on them for the future – history never repeats itself. It is precisely in this that the reality of history consists: to be and to determine us, without ever being able to be mastered through a causal analysis. However, this means that the kind of 'causes' that are at work in history stand in a teleological relationship. To those who are willing and look back, failures appear more salient. History appears to them as a sequence of squandered opportunities and what has happened as their (good or bad) fortune. To those who are willing and look forward, possibilities and tasks to be accomplished appear more salient. History appears to them as that which limits the realm of their own possibilities and what has happened appears as their (good and bad) deed.

2

Historicity and Truth (1991)[1]

[247] As I entered the philosophical discussion of our century as it stood in the early 1920s, there were two problems that concerned us the most. On the one hand, there was the problem of historical consciousness with regard to the universal validity and the universally binding nature of truth. On the other hand, there was the question of the appropriate manner in which philosophers can and, perhaps, must speak about the divine.

The first of these motives was evident since the time that Hegel's predominance had weakened (after Hegel's death), when the historical school turned away from Hegel, leading to the development of the historical sense and its scientific and theoretical legitimation. It was one of the great consequences of modernity, which is most closely related to the radicality of modern enlightenment.[2]

If we start from this first root, Hegel, the way leads beyond the historical school, first of all, to Dilthey, the representative theoretician of the historical school and from him to the Dilthey school and, then, to his influences on Troeltsch and Max Weber. This puts us in the situation in which the discussion stood and in whose throes I myself was caught as a young alumnus of the Marburg school of neo-Kantianism.

As a matter of fact, it was the fundamental philosophical question of so-called historicism. It consisted of the question of how it should even be possible at all to raise claims to truth as thinkers, when we are conscious of our own historical conditioning in any of our attempts to think. How can we answer these questions as thinkers and arrive at some clarity? I hope to be able to show that this is not a problem peculiar to the nineteenth and twentieth centuries, but one that has dominated the whole tradition of metaphysics, including the whole of our thinking, since the time of Plato.

[248] For posing the question in this way, I am particularly indebted to Heidegger, who offered me then for the first time a set of tools for doing so. In the Marburg school too one talked of history, but more in the sense of the field of

all that is contingent, to which one turned only when one could no longer make progress in the great philosophical tasks of thinking and instead broadened the investigation into the 'history of problems'. For me, it was in fact a liberation to see what the young Heidegger was doing in the early 1920s. He had adopted through Husserl a phenomenology influenced by neo-Kantianism, albeit with some distance, and, at the same time, he was returning to Dilthey. As Heidegger himself told me, he hauled home the heavy volumes of the Berlin Academy of Sciences – this was before the Dilthey edition had even appeared – in which Dilthey liked to conceal his groundbreaking works. Then, just after three days, he would receive a recall notice because someone else wanted to read another essay in these thick volumes – obviously not by Dilthey, but, presumably, about some progress in electrophysics or something like it.

Very often, such biographical details shed a certain light on the real situation of the problem. Who was then this young Heidegger? In the meantime, we have come to know much more about the obscure years in which Heidegger had already left behind the work of his academic initiation. This is how I label in very general terms the dissertations that we write. Mine is at its rightful place in the mausoleum of oblivion. These dissertations are merely *oracula ex eventu*[3] if one finds out in the meantime that there was already something sensible in them. Before he came to Marburg and distinguished himself with *Being and Time,* there was little known about Heidegger's philosophical cursus and the true motivations of his thinking. When we look at his so-called 'Duns Scotus' book of 1917, we find in it brilliant logical-phenomenological analyses, but the true motivation that hides behind it was more obscured than clarified by the soft glimmers of the figure of Hegel.

Since then the situation has changed. In recent years, there has appeared a volume of the monumental and controversial giant edition of Heidegger's lectures and writings.[4] It is a lecture given in 1921–22 and so aptly edited by Walter Bröcker and his wife that nobody can find anything to criticize in it. These volumes and even more so the recent publication in the *Dilthey-Jahrbuch* of 1989, for which I wrote an introduction under the title 'Heidegger's early "theological" writing', teach us the following with absolute clarity: what mattered to the young Heidegger was an intellectual [249] justification of his Christian faith. There can absolutely be no question that this religious problem was his main concern. At the time, Heidegger had discovered Schleiermacher. Just like Husserl himself, he had read Rudolf Otto for a long time and with the greatest interest. This reminds me of how, in my earlier years, I became acquainted with Max Scheler through the mediation of my good friend Ernst Robert Curtius.

To my amazement, Max Scheler questioned me not about my revered masters in Marburg, Paul Natorp and Nicolai Hartmann, but about Rudolf Otto. So we can see how at that time, around 1920, the problem of the philosophy of religion in its phenomenological version was part of the discussion. This becomes even more clear when one realizes that the young Heidegger, who was still finding his feet, simultaneously encountered Barth's 'Epistle to the Romans' and the first writings of Gogarten in which he presents himself as a Kierkegaard reader. Of that, we now have a testimony of the first rank: the fact that Heidegger held a lecture on the phenomenology of religion in 1920. In this lecture – this will not surprise those who are acquainted with his early years – he speaks first of all and endlessly about the true concept of phenomenology. Finally, the students complained: he never talked about religion, but only about phenomenology. Heidegger was summoned by the dean. The dean was polite, as people then always were. It should be noted that our humble domains of philosophical teaching, which is the stepchild of the sciences, are not exactly representative of the university made of full professors and it is difficult to imagine that Natorp, my teacher, or Husserl or anybody else might have had something of a Mandarin in them.[5] Yet, the dean told Heidegger: 'I would like to say, first, that obviously you have all the freedom to say *ex cathedra*, what you can justify with your scientific conscience. I will not tell you what to do. But when you announce a lecture on the phenomenology of religion, it should also be about religion.'

What did the young Heidegger do? He threw away the plan he had followed so far for his argument and resumed with the Epistle to the Thessalonians. That is, he began with the famous introduction to the oldest document of Christianity, the letter that Paul wrote to the Thessalonians, among whom he had founded a Christian community. In this letter, Paul writes to his community that it should not incessantly and impatiently wait for the return of the Saviour: 'He will come like a thief in the night.' Thus, Heidegger's confrontation with the problem of time stood under the perspective of Christian expectation and promise. To speak with the concepts of the late Heidegger, this was already a first rejection of calculating thinking, of accounting and measuring, which cover up and suppress the questioning of the authentic understanding of existence and its finitude as being-toward-death.

[250] We now ask ourselves how the two anecdotes are related to each other: of the Heidegger hauling the volumes of Dilthey and the Heidegger inspired by Kierkegaard and forced by Christian revelation to the task of thinking. For an answer, we must begin with the fact that it is about the possibility of metaphysics in the age of enlightenment and science.

Pressed by this problem, Heidegger discovered a 'new' Aristotle. I remember very well how a first compelling intuition, as it appeared to us, was related to us by Heidegger with regard to Greek metaphysics; it was the intuition of how the general question of the sense of Being is necessarily related to the question of the highest being, the divine. It can be said that Book *lambda* of *Metaphysics* presents us with the birth certificate of onto-theology. I emphasize for my part the word *physics*. For, the Aristotelian question of 'being' or the question of first philosophy is founded upon physics and the authentically metaphysical book of antiquity is the *Physics*. The so-called *Metaphysics* of Aristotle is perhaps nothing other than a collection of questions and analyses that resulted from Aristotle's *Physics* and which, so to speak, summarizes everything that concerns the question of the principles at the basis of a teleological physics. When Heidegger calls this, with Feuerbach, an 'onto-theology', this epithet indeed touches an aspect of the Aristotelian project, above all the matters that are laid out in the famous book *lambda* of *Metaphysics*. It would be better to say that the project resolves an unclarity in Book *lambda* of *Metaphysics*. This unclarity resides in the relationship between analogical thinking, on the one hand, and the thinking *pros hen*, pertaining to the prime mover, on the other. These are difficult matters and really open questions. I cannot speak about this theme otherwise than by starting with the questions that are of concern to me.

There was another motivation that accompanied me all the time in the later years and it was my encounter with Leo Strauss,[6] my close friendship with him as well as my intellectual distance from him. This political philosopher, who got a position in the US, but hails from our Hessian homeland, had, in his first work, already tackled a theme that also remained in a certain sense my own life-long theme. It is the theme of the *Querelle des anciens et des modernes*. In the eighteenth century, in the glamorous Paris of Louis XIV, a debate stirred the literati and the poets. The question was: is it really possible to improve upon the model of classical Greek and Latin literature? Do we really have a chance, when we, [251] as *modernes*, enter into such a competition with the *anciens*? This question sparked debates, at first, in the literary field and then, for a long time, influenced the whole discussion in German Enlightenment. This question can be found in Garve, Gellert, Spalding, and all possible popular philosophical authors of the late eighteenth century. The question then was totally obvious: to what extent could the moderns enter into a competition with antiquity at all? Now, my thesis – and not all too bold a thesis – is that it is historical consciousness that provided the solution to this contentious question. Historical consciousness had made us aware of the inner impossibility of any mere imitation of the past; as expressed by Goethe's famous expression: 'Let anyone be a Greek in his own way, but let him be Greek!'[7] Goethe wants to say explicitly that one should not imitate the Greeks and that there can be no 'return'.

Goethe's declaration is based on the insight that we cannot opt for the *anciens* and yet this is something to which we should always look up: to the urgency of the Socratic question and to the clarity of thought that it calls for. It is worth pursuing both. My discussions with Leo Strauss always revolved around this question. Even our correspondence, which has been published in the meantime, treats the same theme. Strauss could not see that a reflection on the temporality of our understanding and the historicity of our existence is not always already at play in this question. Faced with the fact that Plato and Aristotle, the great thinkers of antiquity, had asked the question of the good without any relativization, Strauss was of the opinion that one should not deviate from the ancient immediacy of the question of the good.

The next step in our reflection must verify the claim that I made at the beginning: the modern problem of historicism is not something completely modern, but only presents a specifically modern form. In fact, it corresponds to an interest in a problem that is much older and permeates the history of Western philosophy. One can, I think, show this easily.

First of all, it is clear that Christian revelation demanded from human thinking a totally new type of questioning. Incarnation, the becoming human of God, and the resurrection from the dead cannot simply be thought by using Greek concepts. The great history of the Christian West consists in the constant attempt to do justice to the paradox of Christian revelation with the only conceptual language that the incipient Christian culture came across, namely, Greek and its Latin variants. This is the problem that we see cropping up again in Kierkegaard's critique of Hegel's dialectic and which reaches its culmination in the very contemporaneity of the Christian expiatory death with the demand faith puts on human beings.

[252] In this situation a totally new problem arises and it is what we would call, using scholastic concepts, the problem of contingency. This means that now it is no longer the case, as it was in the great world-view of Greek speculation, that only the regulations in their regularity and in their power to shape things exert their effect on the world we experience and only in this manner become an object of intellectual knowledge. Now, what matters is precisely the inconceivable aspect of what is singular. This is reflected, for example, in a familiar linguistic usage of the present, when the word 'facticity' is used. It is a word in which one hears something if the ear has been trained – and if one wants to

philosophize one must learn how to hearken back to words. To the extent that what I learned in my semantic studies was fruitful, the word 'facticity' appears, for the first time, within the Hegelian dialectical mediation of incarnation with the third member of the trinity, and this means between the faith of Easter – the facticity of the resurrection – and the outpouring of the Holy Spirit – and thus the constant renewal of the wonder exercised by the Pentecost on believers.

One encounters such an extreme solution to singularity [*Einmaligkeit*] in Hegel's philosophy. In opposition to that, on the side of theology, there was an insistence on the singularity of the event, the fact as fact. Thus, the new concept of 'facticity' was coined in order to give the fact as fact its own unique conceptual value. It is really not difficult to see how with this the problem of time too appears in a new light. This 'now' does not only represent a point in the continuum of nows following each other. It is a 'now' that includes in itself its past and its future and is more than the Janus face of a passing by and disappearing, what Eleatic and Hegelian dialectic alone recognized.

Now, my question is the following: what does this problem of temporality mean for the justification or the conceptual treatment of the possibility of faith? Certainly, nothing more than this will ever be granted to the philosopher. I think that we have gained an access here, especially through the hermeneutic turn in phenomenology – this hermeneutic turn that, in fact, goes back to the Heidegger of *Being and Time,* who on this point follows Dilthey and attempts to show that there is no appropriate concept of human existence that is not completely dependent on this wonder and puzzle of the 'there' [*Da*] in existence [*Dasein*].

In 1929 Heidegger published his second book, the Kant-book, in which, to our astonishment, suddenly *Dasein* is no longer written in one word, but as *Da-Sein* (with a hyphen and a capital 'S' for *Sein* [being]). '*Da-Sein*' was thus thought as being in the sense of the being of the there, and not as something that exists [*Daseindes*]. How can this being of the there be thought? What structure of temporality, what structure of presence [*Gegenwärtigkeit*], of existence in the common sense can the 'there' [*Da*] have? If we [**253**] want to get a grip on this question, we have to think through the tradition of Platonic and Christian philosophy as well as that of Aristotle and late antiquity in a new way.

We need to read Aristotle's work not with the eyes of the anti-Reformation systematics – and here our philological friends are not without merit. We should not construe the work of Aristotle as a system, but must read Aristotle as the development of a thinking that tentatively branches out in different directions and is still fully nurtured by the ancient reality of dialogical interlocution.

This is, in my view, the solid starting point of hermeneutic questioning: language has its genuine essence in dialogue. This means that we entrust ourselves to the guidance of language, which is superior to all subjective consciousness. We are, as it were, entangled in language and language for a long time has paved the way for us and inspired us without our knowing it, through its articulation and modulation. Rhetoric is the well-known example for this fact that language constantly threatens to push the speakers ahead of themselves and away from what they mean, and can only with difficulty be brought again to its proper task of saying what the speakers want to say. Thus, when we start with the authenticity of language, which consists in dialogue, we learn that the dialogue with the Greeks is not to be seen as an antiquarian achievement of our historical science; it is also not to be seen as an indication of our embarrassment toward a contemporary theory of knowledge or a theory of science that has been deprived of its metaphysical background. We must rather learn again to enter into a dialogue with the Greeks. It is from Heidegger that I have originally grasped this. Other people may have learned it from others. The *logos* is indeed common to all.

What is the problem here that Plato constantly poses to Aristotle? There is no doubt that the foundation that always supports human thinking about the divine represents the consciousness of our finitude, the consciousness of the fact that we have to resign ourselves. This is the classical expression of the *gnōthi seauton*[8] of the Delphic oracle, whose proper sense consists in not wanting to be God, and it also means for us: not to live in the illusion that we should do everything that our technologically driven civilization has the power to do.

All the same, there lies in it the insight that we have a common foundation. 'To become immortal as much as possible' is a famous Greek expression. One would really have to hear the expression in the way the Greeks uttered it. I do not know how to do this. We, Germans, in fact have our own Greek. Yet, whoever hears *athanatizein*[9] cannot fail to hear the vocalization of the sounds: it is an astonishing crescendo in the sound sequence *athanatizein,* as an echo [254] of *thanatos.*[10] Becoming a hero and thus the *athanatizein*, the becoming immortal was no impossible thought for Greek paganism.

When we start with the presupposition of our finitude, then the philosophical question becomes: how are we going to account for this fundamental structure of our existence in a manner that is conceptually appropriate. Even Luther and the Reformation were critics of Aristotle on this point, because the concept of being culminated in a highest being as the eternally existing divine and dominated the whole of thinking. We have, in the meantime, become conscious of the fact that even the concept of 'eternity' cannot be found in the New Testament. We have here Christian pieces of evidence that have not been utilized. Certainly, it was for good reasons that Greek metaphysics and Christian dogmatics converged into a unified influence. However, even this did not lead to a monolithic unity. I learned from the work of de Muralt[11] what kind of battles between the Scottists and the Thomists in the high Middle Ages pre-determined the ways along which the destiny of modern science would take its course. When Scotism made use of a highest principle of being, it indirectly had an influence on the thinking that is characteristic of early modernity, in the way it operates with principles. Descartes is after all a product of a Jesuit school.

On the basis of my studies of Plato, it has been clear to me for a long time that Aristotelian 'metaphysics' is a physics that goes still further beyond itself. At any rate, it is a kind of thoughtlessness to speak of a Platonic metaphysics. There has not even been a Platonic 'physics'. Plato follows a Pythagorean inspiration in the way he sees order. He contemplates the order of the spheres, the order of the classes in the ideal city, and the order of the powers in the human soul together in one large view. It was a thinking in which, as I have already emphasized, the problem of contingency as such could not be posed legitimately. When we understand it correctly, this means that Plato spoke of the divine always in the neuter: *to theion* – the divine. Certainly, Plato respected the mythical past and the mythical tradition of Greek culture as he worked his own findings into his dialogues in an unforgettable manner: multiple, ironic and playful, reflective and fragmentary. Time and again he also amalgamated the old models of the religion based on Zeus and of Olympus into his critical thinking. However, he considered the world of the gods to be a human invention, as in the famous myth of the *Phaedrus*. The divine itself is certainly not a human invention, but the forms are, in which we represent the divine as a being, as gods and their actions on human beings. All this already belongs [255] to the domain of Greek enlightenment, which is conscious of itself – what Herodotus already stressed and what anyone reading Homer with contemporary eyes can only confirm. There is already a whiff of enlightenment there, a whiff of playful freedom, which the poetry and the thought of the early Greeks took for themselves against the dominant ritual practices, and which Plato also nurtured through the mastery displayed in his thinking and poeticizing.[12]

By contrast, the Aristotelian way leads beyond physics and from there to an unmoved mover, and this means to a highest existent, to God – to the God or the Gods, as the case maybe; at any rate, to a being. The argument rests on the thought of the first mover and on the presence to itself of the moving

God; obviously, as Theophrastus showed, this argument presupposes a loving, striving soul. Let us ask ourselves what this means for the temporal character of the whole.

First, let me make a general remark about the neuter. The neuter is one of the advantages of the Greek and German languages. The neuter has something of a present that can never be localized, and therefore its particular poetic magic moves us, when we read, for example, in Goethe, Hölderlin, Rilke or Trakl such nouns as 'the' serene, or the like. In the neuter 'the', we have the pure presence and the ubiquitous present of a 'there' that encompasses everything and shrouds everything. This is the great power of the neuter that it exercises presence precisely through the fact that it cannot be localized, but can in some way be 'there' everywhere. It is by no means necessarily linked to the pantheistic form of thinking, even if precisely this aspect of the concept of 'the divine' has been attacked as heresy over and over again in history, especially in Christian mysticism. Even the young Heidegger began at that time – it was truly in the air – to turn to Meister Eckhart in order to learn how to pose the question of 'being'. It is in Meister Eckhart's *Opus Tripartitum*, which appeared in 1924, that Heidegger read: *Deus est suum esse.*[13] It strikes me as remarkable that a great thinker and Church dignitary as Nicholas of Cusa dedicated his philosophical work to the task of showing that Meister Eckhart was absolutely not a heretic.

It is not only the question of being, but also the problem of time, which is of particular interest to us, that merits a return to Plato.[14] In the Platonic dialogue *Parmenides* there is a remarkable excursus (or whatever it is), in which the dialectic of being and being one, one and being, is developed. It is then shown that it belongs to being that there is also becoming in it. It is then asked as to when the passage from [**256**] being-in-movement to being-at-rest actually takes place. On this, the Platonic *Parmenides* cites the remarkable essence of *exaiphnes*, the Greek designation for 'the sudden', 'the abrupt'.[15] It is something puzzling. What is it? An ultimate being? A first becoming? Or the other way around? The dialectic of the sudden seems to be a Heraclitean motif that Plato took over, and he used it to describe a fundamental human experience. I am thinking, for example, of the mystery of sleeping and the puzzle of waking up. Suddenly one is awake. There is no transition. One can see in Heraclitean sentences how very closely the mystery of sleep is linked to the mystery of death. We all know the German saying 'he sleeps like a corpse'. The puzzle of this absence in presence and this return to presence when we wake up: it is not a progressive transition, as little as is the loss of consciousness. It is something that we can only describe as being without transition. These matters, it seems to me, were reflected upon by the Greeks very early on with utter lucidity. It stays in the background, even in Aristotle, when God in the sense of Aristotelian theology, the God who thinks itself and maintains itself as present, is distinguished by its continuity, whereas for us, human beings, being awake and perception are never granted without interruption. In these experiences there lies discontinuity, that which is mysteriously sudden and without transition, which challenges our thinking and makes us experience time.

However, this passage of the dialogue *Parmenides* remarkably played no role in the whole history of the Western philosophy of antiquity and after. There is one single testimony that appears in Pseudo-Dionysius and is not essential, because it starts in the usual manner of the late antiquity with etymological plays: 'What breaks out of the invisible' – this is how the sudden is interpreted. A second testimony is a playful 'table talk' in Aulus Gellius.[16] The first one to take the passage in Plato seriously is Kierkegaard. In 'The Concept of Anxiety' he dedicated a long note to this remarkable phenomenon of the sudden, of the moment. This is the problem of time that appears throughout the always disquieting and stimulating attempts made by the late Heidegger. What kind of temporal character is this when it is not 'in' time? I have myself made a few attempts[17] and since Bergson, who goes back to Schelling and romanticism, the theme has lurked on the horizon. The young Heidegger and the young Tillich turned in particular to the Greek concept of *kairos*. It is clear that time should not only be thought with Aristotle in the sense of an uninterrupted continuity of the sequence of nows and in the sense of duration, and certainly not as measured time. Temporality must rather [257] appear in the fulfilled moment or in the 'while' [*Weile*], which stands behind any talk of 'because' [*weil*]. Thus, Heidegger later on, going as far back as the pre-Socratics, tries to extricate the 'while' from Anaximander, in order to find again his own ways of thinking.

I now believe that the problem of historicism, at which the methodological self-consciousness of the modern theory of knowledge and its methodology modeled on the sciences have toiled away in vain, can only be resolved by going back to the oldest questions of being and of time.

How does the problem appear to the historical human sciences? One is used to hearing, for example, from the Vienna Circle, that the human sciences are at most ten percent science and when it comes to the concept of scientificity, as developed in the Vienna Circle, this is probably putting it too mildly. In any case, it is upon the other ninety percent that we rely for our life in common and for human solidarity. This ninety percent opens for us possibilities of dialogue about truth, which is the *logos* that is common to us all, even if only ten percent satisfies the norms of scientificity. Objectivity means objectification. It signifies a constricting prejudice everywhere in that realm where breaking resistance and achieving control are not actually paramount, but rather being together and participating in the hermeneutic universe in which we live with one another. In this regard, I could show how Platonism, in addition to Aristotelianism, makes itself repeatedly relevant for the exegesis of Christian mystery and, altogether, how in the time of the enlightenment the pronouncements of art reach deep into the life of individuals and peoples, beyond all historical distances and differences as well as beyond practical and political decisions.

There were two problems, which, in this manner, prompted a return to the resources in Plato's thought: the problem of historical relativism, on the one hand, and, on the other, the questionable nature of all talk of and about God, as if God were an object offering resistance to our knowledge. In both problems the same presupposition is at work, which stems from an insufficient critique of the modern concept of science and from a wrong application of such a concept. It is to miss the sense of the question of God to think that an anonymous subject would turn God into an object that it could learn to master through knowledge. This is what I tried to make clear when I talked about the divine, which Plato places before all metaphysics. It became clear with Plato how the question of the divine continues to be raised within the experience of human beings and their finitude. To speak like Aristotle, it is a practical knowledge and he even calls it one of the highest forms of praxis, wherein human beings maintain themselves in the 'there' of being, which is not so much a knowing as a **[258]** true being-there-alongside [*Dabeisein*], like the 'being-there-alongside' of participating in a delegation to a celebration that the Greeks called *theoria*.

Here, there is absolutely no problem of relativism. The basis of this problem is the concept of truth that is operative in the sciences and the objectification at work in all fields of research. However, this is no relationship of partnership and such a relationship is imposed upon us by the circumstances of our temporality and our historicity. That is the reason why Plato was helpful. For, he showed the limits of the Aristotelian concept of time and of all measuring, which shapes the concept of objectivity common in the modern sciences.

However, Aristotle himself helps us when he shows us the relevance of practical knowledge, which, in its inseparability from *ethos*, determines all of the accounts we can give about that in which we participate without exercising domination.

3

The History of the Universe and the Historicity of Human Beings (1988)[1]

[206] For a full century, we have attempted to delineate the human sciences by contrasting them with the natural sciences, to the extent that the human sciences have been measured by the scientific character proper to the kind of sciences they are. This was so even though it was clear that the human sciences could not attain a similar level of scientificity as the natural sciences, given that they did not have the same methodological rigour and thus the same concept of objectivity for scientific knowledge. From the perspective of the post-romantic period, in which the natural sciences made their triumphant advance, the human sciences were even called the inexact sciences.

Now, present-day researchers opine that both groups of sciences might eventually merge together again, but not because the so-called human sciences would in the meantime have become more exact, but because the natural sciences themselves would have been transformed. This is the case because the latter would have accepted their temporal dimension. We have learned, the claim continues, to see the history of the universe as one single great process of evolution, leading from its first beginning to our present solar system, and encompassing the history of the earth and with it also all histories. Thus, the opposition between the natural sciences and the historical human sciences would be deprived of its relevance and we would draw closer to a new unified science, which would indeed be the science of the history of the universe. Under the gigantic panorama of one single great process of development, this science would include everything: nature, the spiritual realm, the nature of human beings, and all the vicissitudes of humanity. Such is, roughly, the expectation: the history of the world seen from the vantage-point of such an immense measuring scale would at the same time be world history.

Will those who are familiar with the work of the human sciences be able to share such an expectation or will they have to insist on the obvious difference in the manner in which both of these huge groups of sciences operate? Can one expect anything from such a unified science, which grounds itself on the unity of history in one single time, [207] permeating the whole of reality? The thematic distinction I make between 'history' and 'historicity' should already suggest to those who have an ear for it that I believe I detect a dangerous equivocation here. The word 'historicity' means something different from what the science of the history of the universe, understood in such an encompassing manner, takes as its object.

Let us begin by recalling the status of the discussion. The epistemological debate of the nineteenth century attempted to show how two different methodological ideals and therefore two different concepts of scientific knowledge were in opposition here. Wilhelm Windelband showed in a famous presentation that the nomothetic sciences engage in a research that focuses on laws, whereas in the ideographic sciences the epistemological efforts aim at grasping the individual, the historically singular and the unrepeatable. There is something illuminating in this view. Beginning with this, one can understand how we have come to expect that the methodological opposition between these two classes of sciences would have become meaningless. For indeed, these days, even the natural sciences really take what is singular as their object, namely, the process of the universe, just as the historical sciences attempt to research something singular with 'ideographic' interests. We hear about the history of the universe that it began with the original explosion, the Big Bang,[2] hence with a singular event. At this point we, the feeble-minded scholars in the human sciences, ask the obvious question: and what was there beforehand, prior to this singular event? And the new unity already falls apart. From our counterparts on the other side we elicit only a slight smile. With such a smile they also shove aside the speculative attempts, which play with the idea of conceiving rhythmic models in order to make intelligible the whole process of evolution after the Big Bang, as a pulsation in the recurring rhythm of the course of nature. However, in such a speculation no singular event would remain anymore and it would no longer be the beginning of the universe. Such speculations are, at any rate, far from what science understands by scientificity. It thus remains that in the dialogue with the natural scientists, we have *de facto* to accept a singular process and a universal development, which we call 'evolution', whose secrets the research of the last decades was increasingly able to elucidate. Obviously, we do not deny that this evolution also includes the particular conditions under which life developed on this planet and eventually something like the emergence of the human race, and this means: such beings who do history or cultivate historical memory.

Such a theory of evolution is truly all-encompassing. However, one has [208] to say immediately that this theory of evolution encroaches upon the future, beyond all historical experience. If there is indeed such an evolution, which affects the whole universe, then it follows in fact that this evolution in always pressing onward somehow pulls the future of the totality into our speculation. Here Foucault comes to mind. This may exceed our cognitive capacities, but it is thought 'scientifically' and fundamentally promises a *savoir pour prévoir*.[3] Now, the situation is completely different in the case of history, as indicated by Jacob Burckhardt's famous words about history. Burckhardt said: the benefit of history consists not in in the fact that we become smarter for the next time, but that we become wiser forever.[4] This must sound unusual to the ears of a natural scientist. First of all, natural scientists expect absolutely no kind of benefit from their kind of science, other than an increase in knowledge. When they extend their will to know to the history of the universe so broadly that they also implicate its future, they are indeed again looking for knowledge, but not to become wise or smart.

But how did we come to this? One can wonder about what kind of connection there can be between the history of the universe and the history that human beings experience with one another and in one another. One only needs to realize how little the gigantic history of the universe as disclosed by the sciences coincides with the history that is easily visible since the time the human species came to exist on this planet. This is plainly the case when we mean the history of humanity in the sense in which the human sciences speak of history. Just asking what this connection must be can make us dizzy. How could it make any kind of sense to insert into the totality of the evolutionary process of the universe this tiny portion of a timespan that is illuminated by the light of tradition? Yet, what imposes itself upon us when it comes to broadening the historical horizons is precisely to stop thinking of this gigantic framework into which the little bit of human destiny called world history almost disappears.

By contrast, the horizon of world history, in which we encounter our own history, has been significantly broadened in our century. When I was at school, in the years before the First World War, and held the first historical charts in my hand, everything still began with biblical history, even if not quite with the creation itself and the Flood. It was the history of the Israelites, which could be correlated with Egyptian history. The latter was the only one with which we had a historical connection through the Exodus of the children of Israel from Egypt. This is how the Biblical tradition was presented then and it still resonates today with our account of time according to which [209] we distinguish the centuries or the millennia (or eventually even the millions of years of the history of the universe) through 'BC' and 'AD'.

The situation is completely different today. Our thinking about history has made great strides. Biblical history is no longer immediately followed by Homer and the history of Greece and Rome. When I was a student, I once read a formidable canvas of historical fantasy about the second millennium before Christ painted by the genial dilettante Oswald Spengler. His depiction fascinated me. In the meantime, I have often come across this millennium in my own research into the history of Greek philosophy and science and this led me to ask how it actually came to be that the unique history of Europe started with ancient Greece and Christianity. How could science in our own Western history become the fundamental feature of an advanced culture? There were advanced cultures of the highest rank, as we have known for a long time, and in these cultures too a great deal of scientific knowledge had been compiled, containing in our own eyes important contributions, essentially to geometry and astronomy. Yet, this was something still different. What we have to ponder today is still the fact that we live in a culture, in which science for centuries developed into a determining factor, not only in Europe but also in the whole world. The success and the consequences of our scientific culture have become a global problem. It is the problem of humanity precisely in relation to the future that is hidden from us. We are beginning to be keenly aware of the problem of ecology. We also know very well how many uncertainties lurk when it comes to managing the sustenance of humanity on earth and the conservation of nature, on the survival and equilibrium of which we all depend in ways that are incalculable. For, we can perform many calculations, even if not in specific terms. Since the irreversibility of certain processes must lead to situations of depletion, we can hardly avoid thinking of a limit situation. Here it becomes readily palpable how oddly it sits with the gigantic evolutionary process of the universe that here, on this one heavenly body – as we still refer to the earth in such a charmingly old-fashioned manner – there are thinking beings who constantly harbour in them the question of the where-from and the where-to.

In the end, this broadening of horizons, i.e. the world history of human beings, which used to be called 'universal history' in the eighteenth century, turns out to be rather remarkably modest. We certainly know that, without Egypt and Babylon, no Thales and no Greek sage of ancient times would have been conceivable. Nonetheless, we know equally well that none of these other cultures of ancient times had developed, despite their great [210] achievements in geometry or algebra, anything like the idea of scientific method in the

Western style. How should we properly conceive of the relationship between the history of the universe and what we call world history? If, on the one hand, we have the history of the universe and, on the other, the historicity of human beings, then we have to recognize that it is a specious argument to say that the history of the universe also includes the history of human beings. This may certainly be true in the sense of a mathematical and physicalistic projection of temporal expansion. However, when we question our historical beginnings, this argument suddenly becomes meaningless.

Let us turn again to this authentic historical question of how, from the obscure background of our ignorance, incipient Europe slowly enters our horizon. We recognize here, for example, the significance that the invention of alphabetical writing has had for our civilization. It was certainly not a European invention, but nonetheless something that belongs quite essentially to the great destinal course of the West. Besides other possibilities of writing, there emerged this infinitely abstract development of our alphabetical writing and it spread quickly over Greece and eventually over the whole of our Western culture. Without the invention of writing and the expansion of our alphabet, we would know much less about the historical beginnings into which we inquire. How far back, though, can we really go? To Homer or the Old Testament or to the deciphering of Egyptian hieroglyphs, first made possible by modern science? These are all too modest advances for bringing the early history of humanity closer to the history of the universe.

Let us take another fascinating example. In the time of the Hitlerian insanity about race there was, among other things, a fatal abuse that involved harnessing the results of pre-historical research in the service of racial ideology. The word 'dilettantish' is a mild expression for this. In the meantime, serious research has gained some ground in bringing together pre-historical and archaeological knowledge, which is ultimately also supported by the literary tradition. My friend, the late Vladmir Milojcic, has accomplished something groundbreaking in the Balkans, although he unfortunately could not himself communicate the full fruits of his research. For the first time in the Balkans, he closed the gap between pre-historical and archaeological tradition. It will perhaps also be possible in other cases to come closer to the outer limits of tradition through field research. We would no longer dare say with Hegel that world history began with the linguistic tradition and with texts. True, [211] we will maintain that the dimension of language [*Sprachlichkeit*] and the dimension of writing [*Schriftlichkeit*][5] represent something absolutely decisive for our awareness of the past. Yet, we will hesitate to limit all knowledge of the past to language and to writing. Eventually, the great revolution of modern historical research of the early nineteenth century and its continuation into the twentieth century consisted in breaking away from the mere historical narratives of the Greco-Roman literary tradition or any other literary traditions and in attempting to open up the immediate documents of historical life. It was already something that scholars were no longer content with Herodotus or Thucydides or Livy, that is to say: with historiography, but researched the archives and then, mainly through archaeological excavation, brought the testimonies of the historical past into historical research. This is how Collingwood, the great investigator of the Roman *limes* on the Bristish Isles, acquired world renown through his speculative gifts and, at the same time, as a field archaeologist. When field research was still in its fledgling state, he inaugurated a new era in our knowledge of the past.

All these examples of a broadening of historical memory revolve around the fact of tradition. What indeed is a tradition? What is handed down? What does it mean that something is handed down? A body of testimony? Obviously, it is not the mere retelling of some testimony about something that is no more or a discovery of its traces on the basis of remnants. It is also about monuments. A monument is something that makes us think of something and about which we should think. It is not merely something that has remained or survived in memory. Here we can see that the unity of the history of the universe is something different from the unity of historical memory and its preservation. When looking back in historical recollection or in vague hints of the kinds monuments awaken in us, do we think, for example, about what the emergence of the *homo sapiens* in the history of the universe means? Obviously, there also belongs to the history of the universe the question as to when humanity first appeared on this planet, which we call the Earth, and how the human species evolved – and perhaps also whether and when to expect the extinction of this species. Human beings would then be recorded like key fossils in a chapter of the history of the universe. Yet, this historical past, which we awaken through what monuments and tradition give us as hints, means something else. 'World history' is not a phase in the history of the universe, but is a whole in its own right. It is not primarily through the so-called 'facts',[6] which can be established in objective research with the methods of the natural sciences, that we have a knowledge of this history that we call world history. I have nothing against all of what objective research, even in historical research, attempts to secure as facts with all its methods, circumspection and caution. [212] To this extent, there are methodological procedures even in the human sciences and they are equally indispensable. If we had the rich imagination of a Herodotus or were living in a profusion of streams of legends, as the epic poets of Greece, legend and history would merge into one another. After the fall and rebuilding of so many traditions, as they still live in our historical consciousness, there will always be new facts to awaken our interest. Where does our interest in these facts come from? What kind of question is it for which we only take a fact as an answer?

I would like to say in a very general sense: we know everything from mythical recollection. By this, I have in mind, first of all, only that which is the essence of the mythical, namely this, that it is not checked and verified in terms of correctness. It simply goes against the sense of the mythical to demand such a verification. The mythical is also not provable. Here one should recall the words of Aristotle who said: it is the mark of the educated person to know of what to demand proofs and of what not to demand them.[7] The same is true for the mythical tradition. 'Myth' indeed means nothing other than narrative, but it is a narrative that authenticates itself, that is to say: a narrative that one does not attempt to authenticate and confirm. Yet, caught in our scientific impulse of the nineteenth century we certainly held that, for example, Schliemann started the excavation of Troy in order to demonstrate definitely that Homer had not imagined things. In the meantime, we have learned how much he imagined and how magnificent it is that he imagined it. The demand for authentification and confirmation in fact corresponds to an understandable human desire for knowledge and has its legitimacy. Yet, it can be that we do not see beyond such demands, overlooking what is truly more important for us than stones, bones, tombs with their votive offerings. It is true that all these findings can be monuments and any monument points to something that is to be thought about and is not just something like a fact to be known. In the face of the overwhelming model of natural scientific research, it requires a long and deeper reflection if we have to realize how questionable it is to transfer the self-interpretation that is typical of modern science onto our historical self-understanding and how misunderstandings and misjudgements lurk menacingly in such a move. When Aristotle said that poetry is truer, that is to say, 'more philosophical', and includes more knowledge than 'history', this claim is at first glance hardly intelligible on the basis of the modern concept of science.[8] Yet, this is what a Greek says in the age of an incipient enlightenment and the great unfolding of Greek mathematics and Hellenistic science. It was at this time that science developed, which in many respects still corresponds to what we call science. It was at that time that, in exemplary fashion, Euclidean geometry and [213] inferential logic developed perfectly in all their sophistication. Even now, the mathematics taught in our middle schools is Euclidean. If it is also true that there was a Greek science – and similarly a Greek philology – there also persisted alongside them a broadly dominant presence of mythical recollection, which impressed itself upon the entire world horizon of all those who lived and thought at that time.

We can see today that, for example, a poet like Homer was no theologian and that it is a peculiar misunderstanding to speak of a 'Homeric theology'. In the nineteenth century, entire books were filled with this title, discussing Homeric theology. One often encountered difficulties here, for example, when it is said that Zeus hung all the other Gods on a chain outside Olympus when they did not comply with his will until they eventually caved in. These are nice stories that Homer tells us, but they do not have the value of facts and also not, as in Christian theology, that of truths.

With regard to epic mythology, it is understandable that the research in the history of religion in the nineteenth century preferred to stick to the so-called research into cults. There, one can really find 'facts'. We have fragments of sculptures and pots, inscriptions or a report that was preserved into later times, informing us about cult *mores* in ancient times. These are indeed facts on which one can build something. By contrast, a Protestant scholar, such as Wilamowitz, interpreted Homeric mythology and the Greek world of legends in general as the decline of an authentic religious life. Despite this I would still recommend that we read Homer himself. What he narrates still grabs us today by its humanity. I remember my own experiences in secondary school, when we took the side of either Achilles or Hector. In the militaristically minded Germany before the First World War, our games reflected our childish sympathy for the great underdog Hector. What draws us to these poems over and over again and what in these poems always remains close to us, is that everything is so human. We have at the beginning of the *Illiad* the depiction of a magnificent scene: Agamemnon must give up a slave woman, a prisoner of war who had been promised to him, because she had to be freed on the basis of a revelation by an oracle; now the 'King' Agamemnon demands a prisoner of war in compensation from Achilles. This is how the disastrous feud arises before Troy. We see how Achilles in rage draws his sword from the sheath, but at the last moment the mighty Athena appears to him and warns him. The text continues: and at the last moment he puts the sword back in the sheath and regains his self-control. There are two interpretations of the same process: the warning by the [214] Goddess and the regaining of self-control. This is how enlightenment goes hand in hand with the mythical world and this is in fact the great law of life governing the ancient will to know. The tradition of legend and myth always goes hand in hand with enlightenment. What was then called *historia* meant a knowledge that relied on findings through eyewitnesses or their reports. The Greeks did not call such a form of knowledge 'science'. This is neatly attested to by the sceptics, for example, by Sextus Empiricus. He made all the sciences of his time – and these were philosophy and mathematics – objects of his sceptical critique because of their unreliability. The historical 'sciences' are as little mentioned as the epic tradition. This was not science. Historiography was a way of telling stories just as travelers tell stories. This brings to mind the marvelous sailor slang that Homer put in the mouth of his Ulysses in a magnificent poetic form. Nevertheless, it is in this tradition of Greek story telling that the model of all modern critical history arose – Thucydides. This recollection shows how the magnificent world orientation of the early Western beginnings of scientific culture in Greece was established in equal proportion on myth and history, i.e. on findings, but certainly not on inferential logic, like mathematics or an experience based on mathematical instrumentation.

Something like this was brought about for the first time by the significant turn to the modern concept of science, which began in the seventeenth century. A famous treatise by Galileo, 'The Dialogue on the Two World Systems', can be seen as the fundamental book of a physics that is intelligible, i.e. intelligible for lay-people in the human sciences. Galileo was an educated man. His dialogue is conducted with a partner who has the beautiful name of Simplicio. It is a telling name; one only needs to think of *Sancta Simplicitas*.[9] The play in this name naturally emphasizes simple-mindedness. A second play consists in this that a certain Simplicius, a scholarly commentator of Aristotle, was the man to whom we owe the understanding of Aristotelian physics up into the beginning of modernity. The discussion between Galileo and his partner Simplicio is thus fundamentally the discussion between the modern scientific sensibility and Aristotelian physics. Aristotle appears as the representative of all prejudices. Galileo's dialogue partner Simplicio refuses to look through the telescope or to use the microscope Galileo offers him. This is similar to Goethe, who too did not like such things; for example, he did not like that people wear glasses. A fundamental condition of our being-in-the-world seemed to him to be disturbed if it was not the naturally equipped sensuous being that encountered without any mediation the phenomena that appear in nature. In his unfortunate fight against [215] Newton, Goethe found, as we know, the support of the great German thinkers of his epoch: Schelling, Hegel and Schopenhauer. This is how powerful the great tradition of the Greek cultural heritage was, in which a unified picture of the world was bequeathed to us: a world-picture that encompassed together nature and human destinies. The Greek heritage consisted in this: human beings experience an order that maintains itself and constantly renews itself in nature, in the sky, as in the case of 'meteors', i.e. in terrestrial natural phenomena that indeed do not reach the wonderful regularity of the movements of the stars.

The Greek expression for this experience of order is quite familiar to all of us. It is the concept of 'cosmos', which means the arrangement of order as well as the ornament, the beauty of this order. Beauty itself was retained in the word 'cosmos', and not only in the derived form of 'cosmetics'. In the Greek world-view such a comprehensive idea of order was the universally valid model even for the human soul and for the life of human beings in society. The political unity of Greek life was the *polis*, the city and the city state (if one may say so), and in it order means, above all, the order of justice. This is how the Greeks came to think the equilibrium of the universe (Anaximander) under legal concepts. This is also how eventually even the concept of law, which in fact received the particular connotation of 'natural law' first in late antiquity, is something that survives in modern science.

This idea of order according to laws is already reflected in the mythological tradition of the Greeks when Zeus comes to dominate. In Hesiod it becomes clear how the order of justice founds itself in this manner and simultaneously determines all things in the course of nature. The regular order of day and night, the sequence of the seasons, even the changing conditions of the weather despite all turbulence, all this carries with it our trust in the recurrence of our being-in-the-world. Here in Greek thinking a form of thought was elevated to the level of a concept. The city and the human soul, despite all their passions and confusions, were thought on the model of the order of the universe, a model that we strive to uphold in our human relationships and in the constitution of our community. There is a memorable passage in the *Phaedo* concerning Socrates' refusal of the offer to flee from prison. On the last day of his life, before he has to drink the cup of hemlock, Plato has him recount in long dialogues how he was disappointed by the science of his time and what he had expected from the sciences: that they would allow him to understand why the earth is the steady centre of all worldly occurrences in the same way as he 'would understand' – and this means: why he would deem it good and right – that he stays in jail and lets the unjust judgement on him be [216] carried out. This is also how nature had to be known and understood: it is such as it is because it is good that it is so. What Socrates is demanding here found its response in Aristotelian physics and in the teleological mode of thinking that found its powerful intellectual expression in metaphysics and physics for many centuries. This was the adversary against whom the new science of modernity would have to impose itself. The emergence of modern science was a true revolution, whose precursors have come to be known in the meantime evermore clearly. It imposed itself fully in the seventeenth century. At that time, the homogenous unity of the ancient way of thinking about the world exploded. We still think of this unity today with a form of nostalgia and it continued to exercise its fascination time and time again even on someone like Goethe. This unity that existed in ancient thought between the view of nature, the view of society, and the view of the soul is something that continues to move us, because it is something we are lacking.

This certainly should not mean that there could be a possible return to such a system of ultimate purposes, which the great and triumphant irruption of modern science opposed. It remains that the loss of unity that this irruption signifies has become our destiny. This has been reflected in the very word of 'philosophy' itself. Originally, this word means nothing other than theoretical knowledge in general, which encompasses everything. Even modern research into nature has maintained this meaning of 'philosophy' in one of its classic masterpieces. Newton's work is entitled *Philosophiae Naturalis Principia Mathematica.*[10] Physics was still philosophy for him. In the eighteenth century this was naturally little more than a last glimmer on the horizon. Yet, a great step toward unity was made when Newton recognized the physics of heavenly bodies and the physics of terrestrial bodies as one and the same physics and so could ground a new mechanical-dynamical unity of natural occurrences in their universality. What did this mean, though, for the destiny of thought in modernity? If the order of nature was only a play of forces and energies, what happened then to the orders that human beings established for themselves in social life? They were left deprived of the model provided by the heavenly order that encompassed everything terrestrial. A peculiar rupture was thus made and there was a new need for justification. What imposed itself in the seventeenth century was a new concept of science. Founded upon experimentation and mathematics, it was a new attitude focused on quantification that, in constant progress and lasting self-improvement, eventually transformed science into research.

The entire great heritage of the intellectual tradition of Western culture, a heritage that was of humanistic as well as of Christian origin, was placed under a new compulsion to justify itself. Compared to the claim to universality of the methodological sciences, how can this tradition still prove its own legitimacy? It became the task of modern [217] philosophy to provide such a legitimacy and its visible expression is the appearance of the concept of 'system of philosophy'.

Originally the term 'system' was an astronomical and musical expression, which came to present itself as something else. In the past, in antiquity, what mattered was to conceive in their unity the cyclical movement of a heaven with fixed stars and the clearly deviant movement of the wandering stars, which we designate by the Greek term 'planets'. This is what the concept of 'system' accomplished: to explain the 'connection' of what seems incompatible. In the eighteenth century, this term of 'system' also began to be adopted for naming the new task of philosophy, which consisted in reconciling the great cultural heritage of human knowledge with the claim to universality made by the new empirical sciences. German idealism undertook such a great attempt at reconciliation for the last time and such an attempt has not been repeated until the emergence of academic epigones in the nineteenth and twentieth centuries. For, it is an implacable demand of reason to look for or reach the unity of knowledge. However, if, on the one hand, we have the cultural heritage of the European experience of the world, which stems from the Greeks and Christianity and, on the other, an unstoppable progress in the knowledge and control of nature, then there is no way to integrate the sciences into the conceptual totality of an *a priori* truth. The idea of a universal science that would encompass all truths, as philosophy once was, is obviously irreconcilable with the perspective of experience, whose unending progress refines further and surpasses any established truth. A speculative physics, which knows *a priori* and does not progress along the methodological lines of research, could not reach any durable reconciliation with the empirical sciences (Schelling). This is what Kant recognized in the eighteenth century. He defended a critical limitation of the empirical facts to phenomena. At the same time, he legitimized another sense of facts, which is constituted through the 'fact of reason' that human freedom is.

It was a fundamental insight of the 'critique', which was only understood negatively by philosophy in the age of science and became a turning point only as a critique of the ideal of a dogmatic metaphysics. I was exactly eighteen years old when, in my hometown of Breslau still during the First World War, I attended the first lecture course of a professor of philosophy who rejected dogmatic metaphysics in the Kantian sense. It sent chills down our spine just to hear how the word 'dogmatic metaphysics' sounded. Kant was now seen as the one who grinds everything to dust, as Mendelsohn, a contemporary of Kant, already characterized him. Philosophy then seemed to be confined to the grounding and justification of the empirical sciences and their mathematical foundations. A total reversal of events had thereby been accomplished. Formerly, in the Middle Ages, [218] philosophy and metaphysics were the *ancilla theologiae.*[11] Now, philosophy has become the *ancilla scientiarum*, the handmaiden of the sciences, and was called to service with the ceremonious name of 'theory of knowledge'.

Was this really all that the deliberation of humanity had gathered from experience and insight during the course of its life? The true merit of Kant, which gained full philosophical recognition for the first time in our century, was the fact that the claim to universality proper to the sciences has a limit and that human freedom can never be a fact of experience in the sense of the empirical sciences. Human freedom is only a fact for human beings who are agents. What is totally beyond the concept of experience as it is defined by a method demands a justification that can no longer retrocede behind physics in a 'meta-physics', but rests on the basis of human freedom, which is not a natural fact. This is the great legacy that the human sciences oversee and have to defend in their constant confrontation with the scientific ideal of the natural sciences. The question was: are the human sciences really only inexact sciences? They do not take as their object the 'phenomena', as Kant defined the object of theoretical sciences. As a result, one has attempted to define the 'object' of the human sciences differently by introducing the concept of value. Values belong to the order of what is given, which allows us to find our bearings. Values, thus, possess a normative quality and clearly cannot be grasped as such by the methodological concept of a 'value-free' research.

What was needed was to liberate the human sciences from a direct dependency on the methodological ideal of the natural sciences in order to place them under another ideal. This ideal is certainly not to be measured with the controllable certainty of a science of facts. This precisely explains why the human sciences, for their part, are concerned with something that requires a totally different kind of insightfulness and comprehensibility. What I mean by this is anything but new. Rather, the opposite is the case: the irruption of the new scientific mentality, a research mentality, a quantifying mentality brought modernity under the aegis of modern science. Its knowledge does not find its place in a larger framework of order that is evident to everybody. The questions that had always motivated the human will to know go significantly over and beyond what can find acceptable answers according to the principles of modern scientificity, even beyond what can be asked under those principles. This is not some kind of limit that we impose upon the sciences. These are limits that nature itself has set, to the extent that nature, in the great process of evolution of the universe, caused beings to emerge, human beings, who are so equipped by nature that they not only **[219]** fulfil their natural determination, but also want to know.

Modern science is itself one of the big triumphal products of this freedom and audacity, with which human beings have to configure the order of their life within nature itself. This is how science was born in the Greek world and also how it assumed a new form with modern scientificity. It is the pre-condition of human nature in its drive to question and its capacity to know, and it lies at the basis of the modern scientific mentality as well as at the basis of religious representations, legal organizations, moral organizations, economic forms, and even at the basis of the organization of the activities of war and peace, as they have been developed by human beings. All this belongs to the configuration of reality, which nature left in the hands of human beings and within which human beings stumble everywhere upon their limits. Modern empirical sciences too have their limits. They only reach as far as their empirical scientific methods permit. This does not mean that, in every human cultural formation, the methodological self-discipline of modern scientificity cannot prove itself to be of value. Our human task will always remain to integrate the progress of our human knowledge and our capacity into what is already given to us in terms of a nature and a culture that we inhabit.

As a result, we now face colossal tasks. There are the unforeseen advances made by information systems to which modern technology has led. Increasingly, even the sciences that we call human sciences, share in the progress of this technological development of the means of knowledge and information. How much more complete is a computer generated index of today! How quickly are users serviced at a library thanks to a computer! Any book is quickly available. But is this really only a progress? I have always had my doubts. Although all the information we need is available immediately, I wonder whether it is not better that, when having forgotten something, I have to look for it again and, perhaps, in the process, find something other than what I was looking for. This is what we truly call doing research: to ask questions that always lead to further questions, which we did not anticipate. We are now facing totally new possibilities for alleviating the burden on our memory. This entails that we no longer need our own mental power in order to reawaken what we have forgotten and we no longer nurture recollection. What this will amount to, what kind of changes in the ways human beings live together will befall humanity, as yet we have absolutely no idea. We also do not know how we will come to terms with so many other possibilities that are now newly available to us in managing the organization of our life. It seems as if we have had to pay for the advances in the information systems used in the human sciences [220] with losses in the cultivation of the productive powers of the imagination and creativity.

The situation cannot be totally different in the natural sciences. Yet, where we are dealing with measuring and processing data, things are different. What these advances will make possible in the natural sciences is unforeseeable. In many fields we have come so far with these new advances that research, which previously required twenty years, can now produce results with a computer in a matter of minutes. This has undoubtedly resulted in gains, but also in tasks that turn out to be evermore difficult when it comes to the rational application of our know-how. We only have to think of the beneficial wonder of forgetting and the transfigurative magical power of remembering. The retrieval of data from databases will not give us anything so felicitous. In a gigantic horizontal expansion of memory, we have a new presence at our disposal. Yet, through this, we do not learn any more easily to see the old and the traditional with new eyes and pose new questions, although this remains as before the proper life of historical thinking.

I remember my childhood. My father was a natural scientist and all his life he regretted that I went to the professors of idle talk. One could hear over and over again that the posing of the question is decisive in the sciences. Heaven knows this is true and it holds for all sciences. There is no difference in this regard. Clearly, the imagination that is required for fruitful questioning must always be guided by a self-control, based on well-founded knowledge. However, when we are up to our neck in a crippling mass of information-flows, what is imperative is to continue along pre-planned ways. And yet, looking and finding new ways remain the proper task of research. Technological domination, controllable systems are not all there is to the sciences. All the more so in the praxis of life, where there are always situations that place us before the unknown and, confronted by these situations, we will never dream that any cybernetics or even a rule-governed hermeneutics could help us understand better the new, the other – or the others themselves with whom we have to interact – or even just ourselves.

Let us appeal to our own life experience. What happens when we interrupt people who want to express themselves, with the words: I have already understood. Not only is this not really encouraging for the others, especially when they want to defend their own view with some zeal. To understand the other is truly a difficult art, but also a human task. What the sciences could do to help us in this regard is questionable. The realm in which we evolve is the realm of praxis. However, praxis is not the application of sciences, but on the contrary, an original source of experience and insight. The capacity that matters here is precisely not [221] the mere application of rules. The praxis of life always puts us before situations in which a decision has to be made, but in which we cannot consult the experts and in which the experts cannot even help us in any way. We, thus, have to decide by ourselves and we want to make the right decision. Now, what does it mean to be right? What evidence do we follow here? Certainly not any evidence that can be obtained by applying criteria or by the compelling force of proofs. Obviously, there is another presupposition at play here, which is associated with the proper name for practical philosophy. It is the word 'ethics'. This word is connected with *ethos* and eventually with the habits that we have adopted and that make it so that we can continue to function without thinking. This is often not something that we can reconstruct and control with rules. Rather, we follow processes of adaptation that set in early on, which are now called 'socialization'. *Mores*, orders and customs can also collapse, become ambiguous and questionable, so that some people may be so naive as to call for a new ethics, as if this were the task of philosophy professors. Such a task would clearly be practical. There is a nice ancient poem: 'Yes, if it were so simple, to transplant virtue into the human soul, as it is to heal an ailment with the right medicine, then this person would be celebrated even a lot more than God, even more than Asclepius.' Reasonable people, who do not understand themselves to be on a divine mission, would hardly attempt to play the part of such a divine expert. We know that there are no experts for that and that one cannot unburden oneself of one's own responsibility, even for one's own mistakes, by appealing to another instance. We know that we have to stand for our decisions, for what we say, and perhaps even before all else for ourselves. In a practical life it cannot be our ideal to purge everything that is subjective from reflection and rational examination, so to speak – as it is surely the task of experts, such as researchers – and to give advice and directions on the basis of a knowledge that has become anonymous. Where we are dealing with our ownmost concerns, we do not blindly follow the pre-established model of the upbringing in which we have been formed, but we take a stance. This responsibility obviously belongs so intrinsically to the person that no rule and legal order can reach into this ultimate instance of decision that conscience is.

Now, surely the treatment of the forms of human culture, of the questions of religion, of right, of *mores*, of action, which we find in the sciences, is not the same as the individual decision made by agents in the concretion of their life-situation. Yet, this is the peculiarity that the so-called human sciences introduce into the totality of our scientific activity. It consists in this: all the dealings and

[222] their so-called 'objects' cannot be submitted to an explanatory science in the way such a science enables us to keep track of the orders of nature, as its highest epistemic goal, and allows everything to be known as instances of laws. Human sciences rather belong to orders that constantly configure and reconfigure themselves through our own concrete participation in them and thereby contribute to our knowledge about the human possibilities and normative commonalities that affect us. Thus, the human sciences bring us before ourselves. This, however, always implies a consideration for their own limits. There are no certainties here like the guarantees of the theoretical and 'scientific' kind and here we always need to consider the other side – not only what we have in mind, but also what others think. In our pluralistic world, the other also includes foreign cultures and distant inhabitants of this earth. We will have to learn all this more and more in the future. Our human goal cannot be to use a technological civilization in order to stifle everything that has been handed out to us or to others and has shaped us all in the forms our life has taken. Only when we put the capacities of understanding and mutual acceptance to use in the new tasks that bring and hold the world in equilibrium, will we be able to create new forms of organization. Of all the sciences, it is especially the so-called human sciences that contribute the most to the nurturing of these capacities. They force us to confront constantly in all its richness the entire scale of what is human and all too human.

4

A World without History? (1972)[1]

[317] In this reflection on the theme of 'A World Without History?' it is not my intention to offer a contribution to what will be the work of the next days. What I would like to do is to make the public familiar with the theme and the interest of our colloquium. Although the public is hardly represented here, it is still constantly present in our consciousness. In our meeting in Jerusalem, we extensively discussed the theme of historical knowledge – there is also a publication of these discussions. We now have our meeting in Heidelberg, a few years after this memorable meeting in Jerusalem. It is the first meeting in Germany, one that we had long wished for and are delighted to be able to organize. It may strike us and it should strike us that we have, after such a short period of time since the meeting in Jerusalem, a very similar theme to discuss. We want to have an exchange about truth and historicity. We may feel that this is a repetition of certain problems that formed the core of our discussions in Jerusalem. However, this very fact that the same theme could have become different in the course of a few years, is in itself a contribution to the theme on which I would like to present some reflections.

The contemporary relevance of this theme has now obviously changed compared to what it was some years ago. Stronger than we would have anticipated, public consciousness, to which none of us can be indifferent and which also shapes us, has started to develop new perspectives, new evaluations, and new expectations. What we will discuss with each other in the coming days will not, I think, be the funeral song of historicism. However, the main reason it will not be so is precisely because in a funeral song one abides by the expression: *de mortuis nihil nisi bene.*[2] It will rather appear as the deathblow to a form of spirit that has essentially dominated the intellectual history of Central Europe for a long time. The question will be whether this deathblow hits a living figure or, perhaps, like in a theatre, a deliberately staged marionette. Without a doubt, the relevance of the theme 'Historicity and Truth' cannot be said to be accidental in Heidelberg and in Germany. Historical [318] consciousness and the critical question, which is thereby addressed to philosophy's claim to the truth, has been a privileged theme of philosophical thought in Germany since the days of romanticism and well into our century. However, this historical consciousness is not a fabrication of philosophers and is not curtailed in its significance and influence on us all by the anathemas or the exhortations of philosophers. Behind the problem of historicism, which arose with the decline of the Hegelian philosophy of history, there rather lurks a real transformation of consciousness, as Herder with his immense perceptiveness brings to the fore in an exemplary manner. To the extent that Herder, with his capacity to be sensitive to everything, attempted to harvest the great crop that is modern humanity, he has the great merit of announcing a new historical consciousness as a task for the future. Herder's pathos, which spoke in terms of a universal history, and his free overview of the cultures of the world exerted a overwhelming influence, to which Hegel gave its legitimacy by showing the presence of reason in history. Since Herder and his influence the task of justifying our own proper way of thinking through a historical self-interpretation has become incumbent upon all of us. Especially in the German tradition, this has given rise to what was once called the stifling historical attitude of German philosophy.

Behind the emergence of historical consciousness in the age of romanticism, which certainly marks an epoch-making turning point, stands a much larger event that has marked in equal measure both the friends and the adversaries of historical thinking: this is the dissolution of the traditional form of philosophy as unified science in general. We cannot convince ourselves enough of the fact that, with the emergence of the modern empirical sciences, the situation of philosophy has become precarious. From the moment the word 'philosophy' acquired the particular accent that we now associate with it, a great tradition of Western knowledge in fact came to an end and began to give way to new forms. Even today, the English language and in particular the language that continues to prevail in scholarly literature illustrates this meaning of 'philosophy', which encompassed the totality of all sciences well into the eighteenth century. One only has to think of the title of Isaac Newton's main work *Philosophiae Naturalis Principia Mathematica*.[3] This is what is properly new, which becomes visible as the much older and far-reaching event behind the younger form of historicism and its problems: in contrast to modern science's claims to the truth, the legitimacy of the truth proper to philosophical knowledge has become problematic. It is thus no coincidence that what we call 'philosophy' has never again exercised in modern society the immediate and central function that the all-encompassing concept of science under the name 'philosophy' [319] possessed for the first two thousand years of European history.

What has taken hold of us in the first place, we who have all been shaped by the modern concept of science, and with which we find ourselves constantly confronted in our thinking, is the fact that science has changed our life from the ground up and has taken over the actual administration of the human and social praxis. This relationship is known as the application of science. This relationship corresponds only very roughly to the relationship between theory and praxis. For, the problem of the application of science already presupposes that science as such possesses its autonomous existence with self-certainty before any application and is free from any consideration about possible application. However, precisely by virtue of the fact that it is free from purpose does science make its knowledge available for any arbitrary application: precisely because science cannot decide about its application on the basis of its own scientific competence.

In our linguistic usage this has been framed as the relationship between science and technology. By contrast, the Greek word *technē* and what Aristotle or Plato meant by this word is not in a similar opposition to the 'science' (*epistemē*) of the Greek tradition. Least of all does the Greek concept of *praxis* represent a mere application of knowledge. If *epistemē* is before all else a mathematics that is free from any practical link and distinguished by its demonstrative procedures, then *technē* covers all knowledge that has currency in the learnable process of production. Just as *technē* prepares for the human community a limited multiplicity of what is useful, without being itself in control of the use, similarly, the possibility of 'free' theory does not rely on itself, but demands a free space, which is made possible by a community, and represents in this sense a form of praxis. It represents a change in the situation of human life in general when we, instead, expect an application of science, which itself, as application, cannot be the responsibility of science and for which we still must take responsibility. It is, it seems to me, a characteristic of our modern social cultures that technology, thus the immediate application of science in technique, expresses the proper element of faith within modern consciousness. To be able to make what one can make seems to rip open a large horizon of progress and future, and the alarming question, before which humanity has been standing for a long time, is whether this progress is really or can really become a progress toward the advancement of humanity, to speak with Herder.

It has already been known and deplored for a long time that the great progress in the mastery of nature, which modern science brought about, was not accompanied by a similar progress in the political and social **[320]** life of human beings. A deep concern about freedom and peace arises from this situation of disconnect between what we can do and the knowledge about what we should do or want to do. For some years now, we have become more and more conscious that the expectation we place on science and the role science plays in our world have coalesced into new connections. It is in this sense that the theme of my remarks has to be understood, when I chose to speak of a 'world without history'.

It seems that the hope of survival, which appeared to be for many years, and for good reasons, a very vague and weak hope after the huge trauma of the Hiroshima bombing, is slowly growing stronger for the generations now coming of age. For the younger generations of humanity, it is something like an expectation: science should manage and will manage to ward off the dangers that it has itself generated and will make the future the object of its concern and its knowledge in a manner not yet presently available. The relationship between science and the past is thus beginning to be fundamentally transformed. The past that is passed appears as something slowly fading away compared to the constantly radiant opening up of the utopias of the future. In the contemporary consciousness of the younger generation, a new discipline is, in fact, emerging, the so-called futurology, with a kind of missionary pretention. It is objected in all seriousness that our academic organizations, our universities and our educational systems occupy themselves overwhelmingly with the past that is passed and absolutely not in a systematic and methodic way with all that matters: with the future. This is not only a misunderstanding that is patent in its absurdity – as if we could know what we cannot know and about which we can at best know anything on the basis of a knowledge of what has been. It is also the expression of a transformation in the consciousness of a humanity that has come of age in a highly industrialized society. We are at a point where the work of industry, the broadening of the scientific possibilities of technology does not stop before human society and its forms of life. We are at a point where now experts, who enjoy an uncontested authority in the field of natural sciences, also take over in the field of the social sciences: they are responsible for political and social decisions. At this point and as a matter of fact, there is a transformation in the life-consciousness of everyone, who belongs to such a society. With this transformation, everyone is suddenly a nameless member, deprived of self-responsibility, in a new social machine serviced by social engineers.

To have come to this is not to have gone wrongfully astray, [321] as if we could be found guilty of our wrongfulness by the raised index finger of a schoolmaster. There is instead a sense of a lack, which is deep-seated and precisely for this reason not easy to rectify. It pertains to the idea of the capacity for producing things – and it is unavoidable – that those who produce something themselves do not, through their capacity for production, have the knowledge of how what they can produce will be applied. This is an age-old problem of philosophy that the Platonists among us know very well: *chrēsis* is fundamentally separated from *poiēsis,* at least for a healthy social consciousness, so that the arts of production receive from *chrēsis*, from the use, their instructions and norms. However, when the capacity of production permeates social consciousness as the proper form of knowledge and, most significantly, when what we may need is itself managed again by the producers of our capacity to use, then it is unavoidable that the laws of production, of bringing something about, also gain control of the social existence of human beings. The law of production consists in this that everything made can be made again or, in other words, that everything that can be made is replaceable. I do not need to explain in detail the great extent to which we are aware that everything that we produce in the technological world of production these days is characterized by a rapid replaceability. Nor do I need to explain further the fact that, more importantly, consumption itself, what was called *chrēsis* in the Greek world, is determined more strongly by what we can produce than by the genuine nature of our needs. Just think of the significance publicity and advertisement – and this means persuading and talking people into the belief that they have needs – have gained for the economic life of our modern industrial world. These are not accidental aberrations, resulting from biases of the human cultural development and easily rectifiable. Rather, they are the immediate effects of the idea of science, which has led to the tremendous increase of control over nature in modernity and whose ascetic methodological rigour no longer allows people to know from their own competence what the responsible goals of human activity and work are. A competence for another kind of knowledge than the scientific increasingly disappears from universal consciousness.

We characterize with predilection the physiognomy of our time – and, I think, correctly – through the concept of management. We talk of a 'managed' world. Now, the ideal of a management consists in this that what is done is done in the way it has always been done, that the last justification of a managerial act represents its mere functional fitting into the order of the totality of management; thinking by oneself and personal responsibility for a decision almost contradict the sense of a well-ordered management. I would not like [322] to play the *laudator temporis acti* [4] here. It would be a total misunderstanding of my remarks to hear in them a spiteful cultural critique. I would rather like to understand what challenges us today as thinking beings and what we in the very consciousness of being challenged, cannot facilitate without our own contributions and answers. In this context, it seems that what I called 'a world without history' still needs a counter-formulation or a reply. One should also hear the question mark, which I have always mentally appended to the formulation of this title: can there be a world without history? A world without history does not only represent the quite dangerous political situation of the moment in which the *stalemate*[5] of the superpowers constantly represses and cripples any genuine historical evolutions and in this manner gives rise to a kind of calcified *status quo*. I mean even more than this. Above all else, I have in view the fact that our own consciousness today sees itself exposed to a manipulation to the extent that public opinion is increasingly being given into the hands of the techniques of a productive capacity with its scientific basis. What else can we do in this situation than see for ourselves?

This is the ideal of scientific research in all the orientations of its will to know: it also necessarily includes the great book of the historical tradition, the great book of that which was otherwise. I see more and more – and I think it is not a wrong insight into our situation – a new maturity arising, an oblivion of the fine old art of reading. The omnipresence of a constant flood of information has the immediacy of a violent pressure to conform. Those who today follow the ubiquitous media, from the press to radio and finally to the TV, and understandably cannot escape what these media suggest, will become precisely that into which the technicians of society are trying to turn the human beings of today: they will become a replaceable cog in the great social machine. They are embedded in the functioning of the social apparatus and those who cannot withdraw, through other ways or possibilities, from the information and manufacture of opinion, are helpless. What happens has the features of an unfreedom that is hidden to itself and not assented to, that lulls itself into the illusion of being everywhere, of seeing and hearing what is happening. Is there not really a necessary consequence here that we be humanists in a new consciousness? For, being a humanist means being able to read. Is it not a necessary consequence that in this situation we hold in high esteem the art of reading, which gives us the unique freedom to criticize, a critique that makes so little of the immediate word and image in their imposing actuality? As Platonists, we cannot forget Socrates' answer after hearing the *bombos*[6] of a great speech, for example Protagoras' speech in the dialogue of the same name. **[323]** Socrates must say what he thinks about it: he responds that he unfortunately does not have the memory and the mental power to really understand such a long speech. For him, the speech would have to be given in small parts, in the small play of question and answer. Nowadays, this small play of question and answer is exercised in our literary culture by reading. We are constantly playing when we are reading. This play and what we gain from it is what I call freedom. We who defend reading do not become by that fact a *laudator temporis acti*. For, what we have in mind is our present as well as our future. Without knowledge and without reflecting on our own proper possibilities, there is for us no future. However, this means, not without history. History does not mean an evasion into the past, but is a *memoria vitae*, a memory of life, as Cicero calls historiography.[7] History, the world of history, is not a second world of the past alongside the natural world that surrounds us. History is a completely inexhaustible system of all the worlds that are out there, which are closer to us than the nearby satellite orbiting our earth. For, history is the world of human beings. To study history is to keep open the entire range of what it means to be human. Thanks to history we are not confined to what we know or think by ourselves. History describes all our possibilities. As for what kind of future we will have, it will depend on how broadly we preserve and increase the heritage of the historical tradition from which we all originate and which unifies us all more and more.

5

The Old and the New (1981)[1]

[154] Whenever the puzzle of time enters our consciousness, we are seized by a sense of insecurity and a most profound disquiet. The constants according to which we orient ourselves in the world – number and idea, word and understanding – abandon us. When we go behind all of these identities and reliabilities, which congeal as if in a final crystalline point, in the ineradicable self-certainty of the ego, of the now, of the here, everything is shaken. Memory wanders into the darkness of the past, hope gropes in the twilight of an uncertain future. There is a constant alternation between light and shadow, an uncertain shimmering and this is supposed to be the 'I', this one identical to me, this unique person! Person means: to stand for oneself [*für sich stehen*], to answer for oneself [*einstehen*], to stand [*stehen*]. To stand where everything flows, where not a single hair on our head stays the same. What do I say! Not a single bit of our own bodily matter remains the same in the metabolic processes of life and in much the same way our own biography only becomes clear to us in single flecks of light, like a white crest of foam above an uncertain depth. To sum this all up, how is this bit of personal history embedded and fused beyond recognition into our social existence and its historical course? It may be that a tireless ego consciousness always contrives new self-understanding and constantly builds up its own self-consciousness anew as that which is the same in what is changeable through remembering and forgetting, planning and hoping, and the triumphant certainty of the here and now. Yet, how far does this go?

Already in our being for others, for our neighbours, and, most of all, in the role-play that characterizes our social existence, we do not in the least see ourselves as what we are. If we were to encounter ourselves we would not recognize ourselves, we would reject ourselves. We see this happen in our age of reproducibility when we can hear our own voice on the radio, to our shock and sense of alienation. Although it is already a long process of education to learn at all how to perceive the other or the rational against our own prejudices and interests, when it comes to us, we never really learn to know ourselves. This sounds like a deficiency, but in fact it points to an immeasurable richness. For, it is not so much a resigned acceptance of an excruciating quest for the self as it is a trace of [155] the communities that we are, unbeknownst to ourselves, as children of our parents, as members of our culture and its forms of life, as children of our time, and perhaps even as members of the ultimately final community, as one among the mortals.

Yet, precisely because we are not this self that is certain of itself, to which we like to appeal as a last instance of all certainty, precisely because we are drifting along, constantly being shifted all around indifferently by the soundless flow of time, we are ourselves eager for distinctions. We have more at stake on one side of the divide than on the other and we resolutely cling to it. This means: as those who part this from that [*die Unterscheidenden*], we are also at the same time the ones who depart [*die Scheidenden*]. The fact that we make choices shapes our own existential experience most profoundly as the experience of our finitude. Thus, we are the ones who depart. 'This is how we live and we always take our leave [*nehmen Abschied*]'. For, choosing is always parting [*Scheiden*], giving up something for the sake of something else. At the foundation of the inner certainty of our own self, there lies an ultimate disturbing uncertainty, which springs forth in the particular temporality that is ours. To our distinctive characteristic of being able to choose, there corresponds the vagueness of our wishes and the vacillation of our preferences and preferred values. Constantly do we have to choose and choosing means: not going with the old, but choosing the new without certainty. Clearly, time is for all living beings something other than the parameter by which duration is measured. The Greeks had a specific word for life span and, indeed, the span of existence granted to each individual living entity has its own articulation. There are not only the limits set by birth and death, becoming and passing. Youth and old age and, in-between, the rhythmical alteration of annual seasons and diurnal hours constitute the unity of the organism, of a 'self', which maintains itself as such through change.

One could ask about such a description of the reality of time and the real time, which is granted to higher organisms, plants and animals as well as to human beings: to what extent is it itself only an extrapolation of this experience of time that is the privilege of human consciousness in the restlessness of its questioning and thinking? The life of a star, the life of a cell or the life of an atom or particle sound to us like mere metaphors. However this may be, we experience our own life history really as history, even if, like all history, it is only in a gaze that is turned backward. We experience the self-forgetfulness of our youth perhaps only in the transfiguration of an old age that looks back and we experience being old as something so worthy of attention, only in the reflex of the younger people who find us old. In each phase, we are accompanied by a consciousness of our own time through the years, and truly not as what is counted in a movement, which measures its duration, but rather as an experience of a horizon, in which the horizon [156] shifts imperceptibly but unceasingly. Even this experience may follow its own rhythm of inner seasons and diurnal hours, which does not always correspond to the external rhythm. In productive phases, a larger horizon seems to open up for us, but in other phases the future operates as if it were blocked and without hope. Yet, a direction is maintained, from the sheer boundless openness of the horizon of expectation, at the beginning, to the always increasing richness of that which fills the horizon of memory. The equilibrium that holds sway over all forms of order also seems to dominate our life consciousness: where the future melts away, there the past towers up into a great mountain peak of an inaccessible 'then'. Yet, how unequal are the horizons of our consciousness! The openness of the future is the clarity of our existence itself. The life of memories is like a dream that forgets itself. The openness to what is new, the life in expectation is our constant present. Memory means a 'then' that has been on occasion recaptured from oblivion. If being young and being old are such experiences of horizon, this means at the same time that youth and old age are not determined by the calendar. To be young means to be open for the other, for what is other. This implies that old and young are relative and that this relativity is not a quantitative one, that is, not like big-small, long-short, much-little, which can be correlated to measurable and countable quantities and lose their relativity in relation to them. The relativity of being old and young is of an irreducible sort.

This holds first and foremost for the relativity of old and new, which, in opposition to the relativity of old and young, does not articulate a pregiven shift of horizons, but rather designates qualities of encounter, which materialize at every moment of our experience of the world. The new is what happens at any moment and is experienced as the 'just now'. Inexorably, everything else sinks back into the indifference of what is already known or familiar. Precisely this makes the experience of the new – as well as the experience of the old overshadowed by the new – deeply ambiguous, given that everything new inexorably becomes obsolete. It is the puzzle of time that it is a pure passing away and itself knows no emergence. Indeed, this implies that in time something new always emerges, but also that it inexorably passes away. Often enough, the new is very quickly obsolete and the old appears as new. The quality of the new cannot consist in its newness, but rather in this: it does not become obsolete, not so fast or not at all. Even if the open expectation, with which we live in the future, is constantly after the new, we actually think of it as something supposedly better. Similarly, the old can easily be preferred as something that is better.

Thus, the old and the new are relativized through and through. There is the *laudator temporis acti*.[2] There is the devaluation of the new and the innovator. *Novarum rerum cupidus*[3] was in ancient Rome a clear verdict passed by [157] an enduring republican order. The *homo novus*[4] would like to awaken expectations. But even when these expectations were fulfilled, it was more a disappointed suspicion that passed from success to re-evaluation. The opposing position is no less decisive, for example the rejection of antiquated ideals, the battle against the old traditions – who can still hear in it the pathos of the French revolution, which brought an end to the wig!

There are good arguments for both. The panegyrists of the old can appeal to the fact that it has already been tested by time, that it is not something unknown, untried, whereas the new always remains something risky. Conversely, the persistence of the old often represents the most unreasonable opposition to any innovation depriving it of the test of time, which it would perhaps pass in flying colours. The historical life of human beings seems caught between these two extremes and is always a new way of establishing a balance between the two.

'Always after the new.' The expression betrays us: it is not the old and the new that are up for choice, but this or that, what promises something and because it promises something. It can also be something old. It is in fact never the choice between the old and the new. The old is never up for choice as something old. To the extent that it is old, it has reached the obviousness of what is familiar. Only in light of new possibilities can it be put up for choice at all as a counter-possibility and elicit our attention. It would be a mistake to represent the situation in which we choose as if it were not always about possibilities for the future, regardless of whether it is about preserving the old, which suppresses the new, or about rejecting the old in favour of the new. This is precisely the experience that time is for us: its two dimensions, future and past, are never the present. However, this means that they do not stand in front of us like two equal possibilities. One is the possible, the past is well and truly gone. Even a god cannot make unhappen what has happened. What stands before us [*was vor uns steht*] is what may await us [*was uns bevorstehen mag*]. Even when it is something well-known that awaits us, it is no longer what is usual and known, but appears in a new light.

Here emerges the well-known dialectic of the return [*Rückkehr*].[5] For historical beings there is no going back [*Zurück*]. Even the return is no mere going back and, similarly, a repetition is no recurrence [*Wiederkehr*] of the same. This means that the relativity of the old and the new is far more radical than the relativity of the old and the young. Obviously, it makes a big difference whether the old is meant in relation to the young or in relation to the new. The old is itself old, the young is itself young, even if this is not independent of whether one feels old or young. However, the old, which is not new, and the new are not so in themselves [158] but for us. The old, which stands in opposition to the new, means a universal character of encounter, indeed a character of encounter that follows, like its shadow, the promising and the impressive character of the new. This is so, regardless of the way in which we evaluate the old and the new. We have seen indeed that open expectation is directed toward the new and that the old sinks into the obviousness of what is familiar, even if what is new at a time quickly becomes obsolete and the old turns out to be 'permanent'. What maintains itself in this flux? What is it that cannot be obscured by the new simply because it is new and, conversely, what is it that is not cast aside simply because it is not the old?

What we call culture is the unrelenting effort to provide practical answers to this question. Culture is nothing if it is not such an answer. We certainly have the seemingly enduring forms of organization in our life, the state apparatus and the justice system, the economic system and the organization of the sphere of labour; in addition, we have the free zones of ritual and celebration, of art and play. However, all this does not have a permanence and does not indicate as such a firm stance in the flow of time. Everything in fact becomes obsolete if it is not new in every instant and demonstrates its permanence anew. Restoration and revolution are both misguided. There is nothing old that is good because it is old and there is nothing new that is good because it is not old. Rather, both the old and the new are constantly outdoing and dissimulating each other.

It has always been like this. No innovation gains acceptance without resistance. Indeed, in the end we have to say that the milder the resistance that the new encounters, the quicker the new finds acceptance and the quicker it rushes toward obsolescence.

The new seems almost to draw its strength from the old so that it can acquire permanence. This demands careful consideration. We live in an age where everything new is multiplied technologically, in which even the old is dressed up with the values of novelty that do not belong to it. It is also an age in which everything can be made accessible, even the most distant, which presents itself to us like the newest. All measures have changed. The industrial revolution has become the destiny of the world. Traditions dissolve themselves without anything new making a convincing entry. The new rather becomes the recurrence of the same, even when and precisely when it springs from an unbridled freedom of experimentation. The world everywhere is constantly becoming more and more similar. Is the erasure of the differences between all forms of life in the offing? Or will a new equilibrium between the old and the new, a new 'culture' be constituted under the surface of technological uniformity? We do not know how humanity will deal with the organization of life on this planet. However, I believe that we can know one thing: the productive answers, which the future may bring to this question, [159] depend on the fact that the future comes from its own past. Thus, we also contribute to this future, as the present that we are and the past that we will become. The dialectic between the old and the new is ineradicable.

Will there be art, will art mean anything, beyond occasionally filling up our free time, in the way art meant something when it was not yet in any way intended as art, but was configuring and playing around with all of the forms of life within which human activity took place? When we gaze retrospectively at our culture, we see all this as art – and rightly so, inasmuch as the productive configuration can be experienced as such and makes us experience the old as well as the new. In our century we have experienced in the case of art how a changing world frees itself toward new possibilities of configuration. We see in particular how the universal tendency to bring close together all that is distant has expressed itself in new productive possibilities. Think, for example, of what the plastic arts of our century owe to the African continent or of the impulses from the Far East or Latin America that have newly inspired the European tradition in the most diverse fields.

What would artists such as Giacometti or Henry Moore or Bissier be without such stimulations and what would our music be without the challenge produced by the exotic irruption of rhythm into our musical sensibility? Where linguistic boundaries create barriers, the situation is not so clear. However, there can be no doubt that even there as everywhere, the break with tradition, which took place in our century, blocked the false, historicizing escape routes that our grandparents resorted to, while at the same time, opening our ears to the voices of totally remote traditions.

One could think that it has always been like this. One can think of the eighteenth-century fascination with everything Chinese or of one or the many renaissances that have, as it were, shaped the history of the West. Perhaps something like that will happen again. Who knows along which ways the creative drives will lead us? At any rate, it will be a new situation. Previously, it was within the heritage of a single culture and its religious, philosophical, cultural tradition, that the foreign was formally fused to become the new, while still looking like the old, with the same obviousness with which, for example, Altdorfer in 'The Battle of Alexander at Issus' represents the Persians and Macedonians in the costumes of the German renaissance.[6]

Such a power of transformation, such self-evident submission of the old to the new, of the new to the old, is no longer to be found, not in our small Europe, not in the greater Europe of the world civilization of today. The world that was set into motion exposes all closed historical traditions to new challenges making [160] them question their own identity. What is happening now on a global scale was being played out two hundred years ago within the Western cultural tradition. At that time, in the century of Louis XIV, there arose in the literary field an awareness of the split between the old and the new, between the foreign and the genuine in the famous *Querelle des anciens et des modernes*. At that time, the spirit of modernity was seeking to assert itself laboriously and hesitatingly against the oppressive model of classical antiquity. There were no winners and no losers in this battle. For, there was no choice. Models are unattainable – no, if they have to be models, not only can they not be reached, but they even ought not to be reached. Only the old that is new is preserved at all just as only the new that is not obsolete is.

One may well have controversial thoughts about the uses and the disadvantages of history for life. Many may yearn for the touching innocence of the will to oneself [*Sich-selber-wollen*], which grabs us so much in old drawings or paintings. Conversely, many may want to reject completely the pressure of the past and start over from scratch. This does not help. In the new awareness, which knows how to perceive the old as old and the new as new, we stand in the middle. Surrounded by decayed walls, filled with old recriminations, stuffed with old spectacles, we all look ahead, facing the new day. 'Let anyone be a Greek in his own way, but let him be Greek!'[7] This was the classical solution that the conflict between the old and the new found at the end of the eighteenth century. In our world, transformed beyond all measure, the conflict between the old and the new will be, sure enough, carried out according to new measures. The solution, however, remains the same: 'Let anyone be it!'

6

Death as a Question (1975)[1]

[161] Is death a question? Is there any question that each of us here will die? When forced to think about it, what question can one really ask with respect to the phenomenon of death? I would like to try examining anew the questions and answers around this phenomenon, or better, the upshot of human reflections on the phenomenon of death as they are found in our tradition. In this enterprise I am compelled by necessity to confine my consideration to the Greek-Christian tradition, because I know the original testimonies of other cultures, insofar as they are of a linguistic form, only through translations.

It is thus to our own tradition of Western thought that I turn. However, the preference for one's own tradition is just as much a methodological obstacle because we stand in it and cannot freely look beyond it. Certainly, the herme-neutic effort consists precisely in knowing what is known, to use the formula of the philologist August Boeckh. In fact, this alone makes it possible to speak about death as a question. However, 'knowing the known' is a formula by which Boeckh means at first nothing other than the interpretation of texts. Their content is what is known. But how is it then when we are dealing with death? What is the known here? Can what we find in our tradition really be called answers to a question? Is the advent of death not precisely the fact that it finds us without an answer to its question? The natural or biological process of death is not really a puzzle. Rilke speaks somewhere of the holy inspiration of nature to have discovered the familiar death.[2] Alternatively, he speaks of death as the other side of life. Just as the moon has an unilluminated side that still belongs to the totality of its being, so death would belong to the being of the living. This is how natural death is. If we only possessed the same equanimity toward death as we display when comprehending any other life process!

Death remains a question. There is another instance where the incomprehensibility of death manifests itself. It is this: the certainty of our self-consciousness simply cannot itself be put in an intelligible relationship with the non-existence of this self-consciousness. To speak again with Rilke: 'And what in death takes us away is not revealed to us.' Where [162] is knowledge in this case supposed to be; where the answers of the intellect that we ourselves could comprehend? And still, it seems to be the unrelenting striving of humanity to keep this question alive. As living beings, we are unable to escape it.

If we consider the oldest answers our tradition has offered to the questions of how to experience *thanatos* and *athanasia*, death and immortality, death-lessness, we always encounter the same grand and lugubrious answer: the cult of the dead, the grave. What really distinguishes human beings from all the living beings that nature has produced is that human beings bury their dead and invest the grave with their feelings, their thoughts and their creative works. What a stunning fact it is to see the treasure of votive offerings that comes to light from the graves of previous times, filling us over and over again with incredible aston-ishment! Think, for example, of the Viking graves in Oslo. Entire ships with all their content were covered there with stones and earth in order to preserve for the dead what was theirs. And what variations the view of graves offers, what answers remain concealed in this multiplicity of configurations! We have the colossal stone monuments of the pyramids that were erected by thousands of hands for the sake of a shrinking, tiny something. We have the constantly growing treasure of the grave reliefs coming from the classical period in Greece in the National Museum of Athens. Those who have seen with their own eyes the breathtaking gestures of separation on these columns will never forget this inner awareness of death that the Greek spirit of art presents to us. On Christian graves we find the cross and, later on, verses from the Bible, both referring to the communion of saints, both guaranteeing that the dead live and belong to all others. Or we have the graves in the Islamic world, with their geometrical ornamentation that barely differentiate one particular grave from another. Nothing of the individuality, name or rank, life story or family is revealed. It reminds us of the interpretation of Aristotle, made popular by Arabic philosophy, of the intellect common to all, of the soul common to all into which the individual enters. And yet, the women of Marrakech entrust these graves with their most secret wishes and prayers. Except for the graves of leaders, the gravesites in Islam are completely without any reminder of what was. What do all these graves tell us? Are they answers to the question of what death is? Or is it the case that the answers to this question want to proclaim that death is not or should not be? Is it that these answers do not want to acknowledge death? But death is. What is it? And yet we know death: from where and how?

What does it mean to have knowledge about death? Certainly, what speaks from the trace of the graveyards of this earth, a trace that loses itself in the twilight of prehistoric times, is an authentic distinguishing mark of human beings. Knowing death seems [163] as essential to human beings as their capacity to think. It is true that we say about animals that they know about their death. They hide and withdraw from all sight. We say that they have a sense of when it is the time to do this. But is what we recognize here a real knowledge and not merely the reflex to a human question? Is it not rather a kind of warning-sign that we can discern in the question: we ourselves, do we also know how to accept death in such a way?

Let us ask: how does the knowledge about death occur? And does it occur? Does the certainty of life not have a sovereign primacy and is the certainty of death not always imparted to conscious human beings from the outside, only through a direct or mediated experience? How does this knowledge come to be acquired by children, and what kind of knowledge is this that eventually the poet can say: *Tu sais*, do you know? It is not without reason that I cite a poem of Gottfried Benn, a witness of extreme scepticism.[3] I ask instead: does the child know its knowledge? Does anyone among us know what one knows when one knows that one must die? Is our question about death not always and necessarily a concealment of what we know, a concealment of something unthinkable, of non-being?

If we take this perspective seriously, then is the cult of the grave in the end also such a concealment insofar as it appeals to a sensible present, like those bones for which, to speak with Hegel, there were these sacrificial expeditions to the holy grave, the crusades? Is it always only a matter of not having to think the non-being? Is the cult of the ancestors in the great East Asian cultures itself a not letting go of the dead insofar as one sees oneself returning into a collective being? And how is it in our Christian tradition with the belief that we will see each other once again? What about the ineradicable and seemingly natural expectation that what bound mother and child together in the early years, for example, cannot come to nothing even through the certainty of death? Must this not remain? The hope of seeing again those to whom we belong?

The Greek Hades already had features of such a seeing again. At the end of the *Apology* Socrates himself speaks of how he looks forward to going to Hades because there the great heroes of the mythical tradition of Greece will receive him and he will have the opportunity to ask these people what true virtue is. And if they do not know either – and they will also not know – they will at least not condemn him to death again … And lo and behold we have the Christian idea of paradise or of heaven, which is the heaven of the seeing again. Are all these eventually ways of not wanting to think non-being?

These are questions to which philosophy must devote itself in its own way because the task of philosophy is to want to know what we know without knowing that we know it. This is a precise definition of what philosophy is and an **[164]** apt description of what Plato first recognized: the knowledge with which we are dealing here, *anamnēsis,* is a bringing out of the interior and a raising to consciousness. Let us, thus, ask what one knows without knowing it when one knows about death. What does the philosophical tradition we inhabit have to say about it? Should we also ask about these attempts at thinking whether they are attempts to know or whether they are yet again ways of not wanting to know what we know?

In Homeric religion there is the shadowy character of the souls in Hades – an oppressing sorrow. How did the other cults of the soul differ from the epic and mythical tradition and how did the thinking of the sciences and philosophy finally arise when, first in Pythagoras, in relation to the doctrine of the transmigration of souls in reincarnation, we see the emergence of *anamnēsis,* recalling? What patterns of thought – one can also call them concepts – were prepared here? There are two Greek words that can show us the way here. They are expressions for 'life'. The first one is *zōē,* the other is *bios.* Both are expressions that continue to live in German as foreign words. Both often mean the same. Both words, *zōē* and *bios,* are concepts that gravitate against each other and often intermingle with each other, but even in common usage allow different semantic orientations to resonate. *Zōē* is clearly opposed to what does not have *zōē,* what is not living. What distinguishes it is *psuchē,* soul. In Greek thinking the presence of a 'soul' means that such a being is distinguished by its being animated [*Lebendigkeit*]. 'Being animated' is here like some sort of breath and manifests itself in self-movement. Life, in this sense of being animated, is embodied in ever-new exemplars of living entities. *Zōē* is, from the very outset, free from what we would call individuality. What we call living in the sense of *zōē* is not what we mean by the specific individual, but only in its distinction which contrasts it with a nature deprived of life or with the lifelessness of what is dead.

By contrast, when we mean a being in the specific manner of its being animated, we speak of *bios.* This is so in all the instances where we mean a specific mode of life, including also the mode of life of animals. But it holds true in an eminent sense of human beings. They are living beings who know themselves to be alive. They are thus in a totally new relationship to their own animatedness. This includes the fact that they choose and through their choices – mostly through their unconscious choices – they make decisions about their life. *Bios* is the life that people lead and through which they distinguish themselves from everything else that is also alive, through their mode of living and in particular through their own life history and their own life destiny. To the extent that something new, a self-knowledge, is implied in this concept of the living, we enter the proper ground of the Greek tradition of thinking. This concept [165] of *psuchē* is, since Heraclitus, associated with the guiding concept of *logos*, of knowing and wanting to know, of wanting to provide a foundation. The attempt at thinking that is initiated here puts the knowledge about one's own life and one's own death above the universality of being animated, to which perhaps being dead really belongs as its other side. Now, the problem is that the other side, the properly not being, is ungraspable for such a 'conscious' life.

One could follow this history right up to the concepts of Platonic and Aristotelian philosophy. One could show how the interpretation of 'being animated' on the basis of self-knowledge eventually becomes the doctrine of ideas or the doctrine of the *nous*, what is constantly present and represents. Just as the brightness of the day makes our visible world possible in all its colourfulness, so by means of this inner clarity all being receives its articulation in the thinking that represents, in consciousness. We should also mention the later forms of ancient thought, for example the Stoic stance toward death, which attempts to recall the harmony with nature even in the fact that we have to die; or to argue with Epicurean art for the depreciation of the phenomenon of death to a non-being.

However it seems as if the sum of all such attempts at thinking, which Plato offers us in the *Phaedo* in the form of a large number of proofs for the immortality of the soul, comes down to what Plato puts in the mouth of the doubter: but there is a child in human beings that does not yet feel reassured by all these proofs.[4] In fact, none of the proofs for immortality that we find in Greek thinking is even close to being able to tell us what we want to know when we want to think death from what we know as our own life. The child in the human being is right and Greek philosophy fails before the question of what death is.

This is the broad perspective under which Christianity entered the world. In his 'Hymns to the Night' Novalis has formulated this new element in a poetic manner. It is certainly true that the portrait of the Greeks, which is painted as a celebration of the Gods and a celebration of human beings living in the constant luminous enjoyment of life, does not exhaust the depth of Greek culture. But Novalis correctly saw that Greek thinking had not conquered death, no matter how much the Greek poets had probed all the depths of knowledge about death. The claim of Christianity was precisely not to offer an answer to this question, but to be a promise.

Now we ask: how did philosophy receive this promise of overcoming death that is contained in Christian teaching, and how did it understand this transformation of death into life? Should we [166] not say the following: any attempt that philosophical thought makes to think the transformation of death into life does not really think death? We have an abundance of great intellectual testimonies in which this transformation of death is thought. Some of them even come from a religious background: the mysticism of the Neo-Platonic orientation, negative theology, the thinking of the nothing and of the annihilation of self [*Entwerdung*], through which alone the *unio mystica*,[5] the union with God, can be accomplished.

This is also what we find in poetry: in Novalis there is a new valuation of the night, which is not the withdrawal, the darkening of the bright pleasurable day, but the ground and origin of a higher and more spiritual brightness. We see how Goethe brings love and death together, the being outside of oneself of the lover and the being outside of oneself of the dying who experiences death. 'And as long as you do not have this, this "Die and Become…" But even in this intermingling of 'die' and 'become' is there not an attempt not to take death totally seriously and instead to think it back into the realm of the conceptual, for which in fact our life experience constantly offers us sparkling and fascinating metaphors?

There are essentially two phenomena, which always impose themselves on thinking, sleeping and dreaming. From the standpoint of the inner certainty proper to waking self-consciousness, sleep is as little intelligible as death. The total transformation in the habits of the sleeper, the complete unreachability that the sleeper has for us, who are close to him and awake, seems to be like a kind of pre-figuration of the ultimate unreachability with which the dead terrify us. And the dream? Is not the metaphor of the dream a telling expression of our feeling of life such that the poet could find the expression 'surrounded by the dreams of life?' Does this not mean that our life is filled so much with the images of our imagination and of our worldliness that the question of the nothing, the question that goes beyond our own certainty of living, can no longer be asked?

No matter how much may be captured in these two death metaphors of sleeping and dreaming, both have something decisively in common. They are linked to a state of being awake. To every state of being awake there essentially belongs the fact of going back to sleep, dreaming again, and waking up again. Thus, in such a thinking the experience of death is thought back in terms of *zōē*, of the experience of life, which maintains itself against death in its constant cycle of reproduction; and this happens without the individual living beings having to know themselves in their own finite being. But is this the overcoming of death? The whole attempt at thinking on the part of philosophy seems to be nothing more than a not-willing-to-admit death.

Thus, we ask anew: what do we know when we think death? Here we must introduce a methodological consideration, the seriousness of which cannot be emphasized enough. Does it even make sense to say that we [167] ask the question of what death is seriously? Is it not in the end rather fatal for this question – what holds true for all questions that humans ask – that it remains tied to the certainty human beings have of being alive? Must the thought of death thereby not contain an ultimate existential lack of seriousness because this thought must be endured by the living? A thought about death that allows us to continue to live does not seem to be much different and not essentially distinguishable from all other dreams of our life,[6] which we dream and in which we are caught as long as we live. It seems that we have here an antagonism in which death and thought exclude each other and are held separate. Thinking death already seems to transform death into something that it is not. Perhaps this is only a methodological *aporia* and in fact an answer? Perhaps the question 'what is death?' is not only problematic but is also at the same time and in a certain sense the answer to the question itself because it renders the answer questionable.

Let us take the example of a great and profound myth, the myth of Prometheus as it is portrayed in Aeschylus' drama. The story is well known: Prometheus is chained to the Caucasus, the vulture eats his liver – in the family houses of my generation one could still see this represented in figurines – and Aeschylus shows on the stage how we commiserate with Prometheus. All possible sympathizers queue up to persuade him eventually to renounce his pride against the all-powerful Zeus and spare himself his suffering. It is in this context that Prometheus, acting as his own legal counsel, complains about the terrible injustice he has incurred at the hands of Zeus who owes him so much. Yes, he stole fire from the heavens and brought it to human beings. It is not exactly how it is said, but everybody knows this and, at any rate, he taught human beings how to use fire. The use of fire is without question one of the unequivocal distinctions of human beings among all the things that live. But in what context does Aeschylus make Prometheus say this? Prometheus begins by saying that he has an infinite merit among human beings. For, he has made it so that they do not know about their own death. Clearly, what is meant is that they do not know when they must die. And now Prometheus continues: with this I have transformed their whole life to the extent that I have taught them to observe the stars, to the extent that I taught them numbers, craftsmanship, and techniques, and so on; in short for everything that human beings are able to do, it is I who have accomplished what is decisive; thus have I rendered myself meritorious among human beings.

Even when we add them together as in algebra, myths always remain undecipherable things that tell us something. The obvious question is: how do these two things belong together: veiling the knowledge of death and the new craftsmanship? One can hardly avoid thinking the two together. Aeschylus does not say anything about how Prometheus hid from human beings [168] the certainty of their death and the hour of their death. Did that not happen precisely through the fact that he directed their thinking toward something distant in helping them create enduring works through their planned efforts? This would be the connection between knowing and not knowing and between thinking about death and the idea of progress. Certainly, Aeschylus does not make this connection explicit. He just somehow suggests it. And certainly, Aeschylus still has something totally different in mind when he links the whole boastful discourse of Prometheus to the fact that it is out of love for these poor creatures, the human beings, that Prometheus took upon himself the suffering that was inflicted upon him. This motive is so well worked out that Byzantine Christianity could reconfigure Aeschylus' drama into a Christian drama of the *Christus patiens*[7] by using only Aeschylus' verses.

However, it is without a doubt with the dominion of the highest God that the symbolic figure of human self-help represented by Aeschylus' Prometheus found, in the whole of Aeschylus' trilogy, its limit and its reconciliation. Thus, we ask all the more urgently: what lies behind the curiously enigmatic mythical overcoming of the certainty of death through a belief in the future? I would like to indicate the direction in which I am seeking an answer by the concept of the transcendence of life. This is an expression from Georg Simmel. 'The transcendence of life' means that human life in accordance with its own essence exceeds itself. According to this principle, one can question the standard to which our *aporia* is submitted. Although the thought of death is still a thought that we bear, there is no concealing of death in the certainty of being alive. It is not immediately characteristic of human life to go constantly beyond its state of being alive [*Lebendigkeit*] and the instinctive preservation of such a state into what is without measure and without self. Even the labyrinth of the thought of suicide, in which so many lives end, all too exhausted, is an indirect testimony to this. Suffocating in itself and unable to move beyond itself, life extinguishes itself.

Is the life of human beings in the truest sense of the word not a constant overflow, such that the source of life, which any individual is, overflows? One can think of the famous conversation Goethe had with Falk after the burial of his friend, the poet Wieland. There Goethe discusses why he cannot conceive of life coming completely to an end at death. And he appeals to the fact that he always experiences his own life consciousness, to put it succinctly in a formula, as a phenomenon of excess. As long as life has this character of a phenomenon of excess – Goethe now expresses himself very authoritatively – nature would be obligated to grant us new possibilities for our excess of being. I will not venture to decide how much seriousness and how much play there is in Goethe's conversation.

There are other instances that manifest the transcendence of life and [**169**] refute the thought that life must free itself from its own certainty of being alive when it goes beyond itself. I am thinking here of sacrificial death and also, in particular, sacrificing oneself for one's faith, the martyr. Now, are we as human beings ever in a position to refer to this? We cannot hide from ourselves that what manifests itself in this manner can still be a mode of the excess of life and can find fulfilment in the wild zeal to become a martyr or in the sacrifice that is in truth a flight. There remains an inner ambiguity in the claim that the true emulation of Christ is what manifests itself in such phenomena. Nobody wants to say that it is not and that the sacrifice of one's own life cannot be a real sacrifice. However, one must conversely concede that it does not belong to us to raise ourselves above the ambiguity of our own certainty of being alive.

There is a poem by a modern poet, Paul Celan, that is entitled 'Tenebrae'. The title clearly plays with the darkness that descended over the world when Jesus was on the cross and spoke his last words: 'My God, my God, why have you forsaken me?' The modern poet ventures a new interpretation of this biblical testimony:

We are near, Lord
Near and within reach.

Seized already, Lord,
clawed into one another as though
the body of each of us were
your body, Lord.

Pray, Lord,
pray for us,
we are near.

Tossed by the wind we went,
we went to bend
over hollow and ditch.

To drink we went, Lord.

It was blood, it was
what you shed, Lord.

It gleamed. [**170**]

It cast your image into our eyes, Lord.
Our eyes and
mouths stand so open, Lord.

We have drunk, Lord.
The blood and the image
that was in the blood, Lord.

Pray, Lord.
We are near.[8]

What is monstrous about this poetic idea is that the poet doubtless wants to say the following: when Jesus, in the position of someone dying, calls upon God, it is of no help because God does not know the death of which we all have knowledge. This sounds like a blasphemous reinterpretation of the story of the passion. And yet, in an utterly profound interpretation, can one say the exact opposite: this reading comes very close to the specifically Christian revelation, which announces a message to all in the death of the son of man on the cross? At any rate the poetic expression that a modern poet dares to offer here reflects the fact that a knowledge by which death would become conceivable and bearable should never be presumed. This is precisely what 'we' are. The suffering of death is already granted to everyone. Here we see an intrinsic link between the weakness of human beings and the experience of death. The fact that Jesus feels abandoned on the cross is, as it were, the pre-figuration or paradigm of the abandonment felt by all human beings. The anxiety of life and the anxiety of death are thus intermingled. The flight from one's self constantly springs forth from all anxiety so that one wants to leave behind that about which one is anxious. This flight from one's self is summarized by a symbolic gesture in the experience of Jesus' death on the cross. Jesus poses the question of why he has been abandoned – a citation from Isaiah – while suffering death, although in his prayer at the Mount of Olives, he had given precedence to the will of his father over his own, the will of a creature, and accepted death. Even being ready to be sacrificed is still a possibility of the certainty of one's own being alive.

In our reflections we have presented the great monuments to the meaning of death for human self-consciousness as they are found in the cult of the dead. We have also shown the limitations of the attempts made by thinking to account for the experience of death. In the end we have the following thesis: it belongs to the experience of thinking death that this experience constantly lags behind itself, that it grasps, as it were, a trace of death only in thinking death away and remaining in the certainty of one's own life. What remains an appropriate manner of thinking about death [171] seems to be nothing other than thinking anxiety itself or better: recognizing anxiety itself as thinking.

What is anxiety? What is this mode of being agitated and being outside of oneself in anxiety? About what is one anxious? Heidegger described this in a powerful way: we are anxious about nothing. The uncanniness of being anxious about nothing is precisely the true anxiety. Anxiety is like a thinking of oneself as outside and beyond all beings, beyond everything to which one can cling, to think oneself into nothingness. Thus, it is in the anxiety of life and of death, and not in the thinking beyond and the thinking away of what makes one anxious, that the experience of death coincides with the proper determination of the human being to be the one who thinks. For, what is thinking? It is taking a distance, it is being extirpated from the instinctive processes of natural life. To this extent it is a mode of freedom – not the freedom that we enjoy in being able to change our behaviour arbitrarily, but a freedom from which we, even if we wanted, could not turn away.

The thesis is now the following: the freedom of thinking is the true ground for the fact that death has a necessary unintelligibility. It is the freedom that consists in the fact that I can and must think beyond myself, that I can and must think myself away, that I must constantly extrapolate the inner activity of my intellectual existence. There is nobody here who has an answer to this question: how should I understand the fact that I, an I in which now in this moment there is a thinking activity, one day will not be? Thus, the fact that we are thinking beings seems to be the ground for the unintelligibility of death and, at the same time, seems to include the knowledge of this unintelligibility.

Guardini once said that death is the ontological honour of human beings.[9] As a matter of fact, honour is the fact that one takes pride in oneself. This is not a distinction that one can even renounce. And it is true that such a distinction, which one cannot renounce, without which one cannot live, is for human beings death. Obviously this means that, in contradistinction with other living entities, we have this distinction that death is something for us. The ontological honour of human beings, that to which they unconditionally adhere and which preserves them, so to speak, from the danger of losing themselves and, in the process, of losing also their own capacity to be free, consists in this that they do not conceal from themselves the unintelligibility of death.

Fairy tales are certainly the earliest things that affect children and through which they surmise for the first time what death is. There is, for example, the fairy tale about the house in which the candles of all the living are burning.[10] Visitors to this house who look around themselves, astonished and afraid, eventually also ask about their own life candle – and are struck with terror. Whatever more a fairy tale may tell us about the details, the burning out of the life candles remains, in any case, a revered and apt symbol for human life and its time-span, because in it the finite and ephemeral character of our existence is symbolically presented. [172] The horror of seeing our own life candle is like a flaring up of the innermost anxiety that is given with the certainty of being alive.

However, there is still something else that the symbol of the life candle shows us: it is precisely the very flickering of the candlelight. While a candle quietly burning itself out, its flame moved to and fro by the winds of time, sways back and forth between dimming and a newly rising brightness, the flickering of the candle on the verge of burning itself out seems at times to spread a wee bit more brightness than that of the quietly burning candle: the unintelligibility of death is the highest triumph of life.

Part Two

The Impetus for Thinking Hermeneutically: On the Task of Dilthey

The Problem of Dilthey: Between Romanticism and Positivism (1984)[1]

[406] It is certainly true that Dilthey's *oeuvre*,[2] which is as huge as it is fragmentary, has exercised an influence beyond his own century that is far greater than any other work of a professor of philosophy after the death of Hegel and Schelling. It is indeed even only in our century that his work has really made history due to the fact that it has steadily accompanied the expansion of phenomenological research.

Dilthey's rise to prominence began with his great admiration for Husserl's *Logical Investigations*, passed through the painful conflict brought about by Husserl's publication of the *Logos* essay of 1910 *Philosophy as a Rigorous Science*, casting a shadow on the last year of Dilthey's life, and experienced its true flourishing only after the First World War. At that time, Georg Misch and Bernhard Groethuysen were putting together Dilthey's scattered works.[3] This had far-reaching consequences. It was a significant moment and a true turn in the phenomenological movement occurred when Heidegger emphatically appealed to Dilthey in *Being and Time*, turning the historicity of existence against the transcendental ego.

Husserl's great trend-setting accomplishment was not exhausted when Husserl himself sought to harness his project to the neo-Kantianism of the Marburg school. Many phenomenologists never followed him there. Yet, it remains true that the general turn away from neo-Kantianism after the First World War effectively went hand in hand with the impressive development of Dilthey's intellectual heritage. It may be permitted, precisely in this year, to refer to Ortega y Gasset.[4] His case serves as a good illustration. As a follower of the rigorous Kantian school in Marburg, Ortega, by his own account, discovered Dilthey at the end of the 1920s, finding in his work innumerable confirmations for his own path toward the *razón vital*.[5] It is at the same time that Georg Misch's important [407] work, *Philosophy of Life and Phenomenology*,[6] appeared, opening up a new sphere of influence for Dilthey's ideas within the phenomenological movement between Husserl and Heidegger. It is also the time that saw the first contributions of the younger generation within the phenomenological school, who were open to Dilthey, such as Fritz Kaufmann[7] or Ludwig Landgrebe.[8] It is also at that time that Hans Lipps, Otto Bollnow and myself, among others, started to formulate our own ideas.

From this shift of emphasis that took place after Dilthey's death, it is natural to focus, in Dilthey's work, entirely on the implications of his last creative period. In fact, this is what Dilthey's loyal students already did with the way the first eight volumes of his complete works were laid out, as demonstrated in particular by Groethuysen's introduction to volume 7. This led to the fabrication of the idea of a simple turn in Dilthey from psychology to hermeneutics, from an early neo-Kantianism to a late Hegelianism, making the influence of Husserlian phenomenology the responsible factor for it.

It was inevitable that the one-sided nature of this perspective would in the meantime be revised so that now the continuity of Dilthey's lifework comes to light anew. Such a revision affects not only the historico-biographical aspect but also the philosophy itself, and two directions can be distinguished within the latter. We have, first, the reconnection of philosophy with the positive sciences: the 'politico-moral sciences' as well as the natural sciences – a connection that appeared to have been almost destroyed by Heidegger's radical questioning. Obviously, the proximity of philosophy to the sciences could appear as a new insight only to a generation that had first to rediscover neo-Kantianism and its history for itself. The influence of Heidegger and his turn to a hermeneutic phenomenology, which formulated itself against the epistemological question, had all too fundamentally misrepresented neo-Kantianism. For someone who had gone through the Marburg school, it was no surprise that Dilthey had worked his whole life on the epistemological foundation of the empirical sciences and harboured particularly close affinities for natural scientific research. This was not only the case for Dilthey's earlier years, when people like Friedrich Albert Lange and the great Hermann Helmholtz were preparing a return to Kant. [408] British empiricism and, in particular, the 'inductive logic' of John Stuart Mill exercised a life-long influence on Dilthey. During the Breslau period and the earlier Berlin period, Dilthey was writing the 'Introduction to the Human Sciences', intending it to be a critique of historical reason. It was to represent a decisive movement beyond Kant and was placed entirely at the service of the empirical stand-point. Obviously, one would have to give far more credence to the historicity of experience. Yet, the foundation of the human sciences was never a complete end-in-itself. Rather, Dilthey always had in mind the on-going task of elaborating the common logical and epistemological foundations for both groups of sciences.

There is even a completely different reason for reexamining the fashionable characterization of Dilthey's development as one 'from psychology to hermeneutics'. For, the publication of volumes 18 and 19 of Dilthey's complete works have given us access to important materials. It is well known that Dilthey was deeply upset by the fierce attack launched by Hermann Ebbinghaus against his ideas in 1895. He was equally upset by the ahistorical apriorism of values, upon which precisely Windelband and Rickert erected their theory of the cultural sciences at the time. The preparation of the sequel to the 'Introduction to the Human Sciences' came to a standstill. The psychological foundation and its extension into a 'biological' foundation did not seem sufficient to Dilthey any longer.

This is why Husserl's anti-psychologism must have made a strong impression on him. In the same way, the study of Hegel's early manuscripts could have been a new inspiration for him, which he began[9] at the same time that he resumed his work on his 'Schleiermacher'. We should absolutely not forget that Dilthey from the very beginning carried in himself the rich classical and romantic heritage abandoned by the 'German movement', given how much he detested the 'deductive fallacies' of the idealistic systematizers and how permeated he was by the pathos of the empirical sciences. His devotion to Schleiermacher arose not only from the fact that he was given access to Schleiermacher's correspondence, which he was also going to edit,[10] and to his unpublished manuscripts. This may have played a role in his plan to produce a biography of Schleiermacher.[11] However, the true [409] lines of influence lead us elsewhere. Dilthey was, from early on, attracted by Schleiermacher's free interpretation of Christianity and especially the virtuosity with which he sought his balanced middle way between apriorism and empiricism.

Dilthey was thus from the very beginning a fierce critic of the ahistoricity [*Geschichtslosigkeit*], by means of which British empiricism ran its logical business. This should not surprise us. As fiercely as the historical school rejected the *a priori* historical constructions of a Hegelian variety, the great age of German speculation nevertheless exercised a lasting influence on it. This has been illustrated above all by Erich Rothacker.[12] It was absolutely true for Dilthey, the thinker of the historical school, who, in this respect, came across the schematizing dialectic of a Schleiermacher. This dialectic essentially has only a heuristic and descriptive function and for this reason was certainly not unsuitable to the research mentality of the historical school. The great historical achievements of Schleiermacher and his numerous followers are a testament to this.

The situation for the beginner Dilthey was thus utterly complicated. On the one hand, we had in the Romantic school a nostalgia for the homogeneity of the Christian Middle Ages and most prominently the pathos of Reformation, giving rise to an anti-dogmatic pantheism. On the other hand, we had the critical self-consciousness of modern science and logic, which was connected to this fundamental mood of religiosity. Dilthey, like his contemporaries, stood on shifting grounds. The attempt by German idealism, in the wake of Descartes and Leibniz, to reunify the modern empirical sciences with the metaphysical tradition into a 'system' appeared presumptuous and forbade any emulation – not least the ahistorical positivism of British empiricism: 'Give me a spot on which to stand' [*dos moi pou stō*].[13] How was one to ground philosophical thinking if one wanted to avoid the poverty of an empiricist foundation as well as the aimlessness of historical relativism? We have to start from the fact that philosophy has no place of its own in the age of science if we want to understand the protean capacity of transformation that Dilthey displays in his work. On the one hand, he cannot accept the reduction of philosophy to the role of a theory of knowledge and the reduction of the concept of knowledge to science. On the other hand, he wants to make the empirical standpoint his own and thereby secure the precedence of facts over and above all constructions and hypotheses. This almost compels him to broaden the concept of experience. The outer experience must be completed by inner experience, which amounts to [410] securing the facts of inner experience. Inductive logic proposed by John Stuart Mill as a kind of Bible of scientificity works in the same direction. If one wants to legitimize one's own historical heritage from the standpoint of the empirical sciences, then what matter are the facts of consciousness and in that case the foundations are to be sought in psychology.

It was not Dilthey's particular option to consider the facts of consciousness to be the only things given and to be the only things positive. Grounding his moral philosophy in the 'fact of reason' [*Vernunftfaktum*] that is freedom, Kant took the first step in the direction of a new broadening of the concept of 'fact'. In opposition to Leibniz, Kant conferred upon a fact the distinction of a rational truth, even if it was only a fact founded on nothing other than the autonomous consciousness of duty and responsibility. Fichte raised this 'autonomy' of reason to the level of a principle of 'science' and thereby gave to the 'facts of consciousness' the new sense and the deeper foundation of being an 'activity' [*Tathandlung*]. However, this was the time when the general turn from transcendental philosophy to empiricism was in full swing. After the idealistic movement had run its course, psychology seemed to be the only scientific avenue remaining for philosophy. Psychology had to take possession of the legacy of transcendental philosophy and even borrowed from it the expression 'facts of consciousness', but without retaining the transcendental sense embedded in the activity [*Tathandlung*] that produces all empirical facts of consciousness.

Even the return to Kant continues this empiricist tendency of the time, during which Dilthey began his career. We generally do not see sufficiently clearly how peculiarly two-faced the recognition of Kant by the first pioneers of neo-Kantianism was. When Eduard Zeller introduced the formulation 'theory of knowledge'[14] in favour of the apriorism of the Kantian foundation of knowledge, this was in no way to justify anew the legitimacy of an *a priori* philosophy. It was with the opposite intention: for the sake of the *a posteriori* character of facts. Zeller wanted, in this way, to purify the facts from *a priori* elements and secure the value of 'pure facts', which alone could legitimate the scientific experience. Dilthey's specific [411] question concerning the facts of inner experience and his introduction of the concept of 'lived experience' [*Erlebnis*] are not too far from Zeller's view. He too wants to learn how to avoid the 'deductive fallacies' of the kind committed by Hegel.[15]

Obviously, for Dilthey, the inheritor who was conscious of his idealistic inheritance, the manner in which Herbart and his followers had practised a 'physics of a mental life' [*Physik des Seelenlebens*] had something deeply unsatisfying. He remarks on this psychology: 'it excludes the contents of psychic events, which in the first place decide about the meaning of our existence.'[16] He believes that these contents 'permeate the individuals in a historical movement'. Eventually, he compares the study of these psychic contents 'in a certain manner' with 'the tendency of the phenomenology of spirit'. This is a highly ambitious objective: the commitment to an encyclopedia of the science of the human being, which, so to speak, would be an anthropology based on empirical and historical foundations. Dilthey is fully aware of the far-reaching claim of this project and immediately proclaims that these facts 'include in themselves everything that an idealist philosophy could ever establish'. How exciting is this work plan in itself! These are notes from 1866 in which one can find the bold statement: 'The completed science of history would be the exposition and explanation of the complex of human culture.' This is a utopian goal. Dilthey himself knows that culture is no 'homogeneous totality', like nature. That is the reason why the moral and political sciences can never acquire the closed character of a unified theory, the way it is the uncontested goal of research in the natural sciences. The fragmentary, the incomplete, the protean malleability that distinguishes

Dilthey's own work is preordained, as it were, by the object of investigation. The metaphysics of the individual and its origins in Leibniz lie at the foundations of such an enterprise.[17] Yet, Dilthey once again insists that these moral and political sciences must proceed 'according to a rigorous inductive method'.

The foundations of such a science are the 'facts of consciousness': the facts of inner experience, which must be logically equivalent to those of outer experience. Obviously, it is already implied in the expression 'inner experience' that something of this kind is not accessible to the experimental means of natural science, [412] but can only be described. Eventually, Dilthey will say that only 'understanding' can reach them. Yet, even then 'psychology' remains the foundation.

The introduction of the concept of 'understanding' into Dilthey's vocabulary merits our interest in this regard. This concept can only be distinguished with difficulty from the scientific and theoretical ideal of explanation and when Dilthey finally does manage it, he replaces 'explanation' with 'description'. When it comes to structural connections that are experienced [*erlebt*], he privileges 're-living' [*nacherleben*]. He limits the concept of understanding, first of all, to the alien, the other, be it another person or the sensuous appearance of language and text, on the basis of which one can go back to inner experience. This is remarkable. He had conducted early and well-grounded studies in hermeneutics and Schlegel, Schleiermacher, and later on Droysen had perceived in the expression 'understanding' an almost religious connotation. His own theme was the theme of individuality. Yet, despite all this, he completely submitted his methodological self-understanding to the scientific and theoretical point of view of empiricism. Even his foundation of psychology that is characterized by 'understanding' resulted in a text that had the title 'Ideas toward a Descriptive and Analytic Psychology', which consciously avoids the word 'understanding'. Obviously the foundation of facts must be secured unambiguously and remain free from the problematic of understanding. Regarding the emphasis that the word 'fact' received at that time, the following point seems to me to be somewhat noteworthy. In 1875 Dilthey had planned a chapter on 'The Classification of Mental Facts'. This was obviously due to the influence of Franz Brentano's work of 1874 titled *Psychology from an Empirical Standpoint* that contained a chapter on 'The Classification of Mental Phenomena'.

Dilthey undertook to distinguish the 'inner' facts in their own ontological status simply through their being-inner. Here, we can see the thematic agreement with Franz Brentano. Following Aristotle and against German idealism, Brentano took it that there is a reflection that accompanies the mental act. This reflection does not take as its object the act with which it is linked when accompanying it in its directedness to the object. Rather, this reflection essentially belongs to the execution of the act. It is for this mode of being of these inner facts that Dilthey introduces the word 'lived-experience', which was then entering into parlance, and he characterizes this mode of being as having an immediate unity of experiencing and lived experience. The 'being-inner' expresses the fact that we are not dealing with an 'understanding' with all its hermeneutic implications of divination and interpretation.

Yet, lived experience in Dilthey's view must possess a particular unity that is itself formed as a connection of lived experience, as a structural connection or as a teleological connection and through which the lived experience by virtue of its 'significance' [413] springs out from the totality of a life connection. Obviously Dilthey here describes the concept of 'lived experience' that stands between the following two poles: on the one hand, the temporal immediacy of experiencing, with which we know something not only indirectly – through others, through witnesses, through tradition – but have experienced this immediacy ourselves; on the other hand, a retrospective look seeking to remember, in which its significance comes to the fore. Now, these two aspects of the concept of 'lived experience' are not without an inner relation. As a matter of fact, the significance of a lived experience is obviously already presupposed for the fact that one is even interested at all in immediately experiencing it, directing one's own thought toward it. The experiencing, thus, receives a mediated immediacy. The historian in Dilthey could hardly overlook the fact that the testimony of an eyewitness in any case needs critique and that the significance of what is testified is not determined by the immediacy of having experienced it. Even Dilthey's favourite example – bereavement – can teach us this.[18] The finality of parting company with someone who is dead exercises an idealizing and in any case a stabilizing effect. Because nothing remains, the look turns to a well circumscribed whole, the significance of which appears to one as enduring.

One can see a problem emerge here that was to lead Dilthey eventually from the immediacy of the being-inner to the hermeneutic turn of his thought. It is a deeply temporal and ontological problem. On the one hand, lived-experience must be the absolute givenness, which should not even be called 'givenness' because this would suggest a separation between what is given and that to which it is given. The expression 'being-inner' aims at going beyond all 'givenness'. On the other hand, the unity of the lived experience is precisely not constituted through the mere being-there, which must hold as the being-inner of an inner experience; it is rather constituted through what is particular to what comes to experience and has its significance in the totality of the course of life. This comes clearly to the fore in those lived experiences that we call 'decisive' and which cause a turn, a reversal, a conversion, etc.

Dilthey describes the reality of such a lived experience in the following way: the lived experience emerges out of the experiencing by virtue of its signifi-cance [*Bedeutung*], gaining its enduring unity. 'Significance' is for him truly a category of history or life. Now, Dilthey's thinking will always be in the grip of the dominant presupposition that characterizes the awakening of the West to science as well as the modern [**414**] concept of science with its emphasis on method and objectivity. We know this very well since Heidegger's destruction of the concepts of 'consciousness' and 'subjectivity' and his unveiling of their metaphysical origin. By contrast, Dilthey's reflections are weighed down by the ontological pressure of the metaphysical tradition in a manner that often leads him astray. In Dilthey, it sounds as if it is only at the end of a nexus that the significance of the individual can in fact be determined. This seems to be true in the case of an individual life when the question is whether it was a happy life, or in the case of the totality of history and its sense, or eventually even in the case of the totality of a course of events that has been experienced even if it is only the course of a piece of music. By contrast, since antiquity, the story of Kroisus and Solon has been used to evaluate the sense and nonsense of such an argumentation about happiness.[19] Eventually, Aristotle is right when he neither speaks in favour of Stoic apathy nor sees in the vicissitudes of life what is decisive for assessing happiness; rather, what is decisive for him is the individual fitting into the stability of the moral and political order and this is what is presented as virtue (*aretē*).

The same holds for world history. It is not an objection against it that it must be written anew again and again; rather this is in a certain sense its distinctive feature. So much does it mean for every age. This is entirely clear to Dilthey and he was thus compelled to conclude: it is true that the content of experience undergoes constant change, but something like the character of the present remains and defines itself as a fulfilment with reality. When reality constantly moves forward, what is experienced 'as a force reaching into the present' can acquire its proper character of presence. One has to ask whether, by doing so, Dilthey does justice to the play of forces in which traditions form and transform or whether he does not wrongly absolutize the self-understanding of any present instead of seeing it as a consciousness exposed to the effects of history. He once used the expression 'to be consciously something that is conditioned'.[20] This is all well, but consciousness is itself something conditioned and necessarily lags behind the consciousness of its being conditioned.

What he calls here 'the present' clarifies the ontological preconception [*Vorgriff*] under which he sees reality. Surely, he would count the future, in which human action constantly anticipates itself, as something that determines the reality of the present. Whether what determines the significance of a lived experience is an anticipation toward the future or a reference back to the past [*Vorgriff oder Rückgriff*] or both, the available sum will always be computed 'now'. Thus, his concept of objective knowledge forces him into relativism.

The attempt to avoid relativism often leads us to something surprising. Dilthey describes how repeated visits to a masterwork in painting coalesce together so that the last lived experience is like a taking together of [**415**] the whole. An atemporal ideal end point is thereby once again made the distinctive feature of experience. It is as if darkness and light were not truly interwoven, even during the course of one's life, so that things in a changing light are illuminated in a changing manner and often fall completely into obscurity. There is no light of an enduring day that makes the true significance of everything appear.

However, Dilthey knows very well that a structure or a structural connection has its centre in a middle point, so to speak, and does not form in the sequence of its elements. This is why Dilthey likes the example of a melody in which it is precisely not the last note that in fact makes it possible for us to comprehend it. Nevertheless, we see even here the overemphasis on the retrospective. Of all the things that we experience, music to a strange degree has the distinction of being composed of purely temporal matter. What we understand when we understand music is the structure itself, consisting of notes that are in themselves meaningless. All the elements that configure the whole are 'tempered'. The temporal structure is the fixed law of construction of the musical whole. Now, it is noteworthy how Dilthey at one point describes musical understanding in the image of the particular architecture that is proper to absolute music in its classical apogee. He describes repetition, contrast, and eventually the higher reconciliation of contrasting forces in a victorious finale – a process accomplished with louder temporal forms. One can hardly say more. Meaning elements of a different kind, like those that articulate, for example, the sense of linguistic expressions, cannot be found in pure instrumental music. Thus, all interpretations that assert a univocal content of expression for such a music proceed more or less arbitrarily, as Wolfgang Hildesheimer very recently did in the case of Mozart.[21] What does it really mean to 'understand' a piece of music? What is its meaning when it is nothing other than a pure temporal form? Does

Dilthey correctly describe how music appears in a kind of all-encompassing retrospective look? Can we legitimately compare historical knowledge with the finale in the structure of a symphony? What is the time in which an event is formed in its unity? What is the time in which the event is grasped in its configuration? The time of a memory? A sum?

I have once mentioned another example of the ontological dilemma in which Dilthey finds himself.[22] This is the privilege that Dilthey grants to autobiography when it comes to the formation of the unity of the historical nexus. What he means is that in the autobiography the connection of a life is formed to the extent that one retrospectively knows the meaning of what was experienced. Do those who have experienced something themselves really know the true meaning of what they experienced through retrospection?

[416] This would mean that the eyewitness surpasses the historian and that the autobiography has a greater testimonial value than the result of critical archival research.

One can wonder how a science is at all possible on the basis of such inner facts, which are brought to consciousness in self-reflection. How is the significance of what has been personally experienced to be raised through science to an objective meaning? In the field of our knowledge of nature, it seems that our sensual-linguistic orientation in the world and the mathematical-mechanical construction of natural processes coexist relatively without tension. We only have to think, for example, of the co-existence of Newton's and Goethe's theory of colours. The fact that this coexistence had the character of a conflict was still in the end a misunderstanding, just as the approval that Goethe's sensuous and moral interpretation of reality found among the philosophers of German idealism. Both can be compatible in the end, as long as they mean something different. When we see something that is coloured, we can know all the same that we are affected by real light waves. By contrast, the status of one's own lived experiences as such seems to me to be completely out of reach for science. When we become aware of a lived experience as significant, an objective science can hardly tell us that it is in fact not such, but otherwise. Would the lived experience even be what it is if it could be objectively known as another lived experience, by someone else, as it were? Here, Scheler's theory of the relativity of existence[23] first brought a clarity that seems to me to be missing in Dilthey. This is also manifest in his use of the word 'self-reflection' [*Selbstbesinnung*]. In one sense Dilthey is obviously right: in all knowledge in the human sciences, there is a moment of self-reflection at work. When someone wants to re-live what was experienced, knowledge and science may be involved, for example, with a historical or aesthetic or religious interest. However, it is not so that the lived experience could be subsumed under science and knowledge, as the instance of a rule or a regularity, and reconstrued, so to speak. What is experienced or re-lived has its unique place in the context of a life, which must be experienced or re-experienced as such, but cannot be derived as a mere instance from a rule or a law.

The goal, Dilthey believes, is to make intelligible through the complementary activities of the human sciences in their totality the valuable and meaningful connection [417] that underlies the coexistence and the succession of lived experiences. He also says that, out of this connection, the singular can be grasped. If this is so, then it cannot mean that the connection is derived as an instance out of a rule. Even depth psychology, of whose beginnings Dilthey does not seem to have taken notice, is fully aware that the possibilities of enlightenment that can be arrived at through science are limited. Depth psychology knows that it is itself dependent upon the self-understanding of the patient. Only the patients can recognize themselves by subsuming themselves under a rule. In this sense, it is legitimate for Dilthey to characterize as self-reflection the only procedure that is appropriate with regard to inner facts. However, is there a seamless transition from this self-reflection to the higher generalities of scientific objectivity? It may be the case in psychoanalysis that self-reflection leads back to something hidden, misjudged, forgotten and perhaps even repressed, and which reveals itself as such, that is to say: as the true in reflection. Nevertheless, it is not a self-reflection through science or the elevation of self-reflection to a science.

This is certainly not the case with the famous *anamnēsis*, by way of which Socrates uncovers his partners' ignorance as well as his own, and in this way defines the knowledge of the good, which is at the same time a being good. The Socratic question is a constant exhortation to remember, which sustains itself in all human reflection and in all human acts of giving an account of oneself, whether one may owe such an account to oneself or to another. Aristotle has taken this up in the fundamental principle of his ethics and defines *aretē* as 'a disposition with *logos*' (*hexis meta logou*). That is to say, it is a disposition that contains in itself the Socratic self-reflection, practical rationality, *logos*. This reflection concerns just as much the firmness of a disposition and its normative validity as well as the concrete situation that always demands a decision. The firmness of a moral order and a political constitution, which guarantees the order of justice belongs, according to Aristotle, to the natural needs of the *zōon politikon*. It is on this basis that 'practical philosophy' is founded. This is a very peculiar 'science', which makes the highly peculiar presupposition of an *ethos* that binds us to each other. Only on the basis of this presupposition can we have a seamless generalization of a rationality that is to be expected from anybody. In Aristotle's case, this in no way excludes the all-encompassing empirical character of his studies of the state constitutions or of any other experience. Yet, 'ethics' and 'politics' remain through and through 'practical philosophy'. These are not theories in the sense of allowing us to make any arbitrary application of objective cognitions to praxis. Rather, they are 'theories' only in the Greek sense: they function as a moment in practical self-formation. This is incidentally the deeper reason why Aristotle [418] could eventually also hold on to the utopian mode of thought of the ideal state, of which Plato had availed himself. Every utopia appeals to a peculiar way of thinking because it resists the immediate application to praxis[24] and yet it is meant 'practically'.

This is the point at which a radical conflict arises with the modern concept of science and its founding in method and objectivity. This makes the application of the concept of self-reflection in Dilthey deeply ambivalent. Between the concept of the moral-political sciences, which Dilthey appropriates from the tradition, and the modern concept of science, there opens up a chasm at this point. It is not without reason that the tradition of 'practical philosophy' has met with its demise in the age of science. Consequently, Dilthey does not make use of any reference to the Aristotelian tradition any more. How does he then want to justify the normative claim of the human sciences? Can the passage through the historical world be a substitute for the ground of solidarity, which alone can support a normative science, in the manner that practical philosophy aspires to be a normative science? Dilthey is very well aware of the storm that brews over the attempt at founding science on historical experience. He once calls the passage through the historical world and the plunging into the daydreams of art a 'going to the high seas'.[25] This he knows: 'When unprejudiced spirits want to connect everything that they can re-live in themselves [*nacherleben*], when they would like to look the world in the eye, so to speak, in order to understand its interior, they are then presented with features that will not harmonize in any unified understanding.'[26] Compared to the exemplary but limited truths that research into nature establishes, the unlimited field of historical becoming allows for no unified theoretical interpretation. Dilthey knows that the human sciences do not 'control' their 'object' in the same way. Yet, he will not, on that account, see them as 'inexact' sciences because they fail in their prognoses, like meteorology, which Mill mentions as a point of comparison, but even more than meteorology. It is certainly not a lack of data that hampers objectification and generalization in the human sciences. Let us grant that the data can be multiplied everywhere so enormously that not only long-term weather prognoses, but also perhaps even the prognoses and planning of the social sciences of the future would become more reliable. Would this then [419] be the successful objectification of the self-reflection that Dilthey envisaged as the goal? What is it really that is singular in the inner facts of mental life, on which the human sciences are built? For what reason does Dilthey earnestly expect from the human sciences that they would function as 'a new force in the intellectual life of Europe'?[27] On what does Dilthey ground such a normative claim? On the re-living of everything? Dilthey knew this: if everything that could be re-lived was re-lived and we then gazed at life in its 'inscrutable' [*unergründlich*] visage, we would realize then that life would give us no answer.[28] Are we supposed to expect from the 'historical science in the making'[29] something like a regulative influence on society and on the shaping of the future, the more it approaches the ideal of objective science? In the end, is this historical science supposed to bring about such a measure of magnificent freedom and world peace here on earth that the riddle of transcendence itself would be resolved through a pantheistic godliness of the world?

It cannot be denied that Dilthey really held on to such a claim. He wanted to regulate praxis through the human sciences. Is it possible for any science as science not only to know how to apply its knowledge, but also to direct it toward the good, as 'practical philosophy' could claim, from whose tradition the moral-political sciences originate? When he directed his questions toward experts of all kinds, Socrates showed us once and for all that the objectivity of science releases its results for any random use and is not itself in a position to assume responsibility for its use in the service of the 'good'. Modern science, on this point, has nothing over the knowledge of the craftsmen in an indigenous society. All the control of things through science cannot as such provide an answer to the question of the good. However more objective, scientific knowledge becomes, it does not know, on the basis of that knowledge, whether it 'is right' for individuals to lead their own way of life or for a society or a nation or humanity to exercise the capacities enabled by this knowledge. It seems to me undeniable that Dilthey nonetheless, right up to the very end, held steadfastly to the conviction of his youth: in the sciences and in scientific philosophy, one arrives at the 'transition from the facts of reality to the ought, the purpose, the ideal'.[30] With this conviction, he shares in the ideals of the modern [420] enlightenment. But it is not possible, in fact nonsensical, to expect this transition from the sciences themselves.

Here, radical modern enlightenment has found its limits, which Rousseau pointed out. Kant grasped what Rousseau pointed out, but turned it into a positive point. Rousseau warned us against seeing in the progress of the sciences a progress in our morals and mores. Kant, following him, showed us a way not to be led astray by the eudaimonistic illusions of technical rationality and the imperatives of intelligence. This is the sense of Kant's formalism, which could be better called his 'realism'. In any case, one fails to see how Dilthey's long way through history should have been able to overcome the paradox of a 'normative science' in the sense of modern 'science'. The commitments of Dilthey to his view of the world sound quite peculiar today.

Now, one may readily object that in the age of science a renewal of 'practical philosophy' is simply out of the question. The universalizing of the prevalent mores and norms that Aristotelian ethics and politics undertook was no longer in force at the time of Dilthey. Despite all this, it was not yet afflicted by relativistic scepticism, but could still call itself *philosophia*. After the triumph of Christianity, was Aristotelian teaching, for example the natural character of slave society, worth defending? Is it not simply necessary that, after the advent of historical consciousness and the collapse of all speculative-aprioristic philosophy of history, a philosophical ethics, if grounded only in a particular *ethos*, must lead to complete relativism? Can Dilthey avoid this consequence by a universal expansion of relativity? Can he honestly want to put 'the sciences in the making'[31] in place of the history of salvation or the education of the human race or the progress of world history toward the freedom of all? Can this science imagine that it can lead beyond the relativity of all the forms of *ethos*? How did Dilthey expect to find anything firm there, he being the man who knew himself as someone who could only 'live in the full objectivity of thought'[32] and, for this reason, preferred to put up with the 'bitter situation' of 'renouncing every knowledge about the ultimate nexus of things?'[33]

Dilthey sought an answer to these questions all his life. Could it lie in the doctrine of the many-sidedness of life, as he believed? Dilthey believed that he was beyond all scepticism because he claimed to grasp the relativity of the conceptual systems of philosophy. [421] He reduced philosophy to a few types of world-views. Any of the things taken from another aspect of the fundamental fact of 'life' would emerge from these types and to that extent would not be without truth. Despite this, science would not allow any of them to count as true, that is to say: to fulfil their own claim to know the totality and to legitimate it against the scientific ideal of objectivity. Could one then really *'live* in the full objectivity of thought?' There is no need to have a Count Yorck as a friend to doubt this. Yet, Dilthey's scientific self-understanding insisted upon this.

Given all this, one understands Dilthey's disappointment when, in the '*Logos*' essay of 1910 Husserl, whom Dilthey held in very high regard and decisively supported, openly counts him, Dilthey, among the relativists. Husserl holds him co-responsible for the deadly danger of scepticism, which, according to Husserl, could only be averted through 'philosophy as rigorous science' and on the basis of the transcendental ego.

One must remember how Dilthey had appropriated Husserl's *Logical Investigations* of 1900–1. He drew significant clarity from it, even if he did not at all separate himself from psychology, which in his eyes remained the ultimate foundation at the basis of inner facts. It was liberating for him when he acquainted himself with Husserl's proof of the essential connection between 'expression and meaning [*Bedeutung*]' and in particular the connection of the word to its singular ideal meaning, as well as with Husserl's theory of the *a priori* laws of pure grammar. What Dilthey learned was this: an expression can have a meaning without this having to be the expression of a lived experience. Here we have a structural connection between life and meaning: meaning is in life. Meaning does not come into being only in a 'calm' retrospective look of remembrance, but rather lies in the expression as such, in the word as such, and just as much in life itself. Dilthey did not pay attention to the *aprioristic* claim that Husserl's proofs raised and simply turned his insights into psychological ones. In principle, this did not go against Husserl and the late Husserl would have most certainly tolerated this as a consequence, although not as a foundation. Thus, Dilthey, in his own peculiar way, appropriated, for instance, the idea of meaning-fulfilment, of which Husserl spoke in the *Logical Investigations*, and understood it as the fullness of meaning that gradually enriches itself from inner experiences, a fullness that accrues to experience. In the same way, Dilthey saw with greater accuracy a confirmation of his own theory of the structural connection of mental life in Husserl's analysis of the stream of consciousness in the fourth and fifth of the *Logical Investigations*. Yet, he never adopted the basic Brentanian-Husserlian concept of intentionality.

This expression 'intentionality' was for him not objective enough. [422] Nonetheless, he drew some real benefits for his position from that expression. With the triad lived experience-expression-meaning, he manages to overcome the ambiguity of the immediacy of lived experience that we analysed above. He secured a positive sense for the ambiguity of 'meaning' as it stood between the one ideal meaning and the self-constituting meaningfulness [*Bedeutsamkeit*].

He, thereby, outlines new hermeneutic horizons, into which philosophical reflection would be thrust (Heidegger, Hans Lipps, etc.).

How did Dilthey react to Husserl's criticism of 1910? The publication led to an exchange of letters, but not to a real discussion. The main reason for this is the overly conciliatory presentation that Dilthey's longer letter gives. It formally suggests agreement, and it is accepted by Husserl's response, which even promises to say publicly that in '*Logos*' it was not Dilthey who was the object of his critique of historicism. What remains controversial is how they understood metaphysics. For Dilthey's goal of a universal theory of knowledge, which 'was to provide a firm foundation for the human sciences', 'metaphysics' was impossible as a universally valid science, 'which undertakes to express the connection of the world [*Weltzusammenhang*] through a connection of concepts in a valid way'. In his response, Husserl defends this sense of metaphysics not as traditional ontology, but rather as 'phenomenologically expanded and founded (universal) sciences of existence [*Daseinswissenschaften*]'. He suggested for his part that Dilthey's 'analysis in terms of the human sciences' coincides in 'multiple respects' with his 'phenomenological' analysis.

In Dilthey's published works, I know of only one clear hint of a planned response. It is worth examining the text. In one section of Dilthey's writings on religion from 1911, there is the marginal remark 'See my discussion with Husserl'.[34] In this text we read: 'this connection (which is essential for the problems of the history of religion, and depends on philosophical investigations) must be an objective valid cognition, which stands beyond all unprovable world-views and is thus not metaphysical in the old sense. As every systematic foundation of human science, this connection also needs to encompass only the propositions necessary for such a foundation.'[35] One can detect here that Dilthey wanted to reply: I agree with Husserl that I do not simply do justice to world-views, but inquire behind them with my 'philosophy of philosophy', which, for its part, is secured by way of 'rigorous induction'. On the other hand, I, Dilthey, [423] see no necessity to seek an ultimate foundation in the apodictic evidence of the *ego cogito*. Even in the case of religious experience, there is an inductive process that leads from the facts of consciousness to objectively valid cognition without it requiring a grounding in transcendental subjectivity. This is how Dilthey's discussion could perhaps look and his longer letter to Husserl[36] does not contradict such a picture. One could wonder which passages in Husserl's '*Logos*' essay led him to qualify his empiricism. In any case, one can see that Dilthey too, in a way similar to what Husserl had done in 1913,[37] could have played his part in the fight over true positivism.

This was not without opportunities. It remains astounding how much of the legacy of romanticism Dilthey carried with himself and brought to his philosophy of life, despite all his preoccupation with empiricist scientific theory. 'Meaning' was for him not only the decisive category of historical thinking;[38] but, just as much, the decisive category of poetry.[39] He held on to positivism – certainly not the positivism of 'flattened knowledge' – right up to the very end, but he equally gave hermeneutic reflection the widest possible extent, keeping both directions open till their contours became blurred. With this insight, he still remains close to what a generation, marked by the bloody experiences of the First World War and the shaking up of liberal cultural consciousness, began to seek, precisely through the hopelessness of Dilthey's search at the time. It was a new immediacy that we sought then, which had to break through the hard crust of the scientific culture of the nineteenth century. The puzzling terms of 'life' and 'historicity' began to unsettle university philosophy as well after the First World War. It was above all Heidegger who taught us to recognize in this unrest the essential historicity of human existence and to grasp it as our ontological distinction. Dilthey remains, along with Nietzsche, one of the great figures of European thought, who brought the unifying bond of the humanities [*humanitas*] into the radical questions of our century. At that time we had to thank Georg Misch above all for the fact that Dilthey began to talk to us and not only through the edition of the *Dilthey-Schriften*. More important for us was Misch's own further thinking in terms of a 'Philosophy of Life [424] and Phenomenology', which brought together all the fixed positions of Husserl, Heidegger, and Dilthey, and constantly turned them against each other. The grounding of philosophical hermeneutics gained decisive support through this. Even the discussion presented here of our problems with Dilthey indirectly testifies to his presence as the universal advocate for the historical tradition in which we stand.

8

Dilthey and Ortega: The Philosophy of Life (1985)[1]

[436] The year 1983 saw among others the celebration of two jubilees related to philosophy: the 150th birthday of Wilhelm Dilthey and the 100th birthday of Ortega y Gasset. Further, the birthday of Ortega y Gasset falls on the year Dilthey's central work *Introduction to the Human Sciences* was published. Counting years and jubilees are often a superficial exercise. In the case of Dilthey and Ortega, the situation is different.

It has surely been a long time, a half-century during which a professor from Berlin, who had for long been acclaimed, even highly acclaimed, exercised his overall calm, yet very strong influence. It was also during this time that the young Ortega, at the beginning of this century, came to Germany to pursue his studies in philosophy, mostly in Marburg. Yet, the oft-cited words of Ortega about his reverence for Dilthey as the most significant thinker of the second half of the nineteenth century, expresses in fact a deeper commonality that surpasses historical time. According to Ortega's own testimony, it was only at the end of the 1920s that he actually read Dilthey. For this reason one can surely be confident in the assumption that there was no real influence of Dilthey on the formation of Ortega's own intellectual world. When he was at the peak of his powers Ortega had for long elaborated the fundamentals of his own orientation to the world. It is thus all the more worth asking about the kind of commonalities that existed between Dilthey, the renowned authority in Berlin, who died in 1911, and the cultural philosopher Ortega y Gasset, who was already rising to world renown in the 1920s. It is also worth explaining what led Ortega at the time to acknowledge Dilthey in such an admiring way.

In order to do this one must make two things clear: on the one side, there exists a deep commonality in the distance that the two maintained from the dominant tendencies of academic philosophy in Germany, namely, neo-Kantianism. Obviously, Dilthey may be distinguished as the thinker of the historical school. However, we should not let ourselves be deceived by this honorific title: in academic philosophy at the [**437**] beginning of the twentieth century, and in fact much earlier, Dilthey was rather better known as a genius for his research in the human sciences, but not as a thinker in his own right. Even the most loyal students and disciples of Dilthey, such as Bernhard Groethuysen, have occasionally expressed their surprise when, in the grip of Heidegger's works and influence, we all studied Dilthey from this Heideggerean vantage point as an original thinker who was dealing with the historical reality of life. Even so loyal a student of Dilthey as Groethuysen himself could not suppress his astonishment at the fact that we took Dilthey seriously as a genuine thinker in this context.

It is even more significant that Dilthey, for his part, parted company with neo-Kantianism from the very beginning on one point: its historically-averse transcendentalism. Dilthey attempted to expand neo-Kantianism not only by merely broadening it so as to include historical life, but also to free the concept of experience from the confines of the scientific-theoretical concept of experience prevalent within academic neo-Kantianism. His goal was to extend this concept to life experience and the experience of history. These efforts meant something essentially new. Here one recognizes without any effort an authentic analog to the spiritual history of Ortega. It is well-known that Ortega spent ten years immersed in the philosophy of Kant and was, among other things, introduced to German idealistic philosophy in the most rigorous school of neo-Kantianism in Marburg, under Hermann Cohen and Paul Natorp. In Marburg the work of Dilthey must have remained about as good as unknown to him. Yet, following his own inclination, from the very beginning, from the incipient stages of his own productive work, Ortega pursued the study of the historically saturated life of culture and was not content, as the Marburg school of neo-Kantianism was, to consider the fact of science – the production of 'reality' through the infini-tesimal method – as the foundation of all authentic science. The contact with Dilthey could have only been for him a kind of surprising confirmation of his ownmost tendencies, which he had also encountered at that time in a younger Marburger, Heinz Heimsoeth.

This was the first commonality between Dilthey and Ortega: a critical distance from transcendental philosophy and its concept of 'consciousness in general', which the Neo-Kantians had taken from Kant's *Prolegomena* and elevated into a magical keyword for transcendental consciousness. However, this commonality cannot mean the same for a Dilthey, who was a late product of the romantic cultural tradition in Germany, and an Ortega, who undertook to introduce into European thinking the genuine Latin and Spanish experience of history that had developed over the centuries in Spain. No matter how rich it is and how far it extended into the global aspects of intellectual history, Dilthey's lifework remained, philosophically speaking, in [438] the as yet unresolved duality between the speculative heritage of German idealism and the empirical standpoint. The latter became compelling for him, originating as it did in the spirit of the nineteenth century, and in particular from British empiricism, and from the reinterpretation of Kant in epistemological terms.

Thus, Dilthey, already as a beginner, participated in the reversal that leads from the concept of the 'fact of consciousness', which was of transcendental and idealistic coinage, to the empirical concept of the 'facts of consciousness'. This led him to seek in psychology the original foundation of the human sciences. Obviously, this psychology was not a 'physics of mental life', which had developed since then among his older contemporaries from the reversal of the idealistic theory of the fact of consciousness. Here I have in mind people such as Herbart or Fechner. It is also true that, when he encountered opposition from his peers in psychology, his search for a descriptive and analytic psychology sought a stronger orientation toward hermeneutic phenomena, which for him acquired a fresh relevance first in Husserl's *Logical Investigations,* but also in the resurgent interest in Hegel's *Phenomenology of Spirit.* One could undertake a kind of construction, coming moreover from no less than the oldest and the most loyal disciples of Dilthey, saying that Dilthey had evolved from psychology to a hermeneutics of a phenomenological cast. However, this would certainly underestimate the tenacity and consistency with which Dilthey himself put the phenomenological impulses, which he owed to Husserl's logical genius, at the service of his own empirical standpoint and at the service of founding the human sciences in psychology. This is why, in my own analysis of the Diltheyan position,[2] I could, so to speak, irrefutably demonstrate that for him the *pathos* of empirical science and the ideal of the objectivity of science remained till the very end in an irresolvable conflict with his own point of departure in life experience and the experience of the historical world.

Thus, we must certainly not play down the kind of astonishing resurgence Dilthey's intellectual influence had in the 1920s. This was, on the one hand, a credit to his students, who in the years between the wars had published a well thought out selection of his publications and manuscripts in eight volumes; on the other hand, there was the impression that these historically saturated works made within the school of phenomenology, as well as on people such as Max Scheler, Eduard Spranger, Theodor Litt, Karl [439] Jaspers and, above all, Martin Heidegger. It is only because of the distance, which had been acquired in the meantime, and the newly awakened interest in situating his scientific-theoretical work that Dilthey's proximity to the empirical scientific positivism gained a new value. For those acquainted with the facts, this new discovery is rather comical.

One can look at Ortega, who was fifty years younger, and at his own ten-year imprisonment in the Kantian philosophy of a Marburger cast, to which he remained steadfastly thankful as a peculiar precondition of his intellectual formation. One then encounters an astounding energy for self-liberation that drew him close to Dilthey's late influence. On decisive points, the late Ortega speaks extremely critically of his Marburg teachers, but also of the trailblazer Dilthey, whom he really admired in many respects. In all of them he sees a kind of unconscious positivism. What he means by positivism is naturally the universal scientific positivism, which hindered all of them from taking the path indicated by the things themselves, the path of life experience from which they could have had access to the historical and the cultural world in its true extent. Ortega therefore rightly stresses that Dilthey himself in all the richness of content that he was able to integrate into his studies of intellectual history, never questioned the concept of consciousness and the striving toward a methodical scientificity and objectivity. Even the concept of life, which is supposed to serve as the core and key concept of Dilthey's fundamental position, received in his work the function of a limiting instance of scientific knowability. 'I cannot live without the objectivity of thought', admitted Dilthey. However, he also recognized the inscrutability [*Unergründlichkeit*] of life. In Ortega's reflective incursions into the historical world, no such counter-instance is to be found, not even on the side of Marburg neo-Kantianism. It is also certainly not the case that Ortega's own path of thinking was essentially determined by the reception of Dilthey within hermeneutic phenomenology and therefore by Heidegger. On the contrary, Ortega saw in the Heidegger of *Being and Time*, and also in the impact of Kierkegaard that is to be found in *Being and Time*, as well as later in the whole existential pathos that resonated out of France, a mere concretization and nuancing of the idealistic prejudice with regard to the theory of consciousness. It was precisely from this prejudice that Ortega strove to free himself. This was already clearly to be heard in his Kant lectures of 1924 and in particular in his afterword. Following the development of the Marburg school at the hands of Nicolai Hartmann, Heinz Heimsoeth, Max Wundt and others, Ortega more preferably sought to make fruitful for his own ideas the metaphysical background, which had been hidden up to now and against which Kant had been unilaterally understood in epistemological terms. His critique of historical [440] reason, if one may so characterize his theory of the *razón vital*,[3] was in any event very distant from the epistemological foundation of the human sciences, which Dilthey saw as the task of his life to the end.

It is precisely when one notices this that one wonders about a deeper commonality that was at play in Ortega and Dilthey. This can be clarified if one asks how the philosophical intentions of Dilthey relate to the work of Friedrich Nietzsche, whose true worldwide influence stands in a peculiar contrast to his position as an outsider to the university philosophy of the nineteenth century. The quiet and powerful influence of the successful university scholar Wilhelm Dilthey not in dispute, Nietzsche became the authentic symbolic figure in the thought of the last hundred years, against whom all determinations of greatness have to be measured. The question of the relationship between Dilthey and Nietzsche becomes all the more urgent given that the common background of the two as well as the burgeoning omnipresence of Nietzsche in the course of Ortega's development, are unmistakable.

Now, Nietzsche's and Dilthey's writings represent two very different literary genres. It is telling that Dilthey's reference figure was Schleiermacher and Nietzsche's reference figure was Schopenhauer. We have, on the one side, Schleiermacher, the learned theologian, philologist and historian of philosophy, who has unified in his work all the impulses of the romantic movement and, on top of that, a great speaker and a true genius of friendship, but certainly no great writer in the real sense of the term. We have on the other side the morose recluse Schopenhauer who since his youth was a glowing admirer of Goethe, but at the same time a bitter critic of the university philosophy of his time, to the point of laughable presumptuousness in wanting to outdo his rival Hegel at the University of Berlin. He is a completely different figure from Schleiermacher, certainly no speaker, but a brilliant stylist, moralist, and essayist, whose late influence took its course outside of the university. One thinks of his influence on Nietzsche himself, on Richard Wagner or later perhaps on Sigmund Freud or on Thomas Mann.

Let us first explain Dilthey's stance toward his somewhat younger contemporary Nietzsche. He was in no way blind to the extraordinary intellectual status of Nietzsche. This is shown by testimonies.[4] Yet, he recoiled against Nietzsche's unmasking psychology in a sharply critical way because ultimately nothing better would result from it than the violent humanity of a Cesare Borgia. [441] There seems to have been a corresponding reaction from the side of Nietzsche. In fact, Nietzsche seems to have been once prompted to look into Dilthey's *Introduction to the Human Sciences*, presumably by Heinrich von Stein, an admirer of Richard Wagner and a disciple of Dilthey. Nietzsche did that, but not without being dismayed by the naiveté with which the facts of consciousness are recognized in Dilthey's book as the basis of cognition.

This twofold critical distanciation is not surprising. According to university philosophy and its learned standards, Nietzsche was in fact a dilettante, who, except for the texts of antiquity, derived his philosophical knowledge in general from second hand presentations. At the opposite end, Dilthey was entirely fixated upon the pathos of an empirical scientific attitude and its methodological ideal of objectivity so that he found philosophical value neither in Nietzsche's psychology, which plumbed the depths of consciousness, nor in general in the positive significance of the unconscious, even if he himself recognized it in the negative form of the inscrutability of 'life' and enjoyed its poetic representation.

It is as if what the nineteenth-century metaphysics of will contained in itself had come apart in its extremes in these two men. On the one side, there is Dilthey's unlimited striving to gather the totality of the historical world in himself and to think correctly the manifoldness of life. We have here a rather uncanny phenomenon of the universality of the power of empathy and at the same time the mesmerizing hold exerted by one's own scholarly web. On the other side stands Nietzsche's radicality, which dares not only to give up on all of metaphysics, but even to question behind the concept of truth in the sciences and even more radically to bring into question the concept of the truth of life experience in favour of this true absolute: the will to power, the willing of the will that makes everything the same to the extent that it seeks to overpower everything. Yet, for both 'life' is the fundamental fact and 'cognition' is at the service of life.

It cannot be surprising that Ortega, who had the feeling of being the heir to a rich Latin cultural tradition, reflected further his literary affinity to Nietzsche along the lines of Dilthey and therefore declared his proximity to Dilthey so emphatically. In so doing, he certainly did not entangle himself completely, like Dilthey, in the totality of what is intelligible, but knew how to play one against the other, the reason of life, on the one hand, and the philosophy of consciousness and self-consciousness, as well as the philosophy of science, on the other. Clearly, in this he bears a much stronger resemblance to Nietzsche.

The situation is indeed complicated. When it comes to the philosophical assessment of the two men and of the philosophical movements, which they partly followed and partly initiated, we must expand the framework even further. Behind the commonalities, which are obvious, and the differences, which can be rather clearly grasped, it is necessary to lay out [442] a deeper problematic, which determines them from afar and which finds its designation in the concept of the 'philosophy of life'. The expression characterizes the latest turn of the nineteenth century, with its continued influence into the twentieth century, in its critique of idealism and science. The expression 'philosophy of life' almost sounds like something trivial, as if philosophy did not always mean 'life'. In reality, the expression actually points to a theme of philosophy itself, but one that is anything but trivial. It has occupied thinking for ages and has played a totally central role in German idealism, in a way that cannot be overlooked.

It concerns the relationship between consciousness and life. What is meant by this is not only what Dilthey asserted against the concept of a bloodless subject in modern thought and against which he set out on a long journey through history, which could never come to an end. It also does not only concern how far the concretion of vitality reaches back, behind the limitedness of consciousness and the superficiality of the clarity of consciousness, which was Nietzsche's question concerning the great reason of the body behind the small reason of consciousness. The relationship between life and consciousness remains a deep puzzle, which even today keeps contemporary philosophy on tenterhooks. This was particularly the case for the specialists of ancient philosophy. How did it look from the perspective of modern philosophy?

Ortega rightly said that Descartes had made a false proposition when he distinguished 'thinking' – broadly understood – as the essential feature of a thinking thing, of a *res*. Rather, the concretion of vitality goes far beyond what subjectivity can mean. Dilthey was well aware of this in the critical distance he took from Descartes, Hume and Kant. Even in neo-Kantianism, Paul Natorp above all defended the idea of a transcendental psychology. It had, so to speak, to unify in the concretion of 'being conscious' the differentiated productive capacities of consciousness and therefore the totality of the manners in which it is directed at objects. In a similar way, Bergson in *Matière et mémoire* (in 1886, at the same time as Natorp[5]) had programmatically called for the overcoming of the categories of the natural sciences when dealing with the realm of the reality of the spirit. He was a true heir to romanticism.

The Cartesian distinction of self-consciousness as a substance or the Spinozistic definition of self-consciousness as a mode of the absolute substance remain in essence inadequate to the proper problem of vitality and the relationship between life and consciousness. Even the [443] dissolution of the thought of substance in Fichte's and Hegel's overcoming of Spinozism through dialectic did not really overcome the ontological prejudice, which found its expression in Cartesian dualism. It can be heard unmistakably in the transformation of substance into a subject. Both expressions refer to the same Greek word, the *hupokeimenon*, the *substratum*, that underlies all visible changes and is now applied to the 'I think', 'which must be able to accompany all my representations' (Kant).

Here a glance at ancient thought can be helpful. In ancient thought there is no distinction pertaining to subjectivity or the I. Yet, ancient thought had discovered for the first time the secret essence of self-referentiality or reflex-ivity. It seems compelling that every relation is a relation to something, that every capacity is a capacity for something, that every ability is an ability to do something, directed toward something and not toward itself. Yet, there is the relation to oneself. This could not escape ancient thought. Right down to the name 'reflection', the ancient origin of this insight can be detected. The word comes from optics. It has been handed down to us in the form of a Stoic theory that says that it is the distinctive quality of light to illuminate everything and in so doing even itself.[6] This is the first example of self-referentiality, which can be read off from external phenomena. In reality, self-referentiality encompasses the whole grand theme of ancient ontology in its entirety. For ancient thought, it was purely self-evident that a being is something living insofar as it is properly a being. The living, which means life, is however characterized by the two puzzles of self-movement and the relation to self in the form of awareness, of the inner-being of all awareness, of all perceptions, which is inseparable from any sensible experience. This is well known to us as the psycho-physical problem of modernity. It cannot be cleared away either by the metaphor of reflection, for example in materialism, or through theories of parallelism or through linguistic tricks. Even for modern neurology, self-movement appears to be a peculiar problem. Why and how does the eye see one process of motion as self-movement and the other as being moved? The ontological pre-conception, which animated ancient thought and holding that a being is primarily something living, has clearly become limited in its validity through the turn that the sciences of nature took in modernity in the manner they access reality. However, even Kant in his third critique, which is the most puzzling of all of his critiques and the one that produced the strongest influence on posterity, exceeds the domain of the critique of pure reason and therefore, by the same token, thematizes the limits of the mathematical natural sciences. His successors, Fichte, Schelling [**444**] and Hegel received the impetus for their own thinking precisely from the *Critique of Judgment* and from the muted manner in which it reintroduced teleological structures of thinking. Thus, we find indeed in the whole of German idealism the central place of self-consciousness, the 'I as the principle of philosophy', but at the same time the inner intertwining of life and self-consciousness as a constant theme. It was Hegel who most precisely developed with his dialectical means the transition from the cycle of life to the circularity of the self-referentiality proper to self-consciousness. He traces this structure of self-reference back to a deeper grounding in the concept of the spirit. Self-referentiality unites in itself as much the consciousness that is conscious of itself, namely self-consciousness, as the species, which as the phenomenon of life unites in itself its instances and maintains itself in its instances.

Thus, we can see that in the end the thought of Dilthey as well as that of Ortega is devoted to the problem of vitality, which in a long succession of thought, originating in a distant past, expresses itself time and again in modern subjectivism. The later Dilthey admits this explicitly when, in the text now available 'Life and Cognition', he expands and deepens 'into the biological' the 'psychological standpoint' of his earlier works devoted to the foundation of the human sciences.[7]

It is true that the concept of life already appears in the 1860s when he speaks of his philosophy and sets it apart from the ahistorical *apriorism* of Kant. It is only in the studies devoted to the continuation of the 'Introduction to the Human Sciences' that the philosophical problematic, which lies in the relationship between life and knowledge, fully dawns on him and, with this, he edges closer to Nietzsche.

Dilthey himself characterizes the step toward the grounding of psychology in 'life' as an essential step over and beyond his grounding of psychology so far. The first grounding in 'inner facts' had itself already resulted in a move counter to the intellectualism of the modern philosophy of the subject. However, the expansion into life opens an even wider horizon. We now know, even if only in a rough sketch, the essay that Dilthey drafted as the sequel to his already well-known work on reality under the title 'Life and Cognition'. It has been published in volume 19 of his complete works.[8] The investigation in this work also takes inner experience as its starting point. However, with a critical acuity, Dilthey shows that the concept of inner perception has an intellectual character. This means in a certain sense a step toward hermeneutics. For, [445] 'inner experience' is now explicitly conceived in such a way that it cannot exist without the thinking 'that experiences it as something'. Yet, the goal of this grounding in the 'given' remains the same as in the earlier position. The concern is again to examine critically the manner in which intellectual experience affects the given, to unmask the illusions that in this way creep in and to bring to fruition the capacities that correspond to the normative sense of knowledge. These capacities demand that the real not be transformed by thought, but only be brought to distinct consciousness. This goal is as ever an epistemological goal in the same sense in which Eduard Zeller had long before introduced episte-mology for the purpose of cleansing the given from the *a priori* factors of constitution exhibiting a Kantian lineage. The new turn consists in this that it now concerns the structure of 'life'. Whether it is the active 'I' or the 'I' that experiences the constraint of resistance and in this becomes one with reality, in any case it stands in a functional relationship to reality. This new step toward 'life' signifies an expansion of the horizon, insofar as it is no longer a matter of intellectual processes in themselves, but of the structure of the unity of life and its functional relationships, which is the very 'core of life'. What matters now is the articulation of this unity of life, which unfolds in the 'categories of life'. Such categories are not, as in Aristotle or Kant, fixed moments in the construction of the object of knowledge, but are formed in the flow of life. As such, they stand under the particular epistemological problem concerning the nexus of life and knowing.

Here Dilthey's thought unmistakably comes into contact with Nietzsche's radical emphasis on life and its primacy over all knowing. Dilthey too is aware of the problem that presents itself here. If knowing emerges only in life and serves life, it can never provide a foundation for that by which knowledge itself is supported. This fundamentally changes the meaning of 'category'. A category of life is really defined by the fact that what is articulated in it, precisely life, the original unity of life, cannot be grounded. Rigid categories in the sense of the Aristotelian or the Kantian concepts of category cannot be expected here. The categories of life are in flux and intertwined in the unity of life, which includes the living and its world. Thus, the category of selfhood encompasses both the self that is conscious of itself and the thing that contains its own inwardness, so to speak. This is what is experienced in the experience of resistance. The same holds for acting upon and suffering. They are the original life-forms out of which the category of causality is first derived in its well-defined abstractness. The same goes for concepts, such as essence, goal, value, sense and meaning [*Bedeutung*]. That Dilthey's [**446**] thought about the 'core facts of life' had to lead to such consequences, can certainly be seen already in Dilthey's own published works. In this sense, it prepares Heidegger's starting point in 'being-in-the-world' and his views on the derivative mode of the 'present at hand'.

Now we ask: how is this doctrine of categories related to the underlying problematic of life and knowledge, which Dilthey explicitly presents and characterizes downright as the tragedy of knowledge? All of these categories obviously take full account of the fact that life is unscrutable. Even the concept of type made fashionable by Dilthey is explicitly treated by him as something in the flux of history. The knowledge that emerges in life is thus exposed to the historicity of life. However, the task of knowing is not dissolved in the process. It is only that researchers see themselves inexorably pushed into the path of history. 'What human beings are, only their history can tell.'[9] Thus, all forms of life, which by virtue of these categories result from life, such as religion and philosophy, and, above all, art, are to a certain degree and in their own ways the overcoming of the tragic that is inflicted upon the will to knowledge, in the light of the fact that life is unscrutable. Nevertheless, we are obviously faced with the question of how the objectivity of scientific knowledge relates to all these forms of life, which, as objectivations of life, arise from life itself. Can the relentless expansion of questioning and research into the entire historical world resolve these questions or does this expansion present us in the end with only another form of tragedy, which exalted itself in Nietzsche's destructive extremism against the illusions of knowledge in the name of life? There certainly lies in the expression 'inscrutability' [*Unergründlichkeit*], which constantly accompanies Dilthey's thought, not only the shudder before an uncanny darkness, but also the limit-experience, which constitutes the restless compulsion of grounding. What 'life' and 'vitality' are can only become accessible to a 'description'. This includes the experience that the totality of being can never be completely opened up to the scientific striving for objectivity.

What concerns this totality in the form of the so-called world-views are only projections of vitality. These projections inexorably overstep the bounds of that which scientific objectivity can accomplish. As we saw, Dilthey has ventured in his theory of the types of world-views something like a 'philosophy of philosophy', which he could present as scientific and, in this way, could overcome a mere relativism. Where should the normative power of such an enterprise lie? There is still a deep uncertainty that lies hidden behind Dilthey's unrelenting [447] striving for objectivity and which drives him forward. It is something like the ultimate anxiety, which makes him tremble at the prospect of losing the self-evident ties to the Christian heritage. He is thus like a tragic counterpart in the academic mould to the tragic paradigm that Nietzsche represents for all modernity.

Ortega was the child of another generation for whom the deep intellectual influence of Nietzsche had already entered the whole bloodstream of thinking. The primacy of life and vitality was already recognized and had put limits not only on the false priority of consciousness and self-consciousness, but also on the ideal of positive scientificity and absolute objectivity. This situation had set new tasks for the thought of this epoch. Ortega is one of those who symbolize this new task precisely in this: they question over and beyond Dilthey without sacrificing the breath of Dilthey's historical vision. Thus, Ortega remains indebted to the richness of Dilthey's lifework. Yet, he stays astoundingly close to what a generation, marked by the bloody experiences of the First World War and the shaking-up of liberal cultural consciousness, began to perceive in the late Dilthey: historicity as the ontological distinction of human beings, as Heidegger taught us all. This is what constitutes Ortega's strong resonance in Germany.

He is thus one of the essential figures of European thought that brought forth the great unifying bond of *humanitas*[10] into the radical questions of a Nietzsche and a Heidegger. In teaching us to permeate vitality with rationality and to recognize reason in vitality itself, he correctly read the signs of the twentieth century and brought them to expression in his work on the philosophy of culture. Today, Europe inquires into its tasks under the changed constellation of the declining century and into the possibilities of preserving itself. At this time, it is very precious for us to have a Dilthey as a universal advocate for the historical tradition to which we belong, as well as the European Ortega, who drew his inspiration from the whole of the European history of thought.

9

Hermeneutics and the Diltheyan School (1991)[1]

[185] The Diltheyan School continues to this day as a living intellectual tradition in Göttingen. Frithjof Rodi, a student of Otto Fredrich Bollnow, comes from this school. Georg Misch, who was also a professor in Marburg for a short time, was Dilthey's son-in-law. He was in contact with Paul Natorp in Marburg and with Edmund Husserl. After the First World War he then exerted a long-lasting influence in Göttingen. Today, Rodi belongs to this tradition coming from Bochum. We owe him the efficient continuation of the edition of Wilhelm Dilthey's literary estate, which is not yet exhausted. From the breath of this literary estate alone, Dilthey was one of the last great representatives of a bygone form of erudition, of a tireless capacity for work and an unbroken confidence in the progress of scientific culture.

The present book[2] by Rodi is not only dedicated to the Diltheyan School and the Diltheyan legacy, but in particular to the question of the significance of the contribution of Dilthey and his school to hermeneutics today. It thus concerns an engagement with the impulses that began with Heidegger and continued in the direction of the reception of the late Dilthey since the 1920s. This form that the reception of Dilthey has taken is also connected most closely with the name of Georg Misch. His introduction to the fifth volume of the collected works of Dilthey had already exercised a strong influence on Heidegger. Finally, Misch's book 'The Philosophy of Life and Phenomenology' at the beginning of the 1930s may well represent the only lasting answer to the great event of the publication of Heidegger's *Being and Time*. In his book Misch provides a cautiously balanced and thought-provoking analysis of the phenomenological way of thinking, which was grounded by Husserl and had taken a hermeneutic turn through Heidegger's new book. With the turn, phenomenology comes close to Dilthey's [186] lifework in a compelling way. In addition to Heidegger's explicit validation of the whole of Dilthey's life work in *Being and Time*, the correspondence between Dilthey and Count Yorck von Wartenburg, which already appeared in 1923, also played an important role.[3] While we all, who were young at the time, reacted to this correspondence with great admiration for this aristocratic friend of Dilthey, Heidegger was certainly the first to do this, decisively and bluntly siding with the position that Count Yorck took in this correspondence.

Count Yorck von Wartenburg was a highly cultivated and greatly learned man. As a Silesian landowner, he resided in Klein-Öls. He possessed a degree of self-mastery and independence in the realm of erudite and philosophical discussion that a man from the academic world, a university professor, as Dilthey was, could certainly not possess in the same degree. Under the influence of Heidegger and also many of his students, such as Fritz Kaufmann and Ludwig Landgrebe among others, this correspondence was immediately recognized for its philosophical fruitfulness. The correspondence presents an unmistakable voice, the voice of the Lutheran Count Yorck, deeply rooted in the religious understanding of his position and in the Prussian mentality. In this correspondence he makes a truly devastating critique of the concept of science in the way the historical school understood it. Even the great founder of the school, Leopold von Ranke, who, in general, possessed a commanding reputation, is not spared by the Count. The critique Count Yorck made in that correspondence was as full of conviction as it was convincing in the alacrity of its arguments, the deeply religious mentality in its background, and the author's independent lifestyle. This critique made an indelible impression on Dilthey. It was the inner certainty and freedom of spirit that elicited Dilthey's admiration for this intellectual peer.

A phenomenon such as the one represented by this Count Yorck found enormous resonance in the critical years after the fall of the German empire. It validated above all the critical aspects voiced about the scientific mentality of the nineteenth century and in the human sciences. Even the young Heidegger, as we see ever more clearly from then on, felt at that time and in a similar way an increasing dissatisfaction toward university philosophy and Christian theology of the time. We all saw in the Count a deeply sceptical observer of the whole academic world and, in that sense, a true model for ourselves. By contrast, Dilthey saw himself more as the liberal, who, nonetheless, did not lack admiration for the religious tradition of Christianity and in particular for Luther. However, he was still more firmly in the grip of the scientific mentality of the nineteenth century than the independent landowner from Klein-Öls.

[187] For us, students in philosophy, who were at the time brought up in the *ex cathedra* philosophy of neo-Kantian apriorism and transcendental phenomenology, this correspondence was like a manifesto and a liberation. This is how,

from early on, I too attempted in my own works to contribute to the research direction that Dilthey had opened up and that Heidegger adopted with force and criticism. This appears clearly in some of the chapters of my book from 1960. Later on, in my essay 'Between Romanticism and Positivism' (1984),[4] I once more tried to determine the scientific theoretical position of Dilthey from the perspective of the philosophical questioning proper to hermeneutics.

Rodi's small new book is dedicated to this discussion. The freshly nuanced and precise contributions shed light with great care and knowledge on figures that I have myself treated: Schleiermacher, Droysen, Boeckh, and finally Dilthey himself. The intention of the author is obviously not just to add a scholarly appendix to my own treatment of the pre-history of hermeneutics. It is a critical discussion in the name of Dilthey's heritage.

The book takes as its critical leitmotif the problematic distinction between a traditional hermeneutics and a philosophical hermeneutics that I had proposed. This in fact needs a more precise determination. The expression 'traditional hermeneutics' that I used fits the romantics and the later hermeneutics only insofar as it concerns a further development of the old traditional doctrine of method. This hermeneutics was traditional to the extent that it wanted to be above all a doctrine of method and, as such, had its scientific and theoretical place in jurisprudence, theology, and philology. Schleiermacher and Schlegel, right up to Dilthey and Heidegger, who all play a role in my own analysis, do not all belong to the old doctrine of method. They never claimed to give to the disciplines they practised a new grounding and a new justification for their scientific character. There was in fact no urge for a theory of knowledge. Schleiermacher, who was deeply steeped in the spirit of romanticism, was the first to open the widest extent for the problems pertaining to understanding. We also owe him the emphasis on dialogue as the original living form of all mutual understanding and all comprehension. Along with Friedrich Schlegel, as we know, he recognized in [188] Plato's works the significance of the dialogue-form in its scope and background, allowing his readers to get a feel for it in his translation.

Nevertheless, the old, traditional hermeneutics, in the narrow sense of the term, was still operative in Schleiermacher. Even he treats hermeneutics in conjunction with 'critique', an old philological discipline of method. Only in contradistinction with 'critique' does he make room for 'dialectic'. I myself have to admit that in my presentation I had not sufficiently appreciated the inner connection and inseparability of Schleiermacher's dialectic from the philosophical problems of hermeneutics. However, even Dilthey, who himself presented the emergence of hermeneutics from its beginnings in his well-known treatise from 1900, maintained right into his final works that the conceptual framework within which he undertook to ground the human sciences is psychology and not hermeneutics. For him, hermeneutical problems have their place only within psychology. This is even indicated by the existence of the word itself, as it is clear in the eight-volume edition of Dilthey's works completed in the 1920s: the fundamental position of hermeneutics imposed itself only slowly in its decisive magnitude. It happened essentially only through Dilthey's later influence and above all through his school.

Here Georg Misch receives decisive credit. We owe him his acknowledgement of Heidegger's new impetus, which provided the opportunity to present Dilthey's 'philosophy of life' in its entirety. In so doing, he brought hermeneutical problems to the centre stage and distinguished Dilthey from phenomenology, from Husserl as well as from Heidegger. Even the 'Essential Dilthey Reader', as Bollnow called his commendable early book, followed Misch in this. The same is true of the development of my own philosophical ideas: it is Heidegger's impetus that led me to appropriate Dilthey's ideas. Today, I can hardly still measure the influence that the seeds sowed by Misch in his great critical book had on me in these preparatory years, in which my own hermeneutic philosophy, if I may call it that, showed its first fruits. Hans Lipps' *Hermeneutic Logic* also influenced me afterward. This is how I read the second volume of Bollnow's *Studies in Hermeneutics*[5] in its entirety as a new encounter with my own preparatory years. In the meantime, the long awaited edition of Misch's lecture, of which we have a report by Bollnow, became available.[6]

[189] Since then, volumes 19 and 20 from the Dilthey-edition that Rodi has continued have presented unpublished documents from Dilthey's literary estate.[7] This could shed further light on how much the hermeneutic turn was already in the making in Dilthey himself, something that Misch and Bollnow too attribute to him. At any rate, as it was the case with Heidegger and his students, with Dilthey as well, the hermeneutic turn was long beforehand in the making. Already at the time when volumes 4 and 5 of Dilthey's complete works appeared, we, the younger generation, developed our views in a direction certainly encouraged by Heidegger, but which was in no way to be supported by his own publications. The same could very well be true for the last generation of the Diltheyan School, to which Misch and Nohl belong. For, the old Dilthey already helped many of them develop their views, the initial motivations for which can be found in the works that Dilthey left behind. Let me call up at least one testimony for this: someone as closely associated with Dilthey as Bernhard Groethuysen expressed his astonishment to me in the early 1930s that we had

in the meantime seen in Dilthey not only a historian, but also taken interest in his philosophy. To this corresponds the fact that the quick dissemination of the typology at the hands of Troeltsch, Spranger, Rothacker and Freyer at the time was obviously a late influence of Dilthey.

In the case of Misch, we must undoubtedly admit that he really continued the thought of Dilthey along the lines of Dilthey. This is particularly evident in the increasing significance the poetics and the philosophy of life come to exhibit in Dilthey's later years. It is in fact *Poetry and Experience* that, through its stunning success, brought to the fore for the first time the full presence of Dilthey to the youth of that time. Thus, as the new volumes of Dilthey's complete works as well as Misch's now published lectures show, there is much that could have been a further development of Dilthey's thought.[8]

From all this it emerges that, when we simply oppose or determine the relationship between what I called later in *Truth and Method* 'traditional hermeneutics' and that from which I distinguished it, namely, 'philosophical hermeneutics', we are in fact presented with a common task. This task has a long pre-history. There is no doubt that **[190]** the so-called human sciences acquired their philosophical function only with the end of metaphysics, in the Greek-Medieval sense and in the scholastic sense of modernity, thus only with Kant's critique of 'dogmatic metaphysics', and eventually with Hegel's re-appropriation of metaphysics into his dialectical logic. The human sciences had to contend with the constructive schematic of Hegelian dialectic. It is the rise of historical consciousness in the age of romanticism that gave the philosophical aspects of the historical-philological sciences their philosophical weight.

In this regard, what we have just said is in conformity with the fact that the critical discussion of my own philosophical attempts leads us back mainly to romanticism. Manfred Frank and others are completely right to emphasize that the aspects of scientific theory and the problematic of science within the romantic turn of the European spirit could not yet represent the real counter-force to the human sciences. The words speak here a language that cannot be misunderstood. Only in the concept of *Geisteswissenschaften* ['human sciences'] that is in currency today does one necessarily hear at the same time the counter-concept of the natural sciences. In addition, the legacy of German idealism and in particular the legacy of Hegel still resonates in the term 'spirit' of the *Geisteswissenschaften*. This appears above all in the connotations that lie in the concept of 'spirit'. This is congruent with the fact that it was basically psychology that would come to be called the successor of Hegelian synthesis, when philosophy after the death of Hegel was overtaken by the new turn to the empirical sciences. One only has to think of the influence of Herbart and Lotze. This development has unmistakably made its mark on the philosophical work of Dilthey. As I once again explained in 1984, what I called the intermediary position of Dilthey, I deliberately did not say 'between hermeneutics and positivism', but rather 'between romanticism and positivism'. This was supposed to express the fact that I recognize in Dilthey the rich heritage of romanticism, which the Diltheyan School also preserved. This heritage continued to live in the theories and conceptual constructions of an August Boeckh, Johann Gustav Droysen or even in Dilthey and Misch, and in many others. We all belong to this lineage.

Hence, it is no surprise when in Rodi we encounter Schleiermacher and Schlegel in the series of philosophical contributions to hermeneutics.[9] However, even the masters of philological work that Rodi treats, such as August Boeckh, certainly cannot be confined to their methodological claims, as Rodi presents them,[10] even if his is a lecture course intended for pure philologists, which he repeated for decades **[191]** and finally published as such and not as 'Hermeneutics'. Rodi gives his small book the title *The Knowledge of the Known*, which he takes from Boeckh. He is in fact totally correct when he interprets this concept of 'the known' as a general indication that communicates the entire breath, better still the universality of hermeneutics. Rodi points out that the formula 'knowledge of the known' goes back fundamentally to the Greek word for reading, *anagignoskein*. Reading is, above all, precisely cognizing something again [*Wiedererkennen*] and knowledge is, as I myself have tried to show, always re-cognition [*Wiedererkenntnis*].

With this, we approach the essentially critical point. It concerns the concept of science and the concepts of 'method' and 'objectivity' that are proper to modern science. 'Method' may sound Greek, but, as a modern foreign word, it means something different, namely an instrument for any cognition [*Erkenntnis*], as Descartes has called his *Discours de la méthode*. As a Greek expression, the word means the variety of the manners in which one approaches a field of study, for example as a mathematician or as an architect or as one who philosophizes about ethics.

'Objectivity' too sounds very respectable, but even so it has a somewhat different meaning. It definitely does not mean the real, not the *telos* of everything, but that which is made at every instance into an object, the *objectum*. In the regular usage of 'object', the role of this scientific concept and its background are still expressed, namely the voluntarist attitude [*Willensstellung*] of European culture in modernity.

Modern science is a powerful reality, with which even romantic thought eventually sees itself in constant confrontation and which basically dominates the culture of the enlightenment all over the world. In the correspondence between Yorck and Dilthey, the power of this reality is evident at every turn, not only in the gentle but determined resistance that the Count often exhibits to Dilthey's academic judgements. I do not want to repeat the many instances in Dilthey's understanding of life that speak emphatically of the power of science. They are essentially known to all those acquainted with Dilthey. (I was able to show the reality of these instances right up to a typographical error).[11] By opposing traditional hermeneutics to philosophical hermeneutics, as I undertook to do, what is at issue is not to dispute the philosophical relevance of the great heritage of romanticism, but the fact that those who came afterward were challenged by the claims of the empirical sciences and, as a consequence, had to justify their scientific self-understanding, through method and objectivity. Obviously, they remained susceptible to criticism for a one-sided concept of method and objectivity. What is even less at issue is perhaps the fact that the inscrutability of life, which is one [192] of the fundamental convictions of Dilthey, would be invalidated through the scientific striving toward objectivity and the relative solidity of its results. Even when one hears the pantheistic sense of the Diltheyan concept of life, it still remains a privative characteristic of 'the dark visage of life' [*dunklen Antlitz*][12] and is thought from the perspective of science and with due consideration for its limitedness.

The pressure that the concept of science exercised at the time, as I have emphasized, with regard to the limitations that beset all efforts at objectification, had the net effect of preventing Dilthey himself from remaining consistently clear himself about his own deeper intentions. The task that Misch obviously had set for himself was to plumb these deeper intentions. He somewhat shifted the emphasis away from the fact that life is inscrutable when he stressed the 'logical energy' of the creative powers emerging from life. This exceeds what Dilthey himself said, even when one draws on the materials from volumes 18 and 19 of the Dilthey edition.

If one follows Rodi's presentation and accepts the speculatively exalted 'knowledge of what is known', then one must ask with Rodi the following question: whether the further development that Misch undertook over and beyond Dilthey's position, when he expanded it into a universal hermeneutics, does not in the process at least invalidate its difference from today's hermeneutical movement. We can bring some clarity here by explaining once again the doctrine of the hermeneutic circle. This old truism of rhetoric, which

Melanchton had turned into something hermeneutic, can certainly be extended to hermeneutics, but it can be understood in a narrower and broader sense. Boeckh, as a philologist in pursuit of a doctrine of method, applies to the text to be understood or any article that has been handed down, the circular movement of understanding, which moves back and forth from the part of a whole to the whole. However, there is also a circular movement between the interpreter and the text. The interpreter does not stand outside, but is 'there within life' (Rodi 128). Interpreters are not only theoretical observers, but also belong to the totality of life in which they 'participate'.

It is also in this last sense that Misch in fact goes further in his thinking and consciously exceeds the 'pure theoretical cognitive attitude'. With this we seem to have a complete convergence between Heidegger's adoption of hermeneutics for phenomenology and Dilthey's deeper intentions. Misch and Rodi have also seen this, but they believe that this alleged agreement was eventually deceptive [193]. Rodi speaks of a 'temporary proximity' in the thought of Georg Misch.[13]

Rodi sharpens the closeness that lies here by drawing on a preliminary stage of Heidegger's *Being and Time*: Heidegger's 1924 Kassel lectures on Dilthey, which have become known in the meantime. In this work Heidegger already refers to the large introduction that Misch wrote for volume 5 of Dilthey's writings. Rodi's treatment of this finding of the Kassel lectures is certainly commendable. It is an important chapter in Heidegger's reception of Dilthey, which up until then was only known from *Being and Time*. However, Rodi's planned discussion should not confine itself to *Being and Time* and its preliminary stage. It is well known that Heidegger made little use of the expression 'hermeneutics' in his later years. He clearly wanted to keep his own trajectory oriented toward the question of being, which guided his thinking, from being misunderstood, as though in the question of being only our own questioning was at issue and not rather our being questioned.[14] This is another story to which the reception of Dilthey does not belong.

We must first ask ourselves how things stand with the further development of Dilthey's ideas. Rodi devotes the central chapter of his book to this question and first treats how Misch differentiates himself from 'the common position of Husserl and Heidegger'. With this Rodi wants 'to recall some of the questions that have been asked of phenomenology for over fifty years' (Rodi 127). At that time, in 1931 the work of Georg Misch published under the title 'Philosophy of Life and Phenomenology' presented in fact both of the following: a critical reception of *Being and Time* as well as of the almost contemporaneous Husserlian treatise *Formal and Transcendental Logic*. For Misch both are phenomenology. Misch now puts into question the philosophical grounding that lies in Husserl's claim that phenomenology had arrived at the 'ultimate ground of judgment on which any radical philosophy is to be grounded' (Rodi 130). Misch defends Dilthey against the well-known Husserlian accusation that his starting point in historical life leads to relativism and scepticism. Misch insists that the being-in in life is to be recognized and when he goes beyond the pure theoretical cognitive attitude, **[194]** then it is obvious that the philosophy of life must turn against the transcendental subjectivity of Husserl and its idealistic interpretation of phenomenology.

Rodi, in this regard, gives a very illuminating analysis of the concept of 'meaning' [*Bedeutung*] in Dilthey and Husserl. In fact, Dilthey misunderstood Husserl's *Logical Investigations* and the central concept of meaning, and precisely because of such a misunderstanding makes this concept fruitful for himself. Historical meaning or, better, significance [*Bedeutsamkeit*], which is the fundamental category in Dilthey's research, indicates that it is about something different from what it was for Husserl. This was familiar to every reader of Dilthey at the time. Yet, it remains astonishing that Misch had no misgivings about forcing Heidegger back into this Husserlian position of the *Logical Investigations*. As a whole, *Being and Time* still speaks a clear language. One may perhaps imagine that Heidegger's effort to fit the hermeneutic dimension into the great research programme of phenomenology offered some pretexts for giving him such a shortshrift. One only has to think of the famous remark by Oskar Becker in the Husserl Festschrift, which takes the integration and subordination of hermeneutics to transcendental phenomenology to its extremes. The study of *Being and Time* could certainly teach something better. Already the stylistic transformation of the concept of phenomenon undertaken by Heidegger shows this and the whole argumentative thread in *Being and Time* proves unambiguously that apophantic logic and the mode of being of the present-at-hand did not for Heidegger really 'remain in the back' (Rodi 135). It is even the proper target of Heidegger's overcoming of metaphysics.

The situation is different with Husserl's expansion of his 'Logical Investigations' to pre-predicative logic. Here one can certainly follow Misch when he does not wish to recognize in the 'life of capacities' [*leistenden Leben*] of Husserl's *Formal and Transcendental Logic* Dilthey's philosophy of life. Heidegger's radical critique of the logic of judgement, the decisive pragmatic articulation of the concept of world, and the striving for a hermeneutic of Dasein make it impossible for us to overlook the fact that Heidegger aimed to go beyond Husserl's approach, beyond the requirement for an ultimate foundation. Heidegger explicitly saw in all this a *preparation* for the question of being. It is clear that the concept of being represents the crux for Misch. This is why he misses the problem when he ascribes to Heidegger the 'concept of the original unity of the idea of being'. This sounds more like the philosophy of identity in German idealism and its aftermath. The preparation for the question of being through *Being and Time* is utterly incompatible with such a formulation. Certainly, the fact that Heidegger works with the concept of being is not trivial. Misch is correct about this. But Misch already knew from [195] Heidegger's typescript of 1922, which he received from Heidegger, that this concept of being could not amount to the Aristotelian concept of being.

This 'early theological writing' by Heidegger, which is now for the first time publicly available in the *Dilthey Jahrbuch* of 1989,[15] makes it hardly understandable how someone could see reflected in it a dogmatic metaphysical residue of Aristotelian provenance. Or like us, young folks of the time, who were under the suggestive power of the technical phenomenological interpretation that Heidegger wielded there on Aristotle, had Misch perhaps not recognized either that it was Heidegger's goal to strengthen his opponent in Aristotle and thereby in the Greek concept of being? Heidegger truly had to do this if he wanted to liberate himself not only from the Thomism of his theological upbringing, but also from the pseudo-Hegelianism of his philosophical schooling, which called itself neo-Kantianism. Such a liberation from an epigonal and pseudo-modernized Thomism, as well as from the universal synthesis of neo-Hegelianism demanded a long journey of conceptual struggle, for which Heidegger's typescript of 1922 represented only a first sign-post. Heidegger accepted that this way would often turn out to be a forest path [*Holzweg*]. This was a decade-long confrontation. Because of the disastrous confusions, breakups, and entanglements that the 1930s and 1940s brought upon Germany, it was just not permitted to Misch, who had returned just after the end of the Third Reich, to pursue his research in these directions. He had obviously not realized what Heidegger's 'turn' fundamentally was, namely the rejection of any effort to fit in with Husserl's phenomenological transcendentalism, which *Being and Time* had not yet completely cast off. Later on, all of this would become rather clear, for example, when Heidegger attempted to indicate that 'Being' is a verb, in writing it as Fichte did: 'beyng' [*Seyn*], or when he repeatedly and explicitly said that being is not the being of beings and thus does not mean the concept of essence expressed by *essentia*. Yet, even in *Being and Time* it is clear enough that the question of being is not meant as some kind of highest idea. The hermeneutic structure of Dasein must therefore not be thought only from the side of the projection-character, but rather stands in-between, between projection and thrownness. Here, in the interpretation of the fundamental structure of life, a difference becomes clear, to which we will have to return.

Obviously, it was the particular circumstances of the time that hindered Misch from developing a philosophical account of the differences and convergences that existed in this common ground of life. In the meantime, [196] Misch's influential Göttingen lecture course *Logic and the Introduction to the Theory of Knowledge* was published. The book of 1931 *Philosophy of Life and Phenomenology* grew out of this lecture course. On the other side and in the meantime, Heidegger's early Freiburg lectures became available, which documented the starting point of thought 'in and from life', as in Dilthey, and thereby the influence of Dilthey. Heidegger's later publications would have made it even more clear to Misch how much he had in common with Heidegger in his own project of broadening logic. Obviously, Misch's further development of Dilthey's thought did not take the Heideggerian form of a critical destruction of the conceptuality proper to the language of metaphysics. The tendency to go beyond the discursive toward an evocative language, which Misch advocated at the time, could certainly see itself validated through Heidegger's attitude toward language, and this is clear enough in Misch's book of 1931.

However, the difference between Heidegger and Misch, which opened on the basis of the same starting point of a thinking 'in and from life', would have emerged in all its clarity later. From the very beginning Heidegger's project went beyond the Platonic-Pythagorean polarity of *peras* and *apeiron*, on the basis of which Misch, who saw himself as a Platonist, designed his project. Misch too goes beyond Dilthey, when he assigns the rigidity of form to the inscrutability of life. However, all this is done in the wholly broad sense of a logic of life itself, which also unfolds in creative forms in art and religion, and not only in science.

Heidegger, by contrast, from early on found himself confronted with the ambivalence of life, which loses itself in its care for the world. Already in the early lectures Heidegger speaks of the 'ruination'[16] of life and when he prepares the question of being and elaborates the being of Da-sein as hermeneutic, it is as if he is focusing on a finishing line. He was always aware of this when formulating authenticity and inauthenticity, i.e. the fall of Dasein, in *Being and Time*. Heidegger always maintained the equiprimordiality of authenticity and inauthenticity. In his lectures of the same period, this always produced a surprising effect when he concluded his rather wrathful analysis of 'the They' and of 'idle talk' with the reassurance: 'All of this is said without any pejorative meaning.' The 'moralistic' interpretation of *Being and Time*, which can be used theologically in the sense of protestant eschatology and was so used, did not correspond to his intentions. It is true that the equiprimordiality of the authenticity and inauthenticity of Dasein sounds like a provocation. Or was it a confession of allegiance to Luther?

All of this eventually brings us back to the 'verb' being. Only in this way could one escape the objection of the firm ground that Husserl **[197]** believed to have under his feet against historicism. Husserl himself never put the fundamental validity of the Greek concept of being into question. To shake this fundament was, however, the goal that Heidegger set for himself in the preparation of the question of being. He even undertook the unsuccessful attempt to find a recourse in Greek thought, and even in its very beginnings, for loosening this fundament. Heidegger was looking for testimonies supporting the view that already the Greeks had understood the original word *alētheia* in such a way that it not only meant unconcealment, but also concealment [*Verbergung*] and sheltering [*Bergung*]. Later on he gave up this attempt, even his particular appeal to Parmenides. In any case, it is a mistake to understand being, which was the object of Heidegger's question, in the sense of a highest principle, and then moreover take umbrage at its indeterminateness. Heidegger's intention was directed at something for which the language of metaphysics had no concepts to offer. Even in *Being and Time* Heidegger had caused theological misunderstandings when speaking of the authenticity of Dasein. He meant the being of the 'Da' of the 'Dasein in human beings', as it is called in the Kant-book. 'Being' simply does not mean a being, thus not even the authentic or divine being, but is rather like an event [*Ereignis*], a *pathos*, which opens up the space in which hermeneutics – without ultimate grounding – will become a new universal. This space is the dimension of language.

The word 'there' [*Da*] is certainly the most indeterminate of all words that could ever mean a being that is there. Thus, it is what is common to all words, the proper 'fore-word' [*Vor-wort*] to all other words and their semantic power. However, it is no highest principle and certainly not a solid fundament. Insofar as it is granted to all words to stand in the opening up of the *Da*, the word in language is exposed at the same time to becoming rigid and empty. 'Life is hazy. It clouds itself over and over again.' This is why it is in need of thinking. One may remember Plato's *Phaedrus* here. In that dialogue, in connection with the critique of the dimension of writing [*Schriftlichkeit*], it is said of the living word that it should not remain without assistance, so as to be understood correctly. Such assistance is provided by the other. Obviously, even here word [*Wort*] and answer [*Antwort*] always stand on the sharp boundary between conversation and idle talk. Misch does not ignore this tendency of the word to become trivial and he also emphasizes how expressions must be interpreted in their very performance [*im Vollzuge*],[17] as we all do in the case of reading and as it happens in the case of 'playing music'. Misch obviously had that in mind in his project of loosening the grip of logic. Simmel already hinted at something like this in 1918 and the 'metaphysical chapters' of a dying Simmel also pointed Heidegger in the direction he was to follow. I can still hear Heidegger's admiration for Simmel from the early conversations I had with him in 1923 over in Todtnauberg. Neither [198] in Simmel nor in Misch is the question posed as to what 'being' may then mean. For this, one needed first the logical energy and the destructive powers of thinking that Heidegger directed at the traditional conceptuality of philosophy. With this return to the concept of being in the Greeks and his critique a new way of seeing was opened up.

Now, I do not want to say that I myself stand by all of Heidegger's theses in *Being and Time*. From the very outset I had many difficulties with it, and above all when he sees in 'presence-at-hand' simultaneously the Greek understanding of being and the concept of objectivity in modern science. I had the same problem with the analysis of 'discourse' [*Rede*] in Heidegger's hermeneutics of Dasein. From early on, what was lacking for me in this analysis was the experience one has of others, of their resistance, of their objection, and the guiding force that originates here. I remember one conversation with Heidegger. I was still searching for my own ways and one day I read to Heidegger an essay in which I made the experience of the other the central point. In a friendly and approving way, Heidegger pointed out to me: 'And where is thrownness?' He obviously meant that, in the concept of thrownness, the 'counterpart' is already present, which stands counter to any project. At the time this really took me aback because I could not readily think of 'thrownness' when dealing with the others, who stand face to face with me in dialogue. I should have perhaps recalled then that Heidegger too, like Dilthey himself, readily recognized in Count Yorck von Wartenburg and in his 'thrownness' the character that gave Dilthey's independent friend his own unique freedom and greatness (and certainly also set his boundaries). However, I wanted for my part to hold steadfastly onto the idea that the other in the dialogue is not just the addressee, but also the partner. From *Phaedrus* and also other dialogues, I knew that Plato associated rhetoric with the situation of a dialogue and, in this way, had prepared dialectics.

Thus, I tried to open up even the hermeneutic circle and the use that Heidegger made of it, and apply it to the course of a dialogue. In a dialogue, we are not just dealing with a procedure that one applies to a given text, but with an existential movement that precedes all procedures. In this hermeneutic entanglement one does not yet know oneself in this 'free distance to oneself' through which Dilthey and Misch characterized the attitude in which things may manifest themselves in the way they are. One is rather prompted to answer and this demands the hermeneutic effort in which alone the view opens up and widens. Hermeneutics means first and foremost that something speaks to me and puts me in question in that it poses a question to me. This is why it is only in dialogue that language is always what it can be because **[199]** in the play of question and answer language opens up a view that is offered neither in my perspective nor in the perspective of the other.

My association with Heidegger thus went in this direction. This is not surprising. The kind of central position *phronēsis*, the virtue of moral knowledge, assumes in my thoughts on hermeneutics was indeed clear enough in *Truth and Method*. From early on, I was also interested in the great importance Aristotle's practical philosophy places on friendship. On the other side, I was no less conscious of what Kant's imperative ethics has to teach us. In this regard, one must think above all of the Kantian reconstruction of practical reason, which is grounded in the concept of 'respect'. Respect is something that is demanded of self-love, but at the same time it is that by way of which I and you are able to know and recognize one another. When it is said of some individuals that one can talk to them, then we are not talking about 'idle talk'. We are saying that it is worth having a conversation with them.

It would be a topic in its own right to track how this 'with one another' underlies all religious communities, for example the Christian commandment of love, in which God and the neighbour stand for one another. The same goes for the encounter with art: it entangles one in a conversation and, in this conversation, thinking happens. This was what motivated me in *Truth and Method* to begin with the experience of art, even before I addressed the problem of historicity. For, when we stand before any work of art, we stand in front of something that commands us, before which we are, despite all our protestations, always wrong. This is significant. In my studies of Greek philosophy, I was precisely interested in the primacy of *ethos* over *logos* and I tried to show that, contrary to all doxographical appearances, the Socratic question did not mean the definition, but the dialogue that was opened up by the definition.

While I mention my own efforts to think beyond Heidegger, I would like to speak, with Rodi, about the questionable character of the distinction that I had claimed existed between romantic and philosophical hermeneutics.

Despite all the convergences between them, this distinction also includes the difference of their philosophical aspects. I begin to understand why Heidegger, in opposition to me, characterized my own attempts at thinking not as a philosophical hermeneutics, but rather as hermeneutic philosophy. For my part, my usage of the term 'philosophical hermeneutics' was not a misjudgement of the romantic heritage, which was still operative in my own contribution to thinking. I just did not want to use for myself the pretentious word 'philosophy' and only tried to use it attributively. On the whole, I would acknowledge that I, as in the case of Schleiermacher and also Dilthey, am guilty of partiality for the sake of presenting my own ideas in a sharp manner. **[200]** In my late works, I also had to address the radical problems that compelled Heidegger into an intellectual exchange with Nietzsche. This is how I myself became entangled in a dialogue with the friends of deconstruction. Still, here everything seems to me to be still in the air.

In his small book *Derrida-Nietzsche, Nietzsche-Derrida*,[18] Ernst Behler has included an excellent discussion of the conversation held between Derrida and myself in Paris in 1981. Behler is credited to be one of the architects of the great critical edition of Friedrich Schlegel's works. In his book he, first and foremost, treats Derrida's critique of Heidegger's appropriation and critique of Nietzsche. Derrida sees in this appropriation and critique a relapse back into metaphysics. The exceedingly meticulous and clear analysis of Derrida's critical games provided by Behler is extremely helpful. He himself explains Derrida's deconstruction from the perspective of Friedrich Schlegel and the distance he takes from romantic hermeneutics. Naturally, Dilthey is also included in this discussion, as he should be.

In this regard, the French-German dialogue, which, like any other authentic dialogue, has by no means come to an end, only belongs to our discussion to the extent that Derrida denounces Heidegger and, given the problematic, also Misch, as still being 'metaphysical'. Derrida criticizes Heidegger's interpretation of Nietzsche as a metaphysical construction and imputes the same to hermeneutics. He thus calls it an 'ontohermeneutics'.

If one takes Nietzsche in his ultimate radicality as a basis, this criticism is essentially correct. For, the usurpatory will to power is what 'organizes the totality of the linguistic processes and the symbolic exchange in general, thus including all ontological statements' (Behler 124). Derrida wants to make an exception for Heidegger only insofar as what he says concerning the question of being in 'Time and Being' (1962): that it is the abyssal giving of the 'there is' [*es gibt*]. In fact, this can be found repeatedly in the late Heidegger after the turn: there is only the 'remembrance' [*An-denken*] of being and, thus, only the 'playing along' [*An-spielen*] that temporalizes itself in the play of art. I can definitely recognize in Heidegger's views elements of Derrida's deconstruction and the *dissémination* that fundamentally eludes the deductive systematics of thought. In addition, in my view one must also bring out the evidence that manifests itself when a speculative language of concepts comes close to a poeticizing language of art.

Thus, in the end the question is how this questioning behind the usurpatory *logos,* which stigmatizes all linguistic expressions, is itself motivated and executed. For this purpose, Derrida coined the expression 'deconstruction' [201] in order to emphasize the affirmation, the assent, which must be connected with the annihilation of the metaphysical concepts of being, sense and truth. Derrida undertakes this destruction repeatedly in innumerable disruptions, subversions, and plays on words, which turn customary linguistic sense on its head. Heidegger too did something similar again and again, when he asked, for instance: 'What is called thinking?' and when the sense of this question is changed in a way such that it now asks: 'What is it that calls for thinking?' With this, Heidegger wants to suggest that calculative thinking is not real thinking. Neither Heidegger nor Derrida nor even a hermeneutic philosophy that integrates the critical potential of art and history into thought, can hide the fact that there are processes of coming to an understanding which, in defiance of all usurpatory will to power, raise questions and seek meaningful answers. Even Friedrich Schlegel's plea for incomprehensibility [*Unverständlichkeit*], like all the play with ambiguities, disruptions and subversions, and with the whole of our experience of the world, when it is reflected in art, all these are of the kind that we spin stories about.

It is an enduring motive that is sustained in my own attempt at thinking Heidegger further. From the very beginning I have followed his critique of the concept of consciousness and of an ultimate foundation that could be found in self-consciousness. My studies of Greek philosophy are consistent with this critique and completely so the more I learned from Plato and Aristotle, and recognized in both of them the Socratic question and, with it, the primacy of *ethos* over *logos*. This led me to the sense of performance [*Vollzugssinn*] that a dialogue has. It was already at this time that Plato, especially in his excursus in the seventh letter, pointed out the decisive direction. Neither Heidegger, whose impulses I tried to follow within the limits of my abilities, nor Dilthey rendered me the same help. Heidegger's questioning behind *aphophansis* and his expansion of the hermeneutic structure of Dasein indeed gave language its right place. However, the other was still the mere addressee, not the partner in a dialogue. Heidegger himself only ventured some hints at what a dialogue really is and only by choosing the style of dialogical form in *On the Way to Language*. The same is the case for the Dilthey that Misch further developed, when discursivity (and its overcoming in the evocative) starts with the *proposition*, whose unity and multiplicity is constituted by language, and not by the answer [*Antwort*] that still precedes every word [*Wort*].

What I mean is that every word is an answer and that questioning possesses a fundamental primacy. This is why I appealed to Collingwood in *Truth and Method* and even more to Plato. For, the Socratic dialogue, which is advanced by Plato as an artful overcoming of sophistry and rhetoric, remains itself grounded, despite all its answers, in the overarching [202] primacy of the questioning. It includes the commonality that exists between the two partners. It was in this way that Plato could even meld rhetoric with dialectic in *Phaedrus*.

This is not the famous 'I-thou' problematic, as the talk of 'the I' and 'the thou' appears to me as a semantic violence. The actual truth of the performance of the dialogue remained hidden here. The situation will not improve if one were perhaps to add a 'We' problematic on top of it. Even Husserl's concept of intersubjectivity attests in my view to a residue of ontological dogmatism. By contrast, we have Whitehead's incorporation of the physicalistic concept of the field and the question of being, which is not the concept of essence but means the very 'essencing' [*wesen*] itself. Both of these have the significance of pointing us in another direction. I was not fully aware of this when I undertook to explain concepts, such as play, praxis, the being of the beautiful, and the sense that a word and a concept have in their sense of performance within the horizon of time. Perhaps, early stimulations by Natorp and his starting point in *fieri* have exerted a delayed influence on me.

In the end, the framework of the life-world proper to hermeneutics encompasses all experience, even the human sciences, which can be called hermeneutic sciences. They have a great part of the philosophical tradition of romanticism to manage. For this reason, they do not belong any less than the modern natural sciences to our provenance and our still hidden future.

Afterword

In my works I have presented Dilthey in his intermediary position between the theory of knowledge of the human sciences and the heritage of the romantic-idealist philosophy, which embodied the proximity of life and spirit. This idealist theme experienced in our century a new appropriation and at the same time a transformation through the thematization of the 'life-world'. This influential word was coined by Husserl. It meant the overcoming of the limitations that the concept of objectivity had imposed on the sciences. In its essence, the life-world is a manifold of horizons and, thus, a highly differentiated structure in which obviously objective validity must also have its place, but no longer a position of monopoly. The manifold of human languages begins to manifest itself more and more as one of the ways in which the manifold of life-worlds is articulated. This became increasingly clear with Heidegger's radicalization of the hermeneutic structure of human Dasein. **[203]** Within the framework of Husserl's transcendental philosophy, Oskar Becker still wanted to locate in Heidegger's *Being and Time* simply the elaboration of a layer of constitution, namely, that of history. However, Heidegger's turn toward the dimension of language [*Sprachlichkeit*] meant a rejection of the grounding of phenomenology in the transcendental ego and fundamentally a rejection of the methodological primacy of self-consciousness in contrast to the 'consciousness of something'. This shift occurred with the unfolding of the philosophy of life, which Nietzsche spearheaded with his radical extremism. Heidegger first laid open the ontological pre-conception, which was still at work in the interpretation of a phenomenology, working as it still was with the conceptual tools of Greek metaphysics. Thus, Heidegger had to destroy this conceptuality as well. In the process, the classical hermeneutic circle would no longer be a metaphysical description of a method, of a procedure, through which the sense of performance would be brought to understanding, as was taught since ancient times in rhetoric. The circularity of understanding was certainly always already in opposition to the logical concept of proof, proper to science, and in the succeeding periods could be valid as an appropriate description for the methodological idea of the human sciences. With Heidegger's return to the Greeks, it is no longer just a question about method.[19] The interpreter who seeks to understand the formation of sense is no longer merely someone who accomplishes a reconstruction, as if we learn to reconstruct, say, the Latin period of Cicero. The interpreter is no longer merely an additional researcher, but rather a listener or reader and therefore implicated as a member participating in the sense. The meaningful response that a sense-formation gives is now recognized as an answer to a question and this question is itself again an answer. Thus, there is really no first beginning and no ultimate closure of the so-called subject in favour of the objectivity of science.

As a matter of fact, we know this from the way we all learn how to speak and the way we acquire our experience of the world through linguistic communication and exchange in dialogue. In this, there is no first word. For, no word can mean something by itself. Even the name that designates someone or something can only be so because it is not another name and anything else. It means the one whose name one knows. This is also how the vague pulsating gaze that infants cast on the world, when exercising their senses and ordering their stimuli, gets articulated. This is obviously not a conscious collection of impressions. With the awakening of consciousness and the accompanying consciousness articulated in language we have the continuation of a process that has already been in place for a long time and consists in the satisfaction of desires and their frustration. This is all an **[204]** infinite dialogue, which rises anew again and again and falls silent again and again and never reaches an end.

It is the true fundament of the *linguistic turn*[20] that we just described. There was already a turn toward language when people like Wittgenstein and Austin reversed the logical idea of a formal and univocal language in a turn toward actually spoken language. They freed the latter from its logical constraints by integrating it into the context of acts. There is certainly a great interest in knowing how and in which forms living communication manifests itself. Whether I recognize a proposition critically as correct or whether I praise, rebuke, value, admire, worship, accuse or dispute – all these are forms of response to the world [*Weltantwort*], in which something of practical reason is reflected. However, such a formal theory remains very much on the fringes of what is communicated through language and communication. When Aristotle characterized the essence of the human being as *zōon logon echon*, it took a long time, in fact until Heidegger, for one to clearly realize that here the human being was not defined as 'rational animal', but as the being that has language, in contradistinction to something like the mating and warning calls of birds. States of affairs are made present through language, even if they are not always 'real'. This in fact entails that the living entities called human beings are not governed in their behaviour by rigid instinctual drives, in the way birds, for example, are. In the outbreak of cold from the early winter, birds are compelled to follow their migratory-drive and abandon to starvation their young ones, which they have fed in their nests with self-sacrificing tirelessness. By contrast, human beings must build a common world in constant dialogue with others. We can call this a convention (*sunthēkē*). However, it is not a convention that is closed, but rather one that can be formed and intentionally observed and demanded. What is 'given' is not that which we express and communicate in these exchanges, but rather what we have to say and communicate. This is the whole richness of the commonly shared world and of the experience of the world that is exchanged in conversation.

What does it really mean that something is 'given'? What is 'expressed'? The 'whole truth' of the statement for which we can be hauled up before court and asked to hide nothing and to embellish nothing? Or is it what is meant? Or is it what is repressed? Or is it what is unsaid and unsayable? Certainly, some rigour and responsibility are present in the whole of the culture that is grounded in science and its objectivity. However, even the statement of the witness before the court is always a moral appeal, which points beyond the mere objectivity that science strives for. Even in science, such a striving intersects constantly with the tendencies of the life-world, in which we have to live a common and communal life. This is what is given to us.

[205] Thus, once more: what is the given? Only those who do not answer by saying 'what can be measured' and keep themselves open to this question, will know what hermeneutic philosophy is.

Part Three

Confronting Other Intellectual Movements and Disciplines

Subjectivity and Intersubjectivity, Subject and Person (1975)[1]

[87] The concept of intersubjectivity has come to be known as a problematic aspect of the great Husserlian programme of a transcendental phenomenology. In Husserl's late thought it almost plays the role of an *experimentum crucis*.[2] It is not only that in the meantime the massive amount of his manuscripts on this theme has been published in three impressive volumes.[3] More importantly, it was precisely this problematic aspect that in fact had triggered new developments under the keyphrase of a 'phenomenology of the life-world'. This began already at the end of the 1940s, when Aron Gurwitsch and Alfred Schütz saw in the concept of the life-world a turning away from the principle of transcendental subjectivity and a promising starting point for new developments. They themselves attempted to make the concept of the life-world fruitful for the foundation of the social sciences as this concept had found recognition in American social philosophy in many forms. There are thus good reasons to pay particular attention to the theme of intersubjectivity.

There are, indeed, good reasons to appreciate the Husserlian programme of a transcendental phenomenology for its consistency and radicality. Yet, the way Husserl makes use of the problem of intersubjectivity in the phenomenology of the life-world needs to be questioned.[4] In the end, we cannot overlook the fact that the late Husserl never considered turning away from transcendental idealism. Rather, he saw the specific contribution of phenomenology in the provision of an ultimate foundation through transcendental philosophy. In reacting to the leading school of neo-Kantianism, the Marburg school, Husserl maintained with a high level of confidence that only his unique phenomenological work had produced a real foundation for a systematic transcendental thinking.

Now, we are much more clearly aware that neo-Kantianism, despite its own self-understanding, was never truly [88] a real return to Kant. This became clear in the meantime when we saw how neo-Kantianism internally evolved and collapsed. Neo-Kantianism was rather a return to Fichte. Its progress could, thus, ultimately lead to Hegel and make the concept of 'system of philosophy' a household name in academic philosophy and the history of philosophy up until the beginning of the twentieth century when we arrived at a new critical turn against the concept of system.

This can be easily confirmed when we examine the problem of intersubjectivity. Let us consider the beginnings. At the turn of the century, we had above all the reception of Kierkegaard, which attacked the dominant transcendental philosophy as decisively as Kierkegaard in his time attacked Hegel and his school. The first beginning probably took place in Spain, where Unamuno inspired a whole new generation. With the progress of the Diedrich edition of Schrempf's translation,[5] Kierkegaard's influence was getting continually stronger even in Germany and even on Catholic authors, such as Theodore Haecker, Ferdinand Ebner, but also on Martin Buber, Viktor von Weizsäcker, and others. Last but not the least, the 'Kierkegaard Report' played an important role, which Karl Jaspers presented in his 'Psychology of Worldviews' (1919).[6] Obviously, one did not use the concept of intersubjectivity yet. However, in the name of 'existential philosophy', the concept 'system of philosophy' was being brought to an end.

For a long time, I have followed the methodological principle of not undertaking any investigation without giving an account of the history of the concept. When it comes to our philosophizing, we must account for the capacity of our language to anticipate our philosophizing and we do this by trying to shed light on the implication of the conceptual terms that philosophy deals with. The concept of subjectivity lies unmistakably behind the concept of intersubjectivity. We could even say that the concept of intersubjectivity only becomes intelligible when we address, first, the concepts of subjectivity and subject, as well as their role in phenomenological philosophy. What shaped the word *subiectum* and the concept of subjectivity, which appears self-evident to us all, was the fact that 'subject' means something like relation to self, reflexivity, egoity [*Ichheit*]. Nothing of this can be detected in the Greek word *hupokeimenon,* of which 'subject' is a translation. The word means 'that which lies at the basis'. This is how the word appears in Aristotelian physics and metaphysics, and has had in such contexts a long Latin afterlife as *substantia* or *subiectum*. Both are Latin translations of *hupokeimenon,* which is and means that which lies unchangeably at the basis of the alterations of every change. Aristotle introduces this concept with regard to nature. He distinguishes, on the one hand, that which, in nature, happens to a thing sometimes this way **[89]** and sometimes that way, from, on the other hand, the thing itself, to which this or that happens. This Aristotelian distinction was already prepared by Plato when he differentiated the 'what', the *ti*, from the *quale*, the *poion* [the how]. The Aristotelian turn to physics now brings this concept of subject, which is also a grammatical and logical concept, in the neighbourhood of *hulē* – the concept for matter – and into close proximity with the conceptual framework of Aristotelian substance metaphysics. One can thus ask how the modern concept of subject and subjectivity could take its proper and particular meaning from this fundamental orientation.

The answer is clear. It came through the Cartesian privilege granted to the *cogito me cogitare*,[7] which gained worldwide recognition through John Locke. It was granted a cognitive primacy as the unshakable foundation that has its validity against any possibility of doubt, *quamdiu cogito*, as long as I think – whatever I think. It is, as it were, the substance of all our representations. The concept of subjectivity developed from here. Kant then helped the word and the concept prevail, when he recognized the function of subjectivity in the transcendental synthesis of apperception, which must be able to accompany all our representations, granting them their unity. Just as, in nature, the changing states and processes happen to something that remains unchanging, in the same way the changes in our representations rest on the fact that they belong to an enduring ego. This is the conceptual historical framework in which the transition from the substance to the subject took place.

The structure of reflexivity thereby takes centre stage in philosophy. In terms of etymological formation, reflection and reflexivity derive from the Latin expression *reflexio*, an expression that is known in optics and mirror-making. This expression could not develop into the new conceptual meaning – the one that has become natural to us – before the emergence of scholastic science. Originally, the expression only represented the distinctive feature of light, the fact that it is only what stands in the light that makes light itself visible. This could hold as the decisive trait of the relation to self and of selfhood, which, as self-movement, is proper to life as such and which, for the Greeks, constitutes the concept of soul, *psuchē*. In the case of human beings and animals it is quite obvious that such a structure is proper to life as such. However, even plants form into an organic unity through assimilation and maintain themselves in such a unity. This is what the Aristotelian tradition called the *anima vegetativa*.[8] In this fundamental structure of the organism, there lurk problems, which were already discussed in Plato's time. How can there really be self-movement if everything that is in movement has its mover? How is what is itself moved ever capable of being a mover? What we have here is the whole problem of the *heauto kinoun,*[9] which Aristotle discusses in Book 8 of *Physics.* This is **[90]** what finds its expression in the concept of *nous.*[10] We recognize here the concept of spirit and Hegel closed his system of philosophical sciences, which he called *Encyclopaedia,* with a quotation from Aristotle, almost like a last word. The highest being is the *nous,* which, as *noēsis noēseōs,*[11] as the thinking of thinking, manifests the structure of reflexivity. What is present to itself, what has the structure of reflexivity, presents the highest manifestation of being as present.

It is here that Greek thinking culminates, but not without raising an objection to itself: reflexivity is always a secondary phenomenon compared to the immediate attending to something. Thinking would thus, first of all, be a thinking of something and, only then, also a thinking of thinking. Aristotle saw this problem in its full clarity. The turning back to one's own thinking being is always only an 'aside' (*en parergō*). Aristotle thus saw himself forced, in the onto-theological domain of metaphysics, to make the universe, as the order of all that is in motion, dependent on a highest being, which has the distinctive feature of relating to itself. We can see how differently the apodictic evidence of self-consciousness presents itself to us in the midst of philosophy! Transcendental idealism grants subjectivity the priority of the absolute. It is only when reappropriating Aristotle in the middle of the nineteenth century that Franz Brentano, once again, took issue with the priority of self-consciousness. Max Scheler followed him in insisting on the priority of the givenness of things over self-consciousness.

What motivates the priority of self-consciousness over against the consciousness of things in modern thinking is the primacy of certainty over truth, which was founded on the idea of method in modern science. In contrast to the classical concept of method, since Descartes, method has been understood as a path toward reaching certainty. In this sense, despite all the multiplicity of methods, there is only one method. With the emergence of modern sciences, philosophy is confronted with the enduring task of mediating between the tradition of metaphysics and modern science. It is the task of unifying things as incompatible as the empirical route of science and the eternal truths of metaphysics. This explains why the ancient concept of system found application in philosophy for the first time in modernity. In the old Greek usage, 'system' plays a role only in astronomy and music, that is to say: always in those places like the starry heavens, where we are confronted with the task of bringing into harmony the circular motion of the stars with the irregularities of planetary motion or with the task of distinguishing the different 'tones' in music. The transposition of the concept of system to philosophy now assigns to philosophy the same task of mediating between the constant progress of [91] scientific research and philosophy's claim to the truth. With Leibniz the expression 'system' even makes it to the league of book titles.

The last synthesis to have exerted the greatest influence in philosophy as a systematic construction was without a doubt the synthesis offered by German idealism. This explains why the successors of Kant could make the founding of all knowledge dependent on the first and highest principle of self-consciousness. This was in fact, as Kant called it, nothing short of a 'Copernican turn'. It was the work of Kant's successors to make sure that the formal concept of self-consciousness was filled with a content. Schelling sketched his philosophy of nature, which was supposed to produce the 'physicalistic proof of idealism' to the extent that, in the organization of the potentialities [*Potenzen*], nature reaches its highest potentiality when the thunderbolt from the absolute produces self-consciousness. Continuing beyond Schelling, Hegel assimilates the whole content of historical experience under the concept of idealism and moves from the dialectic of the concept of life to the concept of self-consciousness. Here we see how the role that the concept of life was going to play in the philosophy of the nineteenth and twentieth centuries was prepared. The decisive transition takes place in Hegel's *Phenomenology* in the chapter about master and slave that is as well known as it is misunderstood, where the significance of 'labour' [*Arbeit*] is presented.[12] The genuine consciousness of self founds itself in labour. To the extent that the form produced by labour is impressed on the other, the appropriation of what is alien is accomplished. This is the first higher self-consciousness, from which the path leads to the highest self-consciousness of the spirit.

On this path we find the critique directed at self-consciousness, as exercised by Marx and now by the critique of ideology. Since Nietzsche, this critique has dominated philosophical thinking right up into the present day. In a well-known formulation, Nietzsche bluntly attacks the idealistic principle of self-consciousness when he says, looking back at Descartes: 'Doubt must be exercised more radically.'[13] From then on, it seems to us naive to take the expressions of self-consciousness for granted. Nietzsche already makes reference to what we can call the function of dreams. Freud brought this later to the forefront when he gave the example of someone in deep sleep interpretatively transforming the ringing of the alarm clock into a cannon shot, thus dreaming up a whole battle only to avoid waking up.[14] What is common to Marx, Nietzsche and Freud is clearly the realization that they cannot in good faith take the given of self-consciousness for granted. It is here that the concept of interpretation takes a new role. One thinks of Nietzsche's well-known expression: 'I know of no moral phenomena. I know only of a moral interpretation of phenomena.'[15] [92] Nietzsche's use of the expression 'interpretation' is itself merely the appropriation of a word from the technical language of philologists. The fact that this expression 'interpretation' has expanded well beyond all philological usage and become a fundamental category of modern philosophy is certainly of the greatest significance. Heidegger's adoption of the concept in turn marks, by its very adoption, the critical further development of the concept of phenomenon as it was used in Husserl's phenomenology.

How does the problem of subjectivity look in light of Heidegger and his critique of Husserl? As we know, already in *Being and Time* Heidegger twisted Husserl's usage of the word 'phenomenon' insofar as Heidegger saw the freeing of the phenomenon as the proper task of phenomenology and found that such a task was not sufficiently thought through when Husserl formulated the mere motto of 'back to the things themselves'. For something to show itself, an unveiling of what is concealed is required so that it can come to a self-manifestation. Thus, the word 'phenomenology' does not merely mean 'a description of what is given', but includes the removal of what conceals, which need not only consist of false theoretical constructions. Thus, originally the phenomenological art of description looks somewhat like this: one begins by removing what dogmatically obfuscates what is investigated, for example, mechanistic theories in the theory of perception or a hedonistic theory of instinct. This could be seen as the main motivation for turning to phenomenology, as we find it at work, for example, in Alexander Pfänder and in the school of Theodore Lipps as well as in the young Max Scheler. Husserl himself also spoke of sensualistic elements in the phenomenon of perception and called them the 'hyletic data'. However, this was done for the sake of elaborating the determining formal characters that are at work in perception and bring to manifestation the givenness of the object of perception in its flesh. Heidegger's critique was more radical. It concerned the concept of phenomenon itself and the givenness of the object of perception in its flesh, because this givenness in Husserl is eventually referred back to the apodictic certainty of self-consciousness. By introducing the concept of 'presence-at-hand' [*Vorhandenheit*] and questioning back toward 'readiness–to-hand' [*Zuhandenheit*] and 'Dasein', Heidegger critically moves beyond the horizon of time and thereby also the consciousness of time that Husserl had masterfully described. Heidegger shows that this alleged givenness remains in thrall of the Greek experience of being. This holds true for everything that is subsumed under the concept of the transcendental ego and its apodictic evidence, within which phenomena 'constitute' themselves.

Augustine already elucidated the *aporia* of time-consciousness, in the sense that the now actually 'is' not at all, since already in its [93] self-identification it has cancelled itself as being past. Husserl still saw the essence of self-consciousness in the fact that this consciousness entangles itself in the aporia of temporality when it attempts to bring its own being before itself. The reflecting self falls into a never-ending process of iteration, insofar as reflection can always again reflect on the reflecting self. Thus, it results from the structure of reflexivity itself that it entangles itself in empty iteration. This is due to Husserl's concept of transcendental subjectivity: it includes in itself this unending empty process of iteration. The step Heidegger takes consists only in the fact that he discovers in this very concept of self-consciousness the secret influence of Greek ontology, thereby depriving the concept of consciousness and its fundamental supporting function for transcendental idealism of all validity.

'Being' must be understood not only as that of which I am conscious that it is there or, as the late Heidegger interprets it, that it is present [*anwesend*]. Husserl thought that he could grasp the essence of time-consciousness with the concept of self-presence, and this means: with the self-appearing of the stream of consciousness. Heidegger's critique bears on the narrowness of such an interpretation of being. He shows that such a conception misses the primary fundamental constitution of human existence. Dasein does not consist in the attempt, always retrospective, of bringing oneself before oneself in becoming conscious of one's own self. Dasein is rather a being-given away from itself [*Weggegebenheit*] and this does not only mean being-given away from itself with regard to its representations, but above all with regard to the fact that its future is in the mode of not being given. This is what constitutes human Dasein, as someone like Hermann Cohen also stressed. Whether we want to call this the 'principle of hope' or however else we may emphasize the futural character of human Dasein, Heidegger has shown that, in all this and in the concept of subjectivity, there continues to lurk, unrecognized, an ontological prejudice even if subjectivity is no longer thought as substantiality or presence at hand.

From this critique of the concept of consciousness, which Heidegger later radicalized, the following fact receives particular weight: even before *Being and Time*, Heidegger introduced the expression 'hermeneutics of facticity' in order to set his own questioning against an idealism of consciousness. Facticity is obviously that which cannot be brought to light, that which resists all attempts at rendering it transparent through understanding. From this it becomes clear that in all understanding of sense, there remains something that cannot be explained and that, for this reason, we must question back into what motivates all understanding. In the process, the whole concept of interpretation is transformed and comes closer to the radicality that we found above in the famous words of Nietzsche. My own works proceeded in the direction of finding out what interpretation actually is, if one goes so far as to contest fundamentally the ideal of the self-transparency of subjectivity. What this means is not only that [94] all understanding of sense finds itself *de facto* limited. It rather means that an unlimited understanding of sense would truncate the sense of understanding itself and even basically cancel out such an understanding, in the same way that an all-encompassing perspective would destroy the sense of perspective.

This is of significant import for the problematic issue of so-called intersubjectivity, as we will see. In *Being and Time* it seems at first as if intersubjectivity only represents a marginal appearance in Dasein's authentic mode of being, condemned as inauthenticity, idle-talk, the they, that is to say: intersubjectivity is situated in the tendency of Dasein toward fallenness.

I chose the concept of subjectivity as the object of a reflection about the history of concepts in order to open a new horizon for the problem of intersubjectivity. We stressed at the beginning that transcendental subjectivity forms the enduring foundation in the Husserlian edifice of phenomenology. The concept of 'intersubjectivity' also involves using words in such a way that it points to Husserl's own conceptual difficulties and a whole problematic dimension. What we would perhaps call 'objective Spirit' with Hegel or what we would call, with Marx and under the influence of Hegel's philosophy of right, 'society' falls in Husserl under the concept of intersubjectivity. Husserl's views are so strongly centred on subjectivity that he could only formulate the topic itself on that basis. This is also very clearly manifested by the other concepts that Husserl appeals to in analysing the problems of intersubjectivity. It is telling, in this regard, that Husserl appropriates the Leibnizian concept of the monad and the monadological aspect, which even in Leibniz is marred by the sheer unsolvability of the problem of the co-existence of monads, for which problem Leibniz wanted to prove the existence of God. For his part, Husserl appeals to the meaning of intersubjectivity for the constitution of the world. It is only by having a world in common that we can think the co-existence and the mediation of the monads together, thus on the basis of a consciousness that has a world.

Even without delving into the semantic aspect of the problem, the phenomenological construction of concepts in Husserl gives us something to think about. In the light of the form in which German idealism was discussed here and later on, in the 1920s, and even before, it was as if it were on its last legs. People were then talking about the I-thou problem. To speak of the 'I' or the 'thou' seems to us, at least since Wittgenstein, no longer legitimate. Heidegger also points in the same direction: there is already in such expressions a mystifying substantialization, blocking access to the real problems. We saw that such a critique of the concept of subjectivity in idealism goes back to Kierkegaard. His influence [95] was what inspired in particular the circle around the journal *Kreatur*[16]: Martin Buber, Franz Rosenzweig, Theodore Haecker, Ferdinand Ebner and Friedrich Gogarten. The 'thou' relationship appears here as the counter-instance to the Kantianism of the time and the primacy of the transcendental ego from which Husserl himself for all those years could not escape. It seems to me that it is a significant change when people in the meantime do not say 'the thou' or do not speak simply, as in Fichte, of the 'non-I', which is an expression that sounds like a resistance, a limitation to be surmounted or overcome in some manner. Instead, people speak of the other. The fact that one says 'the other' changes the perspective. There is immediately a reciprocal relationship that permeates into the constitution of the I and the thou. Every other is at the same time the other of the other, as we can learn from Michael Theunissen's book.[17] For my part, I have taken my inspiration from the ancient doctrine of friendship.

On this point, an astounding dogmatism of the phenomenologist manifests itself in the infinitely rich analyses of Husserl. Taking transcendental subjectivity as his starting point, Husserl insists that the other is first intended as a perceptual thing with all the specific formal qualities of perception, which he has presented in his theory of adumbrations. It is only in a second founded act, so to speak, that the perceptual thing is granted the status of being animated. Husserl calls this 'transcendental empathy', obviously consciously borrowing and distancing himself from the psychological theory of empathy and sympathy. This theory had been developed earlier by Theodore Lipps, the psychologist from Munich, to whose school Pfänder, Geiger, Gallinger, Hildebrandt and others belonged, before ending up in the phenomenological movement through Scheler's intervention in the so-called 'toppling' of the Lipps school. Truth be told, this two-level empathy is a very artificial construction. In the living relationship of a life to a life, the sensual givenness of a perceptual thing is a rather secondary construct. Obviously, Husserl is guided by a deconstruction of dogmatic obfuscations and not by the primary givenness of the thing. However, it was the great slogan of phenomenology to go back to the things themselves. At any rate, under the pressure of scientific-theoretical motives, Husserl insisted that the other can only be given, at first, as a perceptual thing and not in its liveliness, as it is given in the flesh. It is on this point that Heidegger directs an ontological critique at Husserl's phenomenology – the point of Husserl's strongest evidence. It very much seems as if an all too narrow pre-conception of givenness – the scientific concept of measurability – has obscured the genius of description that Husserl fundamentally embodies. This has been criticized in many ways. However, only Heidegger [96] drew the ontological consequence: in the shortcomings of such a description we have to see at work the still operative prejudice of Greek ontology and the postulate of measurability prevalent in the modern science.

For Heidegger, what matters is to circumscribe the thinking centred on subjectivity and to unveil the ontological prejudice of phenomenology and philosophical research that stands behind such a thinking. Fundamentally, he proceeds in the right way, in my view. In an era in which all traditions have dissolved and non controversial commonality no longer exists, he does not want to presuppose for this purpose any solidarity other than the one in which all people find themselves obviously united – and this is the limit situation of dying and death, which are always mine. Even this, we should be reminded, could be a presupposition confined to the Christian cultural sphere. In fact, Heidegger's distinction between authenticity and inauthenticity depends on this presupposition. This is not meant to be a fundamental devaluation of the social world. Rather, what should be clear is that what presents itself in the form of idle talk, of the 'They', etc., is absolutely not a common world, but rather a mode of fallenness with which one can hide from the radical individuation of dying and the community that comes to light in it. Heidegger emphasizes this as the finitude of Dasein and explicates it with the sole purpose of preparing the question of being. Here we are not yet dealing with the question of whether the other, and thus the problem of intersubjectivity, receives sufficient consideration in Heidegger. This is not what is in question here for Heidegger. He knows very well that Dasein is also being-with and, in *Being and Time*, he grants being-with the distinction of an equiprimordial constitutive component of Dasein. Dasein is originally as much a being-with as it is Dasein.

However, in Heidegger's approach, what is seen in the horizon of the question of being excludes the primacy of subjectivity so radically that the other can absolutely not become a problem. 'Dasein' is obviously not subjectivity. Hence, Heidegger replaces in his approach the concept of subjectivity with the concept of care [*Sorge*]. At this point, it becomes clear, nonetheless, that the other stands only at the margins and is visible only from a unilateral perspective. Heidegger speaks of care and also about solicitude [*Fürsorge*]. However, solicitude acquires, in his work, a special accent, with which he designates authentic solicitude as a 'liberating solicitude' [*freigebende Fürsorge*]. The word conveys what matters to Heidegger, namely that true solicitude does not consist in caring for others, but rather in liberating the others into their authentic selfhood [*Selbstsein*] – in contradistinction to providing for [*Versorgung*] the others, which would deprive them of the care for their Dasein. What we are dealing with here is absolutely not the social-political **[97]** 'solicitude', as the sociologist Bourdieu claims.[18] Here too Heidegger aims exclusively at the preparation of the question of being, which can only be posed beyond all metaphysics. The formulation of a liberating solicitude is obviously meant as a liberation for that in which the authenticity of Dasein consists and on the basis of which *Being and Time* strives to unfold in a new sense the metaphysical question of being.

One can obviously ask to what extent the project of *Being and Time* itself could grasp the other in an appropriate manner. Here, a reminiscence of mine may be instructive. In 1943 I attempted to show in contradistinction to Heidegger how the understanding of the other has a fundamental significance. This work was to be published later as the first piece of my *Kleine Schriften*.[19] Given the manner Heidegger developed his project in the preparation for the question of being and elaborated understanding as the most authentic existential structure of Dasein, the others could only manifest themselves in their own existence as a limitation. Eventually, as I claimed, it was only when the others are starkly held up against me that the authentic possibility of understanding opened up to me. To let the other stand against oneself – and it is from there that all my herme- neutic works slowly arose – does not only mean to recognize in principle the limitation of one's own project. It also demands simply going beyond one's own possibilities in a dialogical, communicative, and hermeneutic process. When I presented my views to Heidegger at the time, he nodded with approval, but then said: 'Yes, but what about thrownness? [*Geworfenheit*].' Obviously Heidegger meant that the point I was making here was for him completely included in the fact that the existence of Dasein is not only project, but also thrownness. This must mean that Dasein has to take charge of itself in a manner that is never completely transparent.

The word 'thrownness' [*Geworfenheit*] actually presents a semantic field in which very different elements resonate. As a matter of fact, in normal usage we know only of the expression that the cat threw a litter [*Die Katze geworfen hat*]. Her young ones are a throw. This is thrownness. Without a doubt, with this semantic connotation, Heidegger has in mind what is essential to him. One really does not have a free choice to exist. One was thrown into the 'there', just as the litter of the cat. Thus, we have a limitation in principle of the character of project pertaining to authentic Dasein. In such a throw, we are not this single individual and we do not even know who 'we' are, for example, we, 'this generation'. In the expression [98] thrownness, there lies another connotation, which is of a more historical origin: the gnostic components. In gnosis we find an anthropology, which Hans Jonas reconstructed at the time with Heideggerian means. For the Gnostics, 'thrownness' refers to the being of the soul as it is thrown into the world; it is a fundamental determination from which the gnostic meditation takes its point of departure and attempts through meditation to rise up again to reunify with the One. In any case, Heidegger's answer seemed to me to offer too little for the phenomenon that was a concern for me. It is not only this fact that each one of us is in principle something limited. For me, the question was: why must I learn to experience my limitation through the encounter with the other and why do I have to learn to experience it always anew, if I must be able at all to overcome my limitations?

Here, a totally different and new conceptual tradition opens up and we will have to ask how far this conceptual tradition can help. I have in mind everything that is connected with the concept of person. As we know, the expression, like its Greek parallel *prosopon*, is an expression for the mask of the actor and thus also for the role that the actor plays in Attic theatre – and similarly any actor in the theatre of the world. The same is true for its Latin equivalent (*persona*). From there the concept of person migrated into legal language. We can understand that in the field of the law, it is not the individuality as such that is of interest, but the role confined to its legal dimension, a role that one plays in the case under litigation. The history of the concept of person is extremely instructive. Its first formulation can be found in Boethius. According to him, the person is *naturae rationalis individua substantia*.[20] One can see how Greek metaphysics in the later Hellenistic period had penetrated the Latin language and its thought, and has remained at work up until scholasticism. In addition, there is also another highly significant Christian doctrine: the application of this expression to the Trinity. Here, we are dealing with the three persons of God, which is understood as a unity and at the same time as a trinity, as the creator and father, as the saviour and son, and as the propagation of the Holy Spirit. It is obvious that, for the formation of the concept of person in contemporary thinking, what is decisive is not only the conceptual history, which we have just outlined, but above all also the slow development of new social forms, the city and state in the period when we had a consolidation of migrating populations. Thus, especially in late Middle Ages, the English model of the 'free bill'[21] reinforced the social dimension of the concept of person. Luther too exerted an influence in this direction. He associated the concept of person closely with *fides*, the command of faith and thus, at the same time, with the role of moral conscience [*Gewissen*], but absolutely not with the concept of theoretical self-consciousness. [99] Ebeling shows this in his studies of Luther.[22] It is all the more remarkable that, in the technical language of philosophy, the conceptual change, which we have outlined, from substance toward the modern concept of subjectivity had the upper hand. In Descartes as well as in Leibniz and John Locke, the concept of person is defined by the concept of reflection exercised by self-consciousness and the other does not come into view at all. In this regard, it is only in the period of the French revolution that Kant's philosophy opened up new avenues, to the extent that Kant puts the freedom that belongs to the person and the capacity a person has to account for itself above the subjectivity of self-consciousness. Here we first arrive at the political concept of subject as 'vassal'. This also had a retroactive effect on the theological debate. The concept of person enjoyed a new reception in the Lutheran tradition through Schleiermacher as well as through the renewal of the Thomistic tradition in the Catholic philosophy of our century. Schleiermacher even coined the battle cry of 'personalism', through which he sought to eliminate all pantheistic tendencies in the theology of the trinity.[23] The same happened when the Catholic philosophy of our century appropriated personalism, in particular through the influence of Max Scheler and the fruitful distinction that he introduced in philosophical analysis between the private sphere of the person and its social functions. From this, it is easy to understand that the Christian concept of love could be newly interpreted in both confessions – and in particular the third person.

Later on, after he had given up the transcendental interpretation of his project, to which he had clung in *Being and Time*, Heidegger abandoned the dimension of subjectivity even more fundamentally and also eliminated from his thought, after the 'turn' [*Kehre*], the structure of Dasein as care and even the concept of understanding and the concept of hermeneutics. This is the direction that my own works took with an orientation toward the theme of language and the primacy of dialogue. They found their first outline in the delineation of the problem presented in the third part of *Truth and Method*. Whoever thinks about 'language' already operates in a realm that is beyond subjectivity.

11

On the Contemporary Relevance of Husserl's Phenomenology (1974)[1]

[160] In the wake of a lively discussion brought to a close by Paul Ricoeur,[2] the task of a 'summarizing report' is to pay attention to and emphasize the points where the individual contributions converge and common resonances can be discerned.

If we still readily engage Husserl's phenomenology today, the reason for this is a peculiar interplay of historical distance and new relevance. Without taking into consideration the fact that we no longer simply live in the immediate scientific and philosophical stimulation produced by Husserl's work, there is, I think, no way for us to assess the true contemporary relevance of Husserl's thought. I would thus like to sketch briefly, from my perspective, a few specific problems that became apparent even though I am aware that I obviously cannot manage to bring all the motives that we have heard about [in this conference] into a reasonable and substantial convergence.

The first motive, which coincidentally also concerns the first contribution to this conference, is the unity of the idea of method in transcendental phenomenology. This was what Funke's contribution establishes with extensive material.[3] I believe that we can no longer rationally dispute the fact that Husserl maintained the idea of transcendental phenomenology, uncontested and unchanged, from the first conception in *The Idea of Phenomenology* up to his final intellectual efforts. The appearance of a change in Husserl's position on the transcendental self-grounding of phenomenological philosophy comes, as we all know, from the theme of the 'life-world'. However, I believe that we would be mistaken about the facts if we were to think that this theme of the life-world is a new theme in the later development of Husserl's phenomenology. To the contrary, the life-world represents Husserl's earliest position, in contrast to the neo-Kantian epistemology, which was based on the 'fact of the sciences', or positivist epistemology. What Husserl did was to go back to the life-world, and this means to an experience that the sciences can never fully objectify. We must first and foremost bear this firmly in mind [161] if we want to do justice to the question of why the concept and the word 'life-world' came to be articulated only late in Husserl.

This was not because the theme of the 'life-world' was something secondary within his phenomenological enterprise or because it was only acknowledged late. It was rather because this theme suddenly turned for him into a critical question and even a self-critical question addressed to himself, on account of Heidegger's novel enterprise. As one could show in great detail, the whole discussion of the life-world in Husserl is a constant confrontation with the question: can the thematic that Heidegger uncovered really be conceived outside the project of my transcendental phenomenology? You all recall the remark that Oskar Becker made in the *Husserl-festschrift*,[4] a year after the publication of *Being and Time*: he declares that it is a fundamental misunderstanding to count Heidegger's *Being and Time* as a new foundation for philosophy beyond the bounds of Husserl's transcendental phenomenology. It is the elaboration of the stratum of a problem that was sketched within transcendental phenomenology: the stratum characterized by hermeneutic questioning, as well as the interpretation of horizons within the whole of Husserl's research programme, which are given with this stratum. Becker himself, who had certainly become at the time as much a student of Heidegger as he was initially a student of Husserl, wanted to reconcile, so to speak, Heidegger's new approach with the phenomenological programme. It seems to me that it is here that we find the real stimulus in Husserl for confronting the problem of the life-world in an explicit manner.

The *Crisis* volume is, in my view – I know that on this topic I am not in complete agreement with my colleagues Landgrebe and Fink – the continual effort on Husserl's part to show why his own project of a transcendental phenomenology is unavoidable and all-encompassing. If we want to stay with Husserl's theme, we must in any case make a distinction between the role that the theme of the 'life-world' plays within the founding of transcendental phenomenology and the developments of this theme and this research area, which point beyond transcendental phenomenological questioning. It seems to me beyond doubt that Husserl in his own eyes and his own consciousness refuted and rejected any philosophical effort to bring to prominence the theme of the 'life-world' at the expense of his idea of a foundation in the transcendental ego [162]. The whole treatise of the *Crisis* is a monological dialogue wherein Husserl raises objections to himself and refutes them. If we closely analyse volume VI of Husserl's complete works, the *Crisis,* into its component parts, what we see is the following: the most advanced, the boldest, the most radical objections Husserl makes to himself are all in the appendices. By contrast, the main text submits all of them once again to the strict discipline of transcendental phenomenology, wherein it is an established fact that there cannot be any possible problem in philosophy that cannot find its systematic place within the architectonic order of the genetic and constitutive foundation.

The life-world is, thus, in Husserl's eyes not a critical argument. I do not need to repeat here what is essentially covered by this self-critique that Husserl exercises toward himself under the motto of the life-world. It is merely a self-critique of the Cartesian way leading to the transcendental ego, but is never a self-critique of the transcendental ego as the principle of every ultimate foundation. To the contrary, the way of the life-world is meant to lead to the transcendental ego in an 'honest' manner. It does so by rectifying an essential omission, in the sense that it avoids the illusion that it is enough to bracket all positings of the world, all positings of ontic validity [*Seinsgeltung*] in the ontic and mundane sense, so as to retain in this manner pure transcendental subjectivity as the field of valid justification. Husserl saw – and in this regard he may have been assisted by Heidegger's enterprise – his predicament: he could not bring about the intended transcendental foundation of phenomenology in the ego in an irrefutable manner if he did not do the following: thematize explicitly the concept of world pertaining to the life-world as an all-encompassing horizonal character of the world and, thus, to set this concept of world under the *epochē*, bracketing it and putting it in parentheses. He realized and became aware, when facing the claims that Heidegger raised, that the theme of the 'life-world' must be thematized for its own sake and that a typology of life-worlds must be phenomenologically elaborated, if unproven validities are not to seep into the foundation of constitutive phenomenology. From the very beginning, the topic of the 'life-world' is introduced in order to eliminate mistakes that could infiltrate constitutive phenomenology from the side of what is involved in the life-world, that is to say, from the unthematic horizonal character of the world. That could raise the spectre of 'relativism'.

Against this background, it seems to me that, in our exchanges, we have not always been sufficiently clear that it is a totally different question when we ask about the extent to which the ontology of the life-world, which Husserl fully recognized as a legitimate discipline, represents as such, a **[163]** turning [*Umwendung*], to speak with Husserl, in mundane science and how this process of turning is to be conceived. The phenomenological problem of the turning is to be completely severed from the problem of the foundation that culminates in the famous question: 'How do I become an honest philosopher?' How can I grant legitimacy to every step of thinking in an absolute self-responsibility? This problem of legitimation is not put into question by the theme of the 'life-world', but rather deepened in the direction of transcendental phenomenology.

To this extent, I cannot see any argument that goes against the unity of transcendental phenomenology in the theme of the life-world and I find that Funke's opening talk was simply correct on this point.

What I have welcomed is the fact that the theme of 'intersubjectivity' has not been treated in this conference in the same manner as that of the 'life-world', namely as an instance that goes against Husserlian phenomenology. For, the same holds for this topic: Husserl himself was of the opinion that he would bring a perfect resolution to the problem of intersubjectivity on the basis of his transcendental phenomenology. In his eyes, all of these were only objections that he made to himself, which, like all true objections to oneself – I think this is a true statement – have always already anticipated their rebuttal. Even the form Husserl uses for discussing these problems has always already anticipated the refutation of his own objections.

However, there is one point on which I too believe Husserl's phenomenology under the motto of the 'life-world' is in fact caught up in a difficulty. This is the problem of phenomenological self-reference, which, in Husserl, is always under discussion, but, as far as I can understand, not satisfactorily explained, in any case for me. We are dealing with the simple question of whether the life-world as the prior basis for the validity of all naive living-in-the-world, even when it is put into brackets within the transcendental turn in reflection, does not remain the presupposition for the transcendental turn in reflection. What is the meaning of this connection between the origin of reflection in the life-world and the transcendental constitution of the life-world in the ego? From here, there arises the question of the return to the life-world of what is itself a transcendental orientation of thinking. Here the problem seems to me to be as yet unresolved. In the course of our exchanges, we have indirectly come to address some of the points of this problem and I would like to gloss over those points with some remarks in the wider context of my review.

[164] It is a real difficulty to want to break through Husserl's transcendental self-interpretation at any point and it is not enough to have insights into the difficulties that result from this position, for example with regard to the theme of 'praxis'. Nobody has demonstrated this better than Heidegger himself in the way he understood his project in *Being and Time*. Heidegger's was a transcendental self-interpretation. To understand oneself in one's being appeared as the ultimate transcendental basis for the interpretation of metaphysics and its

implications. In my view, Heidegger's later self-critique on this point shows indirectly how compelling the transcendental orientation of thinking is in itself.

I need to explain this a little bit and it will be the second point of my presentation. It concerns the problem of the life-world, as it were, in transcendental terms as well as in terms of the life-world itself. I believe that what we have here is only a repetition of the old question that Schelling had in fact already addressed to Fichte, the discussion of which is now easily available in Walter Schulz's newly edited correspondence between Schelling and Fichte.[5] It is the question of whether transcendental idealism could not and should not give itself a real foundation. Schelling understood his philosophy of nature in this sense of the physicalist proof for idealism. This was supposed to mean that the real foundation for transcendental reflection is not itself to be found again within the framework of transcendental questioning. As we know, Fichte refuted this claim of Schelling's philosophy of nature with unmatched argumentative sharpness. When reading their correspondence, one cannot doubt that Fichte is correct, obviously within the conceptual possibilities that were also the only ones available to Schelling. To the extent that Schelling attempted to defend the autonomous claim of the philosophy of nature against the 'Doctrine of Scientific Knowledge' [*Wissenschaftslehre*], he was at the losing end.

Nowadays, Husserl's phenomenology has experienced a similar critique and has, to some extent, emerged victorious. This is the critique that Scheler directs at phenomenology. Scheler introduces his critique precisely at the same point at which Schelling introduces his own critique against Fichte. Scheler asks: can phenomenology be everything, the whole of philosophy? Obviously, phenomenology still has to answer the question of how one arrives at the very possibility of reflecting philosophically. It is a peculiar distinction of human beings to possess the 'capacity of de-realization' [*Entwirklichung*], which is how Scheler formulates the concept of 'spirit' and which his critique of Husserl's theory of *epochē* explicitly thematizes. His critique refers back to the anthropological foundation on the basis of which the 'spirit' in general, starting with the vital basis of 'drive' [*Drang*], realizes itself. Scheler thus repeats Schelling's objection against the standpoint of transcendental reflection in seeking an anthropological foundation for phenomenology [**165**]. He sought it on the basis of modern anthropological insights into the primacy of the unconscious, but also by drawing on the pragmatic theory of science and the gestalt theory of forms that is found in cognitive and gestalt psychology. Here too Husserl's methodological superiority turns out to be compelling. We cannot comprehend, by means of a scientific-theoretical grounding of the possibility of reflection, that which itself does not recur in reflection. We have grown familiar with this magical circle of the transcendental movement of reflection, not only through Husserl, but above all through Hegel. Hegel's followers used to quote this magical circle always with unmatched success when dealing with his opponents in the 1830s and 1840s. There is not a single conceivable position that does not find its dialectical integration and acknowledgement somewhere in the *Phenomenology of Spirit*. I believe that, in the case of Husserl too, we cannot succeed in critiquing Husserl's phenomenology by proceeding from an extra-phenomenological standpoint.

Despite this, as has become very clear especially in the contribution of our Yugoslavian colleague,[6] there is no doubt that there is a peculiar utopian helplessness in the idea of a new praxis, which Husserl ultimately envisages as the 'consequence' and the end of a successful 'phenomenologization' of humanity. Even here, I would like to defend Husserl against the impression that this were something completely new in his last phase. Here too the situation is different. I believe that Husserl now expresses resolutely what he in fact already meant with his *Philosophy as a Rigorous Science*. Ingarden knew Husserl a full ten years before I met him, but I think he will confirm my views that whoever knew Husserl knows that he had a rather missionary mindset and wanted to heal the whole of human culture on this basis. This comes out clearly in the *Crisis*. I once had a discussion with Husserl that illustrates this point. I was naturally interested in many things having to do with the fine arts and wanted just to know what the eminent Husserl thought about modern art – what I took to be modern art at the time was expressionism. Husserl answered: 'Well, you know, Dr. Gadamer, I enjoy music a great deal too and like poetry quite a lot; I love to go to the theatre and to museums, but the transcendental foundation of phenomenology leaves me no time to continue to engage also with the things that I love.' This was said with a genuine missionary mindset (a side remark by Ingarden: 'Husserl told me that he was a polar explorer and had no time for other matters').

Now, this naturally means that what we have here is, in fact, a theme and a task. The question of turning phenomenological [166] philosophy back toward social praxis in the broadest sense of the term, which Husserl fundamentally demands, can hardly be grasped adequately by means of the self-constitution of phenomenology. This is how we can explain why Husserl exhibits such a weakness in his methodology when using the expression 'synthesis of theory and praxis' in one passage that did not escape the notice of our Yugoslavian colleague.[7] This is in fact not an adequate formulation of what he had in mind. There is more to say about this.

Underlying the question left open by Husserl and not really addressed by him, there is another topic internal to phenomenology, which has manifested itself constantly in our discussion. It began already with the contribution of Enzo Paci.[8] It became apparent that his contribution, along with several others, posed the question – and it is a phenomenological or philosophical question: what is the relationship between the transcendental ego and the concrete ego? Underlying this question, there is the other topic: what is the relationship between transcendental phenomenology and psychology? On this, we actually have answers from Husserl himself, showing the thematic of the 'we' and the 'mind' [*Seele*] to be a legitimate problem. There is also in Husserl a psychological way leading, if understood properly, to the transcendental ego. This is not another challenge to the inner coherence of the architecture of Husserlian phenomenology, but the contrary. The thematization of that which the 'we', the 'mind', and even the 'lived body' are in their *a priori* structure leads to very remarkable theses in Husserl. They all serve the consistent 'reduction' and thus constitutive phenomenology. Obviously – and this is what I believe always leads us astray in these discussions – the possibility of a turn [*Umwendung*] belongs, according to Husserl himself, to every such thematization, once the themes are put into brackets and thus brought to their eidetic thematic and constitutively reduced. Here, we should not confuse what is the possibility of a turning with foundation. Husserl seeks the foundation in the sense of legitimation only along the way that leads to the original presence [*Urpräsenz*], which also constitutes the transcendental ego. In steps that follow logically, he demonstrates this foundation in the theme of 'formal and transcendental logic', which is the only example given of the task he set for himself. As far as I know, Husserl himself considers *Formal and Transcendental Logic* to be the most phenomenologically accomplished of all his works. This is certainly so because the stratification of the constitutive problematic of logic, right up to the logic of truth, is accomplished here on phenomenological grounds. Husserl himself has never offered a problematic of the historical world worked out in a corresponding manner. *Ideas II* obviously did not satisfy his own need for the foundation of such things and for that reason remained unpublished at the time.

[167] The theme of 'phenomenology and psychology' has thus, to repeat, really nothing to do with the issue of concrete genetic questions being raised within psychology. It also has nothing to do with the constitutive genesis that Husserl accomplished in relation to the 'we in general' and 'the mind in general' from the standpoint of transcendental phenomenology. To this extent, it is really a question of terminology and it seems to me entirely correct to say that the

transcendentality of the ego has no different a connection to the concrete ego than any *eidos* to its concrete instantiations. The constitution of the concrete self has no place here. This is a question for psychology and anthropology, and a tremendously important question at that. What was said in our discussion about the difference between the so-called transcendental potentiality of the ego and the 'unique possibility of the self' seems to me to be an important remark. However, these are two different things. One belongs to psychology and the other to the transcendental foundation of psychology.

At this point, I think the question should be posed in a fundamental and general way: to what extent can Husserl's theory be made fruitful for us? It is clear that everything that has been bracketed and set aside by the transcendental reduction can again recover its validity. However, Husserl has never treated this in a detailed analysis. Only Fink had already, very early on, drawn our attention to this theme under the key-expression of a 'streaming in' [*Einströmen*]. Do the things that are bracketed in the transcendental reduction recover, so to speak, their validity? Does science on the basis of the elucidated *a priori* eidetic constitution, become a 'science of a new style', still a mundane science, but one that knows how to justify itself adequately with the help of the transcendental reduction, when it comes to its own idealizations? I am sure that Husserl would have claimed something like this. We, who are older, have all heard this from him in the 1920s. Ludwig Landgrebe was also with Husserl at the time. It was the claim that only through such research into transcendental constitution could the sciences be given their scientific legitimation, while the sciences themselves naturally pursue completely different tasks. As a concrete example, one would perhaps say the following: the transcendental ego is in its constitution totally independent from what was previously called 'the unique possibility that a self has'; this possibility presupposes the concrete life history and its specific mastery of the task of building up the self. What Husserl had in mind with his constitution of the ego was something totally different: it was the analysis of temporality, which still precedes the constitution of the ego and grounds its transcendental validity.

[168] This leads me to the Husserlian grounding of logic. Here, I do not feel competent. I did not quite succeed in my attempt to link Suzanne Bachelard's contribution to my question.[9] I see the problem perfectly well: modern logic is not satisfied with Husserl's distinction between the logic of implication [*Konsequenzlogik*] and the logic of truth; yet, Gödel's theorem somehow lurks in the question concerning the turning of 'apophantic logic' into the logic of truth. Yet, I do not believe that Husserl's distinction can be comprehended

by the means of modern logic. As a matter of fact, the problem of language underlies Husserl's entire effort to ground logic phenomenologically, including the difficulties involved here, even with regard to the problem of semantics. However, the problem of 'language' is not formulated in its actual dimensions through a logic of propositions [*Aussagenlogik*], which even for Husserl remains the clear foundation. Even though Husserl fully recognizes the pre-reflective, pre-predicative structure of the intentionality of experience and perception, the apophantic character of judgement ultimately remains paramount for Husserl. The judgement has the capacity to assimilate all pre-reflective structures. This is the claim and only on this basis can one actually conceive of the logical absurdity of argumentative structures, such as the 'logical circle', but also all talk of a 'hermeneutic circle'. On this point, I would agree in intent with Strasser.[10] Given the way thinking has evolved in the meantime, it does not seem to us possible any longer to narrow down the topic of 'language' in the direction of apophantic perfection and thus to accept objectification as the ultimate *telos* of scientific reason or of reason in general.

If I may refer back to my introductory remarks about the attempt to found transcendental reflection in a life-world, I think that Heidegger is really the only one to have questioned back behind a mere dualistic position, not contenting himself with distinguishing the transcendental reflection from a mundane experience in the life-world. Through his radical ontological critique of the concept of consciousness and its modes of givenness, he prepared the ground for such a questioning. I recall a discussion with Heidegger, still before *Being and Time*. Heidegger said in reference to Scheler that he was a great and genial thinker (Heidegger did not realize this just at the time when he dedicated the Kant-book to him), but that Scheler had never moved beyond the dualism of drive and spirit, of the transcendental science of essences and modern empirical research. In fact, this seems to me to be the point at which Heidegger's critique of the notion of a givenness to consciousness challenges all of us, leading us at least to examine for ourselves what phenomenology can be for us. In his summary, Paul Ricoeur [169] made very clear – and we all know it – that the radicality of Heidegger's questioning has the consequence of steadily wearing out the connection to the sciences. Ricoeur is completely right in saying that it was never Heidegger's understanding of his own project, that he never made the claim to delineate for all the sciences their *a priori* structures in the style of Husserlian transcendental phenomenology and, in this way, to construct, as it were, a reliable and comprehensive picture of our human knowledge. Heidegger had in fact put into question precisely the very idea of a foundation through his question concerning the anticipated concept of being that lies hidden in the idea of foundation. Grounding and founding are recurring themes in Husserl. As always, Funke took great care not to withhold from us even the few places where Heidegger speaks of 'foundation'. At the time, Heidegger could not express himself otherwise. He indeed talked about 'foundation', but his project was, in fact, to show that it was a mistake to ground higher forms of apprehensions on elementary sensory givenness through the lived body in perception. He showed that there lies hidden here an ontological prejudice, as if what is merely there, present, and thus intersubjectively verifiable, had a privileged claim to being, and that, by contrast, forms of apprehension were evidences of a higher order, which should be seen as secondary. It was Heidegger's project to show us what kind of a vague untested ontology of 'values' lay behind this schema of foundation. 'Foundation' certainly appears in Heidegger and quite often in *Being and Time*, occasionally even later. Yet, this idea of foundation is in fact no longer legitimate.

What can take its place? As we know, we all try our own way to promote what we have intuited. Thus, taking the perspective of the hermeneutic movement of interpretation, instead of consciousness and its givenness, I have personally tried to make use of Heidegger's ontological critique in such a way as to come closer once again to the work of the empirical sciences. I believe that I have only elaborated something that lay in the possibilities opened up by Heidegger's more radical questioning. I maintain that to speak of 'being an object for consciousness' is to miss from the outset the authentic question concerning what is. In this, Scheler's concept of reality was productive, despite all the weaknesses of his dualism. Scheler was right when he denied the Husserlian concept of transcendental phenomenology the moment of reality. He was not right, I believe, or rather he did not get the radicality of the questioning opened up by Heidegger, when he wanted to find this task of metaphysics in the synthesis of the empirical sciences and, in the process, let phenomenology simply remain the 'eidetic science'.

We have to begin here, that is to say: we should give up the idea of a foundation, which [170] renders that which is founded dependent once and for all on what provides the foundation. We should abandon this view and put in its place the explanation of what we have always already understood, that of the pre-understanding. When we do this, we can do greater justice to the productive moment in the whole Husserlian problematic of the life-world. In our discussion someone asked: what should the life-world be today, when objectification through technological civilization has transformed our entire

life-world? It is certainly true that this is essentially the most acutely formulated question with regard to which Husserl already conceived his book on the
Crisis. He tried to show how the absolutizing of the scientific attitude based
on Galilean physics narrowed in a disastrous way the questions about human
knowledge. This holds true for us today more than ever when the objectifying
possibilities of reason are targeting social life in its totality. We are now only at
the beginning. This culmination of the situation will indeed make clear the true
motive that Husserl defended when broaching the topic of the 'life-world'.

Here it seems to me that the truly fruitful way of entering into the problem
of our 'hyper-scientific' world is not through a synthesis of theory and praxis,
but by starting analytically from what we know to be 'practical knowledge'. For
my part, I have tried to point out certain prefigurations of hermeneutic thinking
and even of the Heideggerean critique of Husserl, in the question of *phronēsis*
and in the Aristotelian critique of Plato. I concede that my attempt is very
one-sided. In fact, I believe that it is only by going through this self-clarification,
which always already lies in our praxis, that we can manage to assign the objectifying capacities of human reason their rightful place. To speak concretely: our
society's blind faith in experts will not save us from political madness. We have
to recognize a political sense, the practical-political sense in its legitimacy, even
within the objectifying technological civilization. Only such a practical political
sense can guarantee the meaningful application, continuation, promotion and
limitation of such a technological civilization. Of course, experts are indispensable and their technical knowledge shapes our life praxis to a greater and
greater extent. The idea of breaking out of the circle of behavioural patterns
regulated by the sciences is illusory or utopian. Still, it seems to me necessary
that we think a bit deeper about the concept of the 'application' of science.

In this concept of application, as Husserl already developed it in the
Prolegomena, there lies hidden a deep ambiguity. If the application of science is
nothing other than doing everything that one can with the help of science, then
it is not the practical application that we [171] need as human beings for our
society and in our responsibility for the future. Such an application of science
will constantly produce everything that we can produce. I believe, however, that
we start being human first at that point where we ask rational questions of self-
justification about everything that we can produce. To these kinds of questions
empirical research as such offers no answers. In this sense, I would like to
second the moral impulse of Husserl's idea of a 'new kind of praxis' in order to
put it alongside the old impetus of a true common sense *(sensus communis)* that
supports the praxis of our political humanity.

12

'Being and Nothingness'
(Jean-Paul Sartre) (1989)[1]

[110] I have seen Jean-Paul Sartre just once in my life. It was an evening in Siena. We had arrived late. I was wandering through the streets at night and arrived at the famous Piazza del Campo, where the restaurants lean downward toward the place, like in an amphitheatre. There was only one man, sitting there alone, Jean-Paul Sartre. I had always been taught that one should never address a man when he is alone. There was at the same time virtually no overture from Sartre's side. If I dare speak about this, it comes from a motivation that exceeds my personal experiences. I would like to show how difficult it is to understand French philosophical thought for someone who comes from the German tradition and also how the converse is equally difficult. One speaks little of this, out of shyness. This is why I would like to report what it was like when I read Sartre. I later received the first edition of *L'Être et le néant*. It was a gift from Martin Heidegger. He had made it through forty pages of the book.[2] He did not go any further with his reading and this is not so surprising. It has to be said, at the outset, that this book is unbelievably hard to read, even more difficult in translation than in the original, as it is always the case with translations. Now, I have put this to the test. After pretty much forty years I read the book again in its German translation in order to test myself and I want to report some impressions about my take on what was going on at the time and about what may be of documentary interest. I know that I cannot conduct my discussion at the level at which the interrogation of these issues currently stands, but rather perhaps at the level of perennial questions. First of all, I have to remind readers that Sartre is quite probably the first great French thinker since Bergson to have also found a real reception in Germany. His name was associated very quickly with the name of Merleau-Ponty, the founder of the journal *Les Temps Modernes*, whose connection to Husserl became a matter of public knowledge for us at the same time, in the 1940s. Still, there was no doubt that the first impetus for our taking notice came from Sartre.

[111] There was one thing that was of a particular challenge for me and represented a hermeneutic problem. It was that the French philosophers and people of such genius as this great writer Jean-Paul Sartre, took up three great German philosophers at the same time, as if they were their own contemporaries. These three German thinkers are Hegel, Husserl and Heidegger. They are the three great H's, as I am often used to saying. It was an almost impossible task for us to recognize these thinkers, who are so different in our eyes, and to sort out the motives, as they had percolated into Sartre's thought, and finally to grasp what was commonly expressed in them. Clearly, the constellation was meaningful. The book appeared in 1943 during the German occupation of Paris, written in part when Sartre was in a German prison camp. In any case, it was a book whose broad reception in the field of philosophy certainly cannot be compared to the broad reception of the novelist of *La Nausée*³ or with that of the playwright, and finally even to that of the author of a screenplay of so infinitely sad and beautiful a movie as *Les jeux sont faits*.⁴

If today I have to speak of the philosophy of Jean-Paul Sartre and of my efforts to understand it and make it fruitful, we have to bear in mind that this work represents the still semi-academic beginnings, so to speak, of a great writer. Clearly, the theoretical publications before *Being and Nothingness* are the building blocks and the preparatory steps for this work, which must have been prefigured to a great extent by the French university tradition. However, its value and its effect can perhaps be assessed precisely by someone like me who is as clueless about what is going on in academia nowadays as I was at the time. For, we have here philosophical problems in their most general and boldest form put on centre stage by a young thinker and we can in fact recognize many of our own efforts in these philosophical problems.

In order to bring this out clearly, I must first depict the *kairos* or the spirit of the time in which this work appeared and exercised its influence. Obviously, Sartre had also studied in Berlin. We know that he could read German and that he was impressed by the famous seminar of Kojève (at least, through acquaintances), in which almost the whole generation of French names, who are now embedded in the consciousness of the French public, were confronted with Hegel in a new manner. Alexandre Kojève, with whom I was personally well acquainted, was a Russian emigré. While in search of a deeper insight into the grounds of the bloody manner in which the Marxist revolution unfolded in Russia, he pursued his studies of Hegel, first, in Germany and, later on, in France. Iring Fetscher very early on published a minimal outline of the courses that Kojève gave at the time, singling out correctly [112] what interested the young Kojève at the time and during his whole life. I myself heard from Kojève that, as a young man, he could not understand that his father, who was revered in his *latifundium* as a patriarch, as a beloved old father of everyone, was destroyed by the surging revolutionary wave just as ruthlessly and brutally as all the others, among whom there were many who had certainly not lived in such good terms with their peasants. This is what the young Kojève wanted to understand. This is why he studied Marx and naturally Hegel. Obviously, he did not find what he was looking for. How are we supposed to understand all the mysteries of the human soul when we are all a mystery to ourselves?

This is how Sartre came into contact with German philosophy. He was particularly attracted to phenomenology in Germany. At the time, he did not go to Freiburg where one could really learn phenomenology, but only to Berlin, where one could not learn it. However, he surely became quite an avid reader of the things that needed to be read. One finds in his work a cluster of philosophical thoughts woven together and almost impossible for a German philosopher to untangle. This interweaving of thoughts made us see our own thinkers in a new light and from a new perspective. Now, it belongs to a *kairos* that two things come together. We are talking here about Sartre and ourselves in the years after 1945. What was our situation? What was the philosophical tendency at that moment in time? As it could not be expected otherwise, after the official drumbeat and tirades had subsided, public opinion returned to discuss what had occupied us in our academic lectures even during the Third Reich. I was a professor in Leipzig and held exercises on Hegel and Heidegger as well as on Husserl, who was proscribed as a Jew, but nobody took offence at my exercises. Academic teaching at the universities was considerably less disturbed or distorted than what the public now thinks. The Nazis despised intellectuals far too much to bother with our scientific work. In the situation after the end of the war, by contrast, what had been proscribed came to exert its power on public opinion as if it were something new. This explains the effect of the edition of Husserl's works, which began to appear in Louvain. All of a sudden, Husserl, who had disappeared from the public sphere – though not from our philosophical seminars – was again there with his works and was part of the discussion even in Germany.

At the same time, the public experienced another violent surprise. Even Heidegger, who had not been particularly favoured by the Nazi regime in the previous years – he could no longer publish his works – had been completely discredited in the public sphere after 1945, all of a sudden dominated the scene. I once invited Heidegger [113] – it must have been at the end of the 1950s – to give a lecture in Heidelberg. We had to work in the very big lecture hall with programme brochures, which had to be bought for one DM. Only in this way was it possible for Heidegger to have access to the lecture hall, in which he had to speak. We do not need to celebrate that the situation was such. I only want to sketch what was going on and in what conditions we – thus I – read Sartre.

Although I was one of his students, Heidegger certainly did not recognize me as one of the followers of his thinking. I have learned a lot from him and have borrowed a lot from his thought, but he used to say often later on: 'You and your teacher Natorp!' Natorp was the head of the Marburg school under whom I obtained my PhD in 1922 as an immature youngster. Heidegger meant that I was never completely through with Natorp. I say this neither to discredit myself nor to give myself credit, but only to depict once again how we found ourselves at that time in a specific situation that was to leave its mark on us. I was not alone in being steered in the essential stages of my thinking by both Husserl and Heidegger. This was also the case for Ludwig Landgrebe, Eugen Fink, Aron Gurwitsch and Walter Biemel. This was the case for all those possible individuals who survived the Nazi era as a whole or the war years not in Germany, but in emigration or semi-emigration, if we are to add Louvain to the mix as well. They all attempted to work out what was common to Husserl and Heidegger in the strongest possible way, attempting also to show that the opposition between them, which people were terribly eager to see for political reasons, was not tenable as such. And how well they did it! Not in the sense of showing that Heidegger continued entirely in the footsteps of Husserl, but the opposite: that Husserl's philosophical thought in his late years came really close to that of Heidegger. There is an essay by Landgrebe, which I myself published in the *Philosophische Rundschau* and which bears the title 'Farewell to Cartesianism'.[5] In it, Landgrebe wanted to show that Husserl in actuality had ultimately abandoned the Cartesian starting point, which he had constantly emphasized in his recourse to the transcendental ego. He had abandoned it as a result of his own thinking about time and time-consciousness, going in the same direction as Heidegger. This vividly depicts the philosophical situation in which I undertook my reading of Sartre.

Obviously, I read the French original. Translations of philosophical texts are very necessary and offer a certain mediation. However, they can only manage to come close to the original, which they cannot replace. This is a fundamental problem with translations, which should also be addressed in this context. For the moment, I content myself with emphasizing that *Being and Nothingness* is the most significant theoretical [114] and philosophical work of Jean-Paul

Sartre's entire corpus. However, this work in no way circumscribes the totality of his intellectual universe. Even though Sartre is a great writer – a fact that can be recognized as such even in a translation – it is difficult somehow to come to terms with his thought and, thus, with the French philosophical tradition that he represents. This was the expectation with which I began my study of Sartre and experience confirmed this expectation. The Cartesian ideal of *clarté*[6] and the opaque depth of the German romantic tradition from Hamann, via Herder and Hegel, to Heidegger do not go together so easily. The question is always whether it is right for one side to take no notice of the other and whether it is not time to try to lead this dialogue to a better future without the one-sidedness and the prejudice of the stylistic ideals that have been cultivated in the different cultural circles. At any rate, this is the reason why I am here.

Let us try to make clear how Sartre, under the threefold influence of Husserl, Hegel, and Heidegger, succeeded in making these thinkers fit together. As I have already said, the fusion of the three into one is the real puzzle and the real appeal of Sartre's thought. This is where he begins as a phenomenologist. Heidegger read precisely those paragraphs in which Sartre writes about phenomenology and marked some passages. When he offered me the book, these markings were in it. Sartre writes somewhere: 'Husserl or Heidegger would say...' Heidegger had immediately underlined the word 'or' and put a question mark in the margin. Either Husserl or Heidegger, but not both at the same time. Such is the situation in which we all try to make our mark. We must attempt to differentiate the humble steps we take in our own thinking so that they become visible in the first place. In Heidegger's case, there was in fact sufficient reason to insist on the difference. In the end, Heidegger rejected with unbelievable audacity the starting points he had found in Husserl, probably in order to lay out the still deeper motives of his own philosophy. This rejection is generally known as 'the turn' [*Kehre*], in which transcendental questioning in the style of Husserl is rejected. I believe that this turn is a return [*Rückkehr*] and not a change of course [*Umkehr*]: a return to the original, half-religious motives that led Heidegger to involve himself in the business of thinking.

This is at least the way I saw the situation in which I found myself when reading Sartre. Conversely, we have to remind ourselves that we are only studying the academic beginnings of Sartre and that the rest of his works, especially his literary ones, have in a certain sense overshadowed the influence of his philosophical work. These other *genera dicendi*[7] possess a completely different kind of persuasive power and mode of expression, even if *Being and*

Nothingness possesses a significant portion of what we [115] in Germany call the style of the moralists. This style is fundamentally different from what was at play in German philosophy of our day, in Husserl as well as in Heidegger, and in those who attempted to learn from Heidegger.

If we ask ourselves what Sartre has appropriated in his encounter with German philosophy, we have to recognize, first of all, that he adopted a truly phenomenological motive. It is what he calls, with a slight Cartesian accent, the 'pre-reflective cogito'. What he means by this is that reflection is in fact a very secondary act and so is self-consciousness itself a secondary phenomenon with regard to world consciousness. Aristotle was already aware of this. In Book *lambda* of his *Metaphysics*, he speaks of how we are aware of ourselves and our own thinking only obliquely, when we are really focused on something. Such a way of being aware is self-consciousness in a sense that it is not a reflection on the act of thinking. It is the consciousness that accompanies the thinking of something. Aristotle first develops this in *De anima*. Franz Brentano, the forefather of the phenomenological school, points this out forcefully in his *Psychology from an Empirical Standpoint*. When I see something, then I also know that I see it. Does this mean that I turn seeing into an object when I know this? No. It means that such a consciousness accompanies and is always present, animating, so to speak, the acts of our consciousness of the world, of our turning to the other, to other people or to things in the world. Sartre adopted this view. His first starting point is the pre-reflective cogito. This is what he calls 'consciousness'. Consciousness now means, to put it sharply, a primordial quality of human vitality [*Lebendigkeit*] in all its structures of life and modes of behaviour. *Being and Nothingness* is, to a large extent, devoted to the task of precisely showing that there is not just a *cogito me cogitare*[8] as the reflection of self-consciousness, which Descartes developed and which was pushed to the centre stage in German idealism, in Fichte and, later on, in Husserl. Obviously, Husserl also knew something about this other mode of being-conscious that goes along with the consciousness of something. The whole analysis of time-consciousness is steeped in the effort to show that retention – the still keeping in consciousness of something that is no more, but actually was – is not an act of reflection but, as the word beautifully says, 'retention': a retaining of something that tends to fade away and is constantly fading away. To this extent, what Sartre adopted is the good old phenomenological legacy. What obviously does not fit into this ancestral lineage of Sartre is Hegel. For, it is clear that, on this point, Hegel was a Fichtean and this means a Cartesian. Hegel always described reflection as merely a transformation of [116] immediate thinking or experiencing, a transformation that occurs through the objectification of an act. This is the secret of the experience of consciousness that his *Phenomenology of Spirit* describes.

So much for our first finding. We have here a great phenomenological legacy, which is characteristically lacking in the case of Hegel and this, perhaps precisely for this reason, reinforces the affinity between Sartre and German phenomenology. Then comes Heidegger – for Sartre naturally at the same time – and Kojève always stands in the background with Hegel. Heidegger posed the question of being anew. Suddenly, this becomes a central problem. What in Husserl were timid references to a formal ontology and material ontologies of the bodily world [*Leibwelt*] or of mathematics – whatever these may be – is transformed at once into the central question: what does being actually mean? Was this not what metaphysics asked? But had the tradition of metaphysics, from Aristotle onward, grasped this question in its real depth or had it rather obfuscated this question more than it had opened it? This is the well-known destruction of Greek ontology, which distinguishes Heidegger's radicality in the critique of the philosophy of consciousness.

How could Sartre now bring out a Hegelian motive by starting with a radicalized Heideggerean phenomenology? This is in fact what Sartre did. At first, he follows the good phenomenological tradition and thinks consciousness as intentionality. This was the final liberation from the ridiculous representations of consciousness as a box that contains our representations, so that we stand before the precarious question of how we move out of the box toward reality. This theory of consciousness is in fact replaced by a refinement of Brentano's theory and, as a matter of fact, by a return to the Greek conception of things. Consciousness is always already a consciousness of something. I remember a lecture by Heidegger in the lecture hall in Darmstadt in the early 1950s, in which he said that it was a mistake to say, 'I see that the door is there'. 'I' am 'there' when I see the door. What Scheler calls the 'ecstatic' of consciousness, the complete being-outside-of-oneself, appears also in Sartre in all its glory. But now something else emerges. Sartre understood what it means when Husserl asks: what is an object of perception? For example, I can only see this glass from my perspective and you from your perspective. I can turn it, but then again I see it only from my perspective – I do not see the back side – and the same for you. Husserl calls this the 'adumbration' [*Abschattung*] of the object of perception. The object continuously adumbrates itself. Husserl now claims that this is the only tenable sense of the Kantian theory of the thing in itself: what appears in this continuum of adumbrations. When this continuum of aspects presents itself in this way as a continuum, it means that this appearance is [117] the glass itself, and not some essence, a *noumenon* or something from the netherworld. My teacher Natorp said something similar: the thing in itself is nothing other than the infinite task of determining the object of knowledge.

From this neo-Kantian and phenomenological insight, Sartre infers the following: what is decisive in phenomenology is that a phenomenon is an appearance without anything behind it. Being is the being of the appearance itself. This is what he thinks must be interrogated when we pose with Heidegger the question of being. In fact, this is very Hegelian. It is well known that Hegel distinguishes in *The Science of Logic,* first, the logic of being and, then, the logic of the essence. Here, the essence is the truth of being and not something behind it. And when he places the concept beyond essence, the concrete and comprehensive instantiation [*Inbegriff*], this concrete instantiation is the unity of being and essence with absolutely nothing behind them. Sartre took this step too in his own way, without recognizing that it was already in Hegel. What is invoked in this way is not the metaphysics understood as a netherworld 'behind' the world of appearances. Being is itself there in its appearing, so to speak. I am convinced, by the way, that this was also what Plato himself meant, whereas Heidegger saw Plato as being only on the way toward metaphysics as ontotheology. In this regard, Sartre again recognized something in Hegel, namely that the universal is nothing other than the totality of what is concrete. This is what we know from Hegel's terminology as the being-in-and-for-itself. Sartre drew this out quite well from just an analysis of the phenomenon alone.

How have I continued my reading of Sartre? We had Husserl, then we had Hegel, and then Heidegger's question about being. Now I continue reading *Being and Nothingness* and say: what does all this mean? Is Sartre an Eleatic? For, it is indeed the being of Parmenides that Sartre describes; it is Parmenides right up to the way it is phrased. I do not know whether Sartre was fully aware of this, but he probably was. He speaks of a complete being in which there is, so to speak, no tear and no split and no negation. Of what is, one can only say that it is. This is being. This homogeneous sphere of being or this ball of being, as it is called in Parmenides' poem, appears in Sartre as the being-in-itself, the *être-en-soi.* It sounds as bad in French as it does in German. Sartre also reflects on this in-itself. In fact, he does not mean this. There is no 'itself' here. Being is not reflectively related to itself. Sartre here adopts a Hegelian expression. With this in-itself, he means, as he defines it, the presence [*Anwesenheit*] of being in beings. Being-in-itself has an 'in-itself' without being aware of it. Pretty much undetermined, as undetermined as when Plato says that things participate in the Idea either through imitation or representation or community, through mixing or interweaving or in any other way. It does not really matter to Plato [118]. What matters is only that we do not have a reifying, substantializing representation of 'Ideas'. The same goes for 'being' in Sartre.

Sartre here tried to import, via Heidegger, a Hegelian motive into Husserl's phenomenology. Now, it continues in a totally Eleatic manner. We know about Parmenides that he says: stay away from the path of nothingness or of the negative; it is a path not to be trodden. This is a tremendous vision with which Parmenides, as I see it, took the decisive step of the history of Western thought. He posed the question: what are you really thinking, you the great wise men of Miletus, when you say: in the beginning everything was water? What was there before? The nothing? Against this way of thinking I warn you. Sartre certainly does not question like an Eleatic, but like someone who re-effectuates the Eleatic thinking of being on his own, confirming once more the Greek beginning of the ontological question. However, one cannot be satisfied with this. At some point in time, something enters this closed ivory sphere of being, a tear, a tiny sliver of a 'not'. This is an expression of Sartre.[9] When it becomes poetic, it is mostly Sartre, not I. A tiny sliver of 'not' enters being. But from where? And how? Sartre saw something here. Clearly, he is a great writer and so his way of thinking is infused with rhetoric, obviously by another form of rhetoric than our goody two-shoes academic rhetoric in Germany. This is self-evident. However, he saw something that is correct. I mean that we as thinkers introduce the nothing into our ownmost experience. This is indeed what Manfred Frank has in mind when he sees links between Sartre and myself. Certainly, we are not talking here of direct influences, but of the same way of thematizing the question.

The puzzle of the question is indeed this: when the question is raised, every-thing is suddenly thrown into a tizzy. Is it so or not? If not so, then otherwise? Following Hegel, Sartre calls 'negativity' this 'sublation' [*Aufhebung*] of the being that is in-itself into the mere possible, a sublation that is present in any question. Negation is the irruption of the 'not'. The one being is no longer one. This over here is not that, over there. Unfortunately I cannot think without all the time taking my cues from the old stock of the Greek ways of questioning. Thus, I see here again a connection to the Greeks: there is already in Plato the beautiful joke, featuring Parmenides in a dialogue with his student Zeno, who shows with forty proofs that the 'many' does not exist, but only the 'one'. Plato had already seen this clearly and Zeno had already made efforts to show that the negation of the 'not' and the 'no' already implies an interrogation of something and thus a negativity [*Nichtigkeit*], a nihilation [*Nichtung*]. In French this is rendered in a marvelous way. If only Heidegger had been fortunate enough to think his views on the nothing that nihilates in French, Carnap would have lost the game. Recall how [119] Carnap bitterly complains that one cannot write the nothing and the 'not' on the blackboard. The French language can do that. It distinguishes the *rien* from the *néant*. Anyone who has a linguistic sensibility for French hears in *néant* the 'nihilating' [*das Nichten*]. The adverbial ending in *néant* evokes, by comparison to *rien*, the *néantisant*. The 'not' is the *néant néantisant*. What matters is that the experience of the 'not' and the experience of the 'nothing' do not only appear – as Carnap's symbolization consistently indicates – as the semantic character of a judgement. Here, one draws a line over or uses any other such conventional symbol and can say that this proposition, this position is hereby negated and there is absolutely no need for a negation that would be something that, as such, would still need a symbol. There is just this negating. Or are we dealing here with something other than 'propositions', than apophantic logic, than correctness and non-contradictoriness of propositional and argumentative sequences? This is what Sartre, perhaps inspired by Heidegger, demonstrated to us with admirable richness. He has in fact become a great anthropologist and social psychologist. That which nihilates [*das Nichtende*] is present in existence and is not just a matter of question and answer.

I recall that, in my earliest youth and unfortunately without the necessary conceptual capacity, I reflected upon what it means when something comes apart, when something breaks down. From time to time, something almost breaks down, but then nothing really happens. One day, though, it breaks down and then it is final. Here is where we should be able to see the metaphysical problem: this completely unintelligible fact that suddenly no reversibility is possible any longer. In our society, where we simply throw away what we do not need anymore [*Wegwerfgesellschaft*], we are slowly forgetting about this. I was brought up quite strictly at home and attempted to break things as little as possible. In any case, the example of fragility is not only mine, but also Sartre's. I apologize if it sounded as if it were mine. No, it was Sartre's. He distinguishes fragility among others as an example of this *force néantisante*, this nihilating force.

So far we can say: this is going remarkably well, we are close to Heidegger's 'What is Metaphysics?' and everything is in great shape. However, we cannot go that fast. For, Sartre remains a Cartesian. It is certainly true that he does not want to renew the narrowness of a concept of reflection, which derived from Descartes and ultimately from late scholastic logic, flowing thereafter into modern thought. Sartre in fact asked himself how this connection between being and nothingness actually looks like. Is this negating still not a nay-saying, even if there is no real saying, only a nay-doing [*Nein-Tun*] toward being? Is it not essentially the same as with consciousness, this hairline tear in being, through which the uniform sphere of being suddenly turns out to be brittle? Maybe it will shatter [**120**], maybe it will reduce to nothing. This capacity of the being-for-itself, this reflexivity of consciousness, which intends itself and intends all its intentions, representations, and thoughts, is perhaps like some sort of counter-world to the in-itself of the ivory sphere of being. Should we not take seriously the fact that this is the situation of human beings with regard to the constant, unreachable fixedness of the being-in-itself? One cannot negate being, Sartre says, which is full and round. However, in our being-for-itself of the being-in-itself, in our taking over of being, there are not only hairline tears; there are chasms, in which thinking goes astray and loses itself.

When we ask these questions with Sartre we arrive at the thesis that truly, in this being-for-itself, the ambiguity of consciousness spreads over everything. Nothing is spared. Sartre gives examples. He describes anxiety. Significantly he appeals to the Heideggerean concept or the Heideggerean illustration of anxiety as that which annihilates [*das Vernichtende*], but in a completely different sense than in Heidegger. Sartre describes very vividly how I am anxious because I may become dizzy on a steep mountain path. How I resolve to look away from the depth of the abyss as much as possible. He did not describe well how tempting it is to look into the abyss – and this is what is really demonic about vertigo. What makes us dizzy is in fact that we are drawn so irresistibly to that which offers no foothold anymore. However, this peculiarity was certainly familiar to the great psychologist that Sartre was – although in another context. I will in no way lecture him here, but only show that he describes anxiety in the same one-sided way that he describes insincerity. We say 'authenticity' and 'inauthenticity' for what in French is *mauvaise foi*. This does not correspond to our untruthfulness [*Verlogenheit*]. It is rather the fatal indistinguishability within which human beings linger at the margins of truth, used as they are to vacillating between sincerity and insincerity.

Sartre also treats the problem of time in a long essay. It would require a specific analysis to show how Sartre reworks the Husserlian, Heideggerean, Hegelian, even Schellingian motives into his chapter on temporality. Yet, we must concede that we have reached a caesura. From here on, the authentic Sartre begins, if I can put it this way. Everything up to this point, this Eleatism and its subtle splitting up through the modern concept of reflection and consciousness fascinated me at the time. However, the authentic Sartre, as evinced by his lifelong work, is naturally the one that arises at the point where we are no longer dealing with being-for-itself, but with being-for-the-other. It is here that the moralist of great style finds his voice. Here too, Sartre, first and foremost, critically examines his forerunners in order to ascertain their insufficiencies. Unfortunately for my own taste he was very unfair to Hegel, whom he probably read with Marx's eyes. He completely missed the significance [121] of the famous chapter on the dialectic of recognition in the *Phenomenology of Spirit*. In that chapter he accuses Hegel of falling back eventually into the formal idealism of 'I equals I'. This is indeed present in Hegel, but in order to be refuted. Is there anything in Hegel that is not to be refuted? The same also goes for Sartre. Is there anything in Sartre that is not to be refuted? Here too, the situation is different. This dialectic of recognition, this dialectic of self-consciousness, was once the theme of a piece I wrote[10] and I think I really got it right. The dialectic of self-consciousness shows that the one who works has the higher self-consciousness compared to the master, and not the lower. This is the absolutely clear function of the chapter in the context of the *Phenomenology of Spirit*. Sartre did not understand this at all. In this case, he follows his well-motivated rejection of formal idealism and did not see that Hegel himself had accomplished precisely this overcoming of formal idealism. Self-consciousness does not begin with these tricks of formal idealism à la Fichte: 'I equals I' and 'I am who I am' or the like, but with desire, with this vital feeling of oneself as the one who is hungry and satisfies oneself, with this magnificent moment of self-fulfilment in satisfying one's desires. Obviously, those who believe that they can ground their life, their self-consciousness on such a feeling of their selves fail to realize that human beings depend on another kind of validation than the constantly fleeting validation by a sense of satisfaction. This is the recognition by others that only free people can really provide, while slaves cannot dare anything and are for this reason resigned to their lot. We must be very primitive to draw self-consciousness from those who depend on us. Only when recognized by the free and the equal do we experience true validation. Hegel tried to show precisely this: the real self-consciousness of idealism grows out of this concrete experience of living consciousness and of its self-constitution in the dialectic of self-consciousness, and not from formal tricks.

Here we can perhaps omit Husserl. This is because Husserl's theory of inter-subjectivity is one of his shortcomings.[11] Although he himself was convinced that there was no deficiency in his thinking in this regard, intersubjectivity is really one of those points where Husserl always had a hard time doing justice to the phenomenon, given his monadological starting point. This is what I hear when Husserl describes it: I see there an extended something, white, a little bit pink and a little bit brown, then I bestow upon it an interpretation that renders the thing animate and say: there is a man over there. First, I supposedly see [122] that there is something white there and then I recognize in it one of my listeners. No, I really see the listeners and not the whiteness. This means that I am in fact on the same page as Sartre. Everybody knows enough of Sartre to know that he describes the phenomenon of the gaze in a truly genial manner in all its details: what goes on in the exchange of gazes and what happens when we feel that we are being observed, when we are demoted to the status of an object, so to speak, and no longer a partner in the exchange between an I and a you. Even the analyses of corporeality that unfold in this context, especially in the erotic sphere, have to do with the same motive: to make the other an object and to make oneself an object before the gaze of the other, to efface oneself before the other. Sartre described this dialectic wonderfully. These are the things for which one reads Sartre, even when one wants to know or knows little about philosophy.

Now, another word about Heidegger and the 'being-with'. It is hardly believable how differently this topic has been treated in the literature after Heidegger. I should perhaps have intervened in the debate on this topic. For a long time, I wanted to point out that the exchange of gazes and the exchange of words have something in common and that I have perhaps gone a step beyond Sartre, when I show what comes into being in the exchange of words: in a dialogue we have something more than what is realized for a moment in the exchange of gazes, so long as, of course, one does not feel that one is being observed, lapsing into an attitude of estrangement [*Entfremdung*] and alienation [*Verfremdung*]. It is significant that, in his analysis of the being-for-itself, Sartre devotes a rather laborious paragraph to the 'we'. He concedes: there are circumstances in which one really says 'we'. However, most of the time we do not really mean 'us'. We only speak like this as functionaries of society or representatives of public opinion. This is not yet the true conflict between me and you over the being-for-itself and the being-for-the other. It seems to me that Sartre did not treat the 'we' quite correctly. And Heidegger? There is something really interesting here. We all know that the chapter of *Being and Time* on the being-with is characterized, not without merit, as a sparse digression or an incidental paragraph. In *Being and Nothingness* 400 pages out of 750 are dedicated to the being-for-the-other and all that is connected to it, and 350 pages are dedicated to what I have talked about so far. If it is so visibly different in Sartre, it is due, one can say, to the great legacy of Hegel, which Sartre continues. However, it is precisely here that Sartre formally rejects the truly great legacy of Hegel, perhaps like Heidegger too, in that he ignored the extent to which the objective spirit is to be found in the totality of the experience of the other and of the life with others.

One generally criticizes – and this may be correct from an anthropological perspective – Heidegger for formulating his question of being too much [123] in terms of the extreme experience of the nothing as a being, of anxiety, in which nothing remains and where, as a result, the 'there' of beings shines in pure glory before its nothing. For his part, Sartre sees in the 'we', in the being-with of Heidegger, something surprisingly different. Not, as is commonly read, the weak point of Heidegger. We criticize Heidegger for not having noticed institutions, for not having appreciated the objective spirit, for having brushed aside the extent to which the positive life of society and genuine creativity are to be found in all these experiences of the 'we'. In Sartre we read, on the contrary, that the being-with of Heidegger is not a genuine 'we', but rather something like a team. In such a collective unconscious, in which all people say the same things, nobody is properly his or her own self. Heidegger indeed describes the 'They' in this manner, but with the 'being-with' he has in mind the authentic being-oneself and not the other side of our fallen existence. There are still pertinent points in the description of the being-with in Sartre. Yet, it remains remarkable how differently one can read these paragraphs by Heidegger. Most readers see Heidegger shirking away from genuine solidarities in those paragraphs. Sartre sees in it the refusal in the face of the genuine authenticity of the being-oneself. Being-with appears as a kind of party-membership of Dasein. Here, Sartre may have wrongly mixed the analyses of everydayness with the authenticity of Dasein. When we read Sartre's anthropology, we find that it is a conflict of one with the other, for the others or even against the others, for oneself or even against oneself. He even uses the sexual expressions of 'masochism' and 'sadism' to present the two extremes in our relationship to the other. In any case, it is a conflict and Sartre sets it in opposition to the pseudo-solidarity of a team. God knows why Heidegger would say such a thing! Because he supported fascist rabblerousing?

It is immediately clear that Sartre defends the self-certainty of consciousness against this Heideggerean dissolution of the being-ahead-of-oneself, against the mobility of the understanding of oneself in one's being. He quotes a sentence from Heidegger: 'Dasein is that being for whom its being is a concern', and says that here one should say 'consciousnesses' instead of *Dasein*.[12] Consciousness is that for which its being is a concern, to the extent that it makes a representation of everything else and thus negates everything. The Cartesian *cogito* eventually emerges again, not in the manner in which it is usual in the philosophy of science, for example, wherein one appeals to objectivity, certainty, criteria, and all of these fine devices; rather in the sense that for Sartre, as for Descartes, this is the only basis on which one can truly ensure the overcoming of selfhood and thus the possibility of an existence based on freedom.

Who ensures what? It seems to me that in both cases, the Sartrean counter-analysis of corporeality and his analysis of the other, the [124] evidence is stronger on the side of what I have pursued in many instances. The marvel of consciousness is not something ultimate and not something primordial. It is, as Heidegger has shown, a word that has come very late and suggests something very erroneous, as though it were a something. The Greeks were much cleverer when they said: consciousness is the place where all ideas gather. It is sensible for us to hold that this universe in which we are awake includes, at the same time, the unification of all our representations. The Cartesian starting point of the *cogito* cannot perhaps recognize the true puzzle of human existence, which consists precisely in this 'there', in this unfathomable distinction of human beings: the world is 'there' for human beings. This mystery cannot be described in any appropriate conceptuality, but it can always be shown negatively. The world drifts away when we drift into sleep; the world drifts away when we finally close our eyes.

13

Heidegger and Sociology: Bourdieu and Habermas (1979/1985)[1]

[46] The political ontology of Martin Heidegger[2]

In order to be able to evaluate the present book, one would actually need to be a sociologist. Someone belonging to the academic field of philosophy is anything but qualified for this task. For, the real goal of Bourdieu's investigation is precisely the sociological analysis and unmasking of that which happens in the field of philosophy. Philosophical readers, for their part, can only apprise themselves with astonishment or dismay that everything that they themselves deem to be questions of knowledge and truth and for the sake of which they do what they do in their academic field has, in the eyes of Bourdieu, the sociologist, really no proper content and object, and thus no possible truth. In Bourdieu's eyes, philosophy seems to represent a kind of intellectual pretence that has established itself as a respectable social institution. This also applies to the 'Heidegger case'. The fact that Heidegger's philosophy could have been successful in France for a while confronts Bourdieu with the task of a socio-logical and historical explanation of the phenomenon 'Heidegger' in its entirety, and this means: in the light of the critique of 'philosophy' in general.

In this situation it seems pointless to demonstrate to Bourdieu what he not only knows, but also what he prides himself in, namely this: his presentation of the situation in the specific field of philosophy, especially to the extent that it concerns his main theme of Heidegger, often sounds like a caricature in the eyes of one such philosophical reader. In so doing, Bourdieu does not make it easy on himself. On the contrary, he himself criticizes those who hastily mistake Heidegger's thought and mode of speaking for an alleged social and political ideology that would be expressed in it. Bourdieu sees in this manoeuvre a false reasoning 'that characterizes the whole sociology of cultural works, not only that of Adorno' (p. 76). Through the case of 'Heidegger' he would rather like [47] to study philosophical sublimation as such, which, as he writes, stems from the peculiarities of the philosophical field of production. It is on this basis that he would like, then, to uncover the political principles, which find expression in this field and unmask the philosophical alchemy that is practised in the process. This kind of language is already eloquent enough. The sociologist studies a field of production, but one that is of a very peculiar kind. He maintains that this field is about nothing other than alchemy. This means that, in his eyes, we do not find here, for example, a political will or thought that is translated into the true gold of philosophy, but rather the gullibility of a society that is exploited.

Such a sociological questioning necessarily makes a more general claim to validity, which should not hold only with regard to the emergence of Heideggerean thought. This claim may very well not be restricted just to the realm of philosophy. For, as I see it, it holds in a more all-encompassing sense for all forms of discourse that are encountered in the field of scholarly work and literary creation. As we know since Freud, there is always a tension between the interest people have in expressing themselves and a censorship that is exercised by the social field. This always leads to the formation of a compromise, as Bourdieu calls the activity of research [*Akt der Forschung*].[3] (In what follows, I will always resort to the German expressions, which are used in the translation from the French original, and would like particularly to emphasize the readability of Bernd Schwibs' translation, which is something completely uncommon.) Bourdieu envisages a fully universal task. He would like to discover everywhere in the realm of cultural speech the strategies of euphemization that mask the real political motivations. Besides philosophy, his focus is equally directed toward political science. By such strategies of euphemization, he certainly does not mean the conscious deception of the reader or deliberate strategic calculations. On the contrary, 'censorship is never more perfect and more invisible than in the case when all agents have nothing else to say than what they have been objectively authorized to say. In this case, they do not even need to be their own censor.'

Bourdieu would probably not dispute that this general mode of interrogation can also be applied to his own writing.[4] Obviously, the commercial mode of speaking, which he himself likes, is subject to similar conditions of 'imposition of form' [*Formgebung*], with the result that, in the best case scenario, the commercial mode of speaking approximates the ideal case he has just characterized, where one no longer needs to be one's own censor.

[48] What we have here is obviously a general principle of all discourses. We may be familiar with the way it functions, even if we do not consider ourselves to be experts in psychoanalysis or the critique of ideology. This is because this principle concerns nothing other than the way in which rhetoric produces its effects, which has been known to us from the earliest of times, particularly

through the theoretical analysis that Plato and Aristotle have dedicated to it. However, the ancient theory of rhetoric did not claim in the end that, through its theoretical analysis of the way public discourse functions, such discourse or such thinking could no longer lay claim to any relation to the truth. Rather, it is clear since Plato's *Phaedrus* that the adaptation of the arguments to the addressees and the targeting of their emotions, which is present in all public discourse, must be distinguished from the discourse's relationship to knowledge or truth. Perhaps, Bourdieu would be ready to admit this, insofar as it does not concern Heidegger's philosophy?

In these circumstances, one must leave aside the question of whether Heidegger's philosophy is really the purest form of pretence and read Bourdieu's investigations as the application of a general question that is characteristic of sociology. Every discourse possesses its social function and its moment of euphemization. This is true independently of the question of whether the contents of the discourse withstand criticism or not. In this sense, the chapter that bears the heading 'Pure Philosophy and the Zeitgeist' is an interesting socio-historical reading, which makes many convincing points. It would indeed be really absurd if a thinker like Heidegger with the kind of influence that even his bitterest rivals have to grant him, were not a particularly representative expression of the determinate societal situation and attitude of the time, whose censorship he would have experienced in himself. The analogies that Bourdieu draws between Heidegger and the literary representatives of the conservative revolution are rather really clear and convincingly elaborated. Heidegger himself had repeatedly given expression to this in the case of Ernst Jünger, but that was already the case with the huge success of Spengler's *The Decline of the West*. As Bourdieu explains, it is absolutely correct that the success of this book unsettled academic science to an unusual degree and provoked astounding reactions. There was not only the review by Eduard Meyer (in *Deutsche Literaturzeitung*)[5] that Bourdieu mentions – Meyer was one of the great mandarins, to use an expression dear to Bourdieu. There was also the special issue of *Logos,* which launched a full broadside against Spengler.[6] To this extent, Spengler has a peculiar symptomatic value.

Now, Bourdieu amalgamates the analysis of the conservative revolution [49], which he presents with the antipathy that he openly fosters against the academic university structure existing at the time in Germany. The result is that he is not always on target. It is certainly true that the German university system possessed a peculiar exclusivity and monopolistic position. Other avenues to literary success, as they existed in France, seldom played a role in the field of science in Germany. However, Bourdieu uses the expression 'academic proletariat' all too imprecisely. For the nineteenth century until the beginning of the First World War, this expression is not only skewed, but also plainly nonsensical. It is striking that Bourdieu here in a very strange way back-dates the situation and simply omits mentioning the economic causes, which led to the proletarization of the bourgeois middle-class in Germany after the First World War and made possible in the first place something like an academic proletariat. His interest clearly lies somewhere else. He wants to trace the common roots of the nation-alist [*völkisch*], elitist, reactionary ideas and see in them as early as possible the makings of the conservative revolution. This is informative enough and he is by and large convincing in what he takes from Fritz Ringer's book, *The Decline of the German Mandarins: The German Academic Community, 1890–1933*[7] as well as the one by George Mosse, *The Crisis of German Ideology: Intellectual Origins of the Third Reich.*[8]

However, for the reasons cited above, he somehow distorts the case of Spengler into a real caricature. He makes him sound like a poor mathematics teacher in Hamburg who was prevented from succeeding by the academic inbreeding at the university. Are these supposed to be the reasons for Spengler's life taking its course outside of the university? One may hold in very high esteem the unbridled imagination and the synthesizing energy of Spengler, the outsider. However, all of this still came with a congenital lack of criticism and self-control on his part, which was quite evident. I will not rule out that his attempt to take the university route ended in failure for these very reasons. His dissertation on Heraclitus must have really had a very tolerant director. Still, this misses the decisive point, namely that he viscerally despised the academic cursus and, full of self-confidence, preferred to buy his intellectual independence through the professional trade of a schoolmaster. Neither he nor the other conservative revolutionaries who are to be mentioned here really saw themselves as professors who had been hindered. Their self-confidence would have thoroughly rejected that idea.

Even the way in which Bourdieu tries to derive fascistic ideology from the attitude of exclusivity typical of the conservative German university has something skewed about it. His depiction of the fundamentally conservative mood of life in the German university is certainly appropriate. However, it is precisely because of this that the spokespersons and the academic disciples of the burgeoning [50] National Socialism belong to a completely different context. They had little to do with the academic proletariat of the post-war era, which was scraping a living at the university and in the editorial rooms. This is seen already in their enraged anti-intellectualism and the derisive scorn for pure science flaunted by these spokespersons. Bourdieu does not fail to mention this, but, in my view, does not see it in the right context. The tragedy of the Weimar Republic and Hitler's 'legal' power-grab rested precisely on the use of conservative ideology by resolute nihilism for its own purposes.

Incidentally, Bourdieu paints a very vivid picture of the kind and of the scope this conservative ideology had. This picture is presented not only by Spengler, but also most prominently by Ernst Jünger. It is obviously correct that the young Heidegger too, who dissociated himself from the Catholic Jesuit education he received in his youth, felt in many ways the appeal of these 'spokespersons of the Zeitgeist'. Bourdieu explains this correctly.

Bourdieu, then, immediately subjects Heidegger to a sociological analysis in portraying him as an intellectual of the first generation. The palpable anti-urban pathos that pervades Heidegger's bearing and behaviour is conducive to such a generalizing sociological and stylistical analysis. One can without question recognize quite a few things in such an analysis.

Yet, all of this again appears grotesquely distorted. This is obviously due to the methodological premises of Bourdieu's overall approach and only in the smallest part to his peculiar prejudices, such as the above-mentioned feelings that he harbours from the very outset against the German university-system or the incompetence that he manifests when it comes to philosophy. Perhaps, these specific prejudices themselves are not so specific if one asks what of university philosophy can be salvaged under his methodological premises. Bourdieu sees in such a philosophy nothing other than the result of inflated strategies of euphemization and is not in the least bit doubtful about the claim that one simply ought not to see philosophy otherwise than through the eyes of a social scientist, who reduces its tendencies to euphemization and its articulation to socio-political relationships.

There is very little left to argue about this, but the reader may be amazed by the kind of prejudicial slants of which Bourdieu is capable. He specifically furnishes us with an example of this, the context of what Heidegger says about 'solicitude' [*Fürsorge*] in *Being and Time*. Bourdieu not only sees this exposition of the whole lexical field of 'care' [*Sorge*] as pure alchemy. He even goes so far [51] as to opine in all earnestness that Heidegger artfully neutralizes and discusses away the social institutional character of solicitude, which is obviously for Bourdieu the only legitimate one. For Bourdieu solicitude is primarily an institution! In the second edition of his book, in which I read the French text for the first time, Bourdieu briefly touches upon my observation on the sense of 'solicitude'. From this, it appears that he really takes the institutional sense of the word for the 'usual sense' (*ordinaire*), classifying, by contrast, the sense that is natural to us, thus also the famous Heideggerean expression 'liberating solicitude' [*freigebende Fürsorge*], as an alchemy of words. (I easily grant that Heidegger's latter turn of phrase has a very ironic ring for me when I think of the 'Heideggerese' of the many students who have truly lost their freedom in the locutions of Heidegger.) For me, the idea that a word such as 'solicitude' should primarily designate an institution is in fact only a testament to 'sociological construction'.

Here is another example: one may possibly understand that Bourdieu succumbs to the common misunderstanding at the time and understands the distinction between authenticity and inauthenticity of Dasein, which is found in *Being and Time,* by giving it a positive and negative slant. Heidegger himself is certainly not innocent in this regard. However, Bourdieu confuses the dimensions here. He is beholden to the rhetorical staging that Heidegger provided to his philosophical questioning, but is completely blind to the philosophical questioning itself. This becomes easy to see when it comes to the distinction between the ontic and the ontological, namely, the so-called ontological difference. What Bourdieu makes out of it is simply amusing. What is, in his eyes, Heidegger's strategy of euphemization had obviously already started with Aristotle. It would have had more weight if Bourdieu himself had explicitly adopted this thesis.

Even his derivation of Heidegger's strategy from the tendency to assert himself over neo-Kantianism has something very amateurish about it. How does Bourdieu see the situation? Naturally, there was in Heidegger the tendency to assert himself over neo-Kantianism in the post-war era, which he shared with many others. One only has to think of the disbanding of the Marburg school or the turn of the southwest German school toward Hegel. What Bourdieu does not see and what causes him to fail fundamentally in understanding the stature of his object, is that Heidegger became Heidegger only because he, in contrast to all his contemporaries, was able to establish the connection between, on the one hand, the whole problematic of neo-Kantianism in Rickert as well as Natorp and Husserl, and, on the other, its background in Aristotelian metaphysics. It was Heidegger's great fortune, something that Bourdieu never mentions, that he [52] came into proximity with Husserl at the moment he fell out with the Catholic tradition of his philosophical origins. In Husserl, the problems of neo-Kantianism were worked out on an analytic level not found in classical neo-Kantianism. In this way, Husserl could act for the young Heidegger as a near perfect counterpart of almost equal rank to the analytic genius of Aristotle. In any case, Heidegger reached a level of conceptual ability and phenomeno-logical intuitive power that one would search for in vain in epigonal academism, which had for a long time dominated lecture halls. In contrast to this, it was completely secondary that Heidegger, before giving up his transcendental inter-pretation of his project, critically grappled with the neo-Kantian interpretation of Kant.

By the way, we should also note on this occasion how much Mrs. Cassirer was mistaken when she opined that Heidegger was particularly biased against Cohen. Along with the young Emil Lask and Georg Simmel, Hermann Cohen was the one thinker among the neo-Kantian philosophers for whom Heidegger had, without a doubt, the utmost respect and whom he never mistook for an academic epigone, the kind of figure against which he fought. The encounter with Cassirer in Davos still preserves something of that respect, even when the confrontation with Cassirer by the way aptly illustrates the distinction Bourdieu makes between intellectuals of the first and the second generation.

What Bourdieu says there is certainly correct not only about the awkward manner in which Heidegger presented himself in society, but also quite certainly correct about the peculiarity of his style, which had something rural, clumsy, and inelegant when measured from the standpoint of an urbanized taste. Again, it sounds simply comical when Bourdieu says of this intellectual of the first generation that he was not completely at home in the intellectual realm. The unbelievable freshness with which Heidegger approached the old questions and which obviously often carried him away in some violence, was, to put it mildly, the productive counterpoint of such 'insecurity'. Bourdieu would again see in this only examples of successful imposition of form [*Formgebung*]. For him, all this is a posturing and must be so. This follows from his presupposi-tions, for which he elects to give no account. When he entertains us with how many times Heidegger repeats expressions of the type 'original' and 'radical', this is not for him the expression of a real struggle of thought, as it spurs itself forward, but pure mystification. Adorno had limited the jargon of authenticity to the imitators of Heidegger. Bourdieu is free from such restraint. He has decided in advance and would have to stand by the claim that it is only jargon that clothes philosophy everywhere – at least since Aristotle.

Nevertheless, I would like to stress that Bourdieu's whole undertaking [53] has been fruitful in many respects. Heidegger's political 'aberration' in fact reveals itself, as Bourdieu shows, in the many stylistic undertones in the early Heidegger and, beyond that, in the style Heidegger adopted. This is Bourdieu's methodological procedure, which certainly has nothing to do with philosophy, but produces its own cache of knowledge. Yet, I repeat that this method, which bypasses the content of philosophy, could also be applied even to Aristotle, if we only had the historical knowledge at our disposal to see through this stylistical 'imposition of form'. [*Formgebung*]. In the end, I would also have to acknowledge that Bourdieu's 'interpretation' of the ontological difference is coherent from the perspective of the social sciences. This becomes clear to me when I read in the second edition that what is actually philosophically essential for Heidegger is 'l'essentiel impensé social'.[9] I would like to understand this, without any contradiction, as the 'strategy of euphemization' of the social scientist, for whom 'being' must remain an empty word. What an astounding convergence with Heidegger's thesis of the 'oblivion of being'!

Heidegger in the Thinking of Modernity[10]

In his Frankfurt Lectures, which he presented in book form under the title *The Philosophical Discourse of Modernity*, Jürgen Habermas undertakes the task of grounding in detail his relation to modernity and his critique of the cultural criticism of others, above all the neo-conservatives. He does this by offering a critical discussion of the leading figures in philosophy at that time. If we compare this discussion with his former presentation in *Knowledge and Interests*, what is striking at first is the observation that now, after Hegel, it is – and in quite a different measure – Nietzsche who is presented as a turning-point of modernity. He appears outright as the one who introduces postmodernity, heralds it, so to speak. The very beginning of *The Philosophical Discourse of Modernity* indicates this. The book begins with Hegel as the first philosopher who has raised the self-assurance of modernity to the central motive of his thought. This is well-justified. The later split in the Hegelian school into the left and the right shows how much Hegel could be seen as the first philosopher of his epoch, whose universalistic claims through their ambivalence invited, as it were, his successors to take political sides. Even if one speaks of a left and a right also in the case of Aristotle, as Ernst Bloch has done, it is in fact more an indirect confirmation of the exceptional case of Hegel. Now, Nietzsche appears in this new book as a second such figure. The title of a following chapter [54] is precisely 'The Entry into Postmodernity: Nietzsche as a Turning Point'. In this, we should first of all recognize the reflection of the French reception of Nietzsche, welcoming the fact that Derrida and Foucault are being treated here as leading thinkers. These thinkers have in fact opened up a new chapter in the history of the reception of Nietzsche in our time.

Alongside these French heirs to Nietzsche, Habermas now also includes Heidegger under this perspective. This is also fully justified when seen from the standpoint of Heidegger's later writings and the influence of his teachings, especially given the indirect influence that Heidegger himself had exercised on the French scene. This form of interpretation in which Habermas subjects his philosophical questions to the skewed gaze of sociology, seems to me to stand in a strange contradiction to the enduring influence of Nietzsche and Heidegger. Whoever proceeds from the assumption of the end of philosophy and, at best, pursues its evanescent form of appearance in the 'discourse of modernity', establishes a benchmark that must significantly truncate not only Hegel, but also Heidegger. It is true that we can see, for example with Derrida, that Heidegger's placement of Nietzsche in the history of metaphysics and in the beginning of its 'transformation' [*Verwindung*] is an effort doomed to failure. And yet, we do this so that we may, following Hegel, once more grant philosophy (instead of art or myth) the last word. It should cause us to ponder that, for half a century, Heidegger and, first of all naturally, Nietzsche have dominated the present through their philosophical power. In this regard, Heidegger in any case did not benefit from his *zeitgeist*, neither from fascism nor from post-fascism. It was certainly not his so-called mysticism about being or his so-called cultural critique that brought this about and also not his ambivalent and plurivocal transposition [*Umsetzung*] of Nietzsche in his late work. It seems to me that Habermas is in fact placing the cart before the horse when he wishes to detect what Heidegger has to say in the tone of his cultural critique or in the utopianism of his messianic eschatology and when Habermas ascribes these tendencies to Heidegger's essential philosophical achievement (to which Habermas, let it be said, devotes precise and serious analyses). For someone familiar with this issue, the situation is completely upside down when Habermas, following the lead of his own interests, makes Heidegger's late turn dependent on Nietzsche's influence and draws a parallel between Heidegger's turn and Nietzsche's inversion of Platonism, instead of doing the reverse and understanding the interest in Nietzsche from Heidegger himself and the turns in his own thinking.

Naturally, in the process, Heidegger comes out rather badly in Habermas. It is not for me and I do not really even find it new after Bourdieu or beneficial to discuss here the socio-political aspects and the contemporary historical self-staging of Heidegger. Whoever [55] has learned to measure Heidegger not from the standpoint of the discourse of modernity, but from the standpoint of the discourse of antiquity, sees him more in relation to the global development of European civilization, which first arose with Greek thought, and not only with modern enlightenment. Measuring Heidegger on the basis of the discourse of modernity almost seems like someone wanting to measure the philosophical achievement of Kant's *Critique of Judgment* on the basis of Kant's own artistic taste and critical judgement about art. Kant nevertheless remains groundbreaking for philosophical aesthetics. It is often indicative of the genius of thought that a humble and insufficient experience of the real world allows for genial insights. So it seems to me that Heidegger has fundamentally grasped more of the industrialized world of the present than most of those who possess a completely different degree of experience and knowledge of the world of technology. One can also wonder whether Heidegger has not understood the essence of technology better than the spokespersons of progress. I can only read with astonishment in Habermas that Heidegger's representations of art were determined by his preference for classical art. Habermas says this even though we now know of Heidegger's definite interest in Vincent van Gogh, Franz Marc, Paul Klee, Alberto Giacometti, Paul Celan and René Char.

The philosophical categorization of Heidegger that Habermas undertakes, thus, appears most peculiar to me. I have known for long now that Habermas reacts viscerally to the buzzword 'ontological', simply ignoring its phenomenological sense. Thus, he happens to see Scheler and Nicolai Hartmann, the scholastic revival of Thomism, and Christian Wolff together as 'ontological'. Heidegger's use of 'ontological' is completely inapplicable in this context. In Heidegger, the use of the word does in no way mean that he actually wants to renew the ontology of the Greeks. This is to turn things upside down. Here, semantic bias seems to have skewed Habermas's view. Habermas himself studied thoroughly the concept of consciousness in *Being and Time*. Thus, the so-called 'turn' should have appeared to him as arising from the inner difficulties of the young Heidegger's transcendental interpretation of his own project. Instead, Habermas wants to make fascism responsible for the discourse of the destiny of being! On this point, he dates the cause too late.

Instead, if one pays attention to Heidegger's philosophical-religious experiences, one could perceive there his turn away from the imperialism of the Catholic Church and his criticism of the academically educated bourgeoisie, which he encountered when he entered university life. In any case, one should not hastily relate the development of Heidegger's thinking to the events of his time and not underestimate so much the task he set for himself of freeing himself from the Christian influence of his youth and then from the transcendental interpretation of his project, to which he still adhered even in *Being and Time*. *Being and Time*, as I have often stressed, is only a mere stage [56] in Heidegger's path of thinking.[11] As a matter of fact, we only know of the introductory parts of *Being and Time*, which in the end were supposed to lead to the failed attempt culminating in 'Time and Being' and, thereby, in the radical temporalizing of 'being' and 'truth'.

For the alfresco painting of *Being and Time*, that is to say for the outlines of this huge painting, Heidegger obviously employed a Husserlian pattern. This pattern allowed him to present some of the results of his work in finished form and this had its effect and still has today. It is perfectly understandable that someone who is interested in social criticism and observes the colours of time rendered by *Being and Time*, sees Heidegger's massive *pathos* differently than his contemporaries and listeners. At times, it was no different for Heidegger himself, for example when he saw how protestant theology made use of *Being and Time*; or how the Rilke of the *Duino Elegies* was initially interpreted. In this, one sees what such a colour of time brings up. This is truly astounding for later observers. It is the same with the authenticity and inauthenticity of Dasein, whose origins go back to 1920, and which are not meant to present any moralistic appeal. In order to see this, we must really cast our glance elsewhere, when it comes to philosophy. Here, someone like Heidegger has long gone past Nietzsche, because Nietzsche comes up against the conceptuality of conventional metaphysics, and has even gone past Hegel, who too already wanted to overcome subjective idealism. Neither Nietzsche nor Hegel could really help Heidegger in his reflective distress when he was plagued by religion. He had rather to engage in his own intellectual attempt to overcome Greek ontology. All this cannot be derived from the spirit of the time and from fashionable cultural critique. For this, one must see the discourse of modernity in the context of the whole tradition of metaphysics, whose overcoming Hegel like Nietzsche and also Heidegger saw as their essential task. In his time, Bourdieu already attempted – and more correctly than Habermas – to make intelligible the origin of Heidegger's formative influences from the whole of German academic culture and to see him as the intellectual of the first generation, in his weaknesses, but also in his strengths. Bourdieu allows us in this case to recognize the limits of his own approach better than Habermas, because he can only see instrumentalizations and euphemizations in philosophical questioning.

In so doing, Bourdieu leaves Heidegger's philosophical intentions completely to the side, whether one may find them to be religiously motivated or philosophically risky. The social-scientific rejection of all philosophy by Bourdieu is explicit; the sociological recasting of philosophy by Habermas is not. [57] This explains the polemical keywords in both of these authors, such as mysticism about being or alchemy of words, both of which remain equally far from Heidegger's philosophical motivations. Heidegger's critiques of the Catholic theology of his time and of the dull formalism of neo-Kantian transcendental philosophy were not really the life-tasks that the young Heidegger had set for himself in his attempts at thinking. What helped him, in all his critique, was Husserl's phenomenological art of description and the fundamental historical orientation of Dilthey.

How could Heidegger make a contribution himself? His answer was 'destruction'. I must once again emphasize this, because the misunderstanding from other linguistic worlds has taken roots everywhere. For the German linguistic sensibility of those years, destruction in no way meant annihilation [*Zerstörung*], but resolute dismantling of the overlaying layers so that one could return from the dominant terminology to the original experience of thought. One encounters such experiences in no other place than in language as it is really spoken. This is how Heidegger saw himself sent back to the origin and the language of the Greeks, which, via the Latin of the ancients, of the Christian Middle Ages, and in its perpetuation in the forming of modern thought, has continued to operate in natural languages. This is why it is worth going back to original thought experiences, as Heidegger sought to recover them in Greek philosophy. In contrast to all claims to an original conceptuality, he used with predilection the expression 'formal indication' at the time. In doing so, he was following Kierkegaard, who understood himself as a religious writer without authority. We should also read along these lines the later Heidegger when he speaks the language of Nietzsche or Hölderlin. Otherwise, one lands in a mysticism about being.

14

Hermeneutics on the Trail (1994)[1]

[148] The topic of deconstruction certainly falls within the field of hermeneutics. It is just that we should not conceive of hermeneutics as any definite
method that characterizes some group of sciences in contrast to, say, the natural
sciences. Rather, hermeneutics describes the entire realm where human beings
come to an understanding with one another [*Verständingung*]. As a matter of
fact, in my own work it is not just the sciences that are the subject of discussion.
Derrida could very well say the same of deconstruction, namely, that he seeks
to overcome any restriction imposed by a method. This brings us together.
Nevertheless, it seems to me that we have not succeeded thus far in coming
to a mutual understanding between us. Coming to an understanding certainly
does not imply agreement [*Übereinstimmung*]. On the contrary, where people
are already in agreement, they do not need to come to an understanding. We
always reach or seek an understanding with respect to something determinate,
concerning which there is no complete agreement. In our encounters in Paris
and Heidelberg it seems to me that we have not yet found any common ground.
The history of the reception of our respective thinking obviously makes this
clear. From the side of the hermeneuticists, we have the accusation that Derrida
is trying to elude dialogue, whether out of a strategic intent or more or less
unconsciously. The deconstructivists, on the contrary, find that my own contributions, even what I had contributed at the time to the dialogue in Paris and
then reworked into an expanded version for publication,[2] represented no contribution at all to a dialogue with Derrida. Hermeneutic philosophy, they say, is
purely defensive and remains entirely within the framework of metaphysical
thinking. As a consequence, the view is that hermeneutic philosophy, at bottom,
means nothing for the concerns of deconstruction.

In philosophy we cannot in fact proceed in so peaceful and amicable a
manner, as if different ways of thinking could co-exist without any friction
between them. Everyone appeals to experiences that we all could have. We
would, thus, have to come to an understanding with one another over dissenting

opinions through probing questions and tested answers; in other words: through critical dialogue. Hermeneuticists will [149] certainly not dispute that they also know of *dissémination* and they will acknowledge that such a 'dissemination' is present in the way of suggestions, allusions, and overtones in any speech we have to deal with. They will only insist that what this all means is that thinking is, in any case, faced with a new task that invites a new understanding.

When I had presented my own project of a hermeneutic philosophy in 1960 and began to look at the world around me again, I stumbled upon two things that were important to me besides the works of the later Wittgenstein. The first thing was that I became acquainted with Paul Celan, in whose late work I began to immerse myself. The second is that Derrida's essay 'Ousia et grammē', in the festschrift for Beaufret,[3] fell into my hands along with his subsequent books from 1967, which I immediately studied. It then became completely obvious to me how Heidegger's critique of the dissimulation of the concept of being by metaphysics, which he elaborated in the footsteps of Husserl, was fully at work in Derrida. This was certainly the case for the onto-theology of Aristotle, according to which the sense of 'being' could be derived, as it were, from the highest being. I certainly had difficulties afterward with the form that Heidegger's critique of the Greek concept of being took in Derrida and how the motives of the late Heidegger led in Derrida from destruction to deconstruction, partly in a positive and partly in a critical transformation of these motives. I was particularly troubled by how Derrida applied his thought not just to metaphysical constructions, but also to literature, especially since I myself constantly focused on the common ground that nurtures both philosophy and poetry. Even in the works of Heidegger himself, I could often recognize only with difficulty what art and literature could say to me, even if I always found his recourse to such 'texts' very significant. As a matter of fact, both Derrida and Heidegger are rather interpreting themselves instead of what they mean to interpret on a particular occasion. This is no reason to pay less attention to what they do. Heidegger takes artistic expressions so seriously that he ventures to adapt them violently to his own way of thinking. He certainly does not remain stuck in the precincts of aesthetic neutrality. The same is true of the way Heidegger and also Derrida claim Nietzsche for themselves. Through the distinction of the present-at-hand, the ready-to-hand, and Dasein in *Being and Time*, Heidegger developed a critique of the understanding of being by metaphysics and this culminated over time in the rallying cry of 'the overcoming of metaphysics'. This is how Heidegger plunged into a confrontation with Nietzsche, whom he understood then as a kind of ultimate, radical consequence of metaphysics. Against this, in his later contributions, Heidegger tried [150] to prepare a new way of understanding being. For his part, Derrida too called upon Nietzsche. However, he saw in his *Gay Science* the one and only way to freedom and turned all of his efforts not to desist from the enormous task of deconstruction. In this regard, both Heidegger and Derrida were well aware of the fact that philosophy can never be completely extricated from its historical provenance in Western metaphysics. It is in this sense that Heidegger introduces his weaker formulation of a 'transformation [*Verwindung*] of metaphysics' and it is precisely in this transformation that Derrida grounds the inexorability of his deconstructive efforts. These are indeed clear similarities, which offer us food for thought.

This is why I myself have always repeatedly examined the relationship between destruction and deconstruction from out of my own hermeneutical efforts.[4] In fact, it is only in the form of a question that I can attempt to ascertain the common ground that perhaps supports us all.

What is so important about the concept of *présence*, which is the point of Derrida's questioning back, when he speaks about metaphysics? The determination of being as presence represents for Derrida the matrix, as it were, of the history of metaphysics. 'It could be shown', writes Derrida, 'that all the names for "grounding", "principle" or *centre* have always only designated the invariant features of a presence (*eidos, archē, telos, energeia, ousia* – essence, existence, substance, subject, *alētheia*, transcendentality, consciousness, God, human beings, etc.).'[5] As we know, Derrida brings all this together under the umbrella of logocentricism. This is in fact the question: are we dealing here with presence [*Präsenz*] in the real sense of *logos*? Could it be that we are dealing here only with something like propositional truth? If so, then one could at best recognize here the object of Heidegger's destruction. It is true that Derrida introduces the term 'logocentrism' under the influence of what Heidegger meant by his critique of Husserl. This also confirms how close Derrida's views come to the young Heidegger's ownmost task of liberating himself from the shackles of the neo-Kantian logic of judgements. When Heidegger began his studies of Kierkegaard and Aristotle, and focused on the metaphysics of Aristotle, what metaphysics really meant for him at that time was that 'being' is revealed in its beingness on the model of the highest being, the divine. This is also how I understood metaphysics at that time. This also accords with the fact that Heidegger, as he had done again in the appendix to his books on Nietzsche, saw in Plato the preparation toward the Aristotelian position on the question of being as being. However, as I see it now, this is not compelling in the case of

Plato himself, when we see how Plato tried to make dialectic ascend 'beyond being', as it were, and **[151]** toward the Good itself, the beautiful itself or the one itself. If anything, this rather applies more to Aristotle insofar as it is on the basis of his physics that he arrived at the doctrine of the mover-god, even if Heidegger himself, as his later interpretation of Aristotle's *Physics* B1 shows, was always already on the trail of the 'event' [*Ereignis*] of the 'there'.

Be it as it may, through a Christian reinterpretation, the late church doctrine has assimilated the metaphysics of Aristotle into its dogmatics as *theologia rationalis*,[6] whereas Plato in the Christian Middle Ages was always brushing slightly against the limits of heresy.

Now, it is clear that the whole movement of thought of the Greeks does not at all culminate in the Aristotelian doctrine of the first mover. It is rather noteworthy that Heidegger's new appropriation of Aristotle does not start with Aristotle's metaphysics, but with his rhetoric and ethics. In particular, the doctrine of practical knowledge assumed a fundamental significance for Heidegger's own way and it is precisely on this point that Heidegger to a large extent opened the way for me. In fact, he would even have done better if he had appealed to Plato's explicit critique of the logocentrism of metaphysics, which is presented in the excursus of the seventh letter. There we find the well-known critical considerations occasioned by a writing about Plato's teaching, which had been presented at the court of the tyrant Dionysius. On this occasion, as we know, Plato composes a finely crafted statement about the question of how it is at all possible to communicate thoughts to others and how thinking can be taught.[7] It is in this context that the logical definition is also explicitly broached. Such a definition would be as unsatisfactory as the designation or the mere illustration of things. For, even what is communicated in these ways and what is operative in all thinking – and obviously never adequately expressible – takes shape in the soul, becoming knowledge and correct opinion, and finally acquiring a share in the *nous*. All of these are still ways of communicating the thing itself and, as such, they remain embedded in and subordinate to the liveliness [*Lebendigkeit*] of the dialogue. This is the decisive point: it is not through written means alone, but in fact only in dialogue that sparks manage to fly.

Thus, it is no accident that Plato, in view of the liveliness of the dialogue, calls the path of his own thinking 'dialectic'. In the *Republic*, in the education programme for the future rulers, dialectic is expressly required as a step over and above mathematics. Dialectic is also what presents itself in the play of ideas unfolding in the Platonic dialogues. Dialectic is not meant to be a mere critical refutation of arguments and is not supposed **[152]** to consist in the mere technique of argumentation. Rather, it leads the others, the partners in the dialogue, toward the recognition of their ignorance, bringing them to their own thought. To that extent, dialectic has a mere propaedeutic function, perhaps even something like the art that is represented in such a bewildering manner in the Platonic dialogue *Parmenides*. It is difficult to categorize all of this under the common concept of 'metaphysical thinking'. However, if, beginning with Aristotelian physics, we turn to the principles (*Archai*) and move beyond the *logos,* that is to say: toward the *nous*, then this new dimension could very well be called a step toward metaphysics. Insofar as, now, in this metaphysics, the highest *archē* as the first mover is called 'the divine' and this same *archē* is conceived of as pure entelechy, this step toward *nous* acquires a new mode of access. From the perspective of folk religion, this could be understood as the divine in that it can be reached by moving beyond physics. Yet, what can 'metaphysics' really mean in Plato? The 'step beyond', which Plato has in mind (*Rep.* 509 b9) and which finds its expression in transcendence, is literally called a step over and beyond being, toward 'the beyond of being'. Perhaps, Derrida should envisage what he calls metaphysical thinking more from the standpoint of this transcendence than from the standpoint of Aristotle's determinations, which have been rigidly codified as 'substance' or as *essentia*.

I

If one turns back toward Derrida, after this conceptual and historical clarification of what metaphysics in fact is and how it was wrested free from Greek dialectic by logic, one comes closer to what Derrida himself has in mind when he creatively coins the term *différance*. He takes his point of departure from the concept of the sign and how, in every sign, there is a moving-beyond itself. No sign really points only to itself. We must thus ask how Derrida thinks that he can avoid logocentrism when taking such a point of departure. One could expect that the role of structuralism in the thought of French philosophy and the concept of sign, which goes back to its American roots, and everything Derrida has in mind as phonocentrism continued to let the concept of being of metaphysics play its determining role. This is why I wonder whether we have not here hit upon the limits of that community, which could be called 'phenomenology' and which, as phenomenology, is critically directed against all construction. Heidegger already received this impetus from Husserl and passed it on to us in order that we think precisely against that which Derrida calls 'logocentrism'. One only needs to understand the real target of Derrida's critique of Husserl **[153]** when he believes he can identify the dominance of presence not only in *logos*, but also in the voice, through the 'announcement' [*Kundgabe*] that accompanies it. In the end, we will see, following Derrida, that the voice is here a *voix pensée*, a voice that is thought, just as *écriture* is also only a writing that is thought.

From this I draw the following consequence: both voice and writing are in truth inseparable from reading. What would writing be without reading and what would reading be without writing – and without – what is perhaps silent – intonation and articulation? We should only make sure not to be led astray by the manner in which Husserl, in his battle against psychologism, elaborated the ideal unity of meaning. It would be better to listen with French ears. In French, one normally translates 'meaning' [*Bedeutung*] by 'wanting to say' (*vouloir dire*). This is an expression that apparently pulls the rug from under the identity of meaning [*Bedeutung*]. In fact, in 'wanting to say' there resonates the fact that we can never completely say what we wanted to say. There are strong pre-figurations [*Vorprägungen*] that have formed us beforehand, in our speaking as well as our thinking. From the very first words we utter, we are entangled in the whole play of language. In this regard, Heidegger points out what we have all experienced when he says: 'Language speaks.' In the French expression [*vouloir dire*], this is even clearer. It expresses the mere coming close to sense and simply the closeness to sense. What is 'sense' other than that which gives direction and is in this regard determining? Heidegger's critique of metaphysics as well as Derrida's programme of deconstruction must themselves recognize the *differenz* and *différance* that lie in *vouloir-dire*. None of us can simply reflect ourselves out of the mode of thinking in which we have been formed. Even when we come increasingly into contact with the languages and worlds of other cultures, it is first and foremost a gain for ourselves. We are our provenance [*Herkunft*] and we are at home in our mother tongue, which thinks with us.

When Heidegger began his teaching career as Husserl's successor in Freiburg, his inaugural lecture posed a question, which, as any authentic question, leaves something open: 'What is metaphysics?' This was certainly not supposed to be a new pledge of allegiance to metaphysics. Rather, the question may be better understood as: what is truly metaphysics in contradistinction to what metaphysics thinks itself to be? When the question asks about being, it places before itself the entirety of beings, distorting perhaps in the process the very thinking of being – precisely the being about which it asks. Perhaps, one must say for this reason – and this is to be considered also in relation to other cultural worlds – that 'philosophy' can never exist without metaphysics. Philosophy is perhaps only philosophy after it has left metaphysical thinking and propositional logic behind. On this way things are always underway, from Plato's *anamnēsis* to Hegel's logic. In the singularity of 'concept' and 'category', philosophy runs through the whole of the memory that is continually determining itself further and ceaselessly turning back to itself. [154] Heidegger speaks of the mere preparation of the question of being because he always perceives in language and thinking the domination of the understanding of being as entering into presence [*Anwesenheit*] and presence [*Präsenz*]. This also holds true for Nietzsche, as it powerfully comes to the light of day in Heidegger's life long struggle with him.

Heidegger's fundamental ontology, as we can label *Being and Time*, was certainly not to be his last word. Very soon, he did not just leave behind the transcendental interpretation he had of his own project. What followed was a whole series of paths and forest paths [*Holzwege*]. Indeed, Heidegger's own development teaches us how his attempts at thinking are burdened more and more intensely by the distress about language. By this, I certainly do not mean to say that Heidegger was then ready to envisage the path of deconstruction as his ultimate goal. Are there really no other ways to overcome Aristotelian substance metaphysics or even its ultimate completion in Hegel's absolute knowledge than by giving up all conceptual thinking or the *logos* altogether?

What in fact is *logos*? One should certainly not underestimate the fact that already the Socratic-Platonic flight into the *logoi* represents a turn that prepared metaphysics as well as the logic of conceptual definition and of demonstration. Still, is the *logos* not something different? What does *logos* mean in Heraclitus, in Socratic ignorance, in Plato's dialectic? What does the *logos spermatikos* of the Stoics mean and even the other *logos* of the Gospel of John? Here *logos* has completely different dimensions. These dimensions have been better at paving the way for how the New Testament thinks of incarnation than the renewal of Aristotle by the late medieval metaphysics – to say nothing of its modern, post-Kantian death throes. Thus, Heidegger (and whoever followed him) could really turn critically toward the tradition of metaphysics in order to destroy the traditional understanding of being as found in logic and metaphysics. Now, I wonder: does it not generally have to be the case that thinking always has to ask whether the words and concepts, in which it operates, in all the multiplicity of their dissemination, do not always come together again into a coherent configuration of sense? To this question, Derrida would perhaps reply with some hesitation by saying that this is again the logocentrism of our dominant metaphysical tradition. Does he not himself understand Heidegger's ontological difference as rupture [*Bruch*], as opening, as *différance*?

What I mean is that, even for Derrida, the unveiling of ruptures implies a further thinking. His deconstruction can never be taken as an interpretation of a text. He would be the first to see in such a manoeuvre a complete misunderstanding. However, the violence of the rupture indeed ultimately points to an inner composition [*Gefüge*], certainly not in the manner of a propositional truth and not as a system of philosophy. Violent treatments of texts justify themselves [155] only in such instances where a view is open for new horizons – and this can certainly happen for those who think.

It is difficult to think along and think ahead in a linguistic realm that is foreign, not only in the German linguistic realm, but also in the Heideggerian one. One senses in Derrida, especially in his earlier texts, the continued influence of Husserl, but also the objectivizing tendency of structuralism. Here a philosophical bedrock is illuminated. In structuralism we have the logic of the mythical world. However, no Greek has ever meant such a logic or even had a clue about it. This logic shimmers through by way of the strangest transmission, in Levi-Strauss or in Foucault or even already in the linguistic theory of de Saussure. Thus, it is like a step toward a new enlightenment. Doubtless, Derrida also wanted to go further along Husserl's way and, in so doing, radicalized him. Then, he perceived in the late Heidegger and Heidegger's confrontation with Nietzsche the consequences this had for his own way of thinking. Nonetheless, in Derrida as well as in Heidegger, each in his own way, metaphysics hardly ever remains a counter-position that is really completely tenable. It is not possible to speak differently from the way one thinks. The same also goes for me when I now, for example, claim to recognize in the Derridean conceptual constructions, such as *dissémination* and *différance*, the consciousness exposed to the effects of history [*wirkungsgeschichtliches Bewußtsein*] or the fusion of horizons. Heidegger certainly took issue with my use of the word 'consciousness'. In truth, 'the consciousness exposed to the effects of history' was only a provisional expression that was meant to emphasize the temporality of being. What I mean becomes clearer when I speak of the 'dimension of language' [*Sprachlichkeit*] in which the Christian tradition of the *verbum interius*[8] shines through. Here too we have a kind of quasi-transcendental condition of possibility, which is more a condition of impossibility, as incarnation represents a condition of impossibility for human understanding. I now try to further Heidegger's 'transformation' [*Verwindung*] of metaphysics in a phenomenological style and to verify it by using the dialectic of question and answer. This means, however, that we take our point of departure in the dialogue. It is here that *différance* is effectuated, by means of which the alterity of the true is brought to life in the form of question and answer. In this dialectic of question and answer, there is a constant going-beyond. It may be that something unsaid speaks alongside in the question as well as in the answer and can be deconstructively unveiled. However, this speaking alongside does not begin only when it is unveiled. In fact, then, it may no longer speak. In a dialogue there is no rupture, even if new points of view are constantly introducing themselves or new questions and answers are constantly being voiced, which repeatedly put everything out of joint. Despite all this, we are always edging closer. We begin to understand, even when we have no idea where the conversation is leading us.

Certainly, there is a good reason, in the case of philosophy, to say about the conceptual language of metaphysics that we always [156] fall back into it. We only should not think of this as though philosophical concepts were available in some warehouse to be simply hauled out from there. When we are thinking in concepts the situation is rather not as different as when we are using language. When using language, it is also the case that no one can initiate a new use of language. Rather, the use of language initiates itself constitutes itself in the life of the language, until it has acquired a fixed status. Conceptual thinking is always found with blurry edges, as Wittgenstein said. This is why we should follow the semantic life of language and this means: go back to the point where the concept emerges out of speaking itself, out of the 'situatedness in life' [*Sitz im Leben*]. This happens, for example, in Heidegger's destruction as a laying-bare. Deconstruction is in fact not so far removed from this. Indeed, construction is explicitly found in the term 'deconstruction'. Even deconstruction instigates the break with the constructive constraints by means of which language pulls the strings of thinking. The common goal is always to break the conventions of discourse and thinking, and to rip open new horizons. This was the rallying cry of phenomenology: 'Back to the things themselves!' This can happen in very drastic ways. For example, a single word could suddenly turn out to have a different meaning. What was familiar falls apart, but precisely through this, new connections come into view. Ultimately, this is the case any time we have a good idea: the idea dawns on us in the course of thinking in such a way that the entire direction of thought changes. Precisely for this reason, it seems to me that, when we are thinking, no matter how vaguely, a new goal is always in the offing.

In any case one would not call upon Heidegger's laying-bare of the Greek understanding of being, if his only concern was to clear off the Latin equivalents of Greek philosophy, which have come to be used as concepts, such as, for example, *essentia*, subject or substance. This is only the first necessary step. What matters is rather that the sense of the Greek concepts and all the concepts of philosophy that are still speaking and relevant are enriched through their close proximity to language. The same can happen in our own mother tongue: a frozen concept can be enriched, for example, when Heidegger understands being as presencing [*Anwesen*], thereby exposing 'being' [*Sein*] as a verb (or when he simply writes 'beyng' [*Seyn*] in its place). This recourse to language is based precisely on the fact that, in the usage of a word, there lies hidden a wordless experience that is always embedded in the thinking of the word. Of course, thinking can also get entangled in *aporiai*, as Kant shows in his transcendental dialectic. However, it can also be the case that, as in the Greek understanding of the world, a wordless experience, on its own, forces itself into the concept. Then, for those who think Greek, truth dawns on them like an alternate world in the suddenness of a rupture or a flash. When a new word forces a new thought, it is like an event [*Ereignis*], and language often does this effortlessly, when it finds its words. If a real rupture is demanded of thinking, then, by contrast, everything comes [157] crashing down, as when Heidegger, for example, reverses the title 'What is called thinking?' to 'What calls for thinking?' In such a reversal, something fades away and something new arises.

Thus, between deconstructivism and hermeneutics as a philosophy, there exist agreements that should lead us further. Ultimately, both have a common point of departure, namely, the critique opened by Heidegger of this forgotten survival of Greek ontology. As the late Heidegger showed in 'The Age of the World Picture', this philosophical critique also includes modern science, which is grounded on the concepts of method and objectivity. The parallel tones in Heidegger's slogan of destruction and Derrida's slogan of deconstruction are unmistakable. Obviously, the concept of metaphysics, with which Derrida works, as I tried to show, needs to be carefully circumscribed. At bottom, metaphysics for Derrida is nothing Greek. For him, it is what has been associated with the word 'metaphysics' since Kant's *Critique of Pure Reason*. This is what Derrida always has in the mind, in his efforts at deconstructing dialectic: what neo-Kantianism called 'dogmatic metaphysics'. Even in Derrida's language, we can observe how his theory of signs encroaches upon the language of metaphysics, for example when a distinction is made with respect to signs between the sensible and the intelligible realm. However, here is the decisive point: for Kant the critique of the metaphysics of 'pure' concepts undergoes determining limitations from the side of practical reason. The *Critique of Pure Reason* does not wish somehow to prove freedom or, as metaphysics, simply to find support in physics. Rather, we have to build upon the rational fact of freedom. Only as a metaphysics of morals is metaphysics possible – 'at the limits of pure reason' – as Natorp liked to say.

Here, we are far away from the original experience that has shaped the conceptual language of philosophy since Parmenides, Plato, Aristotle, and the re-appropriation of Greek thinking at the beginning of Christianity. It is this experience, along with the nominalism of modernity, that has established the concept of science.

Derrida's works offer particular difficulties for the understanding in that he also applies the dismantling [*Abbau*] of all constructions to himself. From this it follows that, were Derrida himself to undertake the attempt to put his theoretical works into a line of thought, so to speak, he would, it seems, be threatened in turn by a fallback into metaphysical thinking. Yet, he cannot avoid being himself, the one who defends now this and now that view. Thus, one is not only justified, but even forced to persuade Derrida of his own identity so that he can become a partner in a dialogue at all. The identity that the partner in the dialogue has [158] is in fact no rigidly established identity and, as such, absolutely not explicit. It is simply this: a partner reacts to another in a dialogue. In the end, we will always have to insist that the *logos* is not a monologue and that any thinking is a dialogue with oneself and with others.

It seems to me that there lies a particular difficulty in the critique of Husserl, which Derrida had put forward under the title *Voice and Phenomenon*.[9] This sounds astonishing. In an earlier time, as young people and students of Heidegger, long before *Being and Time*, we tried our hand at critiquing Husserl. We felt much closer at the time to Wilhelm von Humboldt and his rudiments of the philosophy of language than to the Husserlian theory of meaning in the *Logical Investigations*. However, at the time we could still not make anything clear out of our feeling of estrangement. Even today my understanding is marred by difficulties, as I look back at Derrida's critique of Husserl. The role that Derrida's critique of Husserl comes to assign to the voice still sounds very peculiar to me. Husserl is much more a mathematician, who transposes into his theory of meaning the ontological sense [*Seinssinn*] of that ideal being that mathematics takes as its object. This had incited us earlier to summon Humboldt's philosophy of language against Husserl. Now, we feel that we suddenly recognize Heidegger's own critique of Husserl in Derrida's critique. Heidegger had taken the masterpiece of Husserlian phenomenological analysis, his treatise on time-consciousness, as the point of departure for his critique. Starting with his concept of Dasein, facticity and futuralness [*Zukünftigkeit*], the ontological force of Heidegger's starting point pulled the rug from underneath the concept of consciousness. How could one find a way from there to Derrida who turns to the concepts of sign and trace?

Even more strongly than our idealistic and phenomenological tradition, to which Derrida belongs, what appears essential in the works of Derrida is the French style of literary criticism. We should not want to understand Derrida only from the standpoint of Husserl and Heidegger. We must also see him from the standpoint of his discussion of the theory of signs and structuralism. This too is a critical discussion. However, as I already indicated, even what is criticized continues to have an effect on the critic, like an unacknowledged presupposition. Derrida speaks of the infinite web of all signs and all references to other things, as if he were a distant observer. This is truly the language of a metaphysics based on nominalism and it can be illustrated in the modern sciences. Think of the gigantic research area before which molecular chemistry finds itself, when, in its research into an incalculable multiplicity of possible connections, it looks for those that are verified experimentally. Now, are we ever the researchers of the universal semiotic world, of which Derrida speaks? We [159] are, rather, already in the midst of it. Without an overview of the whole, we must pursue one trace or another. Thus, for long stretches of time, we do not know whether we are on the way toward the goal that awaits us or whether we have strayed into errant ways. Where should we hope to find an answer? We only have to think of where the traces of the path, the traces of a text, the proclamations of an oracle, the play of fantasy or poetic inspirations may lead us. Paul Celan called poetic language 'multi-faceted' [*vielstellig*]: it leaves many ways open. Yet, at the same time Celan demands from the reader of his poems the 'correct' understanding and for this he advises: 'Just keep reading again and again!' If the proclamations of the oracle are ambiguous, then God is playing with humans. When poets write their hermetically meandering verses, they trust the impalpable nature of their way of weaving sound and sense together and this weave expresses itself in the execution it so prescribes.

II

One understands why Derrida, given his point of departure, wants to grant writing [*Schrift*] and the dimension of what is written [*Schriftlichkeit*] a position of priority. The breath of solitude drifts over all that is written. We have also known for a long time that the relationship between language and writing should not be understood as a relation between something that is given as primary and something that is given as secondary. This much is clear: writing is not the copy of the voice. To the contrary, writing presupposes that one lends voice to what is read. The capacity that language has to be written is thus not a secondary phenomenon. To this extent, it is also significant and at the same time natural that there is really no phonetic writing. The deeper commonality lies ultimately already in the concept of *logos* – certainly not in propositional logic. The primordial meaning of *logos* is, as Heidegger had indeed underlined, reading [*Lesen*], the gathering-together proper to 'harvesting' [*Lese*]. This is why my hermeneutic efforts gravitate toward the concept of reading.[10] In this sense, I fail to see in Derrida the acknowledgement that writing when being read is as vocal as actually spoken language.

What I mean is that, in reading, there is much that points to the dimension of language [*Sprachlichkeit*] as such. Just as the voice becomes articulated as the speaking voice – perhaps even when one only reads without making a sound – in the same way the dimension of what is written, for example with the alphabet, is clearly an articulation of a high level of complexity. It is clear that the voice, which the writer or reader 'hears', reaches an even higher level of articulation than all forms of writing. There are, to be sure, still many other signs, gestures, hints, and traces. Certainly, one can go so far as to say that everything that manifests itself is a sign, in the way Goethe turns the concept of the **[160]** symbolic into something universal. Anything that manifests itself necessarily differentiates itself, in the process, from another thing that manifests itself. It separates itself from another thing just as it relates to that other thing precisely through the separation. This is indeed correct. Such a view from all sides [*Allseitigkeit*] is, however, reserved for the metaphysical concept of God. For us there is only multi-facetedness [*Vielstelligkeit*] and plurivocity [*Mehrdeutigkeit*]. In fact, Derrida was right ultimately to replace the concept of sign with that of the trace. Paul Celan once said: 'Plurivocity accounts for the fact that we see things in neatly cut facets, which show the thing from different angles, in multiple "refractions" and "sections", which are, in no way, just "appearances". I aspire through language to depict at least the sections from the spectral analysis of things, to show them at once in *several* aspects and in their intersections with other things: with neighboring things, subsequent things, opposite things. Because I am unfortunately not in the position to show things from all sides [*allseitig*].'[11]

We understand Celan's ironic regret and we also grasp why Derrida prefers the concept of 'trace'. He thereby frees himself, on the one hand, from all mathematical combinatorics and, on the other, from being entirely limited to the intentional concept of sign. Traces are, indeed, not meant and intended as such, but left behind. This increases, so to speak, their ontological worth. We are not faced here with some random indeterminacy. When a trace is found, one is pointed in a direction – and thus also bound to follow, as in the case of written documents that have been left behind.

In what way is a trace more than what the sign is? The answer seems to me simple: any trace points in a direction and this means: for those who are already on the way and looking for their way. I am certainly not sure that I am adopting Derrida's use of this concept of 'trace' in the sense in which he means it. One can also detect wholly other aspects in the concept of trace. For example, concerning the trace, Levinas rather stresses that the trace is a vanishing trace, like a disappearance into the void, presenting, so to speak, a mute testimony that something has been left behind. It is like the features of pain and suffering that are etched on the face, as traces of a life lived. Such traces are not meant to recall anything. This is the very face, in which the other is encountered, and it is for us always the completely other, so that here our understanding has to remain silent. This is what the trace of the other means in Levinas. The example shows how multi-faceted a word is and how much of its meaning is drawn from its context. What we have here is not a blunt opposition in the meaning of a word. In both cases a trace is what has been left behind. Yet, the encounter with the face points **[161]** in a completely different direction from the connection between speaking and writing, which is the focus of Derrida. In Derrida it sometimes sounds as though the trace (*trace*) is a violent inscription, like an engram that sinks into memory and yet still remains. Often, the trace is transposed into being used as a sign. Then, we only see signs as in need of understanding.

Those who find a trace also know well that something was there and, as it were, has left something behind. Still, they do not just take note of this. They begin from here to search and ask where the trace leads. Only for those who are on the way and search for the right way does the trace stand in connection to searching and tracking [*Spuren*], which begin with the finding of the trace. When a trace is found, we acquire a first direction and it opens onto something. Yet, where the trace will lead is open. We let ourselves be led. We strive not to lose the trace and to stay the course. If we lose the trace we lose our way. Then, we have gone astray and do not know how to continue. As a result, we must search anew for the trace and find it again. Ultimately, there develops around the trace, if it takes the place of a sign, a field of actions of a completely unique kind. The trace constitutes itself, as it were. When it is more often travelled, it becomes a path. Obviously, where the path leads can be totally uncertain. Those who look for the path and finally try one can be on the wrong track. They do not arrive where they really wanted to. Unless they have 'fallen' into the right way.

Now, it is clear that in Derrida it is *écriture* – writing – that plays the role of the trace. The individual signs, which constitute writing, are determined by conventions. When writing is legible, then we have the emergence of a text and it is like a sense-bestowing event. The written signs as such have absolutely as little sense as individual 'words' as such. The sense only emerges when the sense dawns on us, only when we read the whole of the writing and understand it. Then, we will find the right intonation if we really want to continue reading with understanding.

We all know how the evidence for the correctly understood sense is constructed. It goes through several stages, through the deciphering of the individual letters, the correct articulation of the word that is formed and, ultimately, through something like the gathering of the whole, in which the plurality of the signs is grasped together and understood. Then, we immerse ourselves in reading. It is rightly called 'concentration'. We are truly directed into a centre from which the whole falls into place as a sensible arrangement. It is also said then that we are captivated by the reading. We just simply cannot free ourselves from it, at least as long as everything makes sense. We refuse to put the book down because we are really in it in the process of understanding.

[162] In this description we recognize the more general description of what happens when any trace is followed. Readers too are on the way. Many things may occur to them when reading; they may follow their own thoughts and yet they ultimately follow the way that the text prescribes. It is like a dialogue with another person. The text is indeed encountered by us as another person and we try to get closer to it. We try this or that. We have new ideas. The same is often the case with a dialogue: the dialogue literally lives off unforeseen ideas, which take the dialogue in a new direction. The dialogue is indeed no well-crafted treatise. Yet, we try to give the dialogue a direction. We pose a question. Perhaps we understand from the answer what the other person understood or meant. We can only answer insofar as we have understood the other. Otherwise, we speak past each other. Thus, there is a real dialogue only when it constantly leads into the open of a possible continuation. The answer of the other can be surprising. This puts us before a new openness, in which we face something questionable. The possible answers are numerous. The dialogue moves forward and one has the feeling of being on the right track and of getting closer. It is again really like looking for traces. We can come back to something. We pick up

the trace when we have found it again. Even for those who have lost their way, there is, in fact, not just one trace that can be followed. Traces can cross each other. Traces can vanish and come to an end, pointing into a distance for which we remain without a direction. This is something we also know in a dialogue, when there are senseless answers, or when reading a text we come across an incomprehensible development. We lose direction and give up.

Here, we can see the puzzling essence of the question. Questions impose themselves. One must pose questions, because they pose themselves and because the progress of understanding has come to a halt. The secret of the question is truly the wonder of thinking. One knows that to think is to draw distinctions. This means precisely that we have before our eyes one member of the distinction as well as the other. This happens when we ask questions. The question places us before the decision between possibilities. Given the plentitude of all that could be distinguished [*Unterscheidbarkeiten*], a decision [*Entscheidung*] is already implied in the very way in which we ask the question. To ask a question is, thus, not something easy. This is the age-old primordial Platonic theme that those who are questioned, when they can no longer answer, would themselves like to be the questioners, but then they see that questioning is even harder. The responders at least receive guidance in the very question that is posed. By contrast, those who have to ask questions must pick up the trace themselves and remain on the trail. They do not just have the trail of the dialogue partner to pursue. This is why questioning is more difficult than answering.

It is clear that we are not talking about questions seeking information. It must be an [163] open question, but in such a way that the posing of the question is fruitful. According to an old saying, 'in science everything is decided in the way the question is framed'. One certainly does not recognize a way as right only through the fact that it leads to an answer. The opposite can be the case. The one who is on the right way of questioning is not the one to whom the answers come easily. Conversely, the one for whom the answer is difficult learns to see new questions, even when there are stray paths and wrong ways. This is how research is conducted. In science, the ways of conducting research mirror the ways of questioning.

The conditions in a real dialogue are different, because here understanding is immediately confirmed and misunderstanding corrected. In a dialogue we should not weigh precisely every word we say, carefully discarding all possible shifts of meaning and misleading cues. When we try to say something to someone else, we must find the right words that will reach the other. We are always already on the trail and never find ourselves at a distance from where we can see the immeasurable world of signs lying fully spread out before our eyes. We find ourselves being led. This explains why writing is so difficult when we seek to reach a stranger, the reader. In addition, what is written has something terrifyingly irrevocable about it. As a matter of fact, writing is made with signs that are pre-given: they are, as it were, inscribed [*eingeschrieben*] and, in this sense, they are almost prescribed [*vorgeschrieben*].

They constitute texts. In this lies the fact that both the trace and the sign do not stand by themselves for the sense that is meant in individual words. The same characters can represent words of completely different meanings. The context determines the relevant meaning. We call 'texts' only those that can be read and re-read. The text is the unity of a web and presents itself in its texture as a whole, and not in the written signs nor even in the grammatical unities of the sentence structure. Written signs and grammatical unities do not yet constitute a text, but only when it is a whole 'written composition', as we wisely call it. Basically, we understand only when we understand fully and have understood the whole. Those who understand only half may have completely misunderstood. At that point, we do not know whether we agree or how we should really respond. We must then ask again until we have understood, but even this does not mean that we agree with the other.

Musical notation is also similar to the use of writing. There is also the case where linguistic texts are set to music and it may of course happen that, with absolute music, we do not 'understand' a composition. In the case of linguistic texts as in music, not understanding does not only mean that one has not grasped as a whole the word order or the sequence of notes, but also that something that is differentiated in multiple ways cannot present itself as a unified whole. Written compositions, which obviously constitute the text through letters, syllables, words, and sentences, become instructions for [164] understanding the whole. In the same way, musical notation represents the kind of whole that one does not only read, but also follows as instructions for playing. This is why it is difficult and questionable to play a piece of music 'from the page'. Whoever wants to understand music must be familiar with the whole or go along with it. If we go with the music, then we also know when the music has come to an end. However, here we are referring to works of art that form a whole in the eminent sense and which I, for this reason, call 'eminent' texts.

Texts, which are not works of art, leave open the question as to whether a text ever comes to an end or just breaks off, just like a dialogue or like life. Perhaps, there are still other eminent texts, which bring a real closure, such as, for example, a judgement that is issued in court or the good tidings that are announced as a promise, such as the *amen* in church. There is indeed also an art of mere writing and speaking, which, as it were, puts a full stop. Punctuation was a late invention. In any case, it always remains clear that any such text stands in a context. The referential meaning of a sign depends upon that to which it refers. In a same way, even though it may present a unity of sense, a text is still always dependent upon a context, which is often actually what determines in a univocal manner the meaning that is plurivocal. This is an age-old herme-neutic rule that applies to all understanding of texts. One knows this when what surrounds the text, what constitutes the context, is organized anew and the text acquires a new sense. We should be aware of the fact that the lexical unity is determined by the unity of the sentence and the unity of the sentence is itself again determined by larger textual contexts. The same also happens while reading. Whoever has to spell out cannot read and also cannot yet understand. Similarly, if one extracts an individual part of the text from out of its context, this part is rendered mute. It lacks the preeminent power to make sense.

This is the problem in all understanding of citations and most definitely the delicate crossing of borders accounted for by the theory of intertextuality. Not every sentence is by itself a unity. Rather, a sentence belongs to a unity of sense, which lends the whole text its inner dynamic and its own tone. We all know how, in speaking, it is the tone that makes the music[12] and we therefore also know how difficult and what a responsibility it is to put something on record, when we do not know the clear target audience for which to find the right tone. Tone and intonation result precisely from an intangible movement, which plays out between them in their being together. In this regard, we can think of how intangible irony is and how much irony binds us to others as soon as they understand it and how conversely it produces a rift when they do not under-stand it. This exceptional case reminds us of how much the unity of sense of a text or a dialogue is first built up in a being-together.

[165] Here, an entirely new field of problems opens up, which encompasses entirely different complexities than those of the so-called logocentrism. It is indeed the case that not all the random associations and variations, not even all the allusions and suggestions that come to our mind can be made explicit without disturbing the being-with-one-another of the mutual understanding. Even if I recognize what Derrida calls *dissémination*, this cannot yet be the last word. It only names a presupposition on the basis of which a new under-standing of sense can make its claims. I very well recognize this: the power of conventions – or, to speak with Heidegger, the omnipotence of idle talk – but also the demands of logic or the force of convictions that deeply embedded

prejudices have, do not enjoy any legitimacy as such. Conversely, it cannot be the case that we follow random ideas. It may also happen in carefully chosen compositions, both in the rhetorical and the poetic use of language, that many meaningful configurations only play an accessory role. There may also be those that determine the play. It would thus be a false thesis in my view to base all understanding of texts on intertextuality, because this corresponds, in fact, only to the style of a particular period. The style of a period does not always justify a claim to be treated thematically. Rather, one must be mindful that allusions must often remain vague and that the recognition of the allusion will hardly be a contribution to interpretation. It is precisely in its inconspicuousness, in its discretion, and in its harmony that art speaks. *Ars latet arte sua.*[13]

When it comes to language and the art of speaking, we should not be shy of conceiving language rather broadly. Music arises from out of itself. Yet, it is generally the case that art takes on a clearly unified form in its most diverse manifestations – and particularly in the light of the style of the period. One can think, for example, of the dominant role that iconography plays in aesthetics today, which certainly presents an important historical dimension, but overall has still to make the transition toward a 'transformation into structure' [*Verwandlung ins Gebilde*]. This means that iconography has absolutely not reached the realm of art.

Or we can think of contemporary architectural style, in which citation plays a large role. Here, we are at most only able to sense a vague quality of familiarity, but it is precisely in this vagueness that this familiarity represents a contribution to the 'statement' [*Aussage*] made by the building. When we allow such a citation to become the one and only object or when we make it so, then we end up listening past the statement. We are familiar with this, particularly from the historicizing style of the nineteenth century. In this period, we have neo-Gothic churches, we have Romanesque railway stations, we have neo-Classical department stores. In the same way, we also know the response of artistic production in the century that marked the industrial revolution, which eventually led to the complete eradication of all historicizing tendencies [**166**] in art and literature. Now, we must only be clear that, in the experience of art, there is a constant play with the vague stylistic memory of past epochs and we spoil this play if we mix in specific derivations from the past. What can result from a change in tastes and fashions, which move like the play of waves, can be gleaned from the examples of Baroque and even Art Nouveau, in the manner in which they have undergone reevaluation, and this is what assuredly makes other rediscoveries possible.

This may well be the case with intertextuality, which corresponds all too well with the literary citation-style pertaining to the taste of the period. Even in the purest of correspondence, which is perhaps of historical interest, it will really be a matter of not obscuring the unity of what is conveyed in the encounter with the text. It should not, for example, be denied that the contemporary tendencies of taste are something from which artists can hardly ever dissociate themselves completely. As a result, high quality artistic pieces will always be found alongside embarrassingly fashionable imitations. The fundamental principle of intertextuality should not obscure the decisive task of composition. What is threatening here is well known from the plastic arts. The lightness of allusion, which is the creative imperative of artistic composition, will certainly not have an easy task in imposing itself against the need for representation experienced by those living during that time, who do not even think of art. Thus, for example, in the art of portraiture we can hardly expect the commissioner of the portrait to be ever satisfied with the artist when it comes to the result. However, it is also the case that changes in taste from epoch to epoch or even the progress of history, under the dictatorship of iconography's tendency toward reproduction, cannot guard even the greatest masterworks of the plastic arts from being relegated to the storage depot or from being most brutally restored. One need only think of the textbook case of Rembrandt, for instance, of the so-called 'Night Watch', whose clipped sides are now painfully evident as it newly enjoys the light of day today,[14] or think of how wonderfully 'The Conspiracy of Claudius Civilis'[15] was salvaged from an Amsterdam cellar and found refuge in Stockholm.

There is multi-referentiality in the whole world of signs and in particular in the world of language, which is articulated as writing. In light of such a multi-referentiality, the proximity of the trace, the writing, and the reading that follows the writing, gives rise to an unending manifold of possible references. Any reference may open up new perspectives. Yet, are these practicable ways? Deviations, conspicuous by-ways, changing perspectives can take us off course. In a written text it can happen that some secondary overtones come to prominence, although they are simply not intended. On what basis should we actually distinguish whether something belongs to the progression of thought or not? Of all that is inscribed in memory and recognized in the text, although it may not be intended at all, how much of it confuses it all and how much of it enlightens it all! [167] Are there no criteria pertaining to this multiplicity of all the references that words and things have? What is the right way in this situation? Does logical progression only lead to error?

III

It may be good to test the new deconstructive enterprise with some concrete attempts in order to see what can be called right and what must be called erroneous. To that end, I select the discussion of *chōra* found in Derrida's new work, which is highly worth reading. In this work, Derrida is not dealing with the word, but with the concept of *chōra,* as it is known to Platonists from Plato's *Timaeus.* Here we come across a narration of the myth of the demiurge, who constructs the universe according to number and measure. The demiurge constructs the heavenly spheres as well as the terrestrial world, consisting of the four elements. In this context, we encounter something without which the whole event of ordering the world and the interactions between the four elements could simply not take place. This is what gives space and is here called *chōra.* Now, one can naturally wonder what *chōra* actually means. From the usage of the word, one can perhaps stumble into completely different connotations in which *chōra,* for example, denotes a dominion to be administered. In the context of our narrative about the construction of the world, the word is part of a conceptual framework, the framework of the original [*Urbild*] and the copy [*Abbild*]. This is the framework in which the narrative was originally set into motion and which encompasses everything. Now, the notion of the space giver [*Raumgebende*] emerges as something new that had simply not appeared before. What is this third component? One can characterize the perspective, under which this third component opens up, through the language of metaphysics, of which the narrative avails itself. It is said to be something neither spiritual nor material. It is, so to speak, a third genus, of which it can be said that it is neither the one nor the other. What do we now experience of this *chōra*? This extremely tight presentation of the *Timaeus* leaves us rather perplexed, if we have to say what this third genus of being actually is. There is the talk of gold (50a ff.), which can be golden in many ways, and even the talk of the fundamental substance, from which, because of its lack of odor, we produce perfume. Both of these substances make us think far more of the concept of matter, of Aristotle's *hulē* – this prime matter, which has absolutely no formal determination any more – and not of the place that makes space. Certainly, *chōra,* which here encompasses everything, as it is said (50d), is explicitly called 'shapeless', like the shapeless dough out of which the baker or the potter want to make something. Then again this *chōra* is supposed to be like the mother or the wet nurse, who first bears and nurtures the living being that forms itself – again a completely different representational matrix.

[168] In any case, the introduction of this *chōra* in the *Timaeus* produces a surprising interruption in the narrative, in which up to that point the world produced by the *demiurge* with *nous* was depicted as a fitting copy [*Abbild*] of the original [*Urbild*] of the world. Now, all of a sudden, we are also told to put what happens out of necessity besides the *logos*. The emergence of the world would be a mixture of *nous* and *anankē*, of reason and necessity. Reason persuades necessity to relent just enough that in the end something good can come of it. This is the puzzling introduction of this third genus between being and becoming, idea and appearance, original and copy. Clearly, all of these mythical echoes, allusions, and changing forms should leave us perplexed so that what is meant by *chōra* can be something like a new beginning. It is indeed announced, but in such general terms that it is difficult simply to make sense out of this new, completely unique genus. In it we have both being and becoming, what is unchangeable in being and the shapeless, which, on account of its changeability, eludes all easy conceptualization. The latter is introduced as the 'formative cause of what is in flux'.

We are following the hermeneutical principle that says that we should investigate the larger context.[16] What does the context teach us about the text? After the announcement that we now have a completely new start, it is in any case very clear that we are dealing here with what has already been treated and what for Plato are, so to speak, the four pre-given elements and what happens to them (48b5 *pathē*). When we pay closer attention, we see that all these manifold descriptions of what should be the third genus – as the receiver – finally amounts to this: the essence of the third genus is explicitly introduced under the designation *chōra* (52a f). Finally, in the recapitulation, *chōra* is positioned in the middle between being and becoming, and represented as that which mediates between them (52d). In order to explain this, the four elements must be construed with the aid of mathematics and its necessity. These are the four elements that, according to Greek interpretation in Plato's time (since Empedocles), are the constitutive elements of everything. The multifaceted mode of appearance is supposed to constitute the unchanging building blocks of reality for all beings. Now, this is rather unconvincing to the naked eye. For Greek thinking, fire is everywhere where there is warmth, thus not only in the blazing flame, but also in the warmth of life. Water is not only this great infinity of the ocean, of the seas, and the rivers, but also ice in its stone-like hardness. The air is also not merely the blue azure, but equally the wind and the clouds, the fog [169] and the storm. Unchangeable? As he introduced the elements, the narrator had himself emphasized how little these elements in their appearance correspond to the idea of order. None of these elements would be a whole, absolute, and unchangeable 'this'. Fire would not always be pure fire, but, at most, something burning, and the same would be the case with water, air and earth. It is in their completely changing modes of appearance that they are supposed to be the constituent parts of all being. Nevertheless, they have to be shown as what is constant, out of which everything has its being. In order to explain this, mathematics and, in particular, the geometry of triangles is invoked. Mathematics and geometry were the great models of knowledge, cognition, and demonstration, which were in development at the time in the form of Euclidean geometry. Triangles, as building blocks, are supposed to give the elements their constancy. The following mathematical truth of stereometry,[17] which was recognized at the time, is supposed to fulfil this task: there can only be five regular bodies. They are even called the Platonic bodies.

How these five bodies are assigned to the elements is not without its irony. The pyramid stands for the vertical flame; the cube stands for solid earth; the most multi-sided polygon – the icosahedron – stands for water scattered in steam and fog. This is all pretty neat, even if somewhat laborious. However, there is a difficulty. There are only four elements and, yet, five regular mathematical bodies. This is why, in order to avoid embarrassment, the dodecahedron receives a special task, namely that of a scaffolding for the world-sphere! Plato's contemporary readers certainly did not assume that Plato really meant all of this. In every word of the stories told in the *Timaeus* we can sense the lightheartedness of play. When, nonetheless, Aristotle takes the whole thing literally and criticizes it, he gets his own point across with his critique, as he does with the many other dialogical games of Plato, namely, to defend the priority of nature over the secondary character of mathematics. The whole of the *Timaeus* must be taken as a playful game by Plato.

The necessity being discussed in this play now, after the new start, is truly no play at all. Plato is completely serious about the fact that the depiction up to now, which was grounded upon the duality of original and copy, of being and becoming, is not sufficient. Whatever we may say about Aristotle's misunderstanding of Platonism as a two-world theory, we have to admit that Plato had long before anticipated this in the *Parmenides*, in the *Sophist*, and in the *Philebus*. Now, Plato brings this out in a completely explicit way in the *Timaeus* as the 'second beginning' (48b) in this demiurgical tale of the world. Derrida obviously saw this. This is why he was immediately drawn to this third genus, because here the distinction of being and becoming is explicitly declared to be unsatisfactory. The *chōra* of the *Timaeus* makes us actually think of the new natural science grounded in mathematics [170], obstructed as it was by the teleological physics of Aristotle, which had remained valid for a millennium.

What is now the textual basis from which Derrida directs his deconstructive questioning-behind against what he calls metaphysics? Obviously, it is the two-world theory, which Derrida, as metaphysics, makes the basis of his inter-esting and imaginative essay. What do these texts give us? Derrida quotes Plato's *Republic*. There, *chōra* is considered as something that is beyond being. Now, the expression *chōra* is not to be found in the *Republic*. However, because the *chōra* of the *Timaeus* is also about something like a beyond that is neither sensible nor spiritual, Derrida believes that we can recognize the same beyond in the *chōra* of the *Timaeus* as that which the *Republic* introduces as beyond-being. Derrida associates this with the late Platonism of the early Christian epoch. In the depiction of the one and the divine by Dionysius the Areopagite, there is indeed mention of the *chōra*, the place of distinction that the one receives. Now, Derrida believes that he can claim all three testimonies for the same anti-metaphysical sense and pursue a threefold trace. In all three directions something intangible would appear: the beyond of the being of the good, the beyond of the space or place that makes room, and the beyond of the divine one. In his eyes, they constitute a multi-faceted ensemble.

I have my doubts. However, I also greatly admire the fireworks of flashing allusions that Derrida presents when rehearsing the opening scene of the *Timaeus*. In no way do I deny that Plato here calls upon everything in order not to let us forget the intricate connection between the way the world is constructed, the way the state is organized, and the way the soul is struc-tured. He certainly proves himself to be a perfect deconstructivist in his great dialogical drama. In fact, I feel myself in agreement with Heidegger, Derrida, and Vernant (whom I once listened to years ago and with approval) on the point that the conventional explanatory formula 'from *muthos* to *logos*'[18] is misleading and does violence to both. Yet, it seems to me that the context in which the *chōra* is introduced in the *Timaeus*, means something completely different and is a trace that leads us to something totally other than the beyond of the one or the divine. It leads us to the necessity – and there can be no doubt here of the kind of necessity that is in question: it is the necessity of mathematics. The whole construction of Euclidean geometry is certainly something wonderful and stunning, as is the fact that the mathematicians of Plato's time had seen and proved that there can only be five regular bodies that can be inscribed within the sphere. What kind of puzzling rationality is this rationality of the third dimension, according to which what gives space [*Raumgebende*] from itself only permits these five perfect bodies, all of which fit into the perfect sphere of being? What are the limits that show themselves here and at the same time what is the concession [171] necessity manifests here by granting only to these five regular bodies something of the perfection of the sphere? Not even the demiurge can change any of this, so great is the necessity involved here.

I discuss the topic of the *chōra* for the sake of the fundamental question of whether indications, even if they go in a different direction, are to be simply noted or whether we should decide the context in which indications are to be pursued. Traces come with their pre-determinations and are not random. Although I believe I understand the 'beyond' [*Jenseits*] of the Idea of the Good, I certainly do not think of the 'here' [*Diesseits*] of the elements or of the regular bodies. If one considers the 'being beyond' of the one, as it appears in Dionysius the Areopagite and its Christian aftermath, one will rather think of the 'beyond being' that Plato presents in the *Republic*. However, in this we may only see how much we still stand in the neo-Platonic history of the influence exerted by Aristotelian metaphysics, from which we learned to think, in the case of the divine that is beyond [*jenseitige*], as for any being, the space that holds them. We owe this to Aristotle's physics, which introduced God as the first mover. By contrast, when we think of the ideal of symmetry and mathematical order in the five approximations of 'beautiful' bodies to the spherical form of the universe and its construction out of triangles, then here *chōra* serves to illustrate a mathematical necessity. It is this necessity that makes us understand why the elements, despite their changing modes of appearance, are to be understood as being. However, this is not particularly convincing, as the narrator himself concedes. These are superior games that Plato, if also rather gleefully, plays with mathematics. However, it does not follow that mathematics itself is a game.

At the end of the seventh book of the *Republic*, we can see clearly that the Platonic dialogues are to be read as play. There, an obvious solution for the possibility of the ideal city is found with playful lightheartedness: one would just have to throw out of the city all the residents who have reached the age of ten. Then, the paradise of well-trained children will come to be. Through such games, one can point to serious problems and, truly, the decline of the great culture of Athens and the zenith of Greek democracy is reflected in Plato's utopias.[19] That being said, the mathematical construction of the *Timaeus* has exercised a powerful fascination on modern physics and, above all, in our century. The world-play of the *Timaeus* in fact continued to exercise its influence throughout the centuries through Kepler and through Schelling's romantic philosophy of nature up until today. How mathematical relationships can approximate reality remains an actual problem as quantum physics teaches us. However, this is a broad subject.

[172] The dialogical poetry of Plato assiduously avoids rigid determinations and seeks to serve the furthering of thought. The mirror image held out in front of Attic democracy still has for us the full force of a critique. The way Plato stages his ideas preserves something of the secret of language and the mutual understanding that we, human beings, practise every day through language. We have cited above the only authentic words that Plato uttered on this subject in the 'Seventh Letter'. Dialectic must always become dialogue again and thinking must always be authenticated in the back and forth of a dialogue. Even if in Plato there are indeed many traces in play that show complete pride in the logic and mathematics of his time, I am still simply unable to see any logocentrism there. I would rather accept that metaphysics, which became scholastic since Aristotle, could be called 'monologocentrism' under the conditions of the reading culture that prevailed in modernity. Concerning Aristotle himself, we should always note that what we know as the works of Aristotle are merely dictations, which were meant as a basis for his teaching and dialogue. It would require a separate presentation using the assiduous commentators of Aristotle to show how little the methodological ideal of demonstrative logic corresponds to Aristotle's philosophical train of thought and how this methodological ideal has been forced into the commentaries by, as it were, a form of scholasticism. It is in the appendix to the *Posterior Analytics* (B 19) that we find the best account of how research into principles (*archai*) really proceeds. This chapter of Aristotle should be considered as important as the excursus in Plato's seventh letter. Here too, it is shown how concepts are formed and how language and the common knowledge that lives in language exercise their capacities. Aristotle was not wrong in criticizing the demonstrative power of the Platonic dialectic in relation to the concept of *dihairesis*. He is certainly right that the distinctions established in lively dialogue as well as in Plato's dialogical poetry do not at all have the character of logical necessity proper to a demonstration. Now, has Plato ever supposed this? He has dialogue in mind and who does not know that it is only seldom among human beings that a mutual understanding can be reached through strict logical demonstration? We are fully aware of the advantages of logically guaranteed demonstrations in science. However, we are also aware of the room for freedom that human actions have and we are fully aware of the work that creative imagination plays in research itself, as well as all that is granted to the language of poetry. All of this must receive its due. Not everything can be turned into an object of knowledge. There are other

experiences than those of science, when something takes our breath away in the theatre, when we are left pensive before the whole comedy and tragedy of life, when we are a witness of exhilarating events or when we are captivated by thrilling **[173]** narratives. What holds true particularly for the poetic language of lyricism is certainly not confined to it, namely, that it just cannot become an object of science, but, like all experiences of art, it demands our engagement and participation. This is the reason why it seems to me that in these cases the task of deconstruction, which otherwise can open up new horizons, is not required.

Interpretation is always a tricky business. This is already because it is, in accordance with its essence (and with the word), a 'mediating discourse' [*Zwischenrede*]. Interpretation interrupts the exercise of our commerce with the text. We all know this, for example, in the case of poetic texts. Such an interruption is, for this reason, not quite superfluous. Where we bump against something incomprehensible, we need the help of interpretation. However, interpretation fulfils its true purpose only if it aids the exercise of reading the text, which would otherwise be inhibited by incomprehensibility. This is a broad problematic, before which we, in fact, always find ourselves when we are dealing with art. For, where can we find sharp boundaries in art?

Furthermore, the field of language extends over more than just poetic texts. It also includes thoughtful meditation and, thereby, the use of concepts, on which the prose of thinking depends. All this comes to fruition in speech. Ultimately this is even true, to a certain extent, of every interpretation. It may be a mediating speech. However it is what it ought to be only if it interrupts itself so that a thoughtful dialogue may ensue. One should take as a model the manner in which Book *delta* of Aristotle's *Metaphysics* presents itself as a mere propaedeutic. This should absolutely be the model. It holds true not only for poetry. It holds true for all reading. With regard to the texts that Derrida has claimed to deconstruct, it is not without due consideration that I have spoken of what I call the eminent text.[20] I would count under this name the experience, in the widest sense, of all art. This experience encompasses more than what rhymes. Texts and works of art are of such a kind that one does not simply take notice of them. We would most of all like to know lyrics by heart so that we can nurture a dialogue with them. Works of art are all of such a kind that the dialogue with them is never exhausted, but rather always offers itself for new engagement. Philosophical texts are obviously not eminent texts in the same sense. Unless they are like Plato's dialogues, philosophical texts are only 'mediating discourses' in the endless dialogue of thought. We certainly consult them constantly for advice because we all live in the continuous unfolding of our experiences. We certainly do not read philosophical texts as a poem that knows everything. Rather, we study philosophical texts as that which does not know, but whose authors have for a long time pondered and reflected, are thus not so easily distracted by the realities and the spontaneous fashions of their own time [174]. It is thus like a dialogue with another person. 'Whatever I may say, it is not my word.'[21]

Yet, let us return to language and writing. To this entire circle of problems is connected a truly boundless question that has occupied me for a long time: what does the reader have to know? We cannot expect any clear answer here. Perhaps, the question should be posed differently: what should the reader want to know?[22] Perhaps, this is what Socrates meant when, in his conversation with Phaedrus, he at the end directed a prayer to Pan and the other gods. Here, he may have reformulated in a Socratic sense a prayer that also contains the wish for wealth, when he says: 'I would like to consider rich those who are wise and would like to possess a treasure made of such gold that none other than a moderate person could lift it up and carry it away.'[23]

Part Four

Hermeneutics of Beginnings and Returns: The Case of Heidegger

15

Remembering Heidegger's Beginnings (1986)[1]

[3] There has been a renewed interest directed at the pre-Marburg period, the early Freiburg years of Martin Heidegger, when he was still finding his feet as a theologian and as a thinker. This interest was signaled by the publication of an early lecture from the winter semester 1921/22 by Walter Bröcker and his wife. In addition, we are also thankful especially for the works of Thomas Sheehan for a more precise knowledge of Heidegger's beginnings. Through the mediation of Ernst Tugendhat, Sheehan was able to consult the notes of Helene Weiss, who transcribed Heidegger's lecture on the *Phenomenology of Religion.* Sheehan also unearthed other materials from Heidegger's early years. They all complete the picture of the young theologian Heidegger, whose insistence on clarity in life and thought sent him on a path that was arguably to lead him to becoming one of the greatest thinkers of the twentieth century. It is, in particular, thanks to the information about the lecture course on the *Phenomenology of Religion* that we have an important clue as to the nature and extent of the motivation under which the young Heidegger became transfixed by the problem of time in his early Freiburg years.[2]

After overcoming a serious attack of polio, I myself came into personal contact with Heidegger in Freiburg only in 1923. However, reports, 'rumours' of different sorts about a young revolutionary philosopher, who played the role of assistant to Husserl, had already reached us in Marburg. It was probably during my summer semester of 1921 in Munich that I heard the name for the first time. In a seminar held by Moritz Geiger, an advanced student made peculiar remarks. I asked Geiger afterwards what this was all about. He answered with the most natural expression: 'Well! He has become Heideggerized [*verheideggert*].' There was already such a thing then. I remember from the same summer semester of 1921 in Munich noticing in the hallway a serious, dark-eyed, slender student with a big head. [4] I came to know him later on in Marburg. It was Karl Löwith, who, at the time, under Heidegger's recommendation, submitted as his dissertation in Munich an interpretation of Nietzsche that was far too little in line with phenomenological orthodoxy. The second time I heard the name of Heidegger was through a report by a student at Marburg who knew how to say things that were as confusing as they were deep-sounding, and who had spent a semester in Freiburg. Both mentions of his name had not yet really excited me. However, in 1922 my own teacher, Paul Natorp, gave me a manuscript to read that Heidegger had sent him: an introduction to the interpretation of Aristotle. The original unfortunately fell victim to the depredations of war in Leipzig, although in the meantime a partial transcription had been found in the Marbach archives, and it was published after the discovery of another copy. Reading this manuscript hit me like an electric shock. There was not a whole lot about Aristotle, but quite a bit about the young Luther, Gabriel Biel, Augustine, Saint Paul and the Old Testament. What language it was! What a peculiar and, for us at the time, completely novel use of strongly expressive German words and locutions for conceptual purposes! Even what was available at the time, Heidegger's book on the so-called Duns Scotus, *Grammatica speculativa*, of 1917, had nothing yet of this style. I resolved to go to Freiburg immediately after my doctorate, especially since I had myself turned to the study of Aristotle under the encouragement of Nicolai Hartmann.

My first encounter with Heidegger in Freiburg happened in the most peculiar way. I came to his office and heard voices inside. I retreated and waited in the hallway. Then, the door opened and someone was let out by a very short dark-eyed man. I said to myself: What a pity! There is still someone in and I continued to wait patiently. Only after a fairly long time did I listen again against the door and, not hearing any voices anymore, knocked and entered. The short dark man, who simply did not correspond to my expectations, was Martin Heidegger. Obviously, as I conversed with him and saw his eyes, I understood without any explanation that phenomenology has something to do with seeing. In these eyes, there was not only penetrating intelligence but, above all, imagination and intuitive power. It would take a long time before I learned, within the confines of my abilities, to develop in me this phenomenological power of intuition that has almost become unknown nowadays. Naturally, I attended Heidegger's one-hour lecture course on ontology and the undergraduate seminars he offered on Aristotle and on the *Logical Investigations*, as well as the seminar for advanced students on the sixth book of the *Nicomachean Ethics* and even the Saturday seminar that he and Julius Ebbinghaus jointly held on Kant's writings on religion. All five [5] of these academic exercises were formative and unforgettable for me. In his lecture course under what seemed to me the truly unfit title 'ontology', Heidegger lectured on the analysis of the surrounding world [*Umwelt*], which *Being and Time* later made famous. For me, who had been educated in the language of 'general logic' in the Marburg school, these were entirely new ways of speaking. I certainly sensed immediately that, even within the Freiburg phenomenological school, these ways of speaking were unique to Heidegger. What I did not know at the time was how much indirect influences from Nietzsche, on the one hand, and American pragmatism, on the other, were at play. This is a recent insight that I have just gained about Heidegger: he may have been indirectly inspired by American pragmatism. We have known for some time that Emil Lask, whose complete work Heidegger often mentioned with special respect, turned away from his Heidelberg neo-Kantianism and adopted American pragmatism, one year before the First World War broke out, a war that would snatch his life away. It appears that the lecture that Lask held on this topic left its mark not only on György Lukács. God knows in which ways it also left its marks on the young Heidegger. However, it is also true here, as is commonly the case, that the inspirations that turn out to be fruitful are in fact 'in the air' and what is essential is what one does with them. Truly, the independence and the power this young teacher had accumulated were one of a kind. Often with an oblique look through the window, Heidegger would conclude his imposing but convincing pronouncements. There spoke from him a self-consciousness that was at once powerful and legitimate, which vented itself many times in nasty polemic. Max Scheler, in particular, was often treated shabbily, once even in an amusingly mistaken manner. Heidegger referred to a text by Scheler in which a work by Aristotle was mentioned in a footnote: 'Aristotle, *de partibus animae*.' 'Now, my dear friends, such a work by Aristotle does not exist.' Before the next lecture, I had the opportunity to draw Heidegger's attention to the fact that this mistaken citation was nothing more than a typographical error and what the text meant was *De partibus animalium* (the 'l' with which the citation ended was misprinted as 'e'). Heidegger made the correction during the next lecture: it had been pointed out to him and he wanted to share it so that nobody would come to the silly view that he wanted to refute Max Scheler with the help of a typographical error.

In the seminar for beginners that Heidegger held on behalf of Husserl, the object was the *Logical Investigations*. Here again the young teacher already displayed a sovereign mastery in leading a rather large auditorium. I still particularly remember a question and the answer that it received from Heidegger himself. He asked what the [6] intentional object actually is and he rejected all the answers that came from the auditorium to say eventually: 'My dear friends, this is being.' Obviously he meant this in the sense of the tradition of metaphysics: the intentional object would have in Husserl somehow the role that the *ti en einai,* the being-what plays in Aristotelian metaphysics: the essence gathered in its *eidos.* In connection to this answer about being, Heidegger made it clear that being is not the most universal and the highest genus. He then asked another question: who was the first to rediscover the Aristotelian insight that being is not a genus? All possible answers could be heard. I myself in my cheekiness ventured one and suggested Leibniz in view of the concept of monad. However, the answer he gave me was: 'He would have been delighted if he had understood that. No, it was Husserl!' (Heidegger then referred to the sixth of the *Logical Investigations*). Now, I had not yet understood in any way the background of these provoking answers. Today, I would say: we can observe here how Heidegger knew how to connect his thought to Husserl and how he had managed with great diplomatic flair, despite Husserl's insistence and wish, never to engage with *Ideas I* in his 'exercises'. *Ideas I* appeared in 1913 and Heidegger saw it as a relapse into neo-Kantian transcendental idealism. Instead, he engaged with the *Logical Investigations.* He managed to do this with Husserl (as he himself told me) by saying: 'Eminent Professor, students must first go through the phase of the *Logical Investigations.* They are not yet ready for the present stage of your phenomenological insights.' In truth, this obviously amounted to a critical stance, namely that Heidegger did not follow Husserl in his later turn toward transcendental idealism, even if he did not succumb to a shallow relapse into a phenomenological realism in the style of Scheler or the Munich school.

This was precisely what was important to me, especially for my efforts to penetrate Aristotle's philosophy: Heidegger knew how to make it clear to me that Aristotle was not the 'realist' as opposed to Plato, the 'idealist'. I understood this especially when Heidegger was magnanimous enough to invite me on some evenings to a private reading of the so-called substance-books of Aristotle's *Metaphysics.* I was equally fascinated by his introduction to Aristotle's ethics. Here he displayed the full pathos of his 'hermeneutics of facticity' for his interpretation of Aristotle. As we have also just learned from the latest publication of the lecture course from 1921/22,[3] the hermeneutics of facticity means an interpretation of human existence [*menschliches Dasein*], which follows the self-interpretation of this existence in the concreteness of its life-world. Aristotelian ethics could in fact serve in a sense as a parallel for this purpose.

[7] Actually, the rediscovery of Aristotle by phenomenology was not so complete a surprise, as it must have seemed to a neo-Kantian educated in Marburg. The despotic spirit of Hermann Cohen hovered over the Marburg

landscape, even after his death, and in the counter-reaction to him. Cohen loved to say that Aristotle was a 'pharmacist'. With this, he naturally meant the Aristotelian spirit of order based on classification. Cohen was obviously blind – unlike Hegel! – to the speculative content in this all-encompassing empiricism. Natorp and, above all, Nicolai Hartmann, who was distancing himself from the Marburg school, saw much more in Aristotle. Nevertheless, it was like a revelation to me when I realized that the *logos,* the *legomena*, the categories, and, fundamentally, the entirety of the conceptual tradition of metaphysics referred back to the life-world experiences of speaking and language. This was even true for metaphysics and how much more for the analysis of practical reason – if one can express oneself in such a Kantian manner – that Heidegger recognized with compelling force in Aristotelian *phronēsis*. This 'eye of the soul' (as the text once calls it in a metaphorical rendering) was obviously the proper linchpin for the *pathos* of existence, which at the time showed the presence of Kierkegaard in Heidegger's rise. In this respect there was another noteworthy scene in this seminar, which has endured in my memory. It concerns the distinction between *technē* and *phronēsis*, between the knowledge that guides the production of something and the knowledge that directs people in action and politics, thus in the social sphere. We find in Aristotle the formulation of the following distinction: what can be learned in the knowledge of a craft can also be forgotten. Of *phronēsis*, however, there is no *lēthē*, no forgetting. Heidegger asked us: what does this mean? Precisely at the moment the bell rang, indicating the end of the session, Heidegger rose up and said: 'My dear friends, this is conscience [*das Gewissen*]', and left. Dramatic and violent, absolutely! There would be a lot to say about the difference between the concept of conscience and the Aristotelian concept of *phronēsis*. Nevertheless, through this provocative thesis we were inexorably compelled to confront our own questions even if we had eventually to learn how to control the all too violent recognition of our own questions in what we studied and to make distinctions.

The seminar on Kant's writing on religion, which was held together with Ebbinhaus, but in reality completely dominated by the young Heidegger, led us into a completely unknown dimension, a dimension which was completely lacking in my philosophical formation. There, I had the opportunity, but was not able at the time, to assess the inner urgency of the problem of religion and theology in the thought of Heidegger. When Heidegger in many ways [8] distanced the Kantian doctrine of religion more strongly from Luther and drew it closer to Aquinas, I could have already assessed in Heidegger's philosophical efforts the element pertaining to the critique of metaphysics as well as the element pertaining to the critique of Aristotle. However, it was only years later that I realized this.

The unbelievable impression that these first encounters with Heidegger made on me had yet another background, which lay in another direction. In the young Heidegger, I encountered in a lively manner what I had missed in my neo-Kantian formation in Marburg and what I could not fill in through my occasional studies, for example of the works of Dilthey, Max Weber or Ernst Troeltsch. It was no longer a question of the sciences alone and their epistemological justification, not even of the masterly extension of *a priori* analyses to the life-world, which Husserl had introduced. It was essentially about the historicity of human existence, about the solution to the problem of historical relativism; better still: it was about the questioning of the very presuppositions of the framework within which historical relativism appears unsolvable. Dilthey was, for this purpose, the symbolic figure. Heidegger himself, in a manner similar to my young self, attempted to escape the formalist aridity of neo-Kantian systematic thinking and, in particular, also resisted the transcendental-idealistic turn of the Husserlian phenomenological programme. In this situation, he found an essential source of support from early on in the enormously rich and stimulating later work of Dilthey, despite all its conceptual weakness and dullness. It is a mistake to use the citation in *Being and Time* to conclude that Dilthey influenced the development of Heidegger's thought in the mid-1920s. This is already far too late. The way Heidegger sympathetically interprets and makes reference to Dilthey's work, as we find it in *Being and Time,* can put this to rest once and for all. Dilthey's influence did not first come about through the significant introduction by Misch, praised by Heidegger, which appeared in 1924 in the fifth volume of the complete works of Dilthey, by then nearing completion. It did not even come about in the moment, which was epoch-making in its own way, when the correspondence between Count Yorck von Wartenburg and his friend Wilhelm Dilthey appeared.

I experienced this moment in Heidegger very closely when I spent the stormy weeks of the inflation in the fall of 1923 as a guest in his hut. At the time, it was totally clear how Heidegger, with a deep inner satisfaction, even a malicious delight, discovered in these letters the superiority of Count Yorck over the famous scholar Dilthey. Obviously, to be able to perceive this presupposes a precise familiarity with the late output of Wilhelm Dilthey, what Heidegger possessed. Heidegger himself described to me how burdensome [9] it had become always to haul home the heavy volumes of the Berlin Academy edition, in which the late works of Dilthey were to be found and then to haul them back when someone in the Freiburg university library had requested, not Dilthey's essays, but something else in the bulky volumes. (It is only with Volume 5 in 1924 that we have the beginning of the series of volumes that collected the theoretical contributions of Dilthey). The studies of Dilthey, obviously also the late work of Georg Simmel and who knows how many other works, certainly also the work of Kierkegaard, which at the time gained influence through the Diederich edition: all these were, so to speak, the armaments with which Heidegger already in 1919, immediately after the war, battled uncompromisingly against founding everything ultimately in a transcendental ego, as Husserl taught. What he found so convincing in Count Yorck in 1923 – and what put us all under his spell – was that here the idea and faith in the methods of modern critical-historical science stood accused of aesthetic superficiality and were considered with reservation. In *Being and Time* Heidegger cited some of the most massive attacks against the ocularity of the historical school that Count Yorck formulates in his letters. Heidegger did not make as clear in *Being and Time* that this critique also applied to Dilthey himself. To want to apply the famous expression of 'in the spirit of Count Yorck' to the work of Dilthey may look like the subordination of Count Yorck to Dilthey's scholarly work. However, Heidegger really meant the opposite. This is a typical Heideggerean formulation, insofar as it implicitly conveys that whoever engages the work of Dilthey without being immersed in the ideas of Count Yorck, completely misses what is essential. What is essential is the totally obvious fact that Count Yorck fully recognized how the methodological constraints of British empiricism and a neo-Kantianism that was flattened out into an epistemology had adulterated philosophy and the human sciences. The subject-object schema continued to perpetuate itself unquestioned and unshaken in Dilthey's scientific self-interpretation. Count Yorck, by contrast, had no such limitations. Free from any professional sclerosis, he constantly had in mind the heritage of German romanticism and the concept of life, which had been fused with speculative idealism. The meaning of all this was concretely present in his awareness of his tradition and its Lutheran background. This patently confirmed to Heidegger his own deepest concerns, no doubt reducing Dilthey's significance for him. He recognized the weakness of Dilthey's cultural liberalism and the strength of Count Yorck's religious and deeply rooted stature.

Here we can ask whether the greater figure of Hegel is not [10] to be recognized in the background of this encounter and radicalizing confrontation with Dilthey. This was almost in the air at the time, when neo-Kantianism was crumbling. We only need to recall the names of Georg Simmel, Wilhelm

Windelband and his whole circle of students, to which György Lukács and Ernst Bloch belonged as much as Julius Ebbinghaus, Richard Kroner, and many other 'new Hegelians'. Or recall the significant continuation of Ernst Cassirer's work on the history of the problem of knowledge, with its third volume, which was entirely dedicated to Hegel.[4] Thus, it will be no great surprise that the young Heidegger already in 1917 refers to Hegel emphatically with an orientation to the future. It remains that the methodological principle of dialectic was taboo in Husserl's phenomenological school and Heidegger up to the end of his life saw in dialectic the true danger, a risk of fraud for phenomenologically solid work. However, it is obvious that Hegel, his themes and the tasks he set for himself, as well as the conceptual mastery invested in his *Phenomenology of Spirit* and in his *Logic,* were also for Heidegger a constant figure of reference. In this regard, I recall a conversation. It was probably in 1924. As I reconstruct it from the topography of 'the way home' [*Heimweg*], Heidegger still lived in Schwanallee 23, and not yet above, in Barfüsserstrasse. I asked Heidegger then whether his attempt to overcome the subjectivism of modern thought had not already been undertaken by Hegel. Heidegger replied: 'Certainly, his efforts go in this direction, but he lacks the conceptual possibility of separating himself from the inner necessity that lies in the Greek and Cartesian concept of the subject or the concept of consciousness.' As it seems to me, this holds true for many of Heidegger's critical pronouncements about the great thinkers of the tradition: he indeed recognized in them the same concern, the same task for thinking, but they lacked the conceptual possibilities to come through with it.

It is from there that one can particularly understand the influence that Kierkegaard exerted on him and the later fading away of this influence. The characteristically authentic magic words that literally haunt Heidegger's vocabulary in the Marburg years, before the composition of *Being and Time,* were 'the ontological difference'. Here too, I remember a conversation with Heidegger from a very early period, about 1924. Gerhard Krüger was there. We questioned Heidegger about the ontological difference, the differentiation between being and beings, and wanted somehow to know when, where, and how this differentiation is actually made. Then came Heidegger's almost astonished answer, which should have given us something to think about: 'But the ontological difference is not something that we make. It is not we who differentiate between being and beings.' History teaches what is becoming increasingly clear to me in the last decades: Heidegger's so-called 'turn' [*Kehre*] is in fact only the return [*Rückkehr*] to his proper intention, [11] which he had already often anticipated in his youthful internal confrontation with Husserl. I always recall the fact that already in 1920 the young Heidegger had used the following expression while lecturing: 'It worlds' [*es weltet*].

From this point, it becomes even clearer as to what it was that challenged us the most in the Marburg years. I mean Heidegger's demeanor, which to our eyes was something rare and somehow unbelievable, when he presented his strident descriptions of the fall, the 'they', idle talk, the 'frenzy for nearness' [*Tollheit auf die Nähe*], and all that in the tone of a Capuchin preacher, always adding at the end: 'All this is without pejorative meaning.' What this actually means is shown with full clarity by the newly available lecture of 1921/22.[5] The motive proper to Heidegger's thinking did not lie at the time in such dramatic exaggerations to rouse an audience, but in the irresolvable ambiguity that constitutes the essence of the movement of life as such. We already find in the lecture of 1921/22, under the title 'fundamental categories of life', two elements developed in their inseparability: on the one hand, what Heidegger called at the time 'inclination' [*Neigung*], to which corresponds, later on, 'authenticity', and, on the other, 'ruination' [*Ruinanz*], which later came to be called the tendency of Dasein to fall. Life itself has this ambiguity to it.

In the same way, we can only understand Heidegger's quest for the original *alētheia* when we see it in its full ambiguity. First of all, this goes along with what Heidegger always emphatically maintained: *alētheia* and *alēthes* do not lie in propositions, but in being itself, and he appealed to Aristotle to confirm this – obviously this is only partially correct. There is no doubt that he had in mind the fact that it is being itself that shows itself and hides itself. This is also how we need to understand the expression from an earlier time that Bröcker made known to us: 'Life is hazy. It clouds itself over and over again.' The essential point is the inner belongingness of the self-manifesting and self-concealing, of the impetus to authenticity and to falling, a belongingness that is thought by Heidegger in the concept of *alētheia*. It is the essential ambiguity that lies in being itself that leads him to question behind metaphysics. It would be ridiculous to claim that metaphysics had not asked about being if Heidegger were to have understood under 'being' the same as what Aristotle articulated conceptually, the being of beings. Heidegger's questioning behind metaphysics was in search of a pre-metaphysical, inceptual experience of being. This is why, later on, he went back to the pre-Socratics.

His studies of Anaximander, Parmenides and Heraclitus [12] were supposed to render visible the full originality of the experience of being, an experience to which these first steps of Greek thinking were still close. All these indefatigable attempts to call on the pre-Socratics as witnesses could not in the long run deceive Heidegger about the fact that a real thinking of *alētheia*, that is to say, of the dimension in which being discloses itself and which is also the dimension in which being withdraws, was nowhere to be found in Greek thinking. In the statement by Anaximander, one can indeed recognize the temporality of being, 'the while' [*die Weile*] as in an expression on a seal. The didactic poem of Parmenides does not only talk about the heart without a beat of *alētheia*, but also about the absence of being. In the cryptic saying of Heraclitus, the event of being [*Ereignis des Seins*] seems to be absolutely intended, steering everything like lightning. Yet, in the guiding concept of being, which appears in Parmenides for the first time in the singular as 'the being' and appears in Heraclitus for the first time in the singular as 'the one', the temporal structure of being only includes the present [*Gegenwart*], presentness [*Gegenwärtigkeit*], entering into presence [*Anwesenheit*]. Fundamentally speaking, it is absolutely not the statements of these early thinkers, not the utterances that we encounter in their texts that could bring the event of being to concepts. It is rather the semantic resources, the circles of meanings befitting the Greek fundamental words, *logos, phusis, to on, to hen*, which grant the contemporary thinker who attempts to step back, the insight into the oldest experiences still facing all conceptual thinking. It is the primordial history of language that opens itself up meaningfully to this insight. As evinced by these interpretive attempts, the true genius of Heidegger lies less in the interpretation of texts than in the survey of entire semantic fields and in pursuing the secret veins in the primordial sediments of language.

In these attempts at thinking, Heidegger accomplishes as little a beginning before all metaphysics as an overcoming of metaphysics. There is simply no possible perspective from which we could simply leave metaphysics behind, as if it would have nothing more to say to us thinkers, even if we were attempting some new form of thinking. Heidegger himself explicitly stressed this later on, inasmuch as he understood the overcoming of metaphysics as a 'transformation' [*Verwindung*]. In fact, for us today, who stand at the end of the age of metaphysics, there may lie an obscure indication in the secret wisdom of the words. We may feel the intimate inseparability of disclosure [*Entbergen*], concealment [*Verbergen*], and sheltering [*Bergen*], as well as the inseparability between *lēthē* and *alētheia*, and the unity behind all the Heraclitean word plays. In order to bring this to conceptual expression, one needs the whole way of thinking of Western metaphysics and a new re-effectuation of this tradition. Even more than that, one also needs the strength to leave behind the universal synthesis of this path, a synthesis of Greek conceptuality with its

Christian mystical inspiration, which Hegel accomplishes through his dialectical art. [13] What the Aristotelian conclusion of Hegel's *Encyclopaedia of the Philosophical Sciences* tries to bring to expression as if it were its last word is completely different from the vision behind Heidegger's quest. Here we have being understood in the light of the God that is present to itself, understood as the full transparency of being and spirit. We understand the life-long challenge that Hegel posed for Heidegger. This 'last Greek' brought together the Greek experience of being in *logos* with the Christian thought of life and spirit, culminating in a speculative unification in the self-presence of the absolute spirit. Such a dialectic reconciliation must have appeared to the restless Heidegger as an obfuscation and the young Heidegger could not yet find philosophical help to fight it. It became clear to Heidegger only in his Marburg years that there stood behind Kierkegaard's religiously motivated critique of Hegel the theosophically profound insight of a Schelling, which finds its expression in the distinction between ground and existence. Yet, Christian mysticism had held a long attraction for him. Only in his later years in Freiburg did Heidegger assimilate the fact that the limits of metaphysics become visible in Nietzsche's genial dilettantism, when becoming is embossed with the stamp of being. Since then, Nietzsche stands at the centre of the thought of the late Heidegger, like an incarnation of the ontological experience of ambiguity and as the destinal figure of the transition toward another thinking. Still in this final culmination, Heidegger's own efforts at thinking remain in constant dialogue with metaphysics, attempting as they do to return to a point behind it.

16

The Turn in the Path (1985)[1]

[71] It is certainly clear that Martin Heidegger's path of thinking presents itself as *one*, even if it has so many twists and turns. We can see, from the very outset, the goal that motivated his thinking, namely, the overcoming of the subjectivity of modern thought. I have no doubt that these components of modernity also possessed a peculiar relevance for him, given his religious doubt and the manner in which modernism had ensconced itself within the Catholic dogmatics of his time. We should certainly not underestimate the significance that the Catholic dogmatic education of his time, especially the introduction to the history of the dogma of the Christian church, had in the formation of Martin Heidegger. However, he clearly could not be persuaded by how the contemporary Catholic dogmatics dealt with the problems of modern science, especially with the dominant epistemology, and how it tried to reconcile itself with modernity. Thus, we can see that there was something tempting about the situation pertaining to neo-Kantianism, especially in the rather disciplined and concentrated form it had at the time in the figure of the young Rickert in Freiburg, who represented the southwest school of neo-Kantianism in Germany. Thus, he began with Rickert. Then, he thought – and this was still before Husserl's arrival in Freiburg – to have found a road to freedom in Husserl's *Logical Investigations* and in his motto 'back to the things themselves', thus in phenomenology. On closer examination, this turns out to be only partially correct. Obviously, we should not underestimate the impetus Heidegger received thereafter from Husserl's presence in Freiburg and from his access to Husserl's earlier manuscripts. Heidegger saw his true model in the young Husserl's sterling working method.[2]

Yet, Husserl's turn to the *Ideas*, that is to say, his transcendental self-interpretation in association with the neo- [72] Kantianism of Marburg, especially Natorp, was for Heidegger certainly a kind of challenge. It is well known that even as an assistant of Husserl, Heidegger made exclusive use of the *Logical Investigations* as a topic of teaching, and not the *Ideas*. The influence of

Schleiermacher, Dilthey, and Kierkegaard may have also played a role in this period – a period whose fundamental features were quite correctly described by Pöggeler. These influences liberated Heidegger at the decisive moment to recognize Aristotle as a phenomenologist. This was a new turn in his path, whose steps are unmistakably visible in *Being and Time*. However, we cannot simply take this to mean that he had turned further away from his Catholic origins. The theological problem – or rather: the long anti-theological *pathos* in Heidegger – without doubt determined his whole development. At the beginning, this problem made it easier for him to distance himself from Thomism, guarding him against an uncritical appropriation of Aristotelian metaphysics. In this regard, the impetus he received from Kierkegaard was also helpful. This was manifest above all in the chapter on *phronēsis* in the *Nicomachean Ethics*, which was to become so decisive for me. Then, Aristotle's *Rhetoric*, in particular the doctrine of the affects in the second book, provided him with the concretization of the concept of life that he attempted to put in the place of subjectivity. These are well known facts. I mention them only to show the kind of tendency toward freeing himself from the concept of subjectivity that was already at play in Heidegger's early orientations. Today, now that the early lectures are available, we can describe more accurately Heidegger's way, starting with the facticity and the care of life. For this, the transcendental mode of questioning represented an understandable temptation, after his proximity to Luther and his counterpart in Marburg (Bultmann and his proximity to Kierkegaard) did not turn out to be a real opening. Heidegger was left, so to speak, with no other way than to adopt the framework of Husserl's transcendental phenomenology to begin with, even if he was perhaps always trying to render phenomenology more concrete and radical, with the prospect at the back of his mind of advancing along his own way with greater freedom later in Freiburg. It is only with the failure of his overarching programme in the anticipated third part of *Being and Time* that something decisive happened to him.

Without a doubt, the return from Marburg to Freiburg and, thus, to a university that had been powerfully shaped by Catholic theology amounted for Heidegger to a more focused and radical critique of the tradition of metaphysics and thus also of the most recent version of transcendental philosophy incarnated in Husserl. However, he could very well have discovered in Plato, as the epigraph of *Being* [73] *and Time* indicates, the fact that transcendental philosophy continued in his eyes the obfuscation of the true question of being. In Aristotle, he believed to have rediscovered what was preparatory to the new way of posing the question of being. However, how could he manage this from his defensive position? Could the preparation to the question of being really be accomplished by taking one's orientation from Aristotle's *physei onta*? Or from Kant and from the *Da-sein* in human beings? It is possible that the events of the time, such as the worsening of the crisis in the world economy and the radicalization among the ranks of the unemployed, may have awoken vague expectations about possibilities coming from the east. In any case, it appears that the radicalism of a daring thinking came alive in him then and for the first time. More recent presentations have indeed emphasized often enough and with success the two versions of 'On the Essence of Truth' and the relation between 'freedom' and the concealment of being. Instead of speaking of Dasein and its opening of horizons, Heidegger speaks now of the openness [*Offenständigkeit*] of being. This contains an important task that has obviously not been accomplished in its conceptual analysis. It is in this situation, it seems to me, that Heidegger's close and tight association with Hölderlin's mythological and poetic mode of speaking was established as the national socialist 'ascension' fizzled out.

Still, it would be too comfortable to think of this change in Heidegger as a break in his internal consistency up until then: as if his true goal should have been to make a metaphysics of finitude from the transcendental analytic of Dasein or however one wants to envisage the future perspective from what he had sketched out, at the time, in his inaugural lecture in Freiburg. In any case, his flight into poetic concepts does not mean that he had given up, so to speak, on the rigour of the concept from that point on. I myself recall the impression of near shock I received in hearing his lectures on the work of art in Frankfurt. In these lectures, I saw him oppose the 'earth' to the familiar fundamental concept of transcendence, instead of 'beings as a whole'. There was no connection to Aristotle or Hegel to be found when Heidegger, from then on, placed the discourse on 'being' explicitly within Hölderlin's poetry. However, this did not mean that he had abandoned the way of concepts in favour of lyricism. Of course, Heidegger had taught us that metaphysics since Aristotle is a thinking together of the question of being and the question of the highest being. However, the fact that 'being' is not a being had always been true and remained true. Since Heidegger took it upon himself to think being without beings and separated from all beings, this was hardly a mere falling back on an etiolated negative theology, a view that is presented as something obvious in all presently prevalent interpretations, such as the one by Habermas. Instead, one should recognize the impressive multiplicity of the forest paths, which Heidegger had since treaded, as efforts to think and thus lend a better sense to the 'turn'. [74] 'Forest paths' suggest that they lead to no destination and that one has to turn around [*umkehren*] if one is on them. Is the way of thinking that Heidegger attempted really only about such turning [*Umkehren*] and returning [*Rückgang*]? Is it not always followed by a new attempt to start over? Is Dasein not so much a being as the place in which the 'there' shows itself as an event [*Ereignis*] and thus, simultaneously, as the history of being and its concealment? We should conceive of yet another perspective on Heidegger's true path of thinking, fully aware of the changing uses of the concept of 'turn' that researchers have come up with.

In the end, it remains convincing that Heidegger's vision starts from the fact that it is life – and not the subject, not the thinking subject – that lives fully through its tendencies to uncover and always also to conceal. This is indeed the fundamental experience of life as Heidegger had in his earlier years and always tried to retain: 'Life is hazy [*diesig*]. The concept of 'turn' [*Kehre*] implies the following: it is the path that thinking takes and takes in its turning. The path makes a turn that one follows in order to arrive at the actual goal of reaching the top of the mountain. It is not a forced interpretation to reach the view, as I have done, that Heidegger's turn is in truth a return [*Rückkehr*]. It was based on reflections that were without a doubt also fully alive in Heidegger's use of language. At the time, he had given up the transcendental interpretation of his project once and for all and was always looking for new ways leading to the top. We know that, in his own eyes, this was not to become an enduring work: 'Ways, not works.' However, this can perhaps still point to the open. I will not contest that Heidegger himself uses the plurivocal expression of 'turn' in different senses. One must only guard against the temptation of a false nominalism, which goes against Heidegger's own intentions, as if we had several concepts of 'turn' at our disposal. Certainly, Heidegger could often insist precisely on the fact that the turn means a change of direction. However, in truth, Heidegger tries to say only one thing with this: what is it that happens to those who follow their own path of thinking and experience the fact that the path turns? Already in 1930 Heidegger wrote to me, after his new beginning in Freiburg: 'Everything begins to slip away' [*Es kommt alles ins Rutschen*].

In contradistinction to forest paths, we are not even really dealing with a turn around [*Umkehr*] in a path. There have constantly been such turn arounds in Heidegger. This is why he could call his paths of thinking 'forest paths'. This brings to expression precisely the fact that he persistently leads his own thinking in the direction that counts. Because I see things this way, I have never engaged in efforts to differentiate different concepts of 'turn' in Heidegger. What matters is to experience the turn *in actu exercito*, and this means: in doing the thinking, which again means: in the words that language offers us for this purpose. This is how I always come back to my own **[75]** orientation, which can be traced back to how I conceived of my own book. I had initially planned to publish it, not with the title 'Truth and Method', but with the title 'Understanding and Happening' [*Verstehen und Geschehen*]. For, it is precisely not so much our doing that matters as what happens to us when thinking leads us on the way of thinking. I must point out that, in addition to the early testimonies I mentioned in my talk in Messkirch,[3] there is a testimony in *Being and Time* of Heidegger's 'pre-ontological' turn – and this is Heidegger's own way of using language. On this topic, we may read a study by Kathleen Wright on the early linguistic signs of the turn in *Being and Time*, an essay that she undertook under my encouragement. However, the turn does not belong to the things about which one talks. The path turns in thinking and talking. This is all that matters, even for my own contributions, whether they can help us find the direction of the path of thinking pointed to by Heidegger or whether they lead us astray, to a 'liberal' Hegelianism or, instead, to derivative forms of metaphysics. It is no longer within my expertise to make a judgement on this question.[4]

17

On the Beginning of Thought (1986)[1]

[375] There has been a renewed interest directed at the pre-Marburg era, the early years of Martin Heidegger in Freiburg during which he was still fully finding his feet as a theologian and a thinker. What provided the most important impetus for this turn in Heidegger studies was the publication by Walter Bröcker and his wife of an early lecture by Heidegger during the winter semester 1921/22. In addition to this, we are also grateful to the works of Thomas Sheehan for more precise knowledge of Heidegger's beginnings. Through the mediation of Ernst Tugendhat, Sheehan was able to consult the notes of Helen Weiss, who transcribed Heidegger's lecture on the *Phenomenology of Religion*. Sheehan also unearthed other materials from Heidegger's early period. We are seeing a steady flow of new information about Heidegger's early years from this new direction of research, which Otto Pöggeler is meticulously conducting with his many collaborators. It is not for me to take part in this research. It can also not be right for me to wait for its results. All that we have learned in the meantime completes the picture of a Heidegger as a young theologian whose insistence on clarity about life and whose own audacity of thought sent him on the way to becoming purportedly one of the greatest thinkers of the twentieth century. It is thanks, in particular, to the reports on the lecture on the *Phenomenology of Religion* that we have an important clue as to the nature and the extent of the motivation that led the young Heidegger, already in his early Freiburg years, to become absorbed by the problem of time. I have explicated the situation as I see it in my essay titled 'The religious dimension'.[2]

The presence of Heidegger, which is slowly growing in world consciousness, even if it is still lagging far behind in Anglo-Saxon countries in comparison to others, [376] has to deal everywhere with legitimate and understandable counter-forces. One should be aware of this if one wants to understand Heidegger's talk about the beginning of thinking. The question is whether this beginning lies behind us and initiated our thinking from time immemorial or whether it lies in front of us as another thinking. The latter would most definitely mean the end of that kind of philosophy that in the history of the West distinguished itself as science against religion and poetry, eventually distinguishing itself even from modern science as 'philosophy'.

The first significant objection made against Heidegger is his relation to logic. It is not so much the fact that logic has made astounding progress in recent decades, whereas Heidegger, as well as my own generation, was only trained in obsolete Aristotelian logic. We are concerned here with a deeper conflict, which pertains not only to Heidegger, but to continental philosophy in general. We know from Rudolf Carnap that one can pick apart any of Heidegger's sentences. In what has become a famous essay, he indeed completely mistreated Heidegger's inaugural lecture in Freiburg, 'What is Metaphysics?' by using all of the tricks of the trade. In this lecture, as we know, Heidegger talks of the 'nihilating of the nothing' [*das Nichten des Nichts*]. If we attempt with Carnap to write this sentence on the board using mathematical symbols, we find that it does not work. In this formal language, through which everything that can be thought is to be fixed univocally, there is no symbol for the nothing. There is only a symbol for the negation of a sentence. Thus, Heidegger's talk can only be an illegitimate mystification. Such an objection may be correct from the perspective of propositional logic. But what then will become of philosophy?

Hegel does not fare better in the eyes of modern logicians on this score. And Heraclitus the obscure? We have to ask ourselves what philosophical discourse is and how it can claim to escape the laws of propositional logic. In fact, this holds true not only for philosophy, but for any kind of discourse between human beings that falls more precisely under rhetoric. In a still different way, this also holds true for all poetic discourse. In any case, it remains philosophy's highest task to look into why it is that what language permits and what symbolic logic forbids, cannot, as Carnap suggests, be simply brushed aside as 'feeling' or nonrigorous poetic play.

The second objection, which is related to the particular theme of the beginning of philosophy, comes from the side of the philologists. We should not simply consider it unjustified when the classical philologist (of which there is a little bit in me) is often sensitive to the violence of Heidegger's interpretations of Greek texts or [377] establishes the downright incorrectness of his interpretations. We must ask ourselves, I think, whether we must look down superciliously upon this great thinker and whether we ourselves have not perhaps lost sight of something more important when we close ourselves to the power of Heidegger's thought because of such provocations.

The third objection is finally the one originating from the sciences. We have, on the one side, the social sciences, which find their field neglected by Heidegger or believe it to be found in a distorted form in Heidegger: 'society' appears as 'the they' and they find this unreasonable. On the other side, the natural sciences cannot fathom either how Heidegger could say: 'Science does not think.' Perhaps, such a statement demands, if we want to understand it, a thinking that is really of another kind than the one operative in the empirical sciences.

All this congeals into the dominant prejudice: what Heidegger says after *Being and Time* is no longer verifiable; it is poetry or better: a pseudo-mythology. Here it is said of being that 'it gives' [*es gibt*], that 'it sends itself' [*es schickt*], that 'it holds sway' [*es reicht*], and whatever else may be said of this mysterious something, this being. Compared to the 'nihilating nothing' of the inaugural Freiburg lecture, which so infuriated Carnap, this is something still totally different. The 'nothing' appears almost innocuous. Here, we have a question that must occupy us and concerns particularly the role that art and, above all else, Hölderlin's poetry played in the thinking of the later Heidegger.

If I mention these objections against Heidegger, it is to make room for our theme in its overarching contemporary relevance. With this, a question is posed that is directed at our civilization as such. Originating in the West, our civilization has spread over the whole globe more or less like a thick net. It concerns the basic attitude of the sciences and scientificity, which characterizes our age. The inner inexorability of progress based on science and scientificity, despite all that it suggests, is gradually beginning to appear to the general consciousness as something suspicious. It is forty years ago that Heidegger wrote his essay on 'The End of Philosophy' and this essay sounds today as if it gives expression to everything that has in the meantime motivated our thinking and our concerns taken altogether. The same goes for our theme 'The beginning and end of philosophy'. It is a theme that preoccupies us and although it is based on Heidegger's work it directs its questions at us. What does it mean that we are done with philosophy? And that in the best case scenario, philosophy breaks down into a series of individual sciences, which, with a little bit of indulgence, can be tolerated within the whole of our scientific culture alongside the sciences? What is this tendency of our time that the formula 'the end of philosophy' is supposed to describe [378]. And what kind of thinking must begin in the event of this end?

Clearly, this is not to suggest that there is nothing alive among us other than technological frenzy. When Heidegger speaks of the end of philosophy, we immediately understand that we can only talk like this from the Western perspective. Elsewhere, there was no philosophy that set itself apart so much from poetry or religion or science, neither in East Asia nor in India nor in the unknown parts of the earth. 'Philosophy' is an expression of the trajectory of Western destiny. To speak with Heidegger: it is a destiny of being that has in fact become our destiny. The civilization of today, as it appears, finds its fulfilment in this destiny. This is the destiny to which the whole of humanity is submitted under the dictates of the industrial revolution. Whether this revolution is linked to an identical or different economic system plays a secondary role. A centralized economy, as it appears, for instance, in the style of the Russian five-year plan, displays enormous similarities with the imperatives of capitalistic society.

When we hear about the end of philosophy, we understand it from such a situation. We realize that the separation between religion, art, and philosophy, and perhaps even the separation between science and philosophy, are not originally common to all cultures, but precisely shaped the particular history of the Western world. One can ask oneself what kind of destiny this is. Where does it come from? How is it that technology could develop into such an autonomous force of necessity that it has become the hallmark of human culture nowadays? When we question in this manner, Heidegger's surprising and apparently paradoxical thesis suddenly appears to be disturbingly plausible: it is Greek science and metaphysics, whose effects in today's global civilization dominate our present.

Obviously, the technological civilization of today assumes a new character, in contradistinction to the older periods of our history. In his essay on technology, Heidegger himself insisted upon the fact that technology is not merely a continuation of the traditional art of handicraft and a perfecting of humanity's industrial reason, but consolidates into its own system. Heidegger envisaged this system by using the provocative name of 'enframing' [*das Gestell*] – a genuine Heideggerean coinage. We will have more to say about this peculiarity of Heidegger to coin words. In order to understand the concept of 'enframing', we only have to think of some usual uses of the word. Thus, we speak, for example, of the switch tower [*Stellwerk*]. It is the contraption found in all train stations that operates the tracks so that the trains are guided to different platforms. From this everybody understands Heidegger's concept. Enframing is the concept of the totality of such setting and switching [*Stellen und Schalten*], **[379]** ordering and securing [*Bestellen and Sichern*]. Heidegger convincingly explains that we are dealing here with a mode of thinking that determines everything and definitely not just with the peculiarities of the industrial economy as such. His thesis is that philosophy comes to its end, because our thinking has fallen under the complete domination of 'enframing'.

Now, Heidegger asks: where did this come from? What is the beginning of this history? At any rate, the beginning does not lie just at the point where modern science became increasingly dependent on the advancement of technology. Rather, modern science is itself in a certain sense already technology. This means that its relationship to natural beings is that of a constructive trans-formation and thus an attack that seeks to break a resistance. To that extent, science is aggressive inasmuch as it forcibly imposes its conditions for objective knowledge upon beings, whatever they may be, whether nature or society. In order to illustrate this with an example that we are all familiar with because we are indeed living in a society, let us take the survey questionnaire. The question-naire is a visible document for the purpose of forcing questions on people, which they are supposed to answer. It does not matter if one does not want to or cannot responsibly answer. It is like an imposition.[3] Social sciences need their statistics just as the natural sciences apply their quantitative methods to nature. In both cases, it is the dominance of the methods that defines what is capable of providing knowledge and what is worth knowing. This means that the access to knowledge must be controllable. Even if scientific theory develops quite nuanced concepts of how science operates, it is undeniable that the great break-through of the seventeenth century is still at work today. It took its first steps in the physics of Galileo and Huygens, and found its fundamental formulation in the reflections of Descartes. We also know how, through this breakthrough of modern science, the West has brought about a disenchantment of the world. The industrial exploitability of scientific research eventually allowed the West to rise to the status of the pre-eminent power of the whole planet, representing an all-encompassing economic and transport system. However, this was certainly not the first beginning. There is an older, so to speak, a first wave of the 'enlight-enment', in which science and its investigation of the world developed for the first time. This is the beginning that Heidegger has in mind and always has in mind when he speaks of the end of philosophy. It is the awakening of the Greeks to *theoria*. Heidegger's provocative thesis is that this beginning of scientific enlightenment [380] is really the beginning of metaphysics. Modern science is indeed born in a battle against traditional metaphysics, but this, in fact, entails that science is a consequent effect of the physics and metaphysics of the Greeks. Does the true beginning of the destiny hovering over us not lie there, with the Greeks? Heidegger has thereby asked a question that has for a long time occupied the thinking of modernity.

We can illustrate this with a special and well-known case. At the inception of the modern science in the seventeenth century, people began to turn their attention to the most unheralded of the great Greek thinkers, to Democritus. As a matter of fact, the atomic theory, the doctrine of Democritus, has become the triumphant model of modern research into nature. Now, we know almost nothing of Democritus. It was precisely this that led to the fact that, above all in the nineteenth century when the advance of modern science had captivated the general consciousness, Democritus was elevated to the status of the great predecessor, who had been repressed by the obscurantism of a Plato or an Aristotle. Since then, our relation to the Greek beginnings remains broken and contested in a peculiar way. This is especially true for Plato. Aristotle was for a long time held to be a dogmatist blind to experience and Hegel's revival of Aristotelian thinking did not really make him worthy of recommendation. By contrast, Plato was turned into a Kantian before Kant and transformed into a precursor of the mathematical natural sciences, when he was not regarded, on the contrary, as the reactionary destroyer of the promising efforts of Greek research. Now, Heidegger formulated the question of our Greek beginnings in an essentially more radical way than these controversies did. He uncovered a continuity in Western history at a deeper level, emerging earlier and enduring until now. It was this element of continuity that precisely led to the separation of religion, art, and science, and is itself superior in radicality to the European enlightenment. How did Europe take this path? What is this path? How did it begin and how does it lead eventually to being expressed programmatically in Heidegger's 'forest paths' [*Holzwege*] as the end of the path?

Without doubt, this development is connected with what we call in German the 'concept'. To say what a concept is seems to us to be as difficult perhaps as it was for Augustine to say what time is. We all know what it is and, yet, we cannot say what it essentially is. When we are dealing with the concept, the word always already reveals something. In a concept something is put together [*zusammengegriffen*], combined together [*zusammengefasst*]. The word says that the concept seizes [*greifen*], grabs [*zugreifen*], and puts together [*zusammengreifen*] and, in this way, conceives [*begreift*] something. Thinking in concepts is thus an active thinking that is intrusive [*eingreifend*] and far-reaching [*ausgreifend*]. Now, Heidegger has interpreted the history of metaphysics as the expression of an originally Greek experience of [381] being. More precisely he has interpreted it as this very movement of our experience of thinking that grasps beings in their being so that we secure being as that which has been conceived and, to this extent, grasped in hand. This experience finds expression in the task of metaphysics of grasping beings as such in their beingness [*Seiendheit*], leading to the logic of definition, of the *horismos,* in which a being is brought to its concept. This was the great task that thinking set for itself and this Socratic turn is not something like a straying from the right way on which ancient atomism allegedly was. It could only seem like this at the turn toward modernity. When Greek philosophy and all its will to know cross over into Rome and into the Christian Middle Ages, this ultimately leads, through a humanist revival of the Greek tradition at the dawn of modernity, to a new concept of experience and science. This is a long history.

Already in 1923 Heidegger had characterized the feature of modernity as the 'concern for knowledge that is known.' This Heideggerean formulation not yet known in the literature means that the question concerning the truth (*veritas*) is superseded by the concern for certainty (*certitudo*). It is, so to speak, the morality of the method that one prefers to make small, even if humble steps provided they are absolutely controllable and certain. This is how it is in Descartes' *Regulae.* One can say that the Anglo-Saxon analytic philosophy of today has remained more faithful to this scientific morality than Hegel or Heidegger.

Heidegger's claim has now obviously come true. With the full power of his rich imaginative thinking, he was able, from its vantage point, to render really visible the destinal unity of Western history as it arose with Greek metaphysics and culminates in the total domination of technology and industry. Such a claim involves going back behind the logic of propositions. One can hardly escape such a claim when it comes to philosophy, which is in competition with religion and art over the truth. Philosophy is concerned with questions that cannot be avoided and for which one will never indeed find demonstrable answers. We have, for example, the well-known question from Kant's dialectic of pure reason that is formulated in the cosmological antinomy: what was there at the beginning? Physicists cannot ask such questions. When we ask them about what existed before the 'Big Bang,'[4] they can only smile. From the perspective of their scientific self-understanding, it is meaningless to ask such a question. Kant is right about this. Yet, this is what we all do. We are all precisely philosophers, unswerving in our compulsion to question, even where no answer and not even a path toward an answer is to be seen. This is what I mean when I speak of going back behind propositional logic. It is a going back behind that which can be formulated in valid propositions. Such a return has nothing to do with logic itself, its validity, and [382] indisputability. However, it has something to do with the fact that the monologue of rigorous argumentation cannot stifle our thinking that questions imaginatively. The step backward that occurs in such a questioning does not only go back behind the proposition toward that which we, in the language of everyday life, continue to question. It also goes back behind what we can say and question at all in our language. We are always finding ourselves in a tension between what we try to say and what we are not able to put adequately into words. This is the constitutive distress with language [*Sprachnot*], which belongs to human beings. This is the distress into which every true thinker proceeds, who cannot let go of the strenuousness of the concept.

Language was not made for philosophy. Thus, philosophy must borrow words from the language that we inhabit and saddle these words with a proper conceptual sense. These are often technical words, which, in an expanding scholarly culture, diminish more and more into schematic symbols, behind which there is no longer any living linguistic intuition. This corresponds to the tendency of human Dasein to fall, which Heidegger described in *Being and Time*. One uses formulas, normative concepts, scholarly concepts, and conventions, without thinking originally.

In our age of modern science there is thus a new task for thinking, which German idealism already recognized as such, but only partially redeemed. I have learned from Heidegger how to conceive of this task. It consists in becoming aware of the conceptuality in which we think. Where does it come from? What is in it? What is unintended and unconscious when I say, for example, 'subject'? Subject is the same as substance. 'Subject' and 'substance' are both translations of the Aristotelian expression *hupokeimenon*, the foundation. This Greek concept has absolutely nothing to do with the German concept of subject, which means the 'I'. Nevertheless, we say with utter obviousness (even if with contempt) of someone: this is a wretched subject. We also talk as philosophers (with timid deference) about the transcendental subject, in which all the objectivity of knowledge is constituted and which is not supposed to be the empirical ego and also not a collective subject. We see in this example the extent to which the conceptuality of philosophy may be alienated from the original linguistic sense. It was the task of a destruction of this metaphysical conceptual tradition that the young Heidegger resolutely took on. Within the limits of the adequacy of our talents, we learned from him to find the way back from the concept to the word, not with the aim of giving up conceptual thinking, but with the aim of giving back to it its power of intuition. In doing so we follow what the Greeks had already prepared for us. [383] We especially follow Aristotle, who in Book *delta* of his *Physics* analyses fundamental concepts and builds up their plurivocity from out of the way they were used in language. It thus concerns rendering passable again the path from the concept to the word so that thinking speaks to us again. Under the weight of a two-thousand-year-old tradition of thinking, this is no small task. It is difficult to draw a strict line between the precisely elaborated concept and the word that is alive in language. For all of us, there is always the non-arbitrary usage of conceptual words, which originate from metaphysics and continue to perpetuate thoughtlessly in our thinking. Heidegger could summon an unusual linguistic power in order to make language speak to philosophy again. A lot is awakened here. Ultimately, it is a great heritage that is waiting to be taken over. For the German language it is above all the Christian mysticism of Meister Eckhart, Luther's Bible, and the expressive power of our dialects, which have remained untouched by scholarly jargon and academic chatter.

What was new in Heidegger is this: he not only possessed such a great linguistic power, as, for example, the Silesian cobbler Jacob Böhme, but he broke through the whole Latin scholastic tradition of our conceptual language by going back to its Greek beginnings. He succeeded in recognizing in the concept the word that awakens intuition. This was from the beginning Heidegger's peculiar gift. By saying this, I do not contest that the formation of a concept constantly requires the suppression of the historical and semantic implications of a word in favour of the univocal conceptual definition. Even Aristotle proceeded in this manner. Nevertheless, it was a new, a newly sounding Aristotle that Heidegger brought back to language in his works on rhetoric and ethics and who could also shed a new light on metaphysics. Thus, Heidegger succeeded in going back behind the neo-scholastic and Thomistic conceptual language. Finally, one understood that it is not poetry and not the reveries of the mind when one summons linguistic potentialities whose meaning content cannot be written on the board.

The potential that language possesses must serve thinking. This means that, following the word through the analysis of its meanings results in the delineation of a concept. Conceptual analysis, thus, distinguishes several meanings, which are all alive in language, but these meanings only gain their circumscribed determination in the context of speech. This is what the theory of the implicit definition has always noted. Eventually, in a proposition a meaning will take the lead over others in a forceful manner and the other connotations will at most play a subsidiary role. This is what the thoughtful use of words looks like.

In poetry things are not completely different. There, we hear several meanings of a word, but even here the usage of words [384] will happen to have the proper direction of meaning fixed to such a large extent that the unity of the sense of the discourse remains within reach. Nevertheless, there we see the potential of language to develop even further. What really constitutes the volume of poetic discourse is the fact that this discourse enriches itself through the many meanings and many facets that the words have and put into play.

In the case of philosophy language does not stop exercising its productive power. Even here the univocity of the meaning, established by conventions, of a multifaceted expression allows the connotations lying in words to speak alongside in the background. These connotations allow the words to fit the flow of discourse and thought. They can also turn this flow around. This can go so far as to throw thought off its usual course. Hegel often did this consciously in order to take the speculative content of an expression to its culmination in contradiction. Heidegger many a time proceeds even more violently. He even set it up as a requirement when he speaks of the 'leap'. One must, so to speak, force thinking to leap in such a way that one accentuates the secondary senses of words or sentences so that they take on the opposite sense. This can acquire a fundamental significance in the context of philosophical discourse when, for example, a common formulation gains a totally new expressive meaning through the plurivocity of a word. Thus, Heidegger did not read the question, 'What is called thinking?' in the conventional sense of the word 'to call' in the sense of 'to mean'. In an unexpected twist, he liberated from the word the secondary sense of 'to call', meaning 'to call for'. This is obviously not to be imitated. In the case of Heidegger, it is worth pursuing such indications. This does not simply mean to repeat the indication, but to follow it and this means: to take a direction for one's own thinking and to stay the course. This provocative play with the word 'to call' makes us aware as to how much language can open up possibilities for thinking.

Here is another example. In Heidegger's essay on technology, there is a discussion of causality and cause. Heidegger says here: 'In truth, it is an inducing to go forward [*Veranlassung*].'[5] In the context of his exposition, it suddenly dawns on the reader as to what 'to induce to go forward' [*Veranlassung*] actually means. One discovers here that there is a 'letting' [*lassen*]. To let something commence always implies that one lets it happen. Thus, Heidegger loads a normal German word such that this word says something still more from itself. It says: here something is let into being when it starts. Immediately, the word known in the world of automobiles comes to mind: 'starter' [*Anlasser*].

Certainly, in the case of texts, when we are dealing with language in such a way, we are by and large going against the text. The text has its unitary intention.

This must not necessarily be a conscious intention on the part of the writer, but at any rate the one who receives the text, the one who [385] deciphers it is directed toward what the text says. It is clear that Heidegger many a time turns the intention of a sentence on its head. Suddenly, the word goes beyond the usual possibilities of its use and is pressed into making visible something that is no longer thought. Often Heidegger mobilizes etymology to this end. When one relies on scientific research one places oneself, in my mind, in the hands of a rapidly changing scientific validity. In such a case, Heidegger's recourse to etymology easily loses its power to convince. By contrast, in other cases, Heidegger can make us aware of something with the help of etymology, what is still speaking latently in the linguistic sensibility, lending Heidegger confirmation and corroboration. Then, he succeeds in turning words back to an original experience from which these words stem and to make this experience audible anew.

In any case, the exercise is explicitly concerned with words, whose semantic power can be recognized and brought to expression. This exercise has great exemplars, above all in Aristotle. The best-known example is the Greek word for being, *ousia*, which in latinized metaphysics received the conceptual sense of *essentia*. This was the translation of *ousia* that stems from Cicero. What does the word itself mean in the spoken Greek of the time? In this case we can easily reconstruct the context in German: *ousia* means landed property [*Anwesen*], the agricultural real estate, as we also speak about a house or a single farmhouse. Farmers can say of their possessions: 'It is a good property' [*Anwesen*]. The Greek can say the same and can say it right up to the present day. Whoever knows Athens can see this. After the exodus of the Greeks out of Asia Minor at the beginning of the 1920s, the old Athens grew by a million refugees and expanded itself into the countryside. However, all of them are housed in their own small houses. All still have 'what grants them presence' [*Anwesen*]. Thus, what constitutes the being of a being as its *ousia* retains a real intuitive force [*Anschauung*]. Landed property is that which allows what is granted presence [*Das Anwesen ist das Anwesende*]. Landed property [*Anwesen*] constitutes the essence of the dwelling of the farmer. Farmers are aware of their own being in their own *oikos*, in their own enterprises [*Betriebe*], and have their being in the present [*gegenwärtig*]. Here, the word *ousia* manages to make the philosophical conceptual sense clearer in its relation to the original meaning of the word.[6]

When we become aware of the whole semantic field of the words *ousia, parousia, apousia* in this way, we additionally feel that Heidegger's use of the concept of 'presence at hand' [*Vorhandenheit*] is unsatisfactory. I have no better suggestion, but in the expression 'presence at hand' we either hear too much of a mere existing, *existentia* in the sense of the scholastic philosophy of the eighteenth century and, with it, the whole conceptual world that belongs to the empirical sciences of modernity, exclusively dedicated to counting, measuring, and weighing. [386] In that sense, we do violence to the Greek concept. Or we hear too much of the relation to the human hand, which causes the words 'presence at hand' and 'readiness to hand' to mingle together almost indistinguishably in the translation into foreign languages. Both these alternatives do not lie within the sense of 'being' as 'what allows presence' [*Anwesen*]. This does not mean the existence of the object established by measuring and weighing, but also not what is merely linked to use, the *procheiron*, what is at hand. In settling for the expression 'presence at hand',[7] Heidegger neglected the difference in the understanding of being between the modern natural sciences and Greek metaphysics. By contrast, he hits the bull's eye with *Anwesenheit* [coming into presence], because this word still lets resonate the entering into presence [*Anwesenheit*] of the divine in being like the Greek word *parousia*. This is precisely what happens while thinking. When one wants to let words speak, they do not always fit. Sometimes, they go over the proper intention of the speaker. One can learn from Heidegger the possibilities as well as the dangers of such a thinking with language.

In this regard, Heidegger's translation of *alētheia* as 'unconcealment' is particularly instructive. Not because he maintains the privative character of this semantic formation. This is nothing special. It is even childish to want to claim now that this had perhaps been seen elsewhere before Heidegger and that the word had been translated as unconcealment [*Unverborgenheit*], disclosure [*Entborgenheit*] or even unveiling [*Unverhohlenheit*]. Of course, this was true. Even others knew that much of Greek. In fact, the word 'unveiling' [*Unverhohlenheit*] would actually come closest to the original Greek usage. This is how Humboldt translates it. In fact, one finds the word regularly in connection with the *verba sentiendi*.[8] Heidegger stubbornly rejected this linguistic evidence of the connection with the *verba sentiendi* and always emphasized that *alētheia* is not primarily in sentences, but in being itself. He appealed in this regard to Aristotle and ultimately not with full justification. What mattered to him is that it is being that shows itself or conceals itself and not the subject that talks about being. What mattered to him was surely not to preserve the fact that being is independent and out of the reach of subjective knowledge and discourse, for example, in the manner of modern 'realism' that claims something that nobody denies. What mattered to him, on the contrary, was to recognize in 'being' itself not only disclosure [*Entbergung*], but also concealment as an original experience. Self-showing and self-concealing belong inseparably together (just as authenticity and inauthenticity in *Being and Time*). Heidegger's point was about the essential ambiguity that is thought in the concepts of being and *alētheia*, and this he had in mind from early on, as evidenced in the lecture course [387] of 1921/22. Finally, this led him to question behind metaphysics. It would indeed be ridiculous to claim that metaphysics had not questioned after being in the manner Heidegger does, when he understood under 'being' the same as Aristotle, who conceptualized the being of beings.

Heidegger's questioning behind metaphysics rather concerned an experience of being and *alētheia*. This experience was supposed to precede the turn to metaphysics and would be the original experience. He was in search of testimonies for such an experience in the early thinking of the Greeks. His studies of the pre-Socratics, Anaximander, Parmenides, and Heraclitus were supposed to make appear this original experience of being as simultaneously 'what allows presence' [*Anwesen*] and 'what forecloses presence' [*Verwesen*], as '*whiling*' [*Weile*]. He thus wanted to make this experience resonate out of the tradition as 'there', in which being shows itself to thinking. In fact, such an experience has left its trace in the formation of the word *alētheia*. The word includes, through *lēthē*, both sheltering and concealing [*Bergung und Verbergung*]. Heidegger, though, had to recognize eventually that his indefatigable efforts to summon the pre-Socratics as witnesses supporting his views were a failure (*Zur Erfahrung des Denkens*, p. 34). A real thinking of *alētheia* as the dimension in which being happens [*ereignet*], thus also the dimension in which being withdraws itself, is nowhere to be found. Instead of the temporal structure of the 'event', which Heidegger searched for in being and *alētheia*, we always find in the texts only the present [*Gegenwart*], presence [*Anwesenheit*], and absence [*Abwesenheit*] of beings, and not 'what allows presence' [*Anwesen*]. From this we can draw an important conclusion. Fundamentally, it is not the sayings of these early thinkers that appeal to Heidegger; it is not the sentences through the interpretation of which one could conceptualize the 'event' of being. It is rather the semantic findings, the semantic connections inscribed in the fundamental Greek words, such as *logos, phusis, on, hen*, etc., that promise to the thinker of today, who seeks to take a step back, an insight into the oldest experience. These fundamental words explicitly precede conceptual thinking by a wide margin. It is the primordial history of the Greek language (only the hint of it) that opens itself to Heidegger's gaze in a powerfully significant way. Herein lies the true genius of Heidegger, as indicated by the attempts at interpretation I described above, but not only by them. The intensity of Heidegger's thinking concentrates itself not so much in the interpretation of texts as in taking the full measure of words and whole semantic fields, and in pursuing the secret vein in the primordial rock sediments of language, whether it concerns Greek thinking or poetry or the thinking and poetry in our own German mother tongue.

Perhaps one can say that Heidegger uncovered the deeper dialectic of the word behind the artificial dialectic of being, which Hegel articulates in his logic, in order to pass beyond the conceptual language of the Greeks. [388] This dialectic of the word only plays an occasional role in Hegel. Heidegger had cultivated a particularly keen ear for it. In the mother tongue, as in any language, we have an articulation and a schematization of a totality of world experience. If we follow the vein of this work of sedimentation, many a time we hit upon a real source for extraction. Not always. Even in mining, we do not strike gold in all galleries.

What remains decisive in all this is the originality and the radicality with which Heidegger sets his guiding question into motion. In thinking *alētheia* as 'unconcealment', he conjured up his own vision of the Greek beginning, which was to elude his research into the Greek written testimonies receding always further and further into a more obscure pre-history. In 'unconcealment', 'concealment' speaks alongside. This has a connotation that Heidegger wanted to liberate for us and whose true content we grasp only slowly: in unconcealment, there is also the lifting of concealment. What emerges and presents itself in the turning of thinking and in speaking is at the same time something that is sheltered in words and, perhaps, remains sheltered, even when something about it 'comes out' and has been disclosed. The essence of the work of art and, in particular, the essence of poetry stand out in this regard. This coincides with Heidegger's conceptual intention of thinking the experience of being as the counterplay between disclosure and concealment. He thus managed, on the basis of the experience of being as entering into presence [*Anwesenheit*], to make us aware of the destiny of the West, that is to say, the path from the Greeks to the oblivion of being in our days to come. He thus indicated to us the unity of the West as our destiny of being, over and beyond the difference of time-periods, antiquity, Middle Ages and modernity. Already in his interpretation of Aristotle, he presented in the manner of a challenge, which we failed to heed, the fact that being was only conceived as disclosure [*Entborgenheit*] and the coming into presence of what is granted presence [*Anwesenheit des Anwesenden*] and that time was only conceived as the counted number of nows. For someone struggling with an understanding of oneself as a Christian, this would become a challenge. His life-long rejection of Hegel's speculative idealism points in the same direction. The dialectical reconciliation that Hegel had founded between religion and philosophy could indeed be a temptation for someone who was troubled by the problematic nature of Christian theology. Even more, it was Hegel's reconciliation between spirit and history that spoke to the young Heidegger who had been raised mainly in the historical field of Catholic theology. This is why we can in fact find in the so-called *Duns Scotus* book an almost programmatic commitment to Hegel. However, the bland academic way in which the crumbling neo-Kantianism turned to Hegel could not in his view be maintained. Kierkegaard and, preceding him, Luther became decisive figures for the young God-seeker and radical critic of all half-measures. Volume 61 of his [**389**] complete edition gives us clear proof of this. The citation of Kierkegaard, with which the planned volume (which was never finished) began,[9] shows Heidegger on his way to a 'hermeneutics of facticity'. When this book project is titled 'Introduction to Aristotle', we must obviously ask ourselves today how this radical impetus that Kierkegaard represented for Heidegger must have been at work in the interpretations of Aristotle and recognizable in the texts of the *philosophos*.

In retrospect, it is clear how all these discussions of Heidegger have their critical point of reference in the conceptuality of Christian theology and ontology as it is determined by the Greeks. As a result, the kinship that he found between Luther and Aristotle was the real challenge for him. This explains why his critique of those who inspired him, Hegel, Kierkegaard, Dilthey, as well as Augustine and the Aristotle of the practical philosophy, was the same, namely, that their conceptual means were not sufficient to fulfil their essential intentions. This, for Heidegger, granted Aristotle his exceptional position. Although his early students, among whom I counted myself, only understood this later, Heidegger's interpretations proceed from the point of view that Aristotle indeed accomplished the fateful turn to the metaphysics of presence and led it to victory. The young Heidegger understood his calling to be a going beyond such a metaphysics, even though Aristotle was the only one Heidegger credited with having developed a conceptuality commensurate with his intentions. All the others, whom he admired and by whom he was inspired, could not accomplish this, not even the Hegel of the speculative synthesis and not even the Kierkegaard of the 'indirect communication', which the young Heidegger reformulated into the formula of 'formal indication'. This could explain why the one who in conceptual craftsmanship is quite the weakest among his great predecessors, Nietzsche, precisely because his weaknesses were so evident, was in the end to exercise the most enduring fascination on him.

At the time in Marburg we were so taken by Heidegger that he appeared to us as an Aristotle come back to life: he set metaphysics on a new path by taking his point of departure from the *Rhetoric* and the *Nicomachean Ethics,* and found expression for his own experiences by making Aristotle concrete through these experiences. It was a new approach to Aristotle and certainly the only one available if one took really seriously the 'operative sense' [*Vollzugssinn*],[10] to speak with the young Heidegger, against the idealistic metaphysical tradition. Later on, for the concept of 'operative sense', Heidegger employed the scholastic expression *actus exercitus,*[11] a magic word with which he put us all under his spell. There is not only the *actus signatus,*[12] the proposition and its predicative structure, but there is also the *actus exercitus*. It is on this basis that Fink in his later rewriting of Husserl developed the expression 'operative concept'.

[390] We were all too naive at the time and took Heidegger's concretizations of Aristotle as his philosophy. We did not see that Aristotle was for him the adversarial bastion that he invaded with a completely different question. This is the question that arose from the factical life experience of a thinker contemporaneous with us, who was raised as a Christian and was inspired by Kierkegaard. He himself never forgot what Luther's Heidelberg edict meant, namely, that as a Christian one would have to renounce Aristotle. Our identification of Heidegger with Aristotle was, however, understandable if we think of the fundamental principle, according to which he worked and which he inculcated in all of us: one has to strengthen the opponent. He really succeeded in doing so. It was for us like a revelation when we grasped that *zōon logon echon* must not be thought as *animal rationale,* but as the entity that has language. Today, it appears almost unbelievable that the pressure of the scholastic tradition was at the time so heavy that even neo-Kantianism did not manage to see this through the textual evidence of the passage in the *Politics*.[13] One can see how the title of a late publication by Heidegger, *On the Way to Language,* coincided with the direction that Heidegger's own thought took from early on.

What is the upshot of all this for language in the thinking of philosophy? Does the secret of the word and even of the conceptual word not lie in this: the word does not only, like a sign, refer to something else, to which then one can then seek one's own access, but the word essentially always conceals more in itself than it expresses? It is in the nature of the sign to point entirely away from itself. It is no small matter to be able to understand a sign simply as a sign. Dogs cannot do that. They do not look where the finger points but snatch at the finger that points. We are all already thinkers even when we only understand such a pointing. How much more of a thinker are we when we understand words. For, what is at stake here is not only the understanding of the word as a single word, but rather the manner in which the words are spoken in the totality of a melodic flow of discourse, which acquires persuasive force from the articulation of the whole discourse. Words always stand in the context of a discourse. To conduct a discourse is, for its part, not only about running through a constellation of words endowed with meaning. One can think of the meaninglessness of sentences given as examples in a good grammar book of a foreign language. They are deliberately meaningless so that we are not distracted by their objective content, but rather focus on them as words. These sentences are not really discourse. No written discourse is as such real discourse. Discourse is addressed to someone. As 'text', a discourse speaks only when the tone, in which something is said, touches me. There are genuine and false tones, convincing and unconvincing discourses, true and false discourses. There is that which is not all brought out of concealment and presented by discourse, whether spoken or written, and there is that which is not all completely dissimulated by such a presentation.

[391] Heidegger proposed an etymology for the word *logos*: it is supposed to be the 'harvest that gathers' [*legende Lese*]. When I read this for the first time, I rejected it and found that it was a forced explanation of the word to say that, as *logos*, it is both disclosing and sheltering. However, Heidegger's challenge was quite an awakening. Those who follow the excavation of the semantic field, which is at play here, and, from there, go back to the well-known conceptual word *logos,* have at once penetrated a rich background in terms of their conceptual and linguistic sensibilities. I have to concede here that Heidegger has made a word speak. *Logos* is really the 'harvest that gathers',[14] *legein* is 'harvesting', gathering and putting together, so that it is like grapes that are plucked from the vine and stored as the harvest. What are gathered together in the *logos* as the unity of the harvest are certainly not only the words that form a sentence. Any word is itself already such that in it a lot is gathered together into the unity of an *eidos*, as Plato says when he questions the *eidos* according to the *logos.*

What can lie in a sentence or a word is seen in a particularly convincing way in the work of Heraclitus. He was for Heidegger without a doubt the most exciting of all early Greek thinkers. His sentences are like riddles, his words like hints. In Heidegger's small hut in Totnauberg, carved into the bark of the lintel over the door was the inscription in Greek letters: 'The thunderbolt steers all things.' This sentence in fact brings together the fundamental vision of Heidegger, namely that what is granted presence in its entering into presence [*das Anwesende in seiner Anwesenheit*] emerges in a flash of lightning. For a moment everything is clear as day only to fall as instantaneously into the darkest of nights. Heidegger surmised that this suddenness, in which 'what allows presence' [*Anwesen*] is there only for an instantaneous flash of a moment, was the Greek experience of being. The lightning, which in one fell swoop makes everything enter into presence [*anwesen*],[15] grants for a short while the entering into presence [*Anwesenheit*]. In this case it is a whole sentence that in a lightning flash makes visible the belonging together of the unveiling and concealing as a fundamental experience of being. One can understand why Heidegger was so fond of Heraclitus' word. Now, how is this lightning, in which things suddenly become clear, supposed to endure, to be sheltered in words, to become a discourse that explains everything? This is the task and the distress of thinking. Once I was with Heidegger up there in the hut. He read to me from an essay on Nietzsche that he was writing at the time. After a few minutes he interrupted himself, pounded the table with his hand, rattling the tea cups, and exclaimed despairingly: 'This is all Chinese.' To behave like this is truly not the style of a man who would like to be esoteric. Obviously, Heidegger really suffered in his effort to find the words that could be again rendered meaningful to us, beyond the language of metaphysics. How does the fullness of a vision arise out of the dazzling clarity, in which a flash of lightning rends the night? How do a series of thoughts coalesce, in which the words become a new discourse? Truly, it is a fundamental human experience that is expressed here. [**392**]

Here we live in the exceptional situation that even what is absent [*das Abwesende*] is granted presence [*anwesend*], *noō narheonta*, in 'spirit'. All thinking is like a thinking beyond, a planning beyond, and a dreaming beyond the boundaries of our short existence. We can never, as it were, establish – but also not completely forget – that it is only a 'while' and cannot understand how the infinity of the spirit is limited by finitude, by death. From here, Heidegger thinks beyond toward a universal ontological turn. For this experience, he again lets an absolutely simple word speak: 'there is' [*es gibt*]. What is the 'it' that 'gives'? Who gives what here? All this blurs into unclear contours. Nevertheless, everybody understands perfectly well what 'there is' means: 'something is there'. Heidegger has again rendered meaningful the simple turn of phrase and thereby made us aware of an original experience, which is well known from the poetic mystery of the neuter in Greek as well as in German.

Finally, let us ask how the experience of death is to be thought from the perspective of Heidegger's late insights. In *Being and Time*, such an experience was vividly developed in the analysis of anxiety. Can we think the riddle of death from the duality of concealing and sheltering? Heidegger speaks of the 'gathering of sheltering' [*Gebirg*], in which death is sheltered and concealed. This points to a mode of experiencing death, which can perhaps be found in all cultures, even there where, perhaps, the cult of the ancestors dominates everything. Without a doubt, the description offered by *Being and Time* was drawn from the experiential ground of Christianity. Our Western mode of thinking is, however, not the only possible way to think the experience of death. The cult of the ancestors, but also, for example, Islam, seem to think differently. Did the late Heidegger think beyond his own Christian experiential world? Perhaps. At any rate, he came to think back to the Greek beginnings. Who does not keep in mind the significance of Heidegger's Greek beginnings cannot really understand the late Heidegger. This is not due to Heidegger, but due to what 'philosophy' means for us and what our culture determines as worth knowing. We remain determined by this provenance and must, from here, let ourselves be empowered toward the future and toward, so to speak, the possibilities of thinking.

At all times this can be said: what is so moving for us in Greek philosophy is the fact that it ran its course, which was the course of the spoken and responding word, without immediately reflecting on what the speaker is and who this speaker is. The Greeks had no word for the 'subject'. They also had no word for 'language'. *Logos* is what is said, what is named, what is gathered together and laid down. This is not seen from the standpoint of the speakers' capacities, but rather from the standpoint of that in which everything is gathered together and upon which we are in mutual agreement. There is a classical statement by [393] Socrates which goes as follows: 'Whatever I say, it is not my *logos*.' This holds true for Heraclitus as well as for Socrates. The *logos* is common. This is why Aristotle could reject all theories that attributed to words a natural reference. The signs that we call words are *kata sunthēkēn*, which means: they are conventions. This does not mean agreements that were struck at a certain time. Yet, signs are also not from nature. This is a singularity that includes us from the outset and which precedes all linguistic differentiation into this or that word, into this or that language. This is the beginning that has never begun, but is always already. It grounds the ineradicable proximity between thinking and speaking, and itself remains superior to the question of the beginning or the end of philosophy.

18

On the Way Back to the Beginning (1986)[1]

[394] Back to the Greeks: this is a theme that compels our attention not only in relation to the thought of Martin Heidegger. In fact, since the time in which the modern German university was given its current form by the new humanism, the style of philosophy and the ideal of education in Germany have been largely determined by the return to their Greek origins. In our century the development of modern thought has ventured into frontiers in which the word of philosophy has to reckon with a peculiar new situation. I do not mean by this that we are in something like a crisis of the sciences but rather that the age of science and of the belief in its unlimited progress, which is associated with the essence of science and research, is aware of its limiting conditions. The very possibility of maintaining the life of humanity is at stake. Today, this view is gaining ground in the consciousness of everyone.

So it is that a thinker like Martin Heidegger, who for the last two decades has had barely a public presence in Germany, begins to find a new resonance. The great monumental edition of his works, which is currently being published, vividly sets before our eyes and in person Martin Heidegger the teacher. For someone who has accompanied him from his very beginnings as a student, this is a particular satisfaction. In my lifetime I have found myself in a difficult situation when people wanted to know something about Heidegger or even believed to know something against him. I had to ask them whether they had then also listened to Heidegger's Marburg lectures. Whoever did not know the Marburg lectures was, in my eyes, only familiar with one half of Heidegger. Today, these lectures are available to everyone in the form of an edition, for which, despite its quite controversial character, we all cannot be grateful enough. Since very recently, we can go even further back into Heidegger's beginnings than I myself could have experienced in my early years when attending his lectures. A manuscript of Heidegger's lecture from the years 1921/22 was published by Walter Bröcker and his wife, Käte Oltmanns in 1985 as part of the new complete edition. There, Heidegger the teacher [395] becomes accessible to readers. This is even more than what the lecture-manuscripts from his later Freiburg period, which Heidegger himself published, allow us to see. This is especially true for Heidegger's recourse to the Greeks. This recourse to the Greeks is certainly palpable at every turn in that *magnum opus*, his first publication *Being and Time*. In his later publications, however, it is found only at the complete service of his own concerns. This is why we must take a particular look at Heidegger's beginnings if we want to grasp his way back to the Greeks in its peculiarity. It will become clear that this peculiarity documents at the same time his significance as a thinker of our epoch.

Return to the Greeks: this always presupposes the consciousness of a distance, if not an alienation from Greek thought. Such a consciousness could only arise with the new project of science, which in the seventeenth century initiated the triumphant advance of science into modernity. What is the situation of philosophy since then? We all certainly know that Aristotle is not necessarily to be seen as obsolete in the age of modern science, even if it may sound this way in Galileo, who puts in the mouth of a Simplicio the orthodox scholasticism of Aristotelianism and its blindness toward experience. Even in the eyes of those who practise science and have assimilated the new science, Aristotle in fact continues to be a valid point of reference.

This is particularly clear in Leibniz, who recognized that the step back to the Aristotelian tradition of the forms as entelechy was necessary, even after he became convinced of the irrefutable significance of the new Galilean physics, as he himself describes it during a walk in Rosental in the outskirts of Leipzig.[2] Even Hegel's last titanically grand attempt to integrate into an encyclopedia of the philosophical sciences the entire content and substance of our modern scientific knowledge of the world, in particular of the natural sciences, already sounds in its name like the encyclopedic spirit of the 'master of those who know' – like Aristotle.

This is the case to an even stronger degree for the influence and the contemporary relevance of Plato in modern thought. There was above all the neo-Kantian movement, which through Cohen and Natorp, on the one side, and through Windelband and his students, on the other, fashioned Plato into a predecessor of Kant under the buzzword of 'history of the problem'. This was already the case with Hegel, who with his great mediating gaze with which he was able to see everything together, emphasized in a way the whole of the great epoch of Greek philosophy and the inner proximity between Plato and Aristotle, which had basically remained forgotten for 150 years.

[396] In the case of Plato it is not just the ingenious attempt of German idealism to integrate science and metaphysics into a great system that elevated

him to a new relevance. An immediate recourse to the Platonic tradition is already at work in Kant, which is plainly reflected in a critical phase of his own thinking, in the title of his dissertation: *On the Form and Principles of the Sensible and the Intelligible World – de mundi sensibilis atque intelligibilis forma et principiis.*

It is absolutely not the case that this recourse to the Greeks was something peculiar in German intellectual history, and certainly not in the post-Romantic epoch of our modernity so inclined toward history. We do not even have to mention the rich Western tradition of philosophy in the Christian age, which established itself partly in the name of Aristotle and partly in the name of Plato, who was pitted against Aristotle. Nevertheless, Heidegger's return to the Greeks is something different, something new, indeed something simply revolutionary. His return to Aristotle and Plato is not a return aiming at reconnecting or developing further the mode of thinking that these philosophers had opened. Rather, it serves the elaboration of a radically critical questioning, which we hardly perceived in the beginning, but to which we have all grown sensitive in the meantime, having entered an age that can no longer expect all its cures solely from the continuing progress of science.

Heidegger's recourse to the Greeks was anything but a humanistically oriented turning-back. On the contrary, it was a dissatisfaction with this tradition that drove him and finds its semantic expression in such linguistic monstrosities as historicity and facticity or in the reformulation of the traditional concept of 'existence', following in the footsteps of Kierkegaard. It is in this context that we must ask about the true meaning of Heidegger's return to the Greeks and we must ask in particular what this uncommon return undertaken by Heidegger to Aristotle, to Plato, and finally to the beginnings of Greek thought, signified for his own intellectual concerns.

In order to come closer to this question, we need to depict the 'hermeneutic situation' in which the young Heidegger saw himself. With the phrase 'hermeneutic situation' I use an expression that I read with astonishment for the first time in late 1922 in a small manuscript of Heidegger that was given to me by Paul Natorp. This small manuscript was the introduction to an interpretation of Aristotle and carried the title 'The Hermeneutic Situation'. There was a discussion of Luther, of Gabriel Biel and of Augustine, of Paul and the Old Testament. I am not even completely sure if there was a discussion of Aristotle at all in this introductory chapter. From the stages of this way back toward Aristotle, we can perceive clearly the difficulties in which the young Heidegger found himself at the time, when according to his own acknowledgement, [397] he wanted to be a Christian theologian.

What intellectual succour did the philosophy of his day offer him? In the beginning what he had was certainly not so much the metaphysics of Aristotle, with which he was acquainted through his theological studies, but his encounter with Edmund Husserl and his discovery of the phenomenology of the life-world. The phenomenology of the life-world understands phenomena as they are experienced in factical life and gives itself the philosophical task of investigating these phenomena in their immanent *a priori* structures. This phenomenology does not aim any more at the facts permeated by the scientific model upon which Mach, for example, tried to build his 'mechanics of sensations'. In this sense, the task of phenomenology stood under the motto: 'Back to the things themselves', which means: to the phenomena and not to the problems bestowed upon us in the scholarly framework of psychology and the theory of consciousness. The research mentality that is thus formulated is in fact the compensation for a deficit, which had spread by way of the epigonal revival of the intellectual movement of German idealism in the academic philosophy of the nineteenth century. It is certainly true that, when construing a conceptual language for philosophy that was free from scholastic Latin, Fichte as well as Schelling and Hegel, and naturally even Kant had to bear the oppressive burden of the heritage left by the scholastic philosophy of the eighteenth century. Yet, we can be certain that, in all their constructive daredevilry, listening to the lectures of these system-builders brought forth an experience of vividness for all their listeners similar to what I experienced when attending the lectures of Husserl and, even more so, those of Heidegger. We did not have the feeling of progressing from point to point, from argument to argument, but rather believed in the end to have circled around a single object and in such a way that this something finally stood before our eyes in its three dimensions. For this descriptive vividness Heidegger found his decisive model in Husserl, and he always spoke with wonder of Husserl's most trivial investigations regarding sense perception, the adumbration of the perceived object with its horizon of anticipation, and the experience of disappointment that comes with it, etc.

On the other hand, the figure of Husserl certainly presented Heidegger with a challenge. As a student of the great mathematician Weierstrauss, Husserl had started out from the philosophy of arithmetic and through the criticism that Frege had leveled against his philosophy of arithmetic, he became a logician and critic of 'psychologism'. In elaborating the massive research programme that he associated with the idea of phenomenology, he could not summon any systematic help other than by aligning himself with neo-Kantianism. This was **[398]** the way in which he tried to justify the phenomenological criterion of evidence for the intuition of essences. The apodictic evidence of self-consciousness, as the fundamental structure of the transcendental subject was expected to provide legitimacy as evidence. This is how he thought of my own teacher at Marburg, Paul Natorp, as a real comrade in arms or at least as his predecessor.

If Heidegger resisted Husserl on this point without falling back into a naive or metaphysical realism, it is due in no small part to the fact that Heidegger took Wilhelm Dilthey as his supporting figure. It is from the Diltheyan standpoint that Heidegger tried to overcome the excessive neo-Kantian formalism and distortion of Husserl's phenomenological *pathos*, to the extent that he undertook to illuminate by phenomenological means the phenomenon of history and the historicity of our forms of thought and concepts.

If I have characterized the two concepts of historicity and facticity as the keywords of the young Heidegger, then I must immediately mention the name of Kierkegaard alongside Dilthey, who was for Heidegger the essential representative of historical thought. The word facticity goes precisely back to Kierkegaard, as well as the emphatic sense of the concept of 'existence', which Kierkegaard brought to bear against the unending mediation of speculative thinking and thus against Hegel. This was how the hermeneutic situation appeared when Heidegger began his journey. He was disappointed by the scholastic narrowness of the theology current at the time and of the formalistic blandness of the neo-Kantian philosophy of his time; but in the same breath he was inspired by the descriptive genius of Husserl and burdened by the entire problematic of historicity and what people then began to call 'philosophy of life'. Then, he found another, even greater teacher. This teacher turned out to be Aristotle.

This sounds absurd because Heidegger was ultimately one of those who had been educated in the Catholic theology of his time and who, at the beginning, had even held his philosophical lectures in the theological department of Freiburg. Surely, he had been acquainted with an Aristotle there, who had been interpreted by St. Thomas and by the anti-Reformation systematicians in the style of a Suarez. It was, to boot, an Aristotle who had been distorted by what could well be called a wishy-washy compromise into which Catholic dogma had entered in the course of the nineteenth century with neo-Kantianism in particular. A thinker of Heidegger's penetrative power could not feel good about such a mish-mash of ideas. Moreover, he stood as the child of his time in the whole problematic of Christianity in the age of science and did not come to terms with the theoretical stance of his theology. He, thus, found himself confronting the vital question of learning how to connect the modern way toward science and enlightenment with Christian existence. This was obviously the deepest concern for him. How **[399]** then could he hope to find help in this regard from Aristotle, from the one who was always invoked as the authority of the last resort for the official Catholic Church doctrine?

Heidegger in fact found a new and uncommon point of access to Aristotle. He approached Aristotle from the bottom up, so to speak, beginning with factical life. His first lectures did not deal with the *Metaphysics* or the *Physics* of Aristotle but with the *Rhetoric*. In these Aristotelian lectures, he dealt above all with one of the aspects of all authentic rhetoric, as it was first sketched by Plato in the *Phaedrus*, namely, that one must be acquainted with the listeners in order to be able to convince them. Aristotelian rhetoric became for Heidegger an introduction to philosophical anthropology. In the second book of Aristotle's *Rhetoric*, Heidegger found in particular the doctrine of affects, of the *pathē*, the dispositions and resistances that the listener feels toward the speaker. In the light of this Aristotelian model of thought and fuelled by his own vivid experiences, Heidegger acquired an insight into the meaning of 'situatedness' [*Befindlichkeit*]. This is his own expression, which is highly suggestive and yet, at the same time, good German. He elaborated the fundamental meaning of situatedness as one of the most important steps leading beyond the narrow confines of the philosophy of consciousness.

The second point of access that Heidegger found to Aristotle did not immediately lead to the ultimate question of first philosophy either, but concerned ethics. This is easily understandable. The energetic insistence of Aristotle on the separation of the question of 'human good' from all the far-reaching cosmological or metaphysical-mathematical implications, expressed what a man in Heidegger's position and in his hermeneutic situation deeply felt. Thus, the turn to the sixth Book of the *Nicomachean Ethics* in particular, in which what we would call 'practical reason' is offset in a detailed analysis from the exercise of theoretical reason, was to provide Heidegger a true toolkit for his self-understanding. If Kierkegaard's critique of 'understanding from a distance' [*Auf-Abstand-verstehen*], which he makes against how the Christian Church in his country at the time represented the Christian message, expresses a universal truth, then it is most certainly this: the moral-political decisions, which human beings have to make in the concreteness of their life-situation, are no 'understanding from a distance' and not about the mere application of rules and norms that allow the subsumption of the concrete situation under the universal. It is obviously a fundamental insight into the life-praxis of human beings that coming to a judgement and orienting oneself in one's own life-situation is no mere application of knowledge, but is rather co-determined by what human beings themselves are and what they have become.

[400] This is what Aristotle called '*ethos*', the constitution of the being, accrued through time, of those who, in the praxis of their life, have always to decide anew. What Aristotle calls the virtue of *phronēsis*, this judiciousness and circumspection, which is not simply an intellectual capacity, but rather manifests a moral attitude bestowing guidance and discernment, must have also moved a young thinker like Heidegger inspired by Kierkegaard's critique of idealism. Thus, Aristotle was a highlight of his own academic courses and signified for me a first introduction to discipleship when learning from Heidegger. This concerned the interpretation of the sixth Book of the *Nicomachean Ethics*. For all the precision that he brought to bear on his interpretation of Aristotle, Heidegger's access to the material was still completely dominated by the impulse of his own questioning. He was carried away to often violent but also tremendously impressive reformulations [*Aktualisierungen*]. I was myself a witness to this as he one day put up for discussion the opposition between *technē* and *phronēsis*, between the craft and efficiency of technical knowledge, on the one side, and the moral judiciousness of *phronēsis*, on the other, in relation to the following statement by Aristotle: in contradistinction to technical knowledge, there is no forgetting in *phronēsis*, that is to say, no unlearning [*Verlernen*]. He concluded this seminar session, in which these two concepts, *technē* and *phronēsis*, had been delineated against each other, with the challenging statement: 'What does it mean that there is no '*lēthē*' in *phronēsis*? My dear friends, it means that it is conscience.' Certainly, this is to wrench out and transplant a conceptual world configured in a totally different way and, with it, also a conceptual expression into Christian and post-Christian modernity. This presents us in no way with a model for interpreting Aristotle, but rather with a model for a deliberate confrontation with the tradition of philosophizing. Nevertheless, there remained much even for Aristotle to learn, and particularly to take in this fact: what we call leading a life with conscience is based, on the one hand, on the self-interpretation of our life, which illuminates and guides our behaviour, but also, on the other, on the rationality of *logos* and the public community [*Gemeinsamkeit*], in which the understanding of life finds its articulation.

In the field of rhetoric and in the field of practical philosophy, we are certainly very far from the problems that moved and unsettled the young theologian in his own tentative thinking. However, in both these realms it was particularly clear how the Aristotelian construction of concepts arises almost seamlessly from out of the reflective experience of life itself and how the expressive power of the words that are really in use is kept alive in the language of concepts. To this extent, Heidegger's efforts to bring to concepts the experiences of factical life with phenomenological faithfulness can be easily recognized in this Aristotelian model. As a matter of fact, Heidegger saw it as his phenomenological mission to remain true to the motto 'to the things themselves' [401] and study phenomena as they are articulated in human self-interpretation. The greatness and revolutionary nature of his thinking consisted precisely in the fact that he also knew how to bring the conceptuality [*Begrifflichkeit*], which had been developed for millennia in scholastic philosophy, back to its roots in the factical experience of life and its emergence into linguistic expression. He was already conscious of this in a methodologically assured way, and already in his early lectures called his manner of proceeding a 'destruction'.

In this concept, there is no whiff of what, in our vulgar usage, sounds like annihilation [*Zerstörung*]. It means nothing other than the stripping bare of that which needs to be stripped bare so that concepts will speak again. What set the task of destruction for Heidegger's phenomenological drive was above all the conceptual burden of latinized formulations, their transformation and continued development right up into modern languages, as our conceptual language has experienced, which is Greek in origin. It is the jargon in which I myself was still brought up and in which we learned the conventional conceptual structure, the play of categories and modalities, the classification of philosophical positions in the form of idealism, realism or naturalism (or however these different party affiliations go in the scholastic language of philosophy). For a man, who wished to learn how to justify rationally his own religious decisions and who was in this sense animated by the compulsive drive toward philosophizing, namely the striving toward clarity of life, it must have been of a completely decisive significance that he rediscovered in the Greeks a thinking that had built its concepts from out of their factical life-experiences. Such concepts would not be pushed around like symbols on small ivory plates. Heidegger's often ingenious linguistic neologisms and conceptual coinages always arise from the semantic life of spoken language itself and therefore retain an immediate expressivity in their best formations. It belongs to the irony of world history that there is nevertheless something like a Heidegger-scholasticism, which only imitates, fixes the natural-artistic constructions of Heidegger into something like a rigid terminology, and shuffles them this way and that. This is not what Heidegger envisaged under phenomenological philosophy and it is the opposite of that which impelled him to make a return to the Greeks. He read what was really present there, in that he followed the movement of thought and the life of the Greek language.

The famous definition of the human being as *animal rationale,* as *zōon logon echon,* can serve as an example here. Tradition has made us so accustomed to think only of reason and of the equipment of human nature, which consists of the use of reason. In this regard, there is no doubt that this definition is to be found in a context in which *logon echon* means 'having language'. The forms of communication, which [402] nature has granted many of the living beings, is transcended in a decisive manner by human beings. Nature gave them *logos* and this means here language. To have not forgotten this when he wanted to penetrate into the problematic of ontological philosophy in metaphysics was the benefit that Heidegger drew from his phenomenologically oriented relationship to language. It is not from logic and from the rationality of logical thinking, but from language and the commonality of that which is shared and communicated in words, that Heidegger was able to tackle the problems of ontology and the doctrine of being. Aristotle had seen the distinctive characteristic of human language in the fact that it places everything at a distance and makes things present in their distance. Certainly, this distinctive characteristic of language is something that is universally valid. It is an exceptional position of the Greeks and the distinctive characteristic of Greek language that it opened up the way to the concept, along which the Greeks proceeded. Plato and Aristotle above all succeeded in drawing the line that separates philosophy and science from rhetoric and the pragmatics of linguistic usage. However, they have left constantly open the path that returns from the concept back to the word and the path that leads from the word to the concept. One must also take Aristotle at his word and then things show themselves in their original self-givenness. This was why Aristotle became for Heidegger a compelling partner and teacher. Even though there was no place for Aristotle within the framework of the neo-Kantian systematic, Heidegger even managed to convince Husserl of the fact that Aristotle (the lack of a transcendental subject notwithstanding) was a real phenomenologist.

There was in fact an entire series of arguments in favour of this. Despite all the classifications that are attributed to him, Aristotle himself kept an open mind. We are realizing more and more today how much Aristotle tried to penetrate into the openness of the unknown in the full extent of his research fields and teaching areas. It is really the case that in Aristotle there was an authentic phenomenological starting point. There was no system and no compulsion toward a system here. A nice anecdote can illuminate how much this was an inspiration for Heidegger. It is said that Heidegger discovered his incipient path toward becoming a thinker already in the days when he was a student at the gymnasium in Konstanz. There he was one day caught reading a book under his desk, obviously during a class period that was not very interesting. The light fiction he was reading was Kant's *Critique of Pure Reason*! This was like carrying the Marshall's baton in one's knapsack,[3] something hardly any other student in our century had ever done. Obviously, he also had a particularly understanding teacher who encouraged him quite a bit. This teacher did not discipline him, but gave him instead something to read, perhaps as an antidote against Kant. This **[403]** was a book by Franz Brentano *On the Several Senses of Being in Aristotle*. In it the four meanings that Aristotle distinguishes in his conceptual investigations are precisely analysed with the conclusion that in Aristotle they are not really brought together and that there is no general concept of being that could express what is common to all of them. This doctrine of Aristotle is later developed in scholastic philosophy into a significant piece of theological doctrine. The Aristotelian concept of analogy is used for this purpose and one speaks of the *analogia entis*. It allowed theologians to do justice to the ontological distinction between the being of the creator and that of the created. Even if being is not the highest genus, it still makes sense to say that being can appear in different ways: as being-how [*Wie-sein*] (which in scholastic language meant the doctrine of modalities: possibility, actuality, and necessity); as being-what [*Was-sein*] (and this meant the doctrine of substance and categories); and as being-true. All these determinations, which are here accorded to being, have obviously something to do with each other. We are not dealing with mere equivocation, but they are also not specifications of a genus. Heidegger used to say – and I have often heard this from him – 'Yeah, the famous analogy'. With this he indeed wanted to recognize above all the phenomenological *pathos* in Aristotle, who did not try to unify what did not want to be unified. At the same time, there was certainly a challenge for the thinker in Heidegger, for whom what mattered was to develop a conceptuality commensurate with his religious questions. He must have felt challenged by the open incompleteness of Aristotle's question that reveals itself to the uninitiated reader of Aristotelian metaphysics. The challenge was to ask the question of being anew and to do so in a way that it is Dasein, in the awareness of its finitude and historicity, that opens up the horizon of time for the question of being.

The aspect of Aristotle's doctrine of being that accorded the most with Heidegger's guiding interest was obviously the resolution with which Aristotle tried to conceptualize beings in their movement. Aristotle succeeded in doing this with the aid of the concept of *energeia*. This concept is fundamental for the possibility of Aristotelian physics, that is to say: for the ontology of the being that is distinguished by mobility. Heidegger's great achievement lay precisely in recognizing mobility even in the concept of *logos* and in the fundamental metaphysical concepts of Aristotle as well as recognizing in 'being' the 'being produced'. This was the background of *poiēsis* and *producere*, which the Greeks experienced but never reflected upon. Even in the decisive sections of his *Metaphysics,* Aristotle in each case takes beings in their mobility as the guiding thread of his question concerning being as such. Thus, it was particularly the idea of *phusis,* of the self-unfolding of beings into [404] the open in their full bloom and maturity that attracted Heidegger and forced him to make the necessary distinctions. We possess a later reworking of his interpretations of Aristotelian physics, which he treated repeatedly in class. In this reworking the Heideggerian interpretation of Aristotle's train of thought comes to the fore quite clearly. Being is obviously conceived by Aristotle as entering into presence [*Anwesenheit*] and the divine as being present [*anwesend*] to the highest degree. Later on, Heidegger formulated this critically in the concept of the presence-at-hand. Yet, it becomes clear how the orientation of Aristotle toward *phusis* offered the later Heidegger conceptual choices that allowed him to eliminate the concept of subjectivity and consciousness completely from the thematic of ontology. If one wishes to understand the Aristotelian doctrine of being, the relationship to *logos* and the 'proposition' [*Aussage*] is certainly decisive, but not the concept of consciousness or self-consciousness, which remains dominant in Hegel's doctrine of absolute spirit as the *noēsis noēseōs*. Thus, for Heidegger, different from the Hegelians, the distinctive characteristic of *on os alethes* as that of authentic being (*thēta* 10) became a confirmation that unifies *kinesis* and *logos*: being, which is 'there'.

How did Heidegger come to terms with Plato, whose Pythagorean surrender to the number and the numbers clearly did not appear in any way to allow us to think mobility as being? It may astonish us that Heidegger never related to another aspect of Platonic thought, which is found in the concept of the soul as the self-mover and which belongs equally closely to the Pythagorean vision of the numerical order of being. This doctrine could have challenged Heidegger toward a sharpened critique, if he wanted to accentuate the historicity of human thinking for the renewal of the question of being. It is worth noting how Heidegger's reception of Plato is instead always subordinated to the Aristotelian metaphysical question and remains silent about the *psuchē*.

Let us follow the little evidence that attests to Heidegger's recourse to Plato. In his recently published lecture of 1921–2 there is a small section devoted to Plato. There[4] Heidegger praises the expressive power of Plato's style, his manner of speaking, and the style of his thinking, and adds that there is no contrast made yet in what comes to expression in Platonic sayings between the expressive power and the intended meaning, that Plato finds himself, so to speak, in the transition toward concepts. It seems to me telling that Plato is viewed only in this direction, only on the way to the concept and there is not a glance at what Plato's poetic art had held onto in word, speech, [405] and mythical lore, all that was to be lost in the transition toward concepts.

The second piece of evidence for Heidegger's recourse to Plato is his lecture on Plato's *Sophist*. This lecture became famous for the fact that Heidegger took the motto for his first great work *Being and Time* from the *Sophist* in order to introduce the question of being: 'For it is clear that you have known … all along what you wish to designate when you say "being", whereas we formerly thought we knew, but are now perplexed.'[5] The Platonic dialogue, in which this sentence is found, clearly represented a true inspiration for Heidegger. I even believe that I have found the sentence that formulates this inspiration in the strongest manner (Heidegger later confirmed to me that it was the case, but one should never accept the *verba magistri*[6] unconditionally). In the *Sophist* the question of what being is, is confronted with the traditional concepts of that which is at rest and that which changes.[7] These are, as it appears, two mutually exclusive realms. Either something is at rest or it is in motion. Now we read in the text: 'We really do seem to have a vague vision of being [*das 'Seiend'*] as some third thing, when we say that motion and rest are … According to its own nature, then, being [*Seiende*] is neither at rest nor in motion … In which direction should we, who wish to establish within ourselves any clear conception of being, turn our mind?' 'Yes, in which direction?'[8]

This question is obviously asked by Heidegger himself. Certainly, he could not find satisfaction here in the guiding concepts of movement and rest that Plato sharpened into extreme opposites (see the text of the 'Erker Lecture', p. 16).[9] Yet, even in this form what is essential becomes clear: the question of being cannot be asked in the form of a question concerning what is common to things that are so disparate. The question itself: where does one have to look essentially when one says 'being', obviously still had the same perplexity. This is something Heidegger's own attempts at thinking tried to work out, starting with the first vague hints that this could be *time*, as is already manifest in his discussion of the 'Epistle to the Thessalonians'. We certainly cannot stop saying being. Precisely this universality, which lies in the concept of being, is expressed in this constant implication of the use of the word 'being'. This was obviously, for Heidegger, the true challenge of the *Sophist*. It should be noted that even here the nearness, or rather the inner inseparability of rest and mobility, which is meaningfully delineated in the course of the dialogue,[10] [**406**] is not used by Heidegger for his question concerning 'time' and the 'Dasein in the human being'.

The revolutionary resoluteness with which Heidegger took upon himself the challenge of Plato's question may be illustrated well enough through an episode that I remember and can narrate. (This is indeed the prerogative of the elderly to have been the contemporaries of a bygone present.) In the *Sophist,* as is well known, it is an Eleatic who leads the discussion. This is a man who comes from Parmenides, whose didactic poem in fact sets being apart from the emptiness of the talk about negation and the nothing, and manifests being in its purity. This stranger from Elea pleads as to whether it would not be construed that he wished to commit patricide if he now still claims that both being and non-being are justifiable, even unavoidable. According to my memory (and, I believe, not only mine), this sounded differently to Heidegger. I am even guessing that Heidegger himself had something like this in mind. In any case, this was what I heard and took from the real lecture, even if it is the opposite of what is found in the text: the philosopher must dare to commit patricide! I am almost certain that Heidegger said this. We obviously immediately understood it from his relationship to Husserl. In any case, this episode may attest to the fundamental revolutionary disposition in which we received the arrival and the teaching of Heidegger at the time, so much so that we turned the sense of the Platonic text, so to speak, into its opposite. It may show with what kind of immaturity we followed him, but perhaps also how everything that came from Heidegger spoke to us, when we believed to find the Eleatic as the patricide, the philosopher as the patricide in a text that says the opposite. The text suggests that the old Parmenides had already seen much farther than us.

The seductive power that Plato's new formulation of the question concerning being in the *Sophist* represented for Heidegger, had, at that time, clearly extended to the whole history of Platonism, including Christian Platonism. Meister Eckhart, in particular, played a big role for Heidegger. At that time (1924), the *Opus Tripartitum*, the major work of Meister Eckhart had been newly edited in Latin.[11] Heidegger was completely fascinated by this work, obviously because the dissolution of the concept of substance when applied to God pointed in the direction of a temporal and verbal sense of being. This can be seen in the text, which said: *esse est Deus*.[12] At the time Heidegger may have sensed in the Christian mystic a secret ally. One of the first books on the list of readings in the programme of the 'Philosophical Seminar' at Marburg in 1923 was the collection of texts *Les* [**407**] *philosophes belges*[13] by Pierre Mandonnet – an Averroistic heresy! In any case, the force with which Heidegger brought Plato and Aristotle to expression in their continued influence shows how much he followed a Platonic principle, which he likewise found expressed in the *Sophist*: we must make our opponents stronger if we want to overcome them.[14] This is what Heidegger had in mind. He wanted to grasp something and raise it to concepts, what could not be managed with the conceptual means of Greek ontology and the experience of being in Greek thinking. Whether this was now human beings in their temporality or human beings in the light of the Christian promise or whether it was the shadow of nihilism, which had fallen over Europe in our century, or the universal human puzzle of death, in each of these cases we are exposed to still other aspects of temporality than just this one wonderful presence of what is presencing [*Gegenwärtigkeit des Anwesenden*], which Aristotle had conceptualized in his ontology and theology.

It is this Aristotelian perspective that Heidegger also extended to Plato, as a kind of counter-perspective. He could in this regard certainly invoke Plato the mathematician recognizing in him the way to logic, and thereby the turn toward the concept of truth that Plato had delineated for Aristotelian metaphysics. We have the following piece of evidence, showing how his critique of metaphysical thinking and the manner in which he envisaged the question concerning being took their definitive form. It concerns the fact that even before the end of the Second World War, Heidegger published a text about Plato's allegory of the cave, in which he interpreted Plato's doctrine of ideas as a step toward Aristotelian onto-theology.[15] The argument is that Plato, to the extent that he characterized authentic being as the being of the Idea, determined the concept of truth anew insofar as this being of the Idea is to be conceived from the standpoint of the one who is looking. This would not be the being that shows itself and opens itself, and, thus, emerges in the manner of *phusis*, which unfolds in accordance with its pre-determined form: bloom and fruit. Thinking in the old Parmenides remains equally nestled in being, as the most distinguished testimony to being. Plato's turn to the idea signifies, against this, a reorientation away from the question concerning the truth of being, which Heidegger sought at the time in the beginnings of Greek thinking, and toward the question concerning the correct way of seeing being. *Orthotēs*, correctness will rule over truth in the sense of unconcealment. This is what Heidegger formulated in strong terms and, with it, made Plato the precursor of Aristotelian metaphysics.

This is at the same time ingenious and radical. At least since neo-Kantianism and its adaptation to the fact of science,[16] the opposition [408] between Plato and Aristotle was so exaggerated that the new science could indeed be understood as Platonism – right up to the extreme interpretation of the Idea as an anticipation of the law of nature. In opposition to this, Aristotle was considered a 'pharmacist', as Cohen loved to say with contempt about Aristotle. Heidegger understood Aristotle better and recaptured the level of speculative understanding of the Greeks that German idealism, and above all Hegel, had possessed. He was as little accepting of the cheap opposition between the 'realist' Aristotle and the 'idealist' Plato as the assimilation of Plato to the modern theory of science. What was most unique to him, though, was that he did not seek a return to the Greeks, like Hegel, within the tradition of a metaphysics formed with Aristotle, but rather against this tradition. It was above all in the appendices to his Nietzsche work that Heidegger formulated with masterful clarity the fundamental theses of Aristotelian metaphysics: being is always twofold, the what something is [*Was-sein*] and the fact that something is [*Dass-sein*].[17] One could inquire, like Plato, into the 'what', the form, the idea in the sense of that something that is unchangeable in the process of generation and evolution, and one could also inquire into the 'fact that', the *hoti* in its individuality and facticity. Both of these are included in Aristotle and in his understanding of being. In an intricate, difficult discussion, Aristotle in fact distinguishes the first from the second *ousia*.[18] Heidegger now sees in this distinction between the 'being what' and the 'being that', the essential step toward metaphysics as onto-theology. With this, the expression 'metaphysics' becomes something plurivocal. 'Physics' speaks within metaphysics too and this means that there lies in it the step toward a structure of the world, which even identifies the divine, the being that is beyond all other beings, as a being.

When Heidegger applies this concept of metaphysics to Plato, it is for him clearly decisive that if we accept the idea as the what of being, the natural unity of the happening of being [*Seinsgeschehen*] as self-unfolding and self-showing would be distorted. For Heidegger, the turn to the 'what of being' compelled Aristotle's step toward physics, toward the individual that is in motion. It is only through this step toward beings in their mobility that it becomes understandable how the mathematical Pythagorean doctrine of ideas could describe the universal order of all beings. It was certainly clear to Heidegger that Plato himself had still perfectly noticed the unity of his vision of the world when he glimpsed the essential secret of the order in all that happens in his vision of the Idea. However, Heidegger's thesis is that it is precisely because of the fact that he turned his sight toward the idea that Plato made it unavoidable that [409] the realm of the factical-real, of beings in movement would come to be identified as the place of these ideal orders. I would certainly interpret it differently, but the facts concede that Plato never really said anything about how the relationship of the Idea to the individual is to be conceived. He obviously assumes that it is self-evident. From where would we know of the idea if it is not encountered in the forms of order pertaining to the fleeting appearances? Even in the case of mathematical entities, such as triangles and numbers, we do not ask: how is it that we have the many, many triangles (theorems of congruence!) or many numbers and many things that are counted? Plato was aware of the fact that the universal and that in which it appears are two different things and 'separated'. This is what makes the step from the Idea toward physics, from Plato to Aristotle unavoidable. This is how Heidegger saw it.

I wonder whether one must not see things differently in Plato. I am pursuing in this regard a first piece of evidence: anyone who has read Plato knows that Plato has never discussed the divine as though it were a distinct being. For Plato, it obviously went far beyond what human reason could really discern. Greek mythology in its Homeric form created such a heaven of Gods, from which Greek culture has received its radiance and glory right up to the present day. However, in the eyes of a thinker, this obviously remains the work of human beings. This is not the divine toward which Plato was directed by his vision of the ideas. This becomes unambiguously clear in the myth of the *Phaedrus* (246 b f.).

In connection with this, I would like to place the concept of Idea somewhat differently within the whole of our philosophical thought that is concerned with the question of being. It appears to me significant (and I have noted this repeatedly in my works) that Plato never uses the word *eidos* for the 'highest' Idea, the Idea of the good, however obscure it may indeed be. He thus avoids using the word *eidos* in the case of the good, although the word is otherwise very common for him and encourages the traditional, although misleading English translation as 'form'. In Plato, there is otherwise no distinction made between 'Idea' and *eidos*. One can understand why he did not have any need for such a distinction. What he had realized was only this: mathematics is not physics. This was, so to speak, his primordial Pythagorean-anti-Pythagorean intuition. He saw that the Pythagoreans with their wonderful algebraic-numerical imagination saw the universe, music, and the soul in proportions that are expressed by numerical concepts. This is how they meant that the latter was the true reality. Now, we have to distinguish what was Plato's great and decisive step in this regard, when he showed that, out of the sensible as it appears, something is to be discerned and, so to speak, to be contemplated [*Hinschauen*] in its proper being. 'To contemplate' is understood in the active Plotinian sense of *theorein*, in which something is set before our eyes insofar **[410]** as one thinks it.[19] This does not mean that one produces it. What one makes present to oneself in such a way is not any less of a 'being' [*seiend*] than the sensible appearance in which it is found. It is in fact that which appearances only approximate as images.

It is thus on the model of mathematics that the legitimacy and the meaning of the Idea become clear. It seems to me no accident that in the famous seventh letter,[20] in which Plato talks about his teaching of philosophy, the circle explicitly emerges as the paradigmatic example for the authentic seeing of being. It is even a false seeing if one confuses the mathematical circle with the figure that is visible on the board or in the sand. In such a figure, what is round is not round through and through. There is always something straight in it. With the figure, the condition of the definition that really defines the circle is not fulfilled. Here we have the knowledge for which one must, as it were, see through that which appears there as the figure toward something that is. It is this original mathematical experience that Plato first deepens into conceptual consciousness. It is clear that in mathematics, because of the misunderstanding of the role of geometrical figures, we can always have only pseudo-proofs.[21] In such cases, we forget that the figures are nothing other than mere illustrations of what is meant.

Now, I maintain that this also constitutes the proper essence of our experience with language: while thinking we see through all that is said and similarly in conversing with one another we 'contemplate' something that is not in the words and not in the models and illustrations of the putative 'facts'.[22] If this is the case, then it is certainly not so easy to liberate oneself from the apparent images of such a contemplation and above all from the illusion of argumentative conclusions, which entangle themselves in contradictions. We experience this when we are exposed to the suggestive power of words and, fully, when we are exposed to the superior art of argumentation of an expert. Ultimately, this can only succeed in a dialogue, that is to say: in the back and forth of talking with one another and in the seeing with one another of what is common. This is how we learn speaking and writing, as well as all the 'arts' that we master.

Here I would like to chime in and say: in truth, Plato had set foot on a ground that does not necessarily lead to the metaphysical consequences of Aristotle. One can perhaps clarify this in the following way: for oneself alone there is no correct seeing and for oneself alone there is also no 'seen', 'the Idea'. There is no individual Idea.[23] To define an Idea means to circumscribe it and this implies that, with its being, there is an almost infinite non-being, namely everything that the Idea is not. The ideas are – Plato emphasizes this over **[411]** and over again – a framework, a network that cannot be disentangled in its superabundance (as *apeiron*). This means that the task of communicating what is meant is a finite task that can only be conditionally fulfilled. To come to an agreement with oneself and others, to mean something and share it, to communicate what is meant requires that we see together and take apart what is meant in words so that we learn to mean the same. It is always one, it is always many.

This is the theme of the dialogue *Parmenides*. What becomes explicit there as the *aporia* of the one and the many remains from the outset in the background of Plato's writings. This was already so even in the dialogues about definitions with aporetic outcomes, which we attribute to the early Platonic period and which inquire into the Good as if it were one. In any case, it is constantly present as a theme of Platonic dialectic. Even if we did not have the *Greater Hippias* (301 a f.) and the indications of the *Phaedo* (101 f.), we would still be steered from here toward the meaning of number. The number appears as the structural model of *logos*. This gives significant weight to the legacy of the doctrine of ideal numbers, which essentially goes back to Aristotle. The Tübingen school showed with good reasons that there are in truth no historical grounds that stand against accepting the connection between idea and number in Plato from the very beginning. I would also refer to my own presentations, which were first published in the proceedings *Idea and Number* in the series of the Heidelberg Academy of Sciences under the title 'Plato's Unwritten Dialectic'.[24]

There, I had presupposed the correspondence that is elaborated between *arithmos* and *logos*. In the meantime I have come to believe that I can go one step further and in the direction in which Heidegger had sought the beginning, in the direction of *alētheia* itself, when the disclosing-sheltering was still experienced unobstructed. In the end, Heidegger did not find it even in the great Ionian thinkers. It now seems to me that he could have found more in Plato, above all in the *Sophist*. One need only draw the consequences of the analysis of non-being accomplished in the *Sophist*. There it is shown that this 'not' (*mē on*) is a distinct *eidos*, the *eidos* of the 'not this' [*das nicht*], the *heteron*. It is like its positive counterpart, the identity of the 'this', constitutive of thinking, just as vowels are constitutive of language. In the end, it becomes clear here as to what caused the dialogue with Theatetus to founder, namely on the question of how *pseudos*, error, the being false of what is thought and said should be possible at all. The new insight is this: The 'not' is always present when something is 'not this, but that'. A significant step toward the understanding of *logos* lies in this step beyond Parmenides.

Nevertheless, the essential task of the *Sophist* was to characterize the sophist [412] and distinguish him from the true dialectician, the philosopher. This was the true lifework that Plato set for himself after the tragedy of Socrates. Yet, with the elaboration of the positive sense of the *mē on* as 'not that', the *Sophist* had in no way succeeded in making this distinction. At the level of conceptual distinctions, the relationship of the philosopher and the sophist finds no resolution in the whole dialogue. This requires looking at those who want to be such a know-it-all, a 'sophist'. Their 'knowledge' is not an erroneous belief. They do not confuse this with that. Their discourse is not false in this sense. It is rather correct. It pretends to be knowledge, but is a pseudo-knowledge [*Scheinwissen*]. It is 'nothing'. This in no way only means that what is believed and said is a 'not that'. In actuality, nothing is said. Here, the unsayability and unthinkability of the Eleatic 'not' returns again in its full radicality. It is not a 'something' about which one can say something. Yet, it 'is' 'nothing', just as being is not a being and still 'is' 'being' [*'ist' es 'Sein'*].

Thus, the distinction between the sophist and the philosopher appears as the radicalization of the distinction between the true and the false, which constitutes the essence of knowledge for everyone. With this radicalization, the concept of *alētheia* is itself radicalized. Distinguishing between the true and the false certainly constitutes the essence of the dialectician. Plato's dialogue shows how, in making distinctions, identity and difference are inseparably entangled with each other. When we regard something that, on any occasion, is always a 'this' and not a something else, all the other perspectives are necessarily obscured. To that extent, there is already present in the distinction, which says a 'not that', just as much concealment as disclosure. Certainly, this 'antagonism' is not conceived as such, but it is brought to fruition in the effectuation of the distinction. Now, the decisive step consists in the fact that the distinction between the philosopher and the sophist is, first and foremost, not possible through a distinction between true and erroneous discourse. In distinguishing the dialectician from the sophist, we do not say of something that is the true, that it is this and nothing else. Rather, *alētheia* manifests itself in the fullness of its twofold aspect of disclosure and concealment, which is experienced as being and appearance. Certainly, Plato never raises this experience to conceptual intelligibility, neither in the *Sophist* nor in the *Parmenides* nor in the 'Seventh Letter'. Yet, the experience that is described everywhere in these texts seems to me to respond, 'in its very exercise',[25] to the Heideggerian search for the thinking of *alētheia* itself.

Here too, Plato goes beyond the old Parmenides. Plato's renewal of the Parmenidean question does not just go one step beyond Parmenides, leading him to *logos* and the being of beings [413], as Heidegger supposes. It also goes a step back to the 'being' that 'is' nothing, that is not a being and yet distinguishes the philosopher from the sophist.

The Socratic-Platonic dialogue is permeated through and through by this distinction in operation [*Unterscheidung im Vollzug*]. So should we not basically ask: how do we obtain that which, from this perspective, is one and, from that perspective, many? How do we find it? Plato's response is the thoughtful dialogue and the so-called method of *dihairesis* or *divisio*[26] that is found in it.

Here is an example. Socrates converses with his young interlocutor Phaedrus about the essence of love – *Eros* – as Phaedrus, full of enthusiasm, reads him a speech by the famous orator Lysias. Socrates tries to make clear to the young man that the way *eros* is portrayed as the madness of love in Lysias' speech betrays a tacky and business-minded reasonableness.[27] From the perspective of such a reasonableness, the wonder of love may look like a sick overstimulation, an irrational ecstasy. Are there not other forms of ecstasy? That love is a form of ecstasy is indisputable, but not every ecstasy is therefore irrational madness. Perhaps, there is also an ecstasy that exhilarates us, as if we had wings showing us the whole world in a new light. This is in fact what always happens when, with the gaze of the lover enraptured by the magic of love we see the totality of being, radiant in a whole new light. In the end, there is, thus, not only the bad madness, but also the good one. This is how the method of *dihairesis* is practised.

First of all, *collegium logicum*.[28] Now, this is above all a very vivid example of the Platonic or Socratic leading of souls. What we see happening here is the young man being made to realize that he does not know anything yet of true *eros*. When in Lysias' speech, a somewhat sleazy suitor warns of the alleged madness of *eros* in order to seduce the young man, he makes an impression only as long as the young man has not the faintest idea of the true *eros*. After this discussion with Socrates Phaedrus will no longer be like that. What is going on here? To say it in one word: it is a case of *anamnēsis*. What the conceptual tricks in the first oratorical games produced was no thought and recollection. Now, however, we have a case of a successful *anamnēsis*. This is what emerges in the Socratic art of discourse. This is why the mythical recantation that Socrates lets follow his own first oratorical tricks in the *Phaedrus* is like an unveiling. Literally, Socrates unveils his head, which he had covered up by false oratorical games.[29] Now, it will become a successful *anamnēsis*. Likewise, we have [414] a successful *anamnēsis* when Plato in the *Sophist*, at the end of an infinitely creative and refined dialogical discussion, offers a really long, laughably long definition of the determinations of the sophist and thereby clarifies all that philosophers are not and all that they are.[30]

Anamnēsis is nothing else. This is how recollection is. Something dawns on us: 'Yes, this is it.' When Plato introduces the doctrine of *anamnēsis* in his literary work, he depicts it in the discourse of Socrates with the young man, in which the latter learns that the square of the diagonal represents a doubling of a given square. This depiction in the *Meno*[31] is understood by laymen in the following way: the young man succeeds in arriving at this knowledge without Socrates because it is merely 'recollection'. This is a mistake. Even here, Socrates operates as a teacher. He shows the young man the decisive mistakes he made in his attempts to answer and brings him onto the right path. It is through a dialogue that this young man in the end realizes: 'Yes, that is it.' He sees it himself. In the end, he has complete evidence before him for the fact that the doubling of the side resulted in something four times the area and the halving of the side again did not result in the right square. Thus, by squaring the diagonals he comes to see the irrationality of the root of 2, ($\sqrt{2}$) as we would say algebraically.

What I mean is that the Platonic model should give us a glimpse at how we can arrive at a distinct articulated thought that maintains the legacy of metaphysics, insofar as it is fruitful for us. This means that it neglects nothing about which something dawns on us. This certainly implies that we cannot accomplish the step toward metaphysics in the sense of this Aristotelian turn to physics and to meta-physical ontology. It may indeed be true that Heidegger's return to the Greeks had compellingly uncovered the inner unity between the Greek and the modern world-experience and science, and that he had thereby described the way from incipient Greek thought right up to Aristotelian physics. From this physics, the road takes us to philosophy as total science and, eventually, to modern science, which fundamentally disputes philosophy's overarching mission and even the very sense of its questions. Is Plato seen correctly when he is interpreted only as the one who prepares metaphysics? Did the evil Socrates really corrupt him?[32]

It would be better not to call Platonic dialectic metaphysics, but if one must, then it should be called meta-mathematics. In the last instance, it is experiences of order that result from mathematical thinking. These experiences constitute, with all the other experiences of the human being and of being, a totality of our experience of the world, within which we have to find our way. This [415] does not mean that we can calculate anything and everything. It also certainly does not mean that, where we can calculate everything, we should not follow the procedural law of our modern science. Modern science is science in a different, incomparable sense and stands on its own ground, the ground of a constructive projecting experience. Teleological physics and metaphysics, against which modern science acquired its distinction, cannot for their part assert themselves against it. We have rather learned to see – and not least through Heidegger's renewed question concerning what metaphysics essentially is – that a deeper unity holds sway over the history of Western world-experience from its earliest beginnings. The prehistory of modern European civilization, which is global and technological, is not to be sought in the buried impulses of Greek enlightenment, for example in the great unknown Democritus,[33] and thus in an elimination of all metaphysics. We have learned that this unity is rather already at work in these beginnings.

As Heidegger saw that the Platonic-Aristotelian answer to the Socratic question ultimately ran into the dead-end of our world-enlightenment, he tried to return to what lay behind it and inquire into it in the direction of an ever more receding beginning. What can we do, for our part, other than question similarly back until the point where something becomes apparent to us? This is what we all do when we do not believe ourselves to be on the right track. We go back to the beginning where we still know that we were on the right track. Then, perhaps we will find the right track, instead of the wrong one. It is certainly not that simple in our world situation, as if we took a wrong way and knew the right one along which we wanted to go. We know of higher cultures that did not go the way of the Greeks toward mathematical proof and logic, and the subsequent way toward philosophy, metaphysics and modern science. These other cultures did not distinguish between philosophy and religion, between poetry and science, as we have. Thus, one dares to question: have we perhaps missed something on our way? Have we missed something in our thinking? Does the way from Greek mathematics and logic through metaphysics toward modern science, which has become our destinal way, lead us to new tasks of thinking? Such that we should give better consideration to the immemorial, the uncontrollable, the incalculable, which have always accompanied us in all our ways? Should we perhaps learn how to think back more? This must not mean going back to the first beginning or to a completely different beginning. Can we see Plato only as a transition to metaphysics [416] instead of perhaps as the true chief witness of the undeniable unity of knowledge, on the one hand, and the tradition of religion, poetry and wisdom, on the other? Should the latter be true, then we could always learn more from Plato. Even if we ourselves see and recognize that even Plato was already on our way toward the concept, logic and science, on which world history has travelled along with us, we should follow him in the fact that he did not expect everything from this way. This does not mean any kind of renunciation of the will to know, but rather the consciousness that this way does not lead to everything and that there remains a task of thinking that we should not avoid. We indeed all know of the limits of this limitless way of science and research, because we all are forebodingly moved by the beautiful and because we all are similarly moved by the divine.

Appendix: Glossary of German Terms

Abbau: dismantling

Abbild: copy

Abschattung: adumbration (Husserl)

Abwesende, das: what is absent

Abwesenheit: absence

Aktualisierung: reformulation

Allseitigkeit: from all sides

    allseitig: from all sides

An-sich-sein: being-in-itself

anspielen: to play along

Anspielung: allusion

Anwesen: presencing, what grants presence, what allows presence (Heidegger); *ousia* as landed property

    anwesen: to enter into presence (Heidegger)

Anwesende, das: what is granted presence, what is presencing (Heidegger)

    anwesend: present, being present, granted presence (Heidegger)

Anwesenheit: entering into presence, coming into presence, presence (Heidegger)

Anzahl: number

Arbeit: labour

Aufhebung: sublation

aufprägen: to impress

ausgreifend: far-reaching

Ausprägung: expression

Aussage: statement, proposition

Aussagenlogik: propositional logic

Ausweisung: justification

Auszeichnung: distinction

Bedeutsamkeit: meaningfulness, significance

Bedeutung: meaning, significance

Befindlichkeit: situatedness

Befremden, das: estrangement

Begleittöne: overtones

Begreiflichkeit: conceptual intelligibility

Begrifflichkeit: conceptuality

beherrschen: to master, to dominate

Bekenntnis: confession of allegiance
Bergen, das: sheltering
Bergung: sheltering
Besinnung: mental power
beständig: permanent
bestimmen: to determine
Bewegursache: efficient cause
Beweislogik: demonstrative logic
Bewusstsein, wirkungsgeschichtliches: consciousness exposed to the effects of history
bildende Kunst: plastic arts
Da: there
Dabeisein: being-there-alongside
Dasein: existence, *Dasein* (Heidegger)
Daseinswissenschaften: sciences of existence
Dass-sein: that something is
Denkmal: monument
Diesseits, das: the 'here'
Drang: drive (Scheler)
eingreifen: to intervene
   eingreifend: intrusive
Einmaligkeit: singularity
Einsicht: discernment
einströmen: to stream in
Entbergen, das: disclosure
Entbergung: disclosure, unveiling
   Entborgenheit: disclosure
Entfremdung: estrangement
Enthüllung: unveiling
Entwerdung: annihilation
Entwirklichung: de-realization (Scheler)
Erbanlage: genes
Erfahrungswissenschaften: empirical sciences
Ereignis: event (Heidegger)
   Ereignis des Seins: event of being (Heidegger)
Erkenntnis: cognition
Erlebnis: lived experience
Folge: sequence, consequence
Folgezusammenhang: sequential connection
Formgebung: imposition of form (Bourdieu)
Freilegung: laying bare
Fürsorge: solicitude (Heidegger)
   freigebende Fürsorge: liberating solicitude (Heidegger)

Gebirg: gathering of sheltering

Geflecht: web, network

Gefüge: arrangement, composition

Gegebenheit: givenness

Gegenwart: presence

Gegenwärtigkeit: presence, presenceness, presentness

    gegenwärtig: present

Geheimrat: authority, eminent

Geisteswissenschaften: human sciences

Gemeinsamkeit: community

Gemeinwesen: community

Geschehen: event, what happens, occurrence

    Naturgeschehen: course of nature, natural occurrence

    Seinsgeschehen: happening of being

    Weltgeschehen: course of the world, worldly occurrence

Geschichtslosigkeit: ahistoricity

Gesinnung: mentality, intention

Gespräch: dialogue, conversation

Gestaltung: creativity

Gestell, das: enframing (Heidegger)

Gewissen: conscience

Geworfenheit: thrownness

greifen: to seize

Herkunft: provenance

hinausgreifen: to encroach upon

hinschauen: to contemplate

Holzweg: forest path

Ichheit: egoity

Inbegriff: concrete and comprehensive instantiation (Hegel)

Jenseits: beyond

    jenseitig: what is beyond

Kausalbegriff: concept of causality

Kausalnexus: causal nexus

Kehre: turn

Konsequenzlogik: logic of implication

Kunde: testimony, awareness

Kundgabe: announcement

Leben, leistendes: life of capacities

Lebendigkeit: vitality, liveliness, being animated, being alive

Leib: body

Leibwelt: bodily world

Lese: harvest

lückenlos: uninterrupted
Massgesinnung: quantifying mentality
Mehrdeutigkeit: plurivocity
Nacherleben: re-living
Nachgeschichte: aftermath
Naturgeschehen: see '*Geschehen*'
Naturlauf: course of nature
Naturzusammenhang: fabric of nature, natural connection, complex of nature
Neigung: inclination
Neuzeit: modernity
Nichten, das: nihilating
Nichtende, das: that which nihilates
Nichtigkeit: negativity
Nichts, das: the nothing
Nichtung: nihilation
niederschlagen: to reflect, to express
Offenständigkeit: openness
Ort: place
Potenzen: potentialities
Prägung: character, formulation
Raumgebende, das: space giver, that which gives space
Rede: discourse
Rückblick: retrospective look
Rückgang: returning
Rückgriff: reference back
Rückkehr: return
Ruinanz: ruination (Heidegger)
Schriftlichkeit: the dimension of writing, the dimension of what is written
Scheinwissen: pseudo-knowledge
Schuld: guilt
    schuld sein: to be at fault
Selbstbesinnung: self-reflection
Selbstsein: selfhood
Selbstverständlichkeit: obviousness
    selbstverständlich: self-evident, obvious
Seele: mind
    seelischer Akt: mental act
    seelische Tatsache: mental fact
    seelisches Phänomen: mental phenomenon
    Seelenleben: mental life
    Seelenführung: leading of souls
Seiend: a being

seiend: being
   Seiende, das: beings
Seiendheit: beingness
Seinssinn: ontic sense
Seinsgeltung: ontic validity
Seinsgeschehen: see '*Geschehen*'
Seyn: beyng (Heidegger)
Sich-zeigen, das: self-showing
Sich-verbergen, das: self-concealing
Sitz im Leben: situatedness in life
Sorge: care (Heidegger)
Sprachgefühl: linguistic sensiblity
Sprachlichkeit: the dimension of language
Sprachnot: distress with language
Spur: trace, trail
spuren: to track
Tat: deed
Tathandlung: activity
Tollheit auf die Nähe: frenzy for nearness
Übereinstimmung: agreement
Umkehr: change of course, turn around
   umkehren: turn around
Umwelt: surrounding world
Umwendung: turn, turning
unabschliessbar: unending
unabsehbar: unforeseeable
unauslöschlich: ineradicable
unausrottbar: ineradicable
unergründlich: inscrutable
   Unergründlichkeit: inscrutability
unlösbar: ineradicable
Unverborgenheit: unconcealment
Unverholenheit: unveiling
Unverständlichkeit: incomprehensibility
Urbild: original
Urheber: producing agent
Urpräsenz: original presence
veraltete: obsolete
Veranlassung: inducing to go forward
Verbergen: concealment
Verbergung: concealment
Verfremdung: alienation

verhüllt: hidden

Verlogenheit: untruthfulness

Vernichtende, das: that which annihilates

Vernunftfaktum: fact of reason

Versorgung: providing for

Verständigung: coming to an understanding, mutual understanding

verstehen, Auf-abstand: understanding from a distance

Verwandlung ins Gebilde: transformation into structure

Verwesen: what forecloses presence

Verwindung: transformation

Vieldeutigkeit: plurivocity

vielstellig: multi-faceted

    Vielstelligkeit: multi-facetedness

Vollzug: effectuation

    im Vollzug: in its very performance, in its very exercise, in operation

    Vollzugssinn: sense of performance, operative sense

voraussagen: to predict

voraussehen: to foresee, to anticipate

vorauswissen: to anticipate

Vorgang: process

Vorgriff: anticipation, paragon, preconception

Vorhandenheit: presence-at-hand (Heidegger)

Vormeinung: prejudice

Was-sein: being-what, something that is

Weggegebenheit: being-given away from itself

Weile: while, whiling

Weltzusammenhang: connection of the world

Wesen: essencing

Widerstand: resistance

Wie-sein: being-how

Wiederaufnahme: renewal

Wiedererkennen: cognizing something again

Wiedererkenntnis: re-cognition

Wiederkehr: recurrence

Willenstellung: voluntarist attitude

Wissenschaftslehre: scientific doctrine

Wortbildung: semantic formation

Zeitalter: age

Zerstörung: annihilation

Zufallchance: accidental opportunity

Zufallslöcher: gaps of chance

Zuhandenheit: readiness-to-hand (Heidegger)

Zukünftigkeit: futuralness
zusammenfassen: to combine together
zusammengreifen: to put together
Zusammenhang: connection, complex
Zuspitzung: culmination, exaggeration
Zwangsläufigkeit: inexorability
Zweck: purpose
Zwischenrede: mediating discourse

Glossary of Latin and Greek Expressions

actus exercitus: the act exercised (as a performance)

actus signatus: the signate act (considered according to the content expressed by the words)

ancilla scientiarum: the handmaiden of the sciences

ancilla theologiae: the handmaiden of theology

anima vegetativa: the vegetative soul

animal rationale: rational animal. See *zōon logon echon*

ars latet arte sua: art hides in its own art

causa efficiens: efficient cause

Christus patiens: the suffering Christ

cogito me cogitare: I think that I think

de mortuis nihil nisi bene: nothing ill should be said of the dead

Deus est suum esse: God is its very being

dos moi pou stō: give me a spot on which to stand

en parergō: aside

esse est Deus: being is God [existence is God, God is being]

experimentum crucis: the decisive experiment

genera dicendi: kinds of discourse or genres of discourse

gnōthi seauton: know thyself

heauto kinoun: that which moves itself; a self-mover

hexis meta logou: a disposition with *logos*

historia vitae magistra: history is life's teacher

homo novus: the new human being

humanitas: human kind, humanity, human civilization

kata sunthēkēn: by convention

laudator temporis acti: the one who praises the time past

magistra vitae: life's teacher

memoria vitae: the memory of life

naturae rationalis individua substantia: an individual substance of a rational nature

novarum rerum cupidus: the one greedy for new things

oracula ex eventu: pronouncements of the moment

peri theorias: on contemplation

philosophiae naturalis principia mathematica: mathematical principles of natural philosophy

sancta simplicitas: Holy Simplicity

theologia rationalis: rational theology
unio mystica: the mystical union
verba magistri: the master's words
verba sentiendi: verbs of perception
verbum interius: the interior word or speech
zōon logon echon: rational animal, the being that has language
zōon politikon: political animal

Notes

Translators' Preface

1   *Gesammelte Werke,* published in ten volumes by J. C. B. Mohr (Paul Siebeck) in
    Tübingen from 1986 to 1995.

2   Jean Grondin, *Hans-Georg Gadamer, Une biographie.* Paris: Bernard Grasset, 2011,
    p. 16.

3   John McDowell, 'Gadamer and Davidson on Understanding and Relativism',
    in *Gadamer's Century: Essays in Honor of Hans-Georg Gadamer,* edited by Jeff
    Malpas, Ulrich Arnswald, and Jens Kertscher. Cambridge, MA and London: The
    MIT Press, 2002, pp. 173–94.

4   Donald Davidson, 'Gadamer and Plato's *Philebus',* in *The Philosophy of Hans-Georg
    Gadamer,* edited by Lewis Hahn. Chicago, IL: Open Court Publishing Company,
    1997, p. 421.

Introduction

1   Martin Heidegger, *History of the Concept of Time: Prolegomena,* trans. Theodore
    Kisiel. Bloomington, IN: Indiana University Press, 1985, p. 56.

2   See below p. 250.

3   See below p. 235.

4   See below p. 187.

5   See below p. 232.

6   See below p. 6.

7   See below p. 37.

8   See below p. 47.

9   See below p. 7, 9–10, 37.

10 See below p. 231.

11 See below p. 22.

12 *Truth and Method,* 2nd rev. edn., trans. Joel Weinsheimer and Donald G.
    Marshall. New York: Continuum, 1998, p. 218.

13 See below p. 3–4, 92.

14 See below p. 193.

15   See below p. 179.

16   See below p. 121–2.

17   See below p. 193–4.

18   See below p. 6.

19   See below p. 101.

20   See below p. 180–1, 217–18, and especially p. 239.

21   See below p. 245.

22   See below p. 233.

23   'Critique of Hegel's Philosophy of Right: Introduction', in *Marx and the French Revolution*, François Furet, with selections from Karl Marx, ed. and intro. Lucien Calvié, trans. Deborah Kan Furet. Chicago, IL: University of Chicago Press, 1988.

24   Karl Marx, 'Theses on Feuerbach', in *Selected Writings*, ed. Lawrence Simon. Indianapolis, IN: Hackett Publishing Company, 1994, p. 101.

25   Jean Grondin, *Hans-Georg Gadamer. Une bibliographie*. Paris: Bernard Grasset, 2011, p. 400.

26   See below p. 135.

27   See below p. 118–19.

28   See below p. 119.

Is There a Causality in History? (1991)

1   'Kausalität in der Geschichte?' was first published in *Ideen und Form, Festschrift für Hugo Friedrich,* ed. Fritz Schalk. Frankfurt am Main: Klostermann, 1965, pp. 93–104. It was reprinted in:

   (a) Hans-Georg Gadamer, *Kleine Schriften*, vol. 1 *Philosophie, Hermeneutik.* Tübingen: Mohr, 1967, pp. 192–200.

   (b) *Gedanken aus der Zeit, Philosophie im Südwestfunk*, ed. Horst Helmut Kaiser and Jürgen-Eckardt Pleines. Würzburg: Königshausen & Neumann, 1986, pp. 140–51.

   (c) *Gesammelte Werke*, vol. 4 *Neuere Philosophie II Probleme – Gestalten.* Tübingen: Mohr, 1987, n. 6, pp. 107–16.

2   Translators' note: In *Truth and Method* Gadamer cites the entire passage in which Ranke's expression *Szenen der Freiheit*, which we translate as 'scenes of liberty', appears. Here is the relevant portion of the quotation from Ranke: 'The writing of history follows the scenes of freedom. This is its greatest attraction. But freedom involves power, germinal power. Without the latter the former disappears both in world events and in the sphere of ideas. At every moment something new can begin, something whose sole origin is the primary and common source of all

human activity. Nothing exists entirely for the sake of something else. But still a deep inner coherence penetrates everywhere, and no one is entirely independent of it. Besides freedom stands necessity' (*Weltgeschichte*, IX, part 2, xiv, quoted in Hans-Georg Gadamer, *Truth and Method,* 2nd rev. edn., trans. Joel Weinsheimer and Donald G. Marshall. New York: Continuum, 1998, p. 204).

3   Translators' note: The quotation is from Schiller's play *The Bride of Messina; or The Enemy Brothers* (*Die Braut von Messina oder Die feindlichen Brüder*) written in 1803. It is from Act III, scene 5. There are two related passages in the same stanza and Gadamer conflates them in his quotation. The first passage says:

'What are hopes, what are plans

That human beings, in their transience, build?'

(*Was sind die Hoffnungen, was sind Entwürfe,*

Die der Mensch, der vergängliche, baut?)'

The second passage says:

'What are hopes, what are plans

That the human being, ephemeral child of the hours,

Builds on grounds so treacherous?'

(*Was sind Hoffnungen, was sind Entwürfe,*

Die der Mensch, der flüchtige Sohn der Stunde,

Aufbaut auf dem betrüglichen Grunde?)

4   Translators' note: Gadamer seems to make reference to a line in the second stanza of Goethe's poem 'The Harp Player' ('Harfenspieler'). The stanza runs as follows:

'He who never ate his bread with tears,

He who never, through miserable nights,

Sat weeping on his bed –

He does not know you, Heavenly Powers.

You lead us into life,

You let the wretched man feel guilt,

And then you leave him to his pain –

For all guilt avenges itself on earth' (Translation by Emily Ezust, from *The Lied, Art Song, and Choral Texts Archive* [http://www.lieder.net/].

5   Translators' note: 'Efficient cause'.

Historicity and Truth

1   'Geschichtlichkeit und Wahrheit' was first published with the subtitle *Zur versäumten Fortsetzung von Gesprächen in Walberberg,* in *Versöhnung. Versuche zu ihrer Geschichte und Zukunft. Festschrift für Paulus Engelhardt OP,* ed. Thomas Eggensperger, Ulrich Engel and Otto Hermann Pesch. Walberberger Studien.

Philosophische Reihe, vol. 8. Mainz: Matthias Grünewald, 1991, pp. 17–28. It is now in *Gesammelte Werke*, vol. 10 *Hermeneutik im Rückblick*. Tübingen: Mohr, 1995, n. 20, pp. 247–58.

2   This could be a topic of discussion in and for itself. During the week of celebration at my university of Heidelberg, I made some remarks on the connection between enlightenment and romanticism, between the modern scientific attitude and the historical sense. On this, see 'Die Universität Heidelberg und die Geburt der modernen Wissenschaft', now in *Gesammelte Werke*, vol. 10, n. 29, pp. 336–45. [Translators' note: English translation: 'The University of Heidelberg and the Birth of Modern Science', in *Hans-Georg Gadamer on Education, Poetry, and History: Applied Hermeneutics*, trans. Graeme Nicholson, ed. Dieter Misgeld. Albany, NY: State University of New York Press, 1992, pp. 37–46.]

3   Translators' note: 'Pronouncement of the moment'.

4   *Phänomenologische Interpretationen zu Aristoteles. Einführung in die phänomenologische Forschung*, Gesamtausgabe, vol. 61. Frankfurt am Main: Vittorio Klostermann, 1985. [Translators' note: English translation: *Phenomenological Interpretations of Aristotle: Initiation into Phenomenological Research*, trans. Richard Rojcewicz. Bloomington, IN: Indiana University Press, 2001.]

5   Translators' note: This is an allusion to Bourdieu's characterization of university professors who have become part of the academic establishment and have become instruments of power as opposed to researchers. See Gadamer's essay 'Heidegger and Sociology: Bourdieu and Habermas', pp. 167–78.

6   On this, see also 'Hermeneutik und Historismus', *Gesammelte Werke*, vol. 2, n. 27, p. 414f. [Translators' note: English translation: 'Hermeneutics and Historicism Supplement I', in *Truth and Method*, 2nd rev. edn., trans. Joel Weinsheimer and Donald G. Marshall. New York: Continuum, 1998, pp. 505–41], as well as the correspondence with Leo Strauss published in the *Independent Journal of Philosophy* 2 (1978): 5–12.

7   Translators' note: Gadamer replaces *Art* with *Weise* in the quotation from Goethe. It is the last sentence of an essay of 1818, 'Ancient versus Modern' (*Antik und modern*). Here is the full context of Goethe's statement: 'The clarity of the view, the serenity of the perception, the ease of communication – that is what delights us! And if we now say that we find all that in genuine Greek works which represent the noblest subjects, have the most worthy content and are executed to utmost perfection – then it will be understood why we always begin with them and end with them. Let anyone be a Greek in his own way, but let him be Greek!' (*Goethe, The Collected Works vol. 3 Essays on Art and Literature*, ed. John Gearey. Princeton, NJ: Princeton University Press, 1994, p. 93).

8   Translators' note: 'Know thyself'.

9   Translators' note: 'To make immortal or to hold oneself immortal'.

10 Translators' note: 'Death'.

11 André de Muralt, *La métaphysique du phénomène*. Paris: Vrin, 1990, pp. 105–207.

12 On this see also 'Über das Göttliche im frühen Denken der Griechen', in *Gesammelte Werke*, vol. 6, n. 9, pp. 154–70 (*Kleine Schriften*, vol. 3 *Idee und Sprache: Platon, Husserl, Heidegger*. Tübingen: Mohr, 1972, n. 5, pp. 64–79). [Translators' note: English translation: 'On the Divine in Early Greek Thought', in *Hermeneutics, Religion, and Ethics*, ed. and trans. Joel Weinsheimer. New Haven and London: Yale University Press, 1999, pp. 37–57].

13 Translators' note: 'God is its very being'.

14 On this see 'Der platonische *Parmenides* und seine Nachwirkung', now in *Gesammelte Werke*, vol. 7, n. 11, pp. 313–27. [Translators' note: English translation: 'Plato's Parmenides and its Influence', trans. Margaret Kirby, *Dionysius* 7 (1983): 3–16.]

15 Translators' note: This is in the *Parmenides* (156d–e). The passage reads: '"Does this strange thing, then, exist, in which it would be at the moment when it changes" "What sort of thing is that?" "The instant [*to exaiphnes*]. For the instant seems to indicate a something from which there is a change in one direction or the other. For it does not change from rest while it is still at rest, nor from motion while it is still moving; but there is this strange instantaneous nature, something interposed between motion and rest, not existing in any time, and into this and out from this that which is in motion changes into rest and that which is at rest changes into motion"' (in Plato, *Cratylus, Parmenides, Greater Hippias, Lesser Hippias*, trans. H. N. Fowler. The Loeb Classical Library. Cambridge, MA: Harvard University Press, 1926, p. 299).

16 Translators' note: This is in Book VII, xiii of the *Attic Nights*: 'On the brief topics discussed at the table of the philosopher Taurus and called *Sympoticae*, or *Table Talk*.' The questions or 'problems' were meant for amusement at the end of the meal. On one occasion the questions at Taurus' house were the following: 'The question was asked, when a dying man died – when he was already in the grasp of death, or while he still lived? And when did a rising man rise – when he was already standing, or while he was still seated? And when did one who was learning an art become an artist – when he already was one, or when he was still learning? For whichever answer you make, your statement will be absurd and laughable, and it will seem much more absurd, if you say that it is in either case, or in neither' (Aulus Gellius, *Attic Nights*, trans. J. C. Rolfe. Loeb Classical Library. Cambridge, MA: Harvard University Press; London: Heinemann, 1927, p. 125.

17 On this see the essays in Part II of *Gesammelte Werke*, vol. 4, pp. 119f.

The History of the Universe and the Historicity of Human Beings (1988)

1 'Geschichte des Universums und Geschichtlichkeit des Menschen' was presented as the concluding lecture of the lecture series 'Geisteswissenschaften – wozu?' at the University of Mainz in the winter semester 1987–8. It was first published in *Geisteswissenschaften – wozu? Beispiele ihrer Gegenstände und Fragen. Eine Vortragsreihe der Johannes Gutenberg-Universität Mainz im Wintersemester 1987/1988,* ed. Hans-Henrik Krummacher. Stuttgart: Franz Steiner Verlag, 1988, pp. 267–81. Now in *Gesammelte Werke,* vol. 10, n. 17, pp. 206–22.

2 Translators' note: In English in the text.

3 Translators' note: 'To know in order to predict'.

4 Translators' note: Gadamer is paraphrasing a sentence from the first chapter of Burckhardt's *Weltgeschichtliche Betrachtungen.* Here is the passage: 'The mind must transmute into a possession the remembrance of its passage through the ages of the world. What was once joy and sorrow must now become knowledge, as it must in the life of the individual. Therewith the saying *Historia vitae magistra* ['history is life's teacher'] takes on a higher yet a humbler sense. Through experience we want to become not so much smart [*klug*] (for the next time), but wise [*weise*] (for ever)' (Jacob Burckhardt, *Wissenschaftliche Betrachtungen,* ed. Rudolf Stadelman. Pfüllingen: Neske, 1949. [http://gutenberg.spiegel.de/buch/weltgeschichtliche-betrachtungen-4968/1]; English translation *Reflections on History,* trans. M. D. Hottinger. Indianapolis: Liberty Classics, 1979, p. 39. Translation modified).

   The expression *historia vitae magistra* comes from Cicero. In *De oratore* he writes: 'And as History, which bears witness to the passing of the ages, sheds light upon reality, gives life to recollection [*vita memoriae*] and guidance to human existence [*magistra vitae*], and brings tidings of ancient days, whose voice, but the orator's, can entrust her to immortality?' (*De Oratore,* Book 2, Ch. 9, 36, in Cicero, *On the Orator: Books 1–2,* trans. E. W. Sutton and H. Rackham. Cambridge, MA: Harvard University Press, 1942, pp. 225.

5 Translators' note: Usually, the term *Sprachlichkeit* is translated as 'linguisticality' and *Schriftlichkeit* could be translated as 'textuality'. There are, however, two reasons to resist these translations. The first one is linguistic. In German, *Sprachlichkeit* and *Schriftlichkeit* directly derive from the very common words *sprachlich* (verbal, linguistic) and *schriftlich* (written, in writing) and are their nominalizations. In English, 'linguisticality', which does not exist as a word as such, does not have the same direct derivation from 'language', but goes through a change in root: 'linguistic'. In the case of 'textuality', although the word exists, there is no linguistic connection with 'writing'. The second reason

is philosophical. It is the whole argument of Gadamer against any theoretical approach to language and against Derrida's deconstruction that language and writing should not be systematized as some form of means or medium that can be totalized. 'Linguisticality' and 'textuality' may suggest all too much such an effort to offer an equally systematic counter-position to the philosophy of language and conceptual thinking. *Sprachlichkeit* and *Schriftlichkeit* name rather a dimension or an order that is not merely a mediation for concepts, but the soil out of which concepts arise. The verbal as the language in use or as voice is inchoately conceptual precisely because it is connected to a meaning that speakers want to convey. It belongs to what Heidegger calls *Bedeutsamkeit* in *Being and Time*: the significability, but different from Heidegger, this dimension of meaning is not an anonymous feature of the world in which Dasein has been thrown. For Gadamer it is a meaning in action or, as he uses the expression, the verbal is conceptual in its very exercise as verbal. There is thus an inscription in what is merely verbal, but this inscription, against deconstruction, has an existence only in the dialogue in which the verbal lives and unfolds.

6   Translators' note: In English in the text.

7   Translators' note: It is to be found in the *Nicomachean Ethics* Book I, 1094b24–27. Aristotle writes: 'It is the mark of an educated mind to expect that amount of exactness in each kind which the nature of the particular subject admits. It is equally unreasonable to accept merely probable conclusions from a mathematician and to demand strict demonstration from an orator' (*Nicomachean Ethics*, trans. H. Rackham. The Loeb Classical Library. London: William Heinemann, 1926, p. 9).

8   Translators' note: It is to be found in the *Poetics* 1451b3–7. Aristotle writes: 'What we have said already makes it further clear that a poet's object is not to tell what actually happened but what could and would happen either probably or inevitably. The difference between a historian and a poet is not that one writes in prose and the other in verse – indeed the writings of Herodotus could be put into verse and yet would still be a kind of history, whether written in metre or not. The real difference is this: one tells what happened and the other what might happen. For this reason poetry is something more scientific and serious than history, because poetry tends to give general truths while history gives particular facts' (*Poetics, 'Longinus' on the Sublime, Demetrius on Style*, trans. Hamilton Fyfe. The Loeb Classical Library. London: William Heinemann, 1927, p. 35).

9   Translators' note: 'Holy Simplicity'.

10 Translators' note: 'Mathematical Principles of Natural Philosophy'.

11 Translators' note: 'The Handmaiden of Theology'.

A World Without History? (1972)

1   'Welt ohne Geschichte?' is an improvised opening talk given at the conference of
     the Institut International de Philosophie, September 12–16, 1969 in Heidelberg.
     It was first published in *Truth and Historicity/Vérité et historicité. Entretiens
     de Heidelberg, 12–16 septembre 1969*, ed. Hans-Georg Gadamer. The Hague:
     Martinus Nijhoff, 1972, pp. 1–8. It is now in *Gesammelte Werke*, vol. 10, n. 26, pp.
     317–23.

2   Translators' note: 'Nothing ill should be said of the dead'.

3   Translators' note: 'Mathematical Principles of Natural Philosophy'.

4   Translators' note: 'The one who praises the time past'.

5   Translators' note: In English in the text.

6   Translators' note: 'A booming or humming sound'.

7   Translators' note: The famous quotation from Cicero, as quoted by Burckhardt
     (See p. 27), is that history is *magistra vitae*: 'life's teacher'. Gadamer may be
     mixing this expression with another one that appears along with it in *De Oratore*:
     vita memoriae ['the life of memory'], which he may have misread as *memoria
     vitae* ['the memory of life'] on the model of *magistra vitae*. Here is Cicero's text:
     'And as History, which bears witness to the passing of the ages, sheds light upon
     reality, gives life to recollection [*vita memoriae*] and guidance to human existence
     [*magistra vitae*], and brings tidings of ancient days, whose voice, but the orator's,
     can entrust her to immortality?' (*De Oratore*, Book 2, Chapter 9, 36, in Cicero,
     On the Orator: Books 1–2, trans. E. W. Sutton and H. Rackham. Cambridge, MA:
     Harvard University Press, 1942, p. 225. See also note 4 p. 284.

The Old and the New (1981)

1   'Das Alte und das Neue' was presented as the opening speech at the *Salzburger
     Festspiele* in 1981. It was printed in the official programme (Salzburg, 1981,
     pp. 19–28) and reprinted in *Universitas* 38 (1983): 453–60. It is now in
     Gesammelte Werke, vol. 4, n. 9, pp. 154–60.

2   Translators' note: 'The one who praises the time past'.

3   Translators' note: 'The one greedy for new things'.

4   Translators' note: 'The new human being'.

5   See my essay 'Hilde Domin, Dichterin der Rückkehr', *Gesammelte Werke*, vol.
     9 *Ästhetik und Poetik II: Hermeneutik im Vollzug*. Tübingen: Mohr, 1993, n. 28,
     pp. 323–8. [Translators' note: English translation: 'Hilde Domin, Poet of Return',
     trans. Margaret Korzus and Hilde Domin, *The Denver Quarterly* (1972) 6: 4,
     7–17.]

6   Translators' note: Albrecht Altdorfer (1480–1538) painted this in 1529. It was
     commissioned by the Duke of Bavaria.

7   Translators' note: On this statement by Goethe, see note 7 p. 284.

Death as a Question (1975)

1   'Der Tod als Frage' was published in *Kleine Schriften*, vol. 4, *Variationen*. Tübingen:
     Mohr, 1977, pp. 62–73. It is now in *Gesammelte Werke*, vol. 4, n. 10, pp. 161–72.

2   Translators' note: 'This can be found at the end of the ninth Duino Elegy. The poet
     in fact speaks of the "earth" (*Erde*), not nature. The poem says: "You were always
     right and your holy inspiration is the familiar death" (*Immer warst du im Recht,
     und dein heiliger Einfall ist der vertrauliche Tod*).'

3   Translators' note: The poem in question is Gottfried Benn's *Epilog 1949*. The
     phrase 'Tu sais' is found in the third stanza of the fourth part of the poem:
     'Es ist ein Spruch, dem oftmals ich gesonnen,
     der alles sagt, da er dir nichts verheißt,
     ich habe ihn auch in dies Buch versponnen,
     er stand auf einem Grab: 'tu sais' – du weißt'
     ['It is a saying that I have often pondered
     Which says everything, because it does not promise you anything
     I have woven it into the threads of this book too
     It is written on a tomb: 'tu sais' – you know']
     [Gottfried Benn, 'Epilog 1949'. *Gesammelte Werke in acht Bänden: Band I*, ed.
     Dieter Wellershoff. Weisbaden: Limes, 1960, p. 345].

4   Translators' note: Gadamer is referring to Cebes' entreaty to Socrates in the
     Phaedo 77e about assuaging the child in us, human beings, who fears death. Plato
     writes: 'And Cebes laughed and said, "Assume that we have that fear, Socrates, and
     try to convince us; or rather, do not assume that we are afraid, but perhaps there is
     a child within us, who has such fears. Let us try to persuade him not to fear death
     as if it were a hobgoblin."
        "Ah," said Socrates, "you must sing charms to him every day until you charm
     away his fear."
        "Where then, Socrates," said he, "shall we find a good singer of such charms,
     since you are leaving us?"' (*Euthyphro, Apology, Crito, Phaedo, Phaedrus*, trans.
     Harold Fowler. The Loeb Classical Library. London: Heinemann; New York:
     Putnam's Sons, 1914, p. 271).

5   Translators' note: 'mystical union'.

6   Translators' note: We take *Lebensräumen* ('living spaces') as a misprint of
     Lebensträumen.

7   Translators' note: 'the suffering Christ'.

8   Translators' note: Paul Celan, *Tenebrae*, first published in *Sprachgitter*, Frankfurt am Main: S. Fischer, 1959 and also in *Gesammelte Werke*, vol. 1, ed. Beda Allemann, Stefan Reichert, and Rolf Bücher. Frankfurt am Main: Suhrkamp, 1983, p. 163. English Translation: "Tenebrae," in *Harper's Magazine*, trans. Scott Horton, 2008 (http://harpers.org/archive/2008/03/hbc-90002696). Translation modified.

9   Romano Guardini (1885–1968) was an influential Catholic theologian and professor of theology in Germany. As an anecdote, when Heidegger tried to have Gadamer appointed at the University of Freiburg as his successor in 1945, the position was first offered to Guardini, who turned it down. See Jean Grondin, *Hans-Georg Gadamer. Une biographie.* Paris: Bernard Grasset, 2011, p. 332.

10 The fairy tale being referred to here is 'Godfather Death [Der *Gevatter Tod*]', in *The Complete Grimm's Fairy Tales*, New York: Pantheon Books, 1972, pp. 209–12.

The Problem of Dilthey: Between Romanticism and Positivism (1984)

1   'Das Problem Diltheys. Zwischen Romantik und Positivismus' was first presented as a lecture in Italian at the International Dilthey Congress in Rome and as a lecture in German at the phenomenological society in Trier in 1983. It appeared under the title 'Wilhelm Dilthey nach 150 Jahren (Zwischen Romantik und Positivismus. Ein Diskussionsbeitrag)', in Ernst Wolfgang Orth (ed.), *Dilthey und die Philosophie der Gegenwart.* Freiburg/Munich: Karl Alber, 1985, pp. 157–82. It is now in *Gesammelte Werke*, vol. 4, n. 28, pp. 406–24.

2   Translators' note: Gadamer uses the French word.

3   Wilhelm Dilthey, *Gesammelte Schriften*, 8 vols, ed. Bernhard Groethuysen and Georg Misch. Berlin/Leipzig: Teubner, 1923–31 (continued since then).

4   Translators' note: Gadamer makes a reference to an essay 'Ortega und das Problem des Lebens' in *Gesammelte Werke*, vol. 4, n. 30, pp. 451–62 that is not to be found there. In that volume 4 there is, however, the essay 'Dilthey and Ortega: The Philosophy of life', translated in this volume pp. 91–102.

5   Translators' note: 'Vital reason' or 'reason with life at its basis'.

6   *Lebensphilosophie und Phänomenologie. Eine Auseinandersetzung der Dilthe'schen Richtung mit Heidegger und Husserl.* Leipzig: Teubner, 1930.

7   Fritz Kaufmann, 'Die Philosophie des Grafen Paul Yorck von Wartenburg', *Jahrbuch für Phänomenologie und phänomenologische Forschung* 9 (1928): 1–235.

8   Ludwig Landgrebe, 'Wilhelm Diltheys Theorie der Geisteswissenschaften (Analyse ihrer Grundbegriffe)', *Jahrbuch für Phänomenologie und phänomenologische Forschung* 9 (1928): 237–366.

9   Wilhelm Dilthey, *Gesammelten Schriften,* vol. 4 *Die Jugendgeschichte Hegels.* Berlin: Verlag der Königlichen Preussischen Akademie der Wissenschaften, 1905.

10 Wilhelm Dilthey (ed.), *Aus Schleiermachers Leben in Briefen,* 4 vols, prepared for publication by Ludwig Jonas. Berlin: Reimer, 1863. [Translators' note: New publication: Berlin: de Gruyter, 1974.]

11 Wilhelm Dilthey, *Leben Schleiermachers,* 2 vols. Leipzig: Teubner, 1922 (2nd edn. by Hermann Mulert expanded with fragments of the posthumous works). In the meantime, we have vols 13 and 14 of the *Gesammelte Schriften,* ed. Martin Redeker. 4 books in two vols. Berlin: de Gruyter, 3rd edn., 1970.

12 Erich Rothacker, *Einleitung in die Geisteswissenschaft.* Tübingen: Mohr, 1920.

13 Translators' note: This is the famous statement by Archimedes that he could move the earth if he had a point of support.

14 Eduard Zeller, *Über Bedeutung und Aufgabe der Erkenntnisstheorie: Ein Akademischer Vortrag.* Heidelberg: K. Groos, 1862. Now in Eduard Zeller, *Vorträge and Abhandlungen,* 3 vols. Leipzig: Fues, 1875–84. See vol. 2, pp. 479–526.
    See also Klaus Christian Köhnke, 'Über den Ursprung des Wortes Erkenntnistheorie – und dessen vermeintliche Synonyme', *Archiv für Begriffsgeschichte* 25 (1981): 132–157, and my contribution to the Festschrift *Semper Apertus zur 547 Jahrfeier der Universität Heidelberg* (6 vols), ed. Wilhelm Dörr. Heidelberg, 1986. My contribution 'Eduard Zeller. Der Weg eines Liberalen von der Theologie zur Philosophie' is in vol. 2, pp. 406–12 (See 'Die Universität Heidelberg und die Geburt der modernen Wissenschaft', *Gesammelte Werke,* vol. 10, n. 29, pp. 336–45. [Translators' note: English translation: 'The University of Heidelberg and the Birth of Modern Science', in *Hans-Georg Gadamer on Education, Poetry, and History: Applied Hermeneutics,* trans. Lawrence Schmidt and Monica Reuss, ed. Dieter Misgeld and Graeme Nicholson. Albany: State University of New York Press, 1992, pp. 37–46].)

15 As stated in the drafts to 'Leben und Erkennen', in Wilhelm Dilthey, *Gesammelte Schriften,* vol. 19. Göttingen: Vandenhoeck & Ruprecht, 1982, pp. 341–8. [Translators' note: English translation: 'Life and Cognition', in *Selected Works,* vol. II: *Understanding the Human World,* ed. Rudolf A. Makkreel and Frithjof Rodi. Princeton, NJ: Princeton University Press, 2010, pp. 58–114.]

16 Wilhelm Dilthey, *Gesammelte Schriften,* vol. 18. *Die Wissenschaften vom Menschen, der Gesellschaft und der Geschichte. Vorarbeiten zur Einleitung in die Geisteswissenschaften (1865–1880),* ed. Helmut Johach and Frithjof Rodi. Göttingen: Vandenhoeck & Ruprecht, 1977, pp. 5f.

17 See Manfred Riedel's excellent contribution on *ens positivum*: 'Diltheys Kritik der begründenden Vernunft', in Karl-Otto Apel and Ernst Wolfgang Orth, *Dilthey und die Philosophie der Gegenwart: Beiträge.* Freiburg im Breisgau: Karl Alber, 1985, pp. 185–210.

18   Wilhelm Dilthey, *Gesammelte Schriften,* vol. 8 *Weltanschaungslehre. Abhandlungen zur Philosophie der Philosophie,* ed. Bernhard Groethuysen. Leipzig/Berlin: Teubner, 1931, p. 45.

    See also Wilhelm Dilthey, *Gesammelte Schriften,* vol. 7 *Der Aufbau der geschichtlichen Welt in den Geisteswissenschaften,* ed. Bernhard Groethuysen, Helmut Johach and Martin Redeker. Berlin/Leipzig: Teubner, 1927, pp. 233, 237. [Translators' note: English translation: *The Formation of the Historical World in the Human Sciences,* in *Wilhelm Dilthey: Selected Works,* vol. III, ed. Rudolf Makkreel and Frithjof Rodi. Princeton, NJ: Princeton University Press, 2010.]

19   See Aristotle, *Nicomachean Ethics,* 1100a 10–15. [Translators' note: Aristotle writes: 'Are we then to count no other human being happy either, as long as he is alive? Must we obey Solon's warning, and look to the end? And if we are indeed to lay down this rule, can a man really be happy even after he is dead? Surely that is an extremely strange notion, especially for us who define happiness as a form of activity' (*Nicomachean Ethics,* trans. H. Rackham. The Loeb Classical Library. London: William Heinemann, 1926, pp. 47–9).]

20   From Wilhelm Dilthey, 'Schluss auf das Wesen der Philosophie', in *Gesammelte Schriften,* vol. 5, part 1 *Abhandlungen zur Grundlegung der Geistewissenschaften.* Stuttgart: Teubner, 1990, p. 364.

21   Translators' note: Gadamer is referring to Wolfgang Hildesheimer, *Mozart,* Frankfurt am Main: Suhrkamp Verlag, 1977. English translation: *Mozart,* trans. Marion Faber. New York: Farrar, Straus and Giroux, 1982.

22   Hans-Georg Gadamer, *Wahrheit und Methode. Grundzüge einer philosophischen Hermeneutik.* Tübingen: Mohr, 1960. p. 205f, in particular p. 211 (*Gesammelte Werke,* vol. 1, pp. 222ff., p. 228). [Translators' note: English translation: *Truth and Method,* 2nd rev. edn., trans. Joel Weinsheimer and Donald G. Marshall. New York: Continuum, 1998, pp. 218f., p. 224.]

23   For a doctrine of the relativity of existence, see Scheler's scattered remarks in Max Scheler, *Gesammelte Werke,* vol. 2 *Der Formalismus in der Ethik und die materiale Wertethik,* ed. Maria Scheler. Bern/Munich: Francke Verlag, 1966, pp. 392f. [Translators' note: English translation: *Formalism in Ethics and Non-Formal Ethics of Values: A New Attempt Toward the Foundation of an Ethical Personalism,* trans. Manfred S. Frings and Roger L. Funk. Evanston, IL: Northwestern University Press, 1973.] See the section, 'Das Problem der Seinsrelativität', in Max Scheler, *Gesammelte Werke,* vol. 9 *Späte Schriften,* ed. Manfred S. Frings. Bern/Munich: Francke, 1976, pp. 196–200. See also Max Scheler, *Gesammelte Werke,* vol. 8 *Die Wissensformen und die Gesellschaft,* ed. Maria Scheler. Bern/Munich: Francke Verlag, 1960 (2nd edn.), pp. 202, 271.

24   For these questions, see, among others, 'Lob der Theorie', in *Gesammelte Werke,* vol. 4, n. 3, pp. 37–51. [Translators' note: English translation: 'Praise of Theory', in

Praise of Theory: Speeches and Essays, ed. and trans. Chris Dawson. New Haven, CT: Yale University Press, 1998, pp. 16–36.]

25   Wilhelm Dilthey, *Gesammelte Schriften,* vol. 19 *Grundlegung der Wissenschaften vom Menschen, der Gesellschaft und der Geschichte. Ausarbeitungen und Entwürfe zum zweiten Band der Einleitung in die Geisteswissenschaften (ca. 1870–1895),* ed. Helmut Johach and Frithjof Rodi. Göttingen: Vandenhoeck & Ruprecht, 1982, p. 42.

26   Wilhelm Dilthey, *Gesammelte Schriften,* vol. 8, p. 233.

27   Wilhelm Dilthey, *Gesammelte Schriften,* vol. 19, p. 275.

28   Wilhelm Dilthey, *Gesammelte Schriften,* vol. 18, pp. 66f.

29   Wilhelm Dilthey, *Gesammelte Schriften,* vol. 8, p. 232.

30   Wilhelm Dilthey, *Gesammelte Schriften,* vol. 5 *Die geistige Welt: Einleitung in die Philosophie des Lebens.* First part: *Abhandlungen zur Grundlegung der Geisteswissenschaften,* ed. Georg Misch. Leipzig/Berlin: Teubner, 1924, p. 64.

31   Wilhelm Dilthey, *Gesammelte Schriften,* vol. 8, p. 232.

32   Wilhelm Dilthey, *Gesammelte Schriften,* vol. 8, p. 231.

33   Wilhelm Dilthey, *Gesammelte Schriften,* vol. 8, p. 225.

34   Wilhelm Dilthey, *Gesammelte Schriften,* vol. 6 *Die Geistige Welt. Einleitung in die Philosophie des Lebens.* 2. Häfte, *Abhandlungen zur Poetik, Ethik und Pädagogik.* Leipzig/Berlin: Teubner, 1924, p. 321.

35   Wilhelm Dilthey, *Gesammelte Schriften,* vol. 6, p. 303.

36   The letter to Husserl of June 29, 1911 has been published in Frithjof Rodi and Hans-Ulrich Lessing (eds), *Materialien zur Philosophie Wilhelm Diltheys.* Frankfurt am Main: Suhrkamp, 1984, pp. 110ff.

37   Edmund Husserl, *Ideen zu einer reinen Phänomenologie und phänomenologischen Philosophie I, Jahrbuch für Phänomenologie und phänomenologische Forschung* 1 (1913). See also Edmund Husserl, *Gesammelte Werke.* Husserliana vol. 3, ed. Karl Schumann. The Hague: Martinus Nijhoff, 1976. [Translators' note: English translation: *Ideas Pertaining to a Pure Phenomenology and to a Phenomenological Philosophy: First Book,* trans. Fred Kersten. The Hague: Martinus Nijhoff, 1983.]

38   See Wilhelm Dilthey, *Gesammelte Schriften,* vol. 7, p. 202.

39   See Wilhelm Dilthey, *Gesammelte Schriften,* vol. 6, p. 319.

Dilthey and Ortega: The Philosophy of Life (1985)

1   'Dilthey und Ortega: Philosophie des Lebens' was presented at the Ortega Congress in Madrid in 1983. It was first published under the title 'Wilhelm Dilthey e Ortega y Gasset: un capítulo de la historia intelectual de Europa', in

Revista de Occidente 48/49 (1985): 77–88. It is now in *Gesammelte Werke*, vol. 4, n. 29, pp. 436–47.

2   See *Wahrheit und Methode*, p. 205 (*Gesammelte Werke*, vol. 1, pp. 222ff.) [Translators' note: English translation: *Truth and Method*, pp. 218f.] and here in this volume 'The Problem of Dilthey: Between Romanticism and Postivism', pp. 73–89.

3   Translators' note: 'Vital reason' or 'reason with life at its basis'.

4   In this regard, see Otto Friedrich Bollnow, '*Der Ausdruck und das Verstehen*', in Frithjof Rodi and Hans-Ulrich Lessing (eds.), *Materialien zur Philosophie Wilhelm Diltheys*, pp. 267–74.

5   See Paul Natorp, *Einleitung in die Psychologie nach kritischer Methode*. Freiburg: Mohr, 1888. It is the precursor of *Allgemeine Psychologie* of 1912, which became significant for Husserl.

6   Hans Friedrich August von Arnim, *Stoicorum veterum fragmenta*, vol. 2, 24, 36 and 36, 9. Leipzig: Teubner, 1903.

7   Wilhelm Dilthey, *Gesammelte Schriften*, vol. 19, p. 345. [Translators' note: English translation: 'Life and Cognition', in *Selected Works*, vol. II: *Understanding the Human World*, ed. Rudolf A. Makkreel and Frithjof Rodi. Princeton, NJ: Princeton University Press, 2010, pp. 58–114.]

8   See Wilhelm Dilthey, *Gesammelte Schriften*, vol. 19, pp. 333–88.

9   Wilhelm Dilthey, *Gesammelte Schriften*, vol. 8, p. 226.

10   Translators' note: 'Human kind, humanity, human civilization'.

Hermeneutics and the Diltheyan School

1   'Die Hermeneutik und die Dilthey-Schule' was published under the same title as a review of several books with an 'Afterword' in *Philosophische Rundschau* 38 (1991) 3: 161–77. It is now in *Gesammelte Werke*, vol. 10, n. 16, pp. 185–205.

2   Frithjof Rodi, *Die Erkenntnis des Erkannten. Zur Hermeneutik des 19. and 20. Jahrhunderts*. Frankfurt am Main: Suhrkamp, 1990.

3   Wilhelm Dilthey and Paul Yorck von Wartenburg, *Briefwechsel zwischen Wilhelm Dilthey und dem Grafen Paul Yorck v. Wartenburg, 1877–1897*, ed. Erich Rothacker. Halle (Saale): Max Niemeyer, 1923.

4   On this, see 'The Problem of Dilthey: Between Romanticism and Positivism', in this volume pp. 73–89.

5   Otto Friedrich Bollnow, *Studien zur Hermeneutik*, vol. 2 *Zur hermeneutischen Logik von Georg Misch und Hans Lipps*. Freiburg/Munich: Karl Alber, 1983.

6   Georg Misch, *Der Aufbau der Logik auf dem Boden der Philosophie des Lebens. Göttinger Vorlesungen über Logik und Einleitung in die Theorie des Wissens*, ed. Gudrun Kühne-Bertram and Frithjof Rodi. Freiburg/Munich: Karl Alber, 1994.

7   Wilhelm Dilthey, *Gesammelte Schriften,* vol. 20 *Logik und System der philo-
    sophischen Wissenschaften. Vorlesung zur erkenntnistheoretischen Logik und
    Methodologie (1864–1903),* ed. Hans-Ulrich Lessing and Frithjof Rodi. Göttingen:
    Vandenhoeck and Ruprecht, 1990.

8   The special significance of the new volume 20 lies in the fact that it now completes
    the fragmented transmission of Dilthey's unfinished works, presented in volume
    19, with the help of the transcripts of the lectures. It thus makes the systematic
    coherence of the whole clearer. Furthermore, the editor correctly points to the
    later draft of the Basel *Logic* where we encounter §27 on 'Intuition', which already
    announces the great plan of work to which Dilthey devoted his entire life.

9   It is only recently that we are really beginning to bring Schlegel to his full presence
    thanks to Ernst Behler's new edition.

10 Translators' note: We read *sich präsentiert* as *sie präsentiert.*

11 Translators' note: Jean Grondin notes that Gadamer here makes an allusion to
    what he says in a footnote in *Truth and Method* about Dilthey's work *Das Leben
    Schleiermachers.* Gadamer writes: 'It is interesting that the reading *Erlebnisse*
    (which I consider the right one) is a correction given in the second edn. (1922,
    by Mulert) for *Ergebnisse* in the original edn. of 1870 (1st edn., p. 305). If this is
    a misprint in the first edition, it results from the closeness of meaning between
    Erlebnis and *Ergebnis* that we saw above' (*Truth and Method,* 2nd rev. edn., trans.
    Joel Weinsheimer and Donald G. Marshall. New York: Continuum, 1998, p. 64).
    Jean Grondin's note is in H.-G. Gadamer, *L'herméneutique en rétrospective* Ire et
    IIe Parties, trans. Jean Grondin. Paris: Vrin, 2005, p. 242.

12 Translators' note: Dilthey also speaks of the 'unfathomable visage' of life
    (*unergründliches Antlitz*) (Wilhelm Dilthey, *Poetry and Experience, Selected Works,*
    vol. 5, ed. Rudolf Makkreel and Frithjof Rodi. Princeton, NJ: Princeton University
    Press, 1997, p. 254). We have translated *unergründlich* as 'inscrutable'.

13 When I read these explanations in Rodi, I seems to me that the picture of
    Heidegger and the interpretation of hermeneutics that can be derived from this
    picture are in the end inappropriately limited to the generation of Dilthey's and
    Misch's students. Whoever reflects further upon Dilthey would also have to
    attempt to reflect further upon *Being and Time,* and it would be decisively easier
    for the younger generation to do this today than it was for Misch. Meanwhile, the
    further developments of Heidegger (as also my own efforts) have for long been
    publicly available. We should no longer be concerned just with *Being and Time.*

14 See *Unterwegs zur Sprache.* Pfüllingen: Neske, 1959, pp. 95ff., p. 120. [Translators'
    note: English translation: *On the Way to Language,* trans. Peter D. Hertz. New
    York: Harper & Row, 1971, pp. 9, 28.]

15 On this, see my opening remarks in 'Heideggers "theologische Jugendschrift"', in
    Dilthey Jahrbuch, vol. 6 (1989): 228–34.

16 Translators' note: As Gadamer notes in another essay, 'Remembering Heidegger's
    Beginnings', Heidegger uses the term *Ruinanz* in association with *Neigung*,
    'inclination' in his lecture course of 1921–2 on *Phenomenology of Religion*.
    Both of these designate fundamental categories of life and these two terms will
    be replaced in *Being and Time* by *Verfall*, 'fallenness' and 'authenticity', respectively.

17 Translators' note: Gadamer uses the expression *im Vollzug* to translate the
    Latin *in actu exercito*, 'in the very exercise of the act', 'in its enactment' or 'in
    its performance', as opposed to the act that is signified, the *actus signatus*, the
    signate act considered according to the content expressed by the words. There is
    what is said both in the content of what is said – *actus signatus* – and in the very
    fact of saying it – *actus exercitus*. Gadamer takes this scholastic distinction from
    Heidegger. In *Die Kategorien- und Bedeutungslehre des Duns Scotus*, Heidegger
    gives the example of negation: 'When saying *nego* ['I deny'], for example, what
    is communicated is that I accomplish an act of negation. When saying *non* the
    act itself accomplishes itself. When calling out "O Henrice" there lies in the
    "O" the accomplishment of the act. The act is not first communicated by the
    "O", but accomplished' (*Frühe Schriften*, ed. Friedrich-Wilhelm von Herrmann,
    Gesamtausgabe 1. Frankfurt am Main: Klostermann, 1978, 313).

     Gadamer considers Fink's use of the expression 'operative concept' to be an
    illustration of this *actus exercitus*. See p. 242 for more on this expression.

18 Ernst Behler, *Derrida-Nietzsche, Nietzsche-Derrida*. Paderborn/Munich: Ferdinand
    Schöningh, 1988, pp. 138ff. See also the afterword 'Dekonstruktion und
    Hermeneutik', pp. 147ff.

19 I already presented these views in 1959 in my essay 'Vom Zirkel des Verstehens'
    (now in *Gesammelte Werke*, vol. 2, pp. 57–65).

20 Translators' note: In English in the text.

Subjectivity and Intersubjectivity, Subject and Person (1975)

1 'Subjektivität und Intersubjektivität, Subjekt und Person' was presented as a
   lecture in Dubrovnik in 1975. It was first published in *Gesammelte Werke*,
   vol. 10, n. 8, 1995, pp. 87–99. [Translators' note: A first translation was
   made by Peter Adamson and David Vessey under the title 'Subjectivity and
   Intersubjectivity, Subject and Person' (*Continental Philosophy Review* 33 (2000):
   pp. 275–87.]

2 Translators' note: 'The decisive experiment'. Literally: 'experience of the cross'.

3 Translators' note: These volumes are the following:
    Zur Phänomenologie der Intersubjektivität. Texte aus dem Nachlass. Erster Teil:
    1905–1920, Hua 13, ed. Iso Kern. The Hague: Martinus Nijhoff, 1973.

Zur Phänomenologie der Intersubjektivität. Texte aus dem Nachlass. Zweiter Teil: 1921-1928, Hua 14, ed. Iso Kern. The Hague: Martinus Nijhoff, 1973.

Zur Phänomenologie der Intersubjektivität. Texte aus dem Nachlass. Dritter Teil: 1929-1935, Hua 14, ed. Iso Kern. The Hague: Martinus Nijhoff, 1973.

4 See here and for what follows the essay 'Die phänomenologische Bewegung', essentially parts II and III, in *Gesammelte Werke*, vol. 3 *Neuere Philosophie I (Hegel/Husserl/Heidegger)*. Tübingen: Mohr, 1985, n. 6, pp. 105–46. [Translators' note: English translation: 'The Phenomenological Movement', in *Philosophical Hermeneutics*, trans. and ed. David Linge. Berkeley, CA: University of California Press, 1976, pp. 130–81.]

5 Translators' note: Søren Kierkegaard, *Gesammelte Werke*, trans. Christoff Schrempf, Wolfgang Pfleiderer, Heinrich Cornelius Ketels, and Hermann Gottsched. Jena: Eugen Diedrich, 1910–38.

6 Translators' note: 'Referat Kierkegaards', in Karl Jaspers, *Psychologie der Weltanschauungen*. Berlin: Julius Springer, 1919, pp. 370–80.

7 Translators' note: 'I think that I think'.

8 Translators' note: 'Vegetative soul'.

9 Translators' note: 'That which moves itself'.

10 Translators' note: 'Mind or intellect'.

11 Translators' note: 'Thought thinking itself'.

12 On this, see my contribution on Hegel, 'Die Dialektik des Selbsbewusstseins' (1973), in *Gesammelte Werke*, vol. 3, n. 3, pp. 47–64. [Translators' note: English translation: 'Hegel's Dialectic of Self-Consciousness', in *Hegel's Dialectic. Five Hermeneutic Studies*, trans. P. Christopher Smith. New Haven, CT: Yale University Press, 1976, pp. 54–74.]

13 Translators' note: In his essay 'Philosophische Bemerkungen zum Problem der Intelligenz', Gadamer uses the same quotation by Nietzsche and gives the following reference in a footnote: 'KGW VII/3, 40 [25]; see also 40 [10], [20]' (*Gesammelte Werke*, vol. 4, p. 280). The reference he gives is of *Nietzsche Werke. Kritische Gesamtausgabe*, vol. VII 3 *Nachgelassene Fragmente Herbst 1884–Herbst 1885*, ed. Giorgio Colli and Mazzino Montinari (Berlin: de Gruyter, 1974). The quotation is of a posthumous fragment of August–September 1885 that does not say *gründlicher* ('more fundamentally'), as Gadamer quotes it, but *besser* ('better'): 'We must doubt better than Descartes' (*es muss besser gezweifelt werden als Descartes*)' (p. 563). The second passage Gadamer references ('40 [10]') includes the statement: 'Descartes is not radical enough for me' (*Descartes ist mir nicht radikal genug*, p. 554) and the third passage referenced ('40 [20]') ends with the statement: 'It is to be doubted that 'the subject' can prove itself' (*es ist zu bezweifeln, dass 'das Subjekt' sich selber beweisen kann*, p. 560).

14 Translators' note: In *The Interpretation of Dreams*, Freud refers to a collection of

dreams by Jessen that are 'traceable to more or less accidental objective sensory stimuli'. Freud quotes Jessen: 'Every indistinctly perceived noise gives rise to corresponding dream pictures; the rolling of thunder takes us into the thick of battle, the crowing of a cock may be transformed into human shrieks of terror, and the creaking of a door may conjure up dreams of burglars breaking into the house' (Sigmund Freud, *The Interpretation of Dreams*, trans. A. A. Brill. New York: Macmillan, 1913, p. 18).

15 Translators' note: This is an aphorism from part 4, section 108 of Nietzsche's 'Beyond Good and Evil' (*Basic Writings of Nietzsche*, trans. Walter Kaufmann. New York: The Modern Library, 2000, p. 275). It runs as follows: 'There are no moral phenomena at all, but only a moral interpretation of phenomena' [*Es giebt gar keine moralischen Phänomene, sondern nur eine moralische Ausdeutung von Phänomenen*] (*Jenseits von Gut und Böse*. Stuttgart: Reclam, 1988, p. 78).

16 Translators' note: *Die Kreatur: Eine Zeitschrift* was a journal published in Berlin from 1926 to 1930 and dedicated to an encounter between Jews and Christians. It was edited by Martin Buber, Joseph Wittig and Viktor von Weizsäcker, representatives of the Jewish, Catholic and Protestant communities respectively. The editors encouraged the discussion of social and political issues.

17 Translators' note: Michael Theunissen. *The Other: Studies in the Social Ontology of Husserl, Heidegger, Sartre, and Buber*, trans. Christopher Macann. Cambridge, MA: The MIT Press, 1984.

18 On this, see in this volume the essay 'Heidegger and Sociology: Bourdieu and Habermas', pp. 167–78.

19 'Das Problem der Geschichte in der neueren deutschen Philosophie', *Gesammelte Werke*, vol. 2, n. 2, pp. 27–36.

20 Translators' note: 'An individual substance of a rational nature'.

21 Translators' note: In English in the text.

22 Gerhard Ebeling, *Evangelische Evangelienauslegung: eine Untersuchung zu Luthers Hermeneutik*. Darmstadt: Wissenschaftliche Buchgesellschaft, [1st edn. 1942] 1962.

23 Translators' note: Scheiermacher is credited to be the first to use the term *Personalismus* in *Über die Religion. Reden an die Gebildeten unter ihren Verächtern* (Berlin: de Gruyter, 1995); English translation *On Religion: Speeches to its Cultured Despisers*. Cambridge: Cambridge University Press, 1996.

On the Contemporary Relevance of Husserl's Phenomenology (1974)

1 'Zur Aktualität der Husserlschen Phänomenologie' was presented at the Phänomenologen-Kongress in Schwäbisch-Hall in 1969, which took place 8–11 September. It was first published in Herman Van Breda (ed.), *Vérité et vérification*

– *Wahrheit und Verifikation.* The Hague: Martinus Nijhoff, 1974, pp. 210–23. It is now in *Gesammelte Werke*, vol. 3, n. 8, pp. 160–71. [References corrected by translators.]

2   Translators' note: Ricoeur's talk was titled 'Conclusions' (*Vérité et vérification – Wahrheit und Verifikation*, pp. 190–209).

3   Translators' note: Gerhard Funke's essay was titled 'Bewusstseinswissenschaft' (*Vérité et vérification – Wahrheit und Verifikation*, pp. 3–58).

4   See Oskar Becker, 'Von der Hinfälligkeit des Schönen und der Abenteuerlichkeit des Künstlers', in *Supplement* to the *Jahrbuch für Philosophie und phänomenologische Forschung* 1929: pp. 27–52. It is in footnote 2, p. 39. This essay was reprinted in Oskar Becker, *Dasein und Dawesen.* Pfüllingen: Neske, 1963, pp. 11–40.

5   Johann G. Fichte, *Fichte-Schelling-Briefwechsel (Auswahl)*, ed. Walter Schulz. Frankfurt am Main: Suhrkamp, 1968.

6   Translators' note: Gadamer is referring to Ante Pažanin's contribution titled 'Wahrheit und Lebenswelt beim späten Husserl' (*Vérité et vérification – Wahrheit und Verifikation*, pp. 71–116).

7   Translators' note: Ante Pažanin.

8   Translators' note: Enzo Paci's contribution was titled 'Vérification empirique et transcendance de la vérité' (*Vérité et vérification – Wahrheit und Verifikation*, pp. 59–70).

9   Translators' note: The contribution by Suzanne Bachelard was titled 'Logique husserlienne et sémantique' (*Vérité et vérification – Wahrheit und Verifikation*, pp. 117–31).

10 Translators' note: Stefan Strasser's contribution was titled 'Probleme des 'Verstehens' in neuer Sicht' (*Vérité et vérification – Wahrheit und Verifikation*, pp. 132–89).

'Being and Nothingness' (Jean-Paul Sartre) (1989)

1   "Das Sein and das Nichts' (J. P. Sartre)' was presented at the International Sartre Conference at the Johann-Goethe-Universität in Frankfurt am Main, 9–12 July 1987. It was first published in *Sartre: Ein Kongress,* ed. Traugott König. Hamburg: Rowohlts Taschenbuch Verlag, 1988, pp. 37–52. It is now in *Gesammelte Werke*, vol. 10, n. 10, pp. 110–24.

2   Translators' note: Literally: 'He had cut forty leaves', printed volumes at the time being often bound with folded leaves that needed to be cut.

3   Translators' note: Jean-Paul Sartre, *La Nausée.* Paris: Gallimard, 1938. English translation: *Nausea*, trans. Lloyd Alexander. New York: New Directions Publishing Company, 1964.

4   Translators' note: *Les jeux sont faits* was a screenplay published in 1947. An English translation by Louis Varese under the title *The Chips Are Down* was published in 1948. The movie *Les jeux sont faits* was directed by Jean Delannoy in 1948.

5   Translators' note: Ludwig Landgrebe, 'Husserls Abschied von Cartesianismus', *Philosophische Rundschau* 9 (1961): 133–77.

6   Translators' note: 'Clarity'.

7   Translators' note: 'The kinds of discourse' or 'the genres of discourse'.

8   Translators' note: 'I think that I think'.

9   Translators' note: Sartre's text says: '... time is revealed as the shimmer of nothingness on the surface of a strictly atemporal being' (*Being and Nothingness: A Phenomenological Essay on Ontology*, trans. Hazel E. Barnes. New York: Pocket Books, 1972, p. 294). The French text says: 'Le temps se révèle comme châtoiement de néant à la surface d'un être rigoureusement a-temporel' (*L'Être et le néant. Essai d'ontologie phénoménologique*. Paris: Gallimard, 1943, p. 258).

10   'Die Dialektik des Selbstbewusstseins' (1973), in *Gesammelte Werke*, vol. 3, n. 3, pp. 47–64. [Translators' note: English translation: 'Hegel's Dialectic of Self-consciousness', in *Hegel's Dialectic: Five Hermeneutical Studies*, trans. P. Christopher Smith. New Haven, CT: Yale University Press, 1976, pp. 54–72.]

11   On this see also in this volume 'Subjectivity and Intersubjectivity, Subject and Person', pp. 125–37.

12   Translators' note: Sartre uses the German term *Dasein* in this passage (*L'Être et le néant. Essai d'ontologie phénoménologique*. Paris: Gallimard, 1943, p. 29).

Heidegger and Sociology: Bourdieu and Habermas (1979/85)

1   'Heidegger und die Soziologie: Bourdieu und Habermas' first appeared as a review of Pierre Bourdieu's book *Die politische Ontologie Martin Heideggers* in *Philosophische Rundschau* 26 (1–2) (1979) 143–9. The review of the chapter on Heidegger in Jürgen Habermas' book *Der philosophische Diskurs der Moderne. Zwölf Vorlesungen* was first published along with the review of Bourdieu's book in *Gesammelte Werke*, vol. 10, n. 4, pp. 46–57.

2   Pierre Bourdieu, *L'ontologie politique de Martin Heidegger*. Paris: Les Editions de Minuit, 1988. [Translators' note: English translation: *The Political Ontology of Martin Heidegger*, trans. Peter Collier. Cambridge: Polity Press, 1990.]

3   Translators' note: What Gadamer renders as the 'activity of research' (*Akt der Forschung*) is what Bourdieu in the French original (*L'ontologie politique de Martin Heidegger*. Paris: Editions de Minuit, 1988), calls 'academic discourse' (*le discours savant*, p. 83) or 'philosophical discourse' (*le discours philosophique*, on the dustjacket of the book), about which there is the 'formation of a

compromise' or which is the result of a compromise. The English translation
says 'learned discourse' (*The Political Ontology of Martin Heidegger*, trans. Peter
Collier. Cambridge: Polity Press, 1990, p. 70). Bourdieu also calls this formation
of a compromise a 'transaction' between what the author wants to express
and the structural constraints of the field in which this discourse takes place.
Academic discourse is thus a 'transaction' at the unconscious level between
authorial intent and what the social and cultural milieu allows. It is to be
underscored that this transaction is not consciously negotiated, neither on the
side of society or culture nor on the side of the author. It is rather a matter of the
constraints that social and cultural forms exert on anything that is to be said and
published, and a matter of unconscious censorship or self-censorship on the part
of the author.

4   The present text does not make suggestions leading in that direction. However,
methodological reflections in his *Outline of a Theory of Practice* (trans. Richard
Nice. Cambridge: Cambridge University Press, 1977) makes a principled critique
of the naiveté of 'objectivism', which in my view implies such a consequence.

5   Translators' note: Eduard Meyer, 'Spenglers Untergang des Abendlandes', *Deutsche
Literaturzeitung* 25 (1924): 1759–80.

6   Translators' note: The journal is named *Logos. Internationale Zeitschrift für
Philosophie der Kultur* and the issue was from 1920/21, n. 9. It included essays by
Gustav Becking ('Die Musikgeschichte in Spenglers "Untergang des Abendlandes"',
pp. 284–95), Ludwig Curtius ('Morphologie der antiken Kunst', pp. 195–221),
Erich Frank ('Mathematik und Musik und der griechische Geist', pp. 222–59), Karl
Joël ('Die Philosophie in Spenglers "Untergangs des Abendlandes"', pp. 135–70),
Edmund Mezger ('Oswald Spenglers "Untergang des Abendlandes"', pp. 260–83),
Eduard Schwartz, ('Über das Verhältnis der Hellenen zur Geschichte', pp. 171–87),
Wilhelm Spiegelberg ('Aegyptologische Kritik an Spenglers Untergang des
Abendlandes', pp. 188–94).

7   Cambridge, MA: Harvard University Press, 1969.

8   New York: Grosset & Dunlap, 1964. [References corrected by translators.]

9   Translators' note: 'The essential social unthought'.

10   Notes after a first reading of Jürgen Habermas, *Der Philosophische Diskurs Der
Moderne: Zwölf Vorlesungen*. Frankfurt am Main: Suhrkamp, 1985. [Translators'
note: English translation: *Philosophical Discourse of Modernity: Twelve Lectures*,
trans. Frederick Lawrence. Cambridge, MA: MIT Press, 1987.]

11   On this, see for example 'Der eine Weg Martin Heideggers' in *Gesammelte Werke*,
vol. 3, n. 28. [Translators' note: English translation: 'Martin Heidegger's One Path',
in Theodore Kisiel and John van Buren (eds), *Reading Heidegger from the Start:
Essays in His Earliest Thought*. Albany, NY: State University of New York Press,
1994, pp. 19–34.]

Hermeneutics on the Trail (1994)

1   *Hermeneutik auf der Spur* was written in 1994 and first published in *Gesammelte*
     Werke, vol. 10, n. 13, pp. 148–74. [Translators' note: A first translation appeared
     under the title 'Hermeneutics Tracking the Trace [On Derrida]', in *The*
     Gadamer Reader: A Bouquet of Later Writings, ed. Richard Palmer. Evanston, IL:
     Northwestern University Press, 2007, pp. 372–406.

     In his title Gadamer plays with the expression *Hermeneutik auf der Spur*. The
     word *Hermeneutik* can be the object: 'on the trace of hermeneutics', 'exploring
     hermeneutics', as in the expression *der Natur auf der Spur* (exploring nature).
     This is how Jean Grondin translates the title into French: 'Sur la trace de
     l'herméneutique'. However, in the essay Gadamer also argues for the specific
     way hermeneutics investigates its object and how it can reveal more than, for
     example, deconstruction, which makes abundant use of the notion of 'trace'.
     Hermeneutics can 'follow the trace', as deconstruction claims to do, but, unlike
     deconstruction, hermeneutics is not a celebration of the multiplicity of traces
     and a simple affirmation of the dissolution of meaning altogether. For Gadamer,
     to be on the trail as hermeneutics is, is to be in a constant dialogue, asking
     questions, answering, being asked other questions, led astray, led toward dead
     ends, but never giving up on the prospect of meaning itself, which is for him
     the cornerstone of shared existence. Thus, the title also means, as Richard
     Palmer translates it into English, 'Hermeneutics Tracking the Trace'. We choose
     'Hermeneutics on the Trail'.]

2   See 'Text und Interpretation', in *Gesammelte Werke*, vol. 2, n. 24, pp. 330–60.
     [Translators' note: English translation: 'Text and Interpretation', in *Dialogue and*
     Deconstruction: The Gadamer-Derrida Encounter, ed. Diane Michelfelder and
     Richard Palmer. Albany, NY: State University of New York Press, 1989, pp. 21–51.]

3   Now also in Jacques Derrida, *Marges de la philosophie*. Paris. 1972, pp. 31–78.
     [Translators' note: English Translation: *Margins of Philosophy*, trans. Alan Bass.
     Chicago: University of Chicago Press, 1982, pp. 29–67.]

4   See, among others, 'Destruktion und Dekonstruktion', in *Gesammelte Werke*, vol.
     2, n. 25, pp. 361–72 as well as 'Frühromantik, Hermeneutic, Dekonstruktivismus'
     (1987), in *Gesammelte Werke,* vol. 10, n. 11, pp. 125–37, and 'Dekonstruktion
     und Hermeneutik' (1988), in *Gesammelte Werke,* vol. 10, n. 12, pp. 138–47.
     [Translators' note: These three essays have been translated in the volume *Dialogue*
     and Deconstruction: The Gadamer-Derrida Encounter under the following titles,
     respectively: 'Destruction and Deconstruction', pp. 102–13; 'Hermeneutics and
     logocentrism', pp. 114–25; and 'Letter to Dallmayr', pp. 93–101.]

5   Translators' note: This is taken from the essay 'Structure, Sign and Play in the
     Discourse of the Human Sciences'. Here is the translation by Alan Bass: 'It could

be shown that all the names related to fundamentals, to principles, or to the centre have always designated an invariable presence – *eidos, archē, telos, energeia, ousia* (essence, existence, substance, subject) *alētheia*, transcendentality, consciousness, God, man, and so forth' (*Writing and Difference*, trans. Alan Bass. London: Routledge, 2001, p. 353). Note that Gadamer changes the opening as well as the closing parenthesis.

6 Translators' note: 'Rational theology'.

7 For something more detailed in this regard, see 'Dialektik und Sophistik im siebenten platonischen Brief', in *Gesammelte Werke,* vol. 6, n. 6, pp. 90–115. [Translators' note: English translation: 'Dialectic and Sophism in Plato's Seventh Letter', in *Dialogue and Dialectic: Eight Hermeneutical Studies on Plato*, trans. P. Christopher Smith. New Haven, CT: Yale University Press, 1980, pp. 93–123.]

8 Translators' note: 'Interior speech'.

9 Translators' note: *Voice and Phenomenon. Introduction to the Problem of the Sign in Husserl's Phenomenology*, trans. Leonard Lawlor. Evanston, IL: Northwestern University Press, 2010.

10 See also the relevant works in *Gesammelte Werke,* vol. 8: among others, 'Stimme und Sprache' ['Voice and Language'] (n. 22), 'Hören – Sehen – Lesen' ['Listening, Seeing, Reading'] (n. 23), 'Lesen ist wie Übersetzen' ['Reading is like Translating'] (n. 24).

11 See Hugo Huppert, '"Spirituell". Ein Gespräch mit Paul Celan' ['"Spiritual": A Conversation with Paul Celan'], in Werner Hamacher and Winfried Menninghaus (eds.), *Paul Celan*. Frankfurt am Main: Suhrkamp, 1988, p. 321.

12 Translators' note: The German text says: *der Ton macht die Musik*. This idiom means that the manner in which something is said is necessary for understanding the content of what is said; only through the manner of speaking will the content be fully understood.

13 Translators' note: 'Art hides in its own art'.

14 Translators' note: In 1715, the sides of the 'Night Watch' painting were trimmed, most significantly from the left-hand side, in order for it to fit its new space in Amsterdam's town hall when it was moved there from its original location, the Kloveniersdoelen.

15 Translators' note: Gadamer says 'The Conspiracy of Auricius' [*Verschörung des Auricius*]. 'The Conspiracy of the Batavians Under Claudius Civilis' was Rembrandt's largest painting, made in 1661–2. It was later cut down drastically by the artist himself in order to sell it. Its whereabouts were unknown up until 1662. In 1734 it was purchased by Nicolaas Kohl and Sophia Grill who resided in Amsterdam until the painting was most probably taken to Sweden in 1766 and donated to the local Royal Swedish Academy of Fine Arts in 1798 by Anna Johanna Grill in the memory of her late husband Henrick Wilhelm Peill. (See

'Rembrandt's Claudius Civilis temporarily at view at the Rijksmuseum', https://
www.rijksmuseum.nl/en/press/press-releases/rembrandts-claudius-civilis-
temporarily-on-view-at-the-rijksmuseum [accessed 28 May 2015].)

16 For a more detailed account of this, see my contribution 'Idee und Wirklichkeit in
    Platos Timaios', in *Gesammelte Werke*, vol. 6, n. 15, pp. 242–70. [Translators' note:
    English translation: 'Idea and Reality in Plato's *Timaeus*', in *Dialogue and Dialectic*,
    pp. 156–93.]

17 Translators' note: The science of the measurement of volumes and other
    characteristics of solid figures, to be contrasted to planimetry. From *stereos* (solid)
    and *metron* (measure).

18 Translators' note: 'From myth to reason'.

19 See also 'Platos Denken in Utopien', in *Gesammelte Werke*, vol. 7, n. 9, pp. 270–89.

20 See in this regard, 'Der "eminente Text" und seine Wahrheit', in *Gesammelte Werke*,
    vol. 8, n. 25, pp. 286–95. [Translators' note: English translation: 'The "Eminent
    Text" and its Truth', trans. Geoffrey Waite, in *The Horizon of Literature*, ed. Paul
    Hernadi. Lincoln, NE: University of Nebraska Press, 1982, pp. 337–47.]

21 Translators' note: Statement by Socrates, which Gadamer explains a little bit in the
    essay 'On the Beginnings of Thought', p. 245. There he formulates it as: 'Whatever
    I say, it is not my *logos*.'

22 With regard to the interpretations of Celan, see the essay 'Was muss der Leser
    Wissen?' ['What must the Reader Know?'] in 'Wer bin Ich und wer bist Du?:
    Kommentar zu Celans Gedichtfolge "Atemkristall"', *Gesammelte Werke*, vol. 9.
    Tübingen: Mohr, 1993, n. 36, pp. 443ff. [Translators' note: English translation:
    'Who Am I and Who Are You?' in *Gadamer on Celan: 'Who Am I and Who Are
    You?' and Other Essays*, trans. Richard Heinemann and Bruce Krajewski. Albany,
    NY: State University of New York Press, 1997, pp. 67–126.]

23 Translators' note: *Phaedrus* 279c. Here is the translation in The Loeb Classical
    Library: 'May I consider the wise man rich; and may I have such wealth as only
    the self-restrained person can bear or endure' (Plato, *Euthyphro: Apology; Crito;
    Phaedo; Phaedrus*, trans. Harold N. Fowler and Walter R. M. Lamb. The Loeb
    Classical Library. Cambridge, MA: Harvard University Press, 1914, p. 579).

Remembering Heidegger's Beginnings (1986)

1   'Erinnerungen an Heideggers Anfänge' was written on the basis of a lecture
    presented at a symposium in Bochum, 16–17 September 1985 on the topic of
    'Faktizität und Geschichtlichkeit' [Facticity and Historicity]. A revised version
    of the lecture first appeared in *Heideggeriana: Saggi e poesie nel decennale della
    morte di Martin Heidegger (1976–1986)*, ed. Giampero Moretti. Lanciano: Editrice

Itinerari, 25 (1986) 1–2: 5–16. It is now in *Gesammelte Werke,* vol. 10, n. 1, pp. 3–13.

2   I wrote something about this in my essay 'Die religiöse Dimension' (now in *Gesammelte Werke,* vol. 3, n. 22, pp. 308ff. [Translators' note: English translation: 'The Religious Dimension', in Hans-Georg Gadamer, *Heidegger's Ways,* trans. John W. Stanley. Albany, NY: State University of New York Press, 1994, pp. 167–80.]

3   *Phänomenologische Interpretationen zu Aristoteles. Einführung in die phänomenologische Forschung* (Wintersemester 1921/22), ed. Walter Bröcker und Käte Bröcker-Oltmanns. Gesamtausgabe 61. Frankfurt am Main: Klostermann, 1985. [Translators' note: English translation: *Phenomenological Interpretations of Aristotle: Initiation into Phenomenological Research,* trans. Richard Rojcewicz. Bloomington, IN: Indiana University Press, 2008.]

4   *Das Erkenntnisproblem in der Philosophie und Wissenschaft der neueren Zeit,* vols 2, 3 and 4 of Ernst Cassirer, *Gesammelte Werke.* Hamburg: Meiner, 1998. [Translators' note: The third volume does not seem to be entirely dedicated to Hegel but to the idealists Fichte, Schelling, Hegel, Herbart, Schopenhauer, Fries.]

5   *Phänomenologische Interpretationen zu Aristoteles,* pp. 79ff; *Phenomenological Interpretations of Aristotle,* p. 61.

The Turn in the Path (1985)

1   'Die Kehre des Weges' was first published in *Gesammelte Werke,* vol. 10, n. 6, pp. 71–5.

2   For a long time now, I have explicated (*Gesammelte Werke,* vol. 3, pp. 271f.) how Heidegger's turn can be understood as a way of bringing to resolution his early opposition to the transcendental self-interpretation of Husserl and thus as a return [*Rückkehr*] to his own mission.

3   See 'Der eine Weg Martin Heideggers' (in *Gesammelte Werke,* vol. 3, n. 28). [Translators' note: English translation: 'Martin Heidegger's One Path', in Theodore Kisiel and John van Buren (eds.), *Reading Heidegger from the Start: Essays in His Earliest Thought.* Albany, NY: State University of New York Press, 1994, pp. 19–34.]

4   In the meantime, in the proceedings of the Heidegger-Symposium organized by the Alexander von Humboldt Foundation in Bonn-Bad Godesberg in 1989, we can read a very important essay by Alberto Rosales on this topic ('Heideggers Kehre im Lichte ihrer Interpretationen', in Dietrich Papenfuss and Otto Pöggeler (eds.), *Zur philosophischen Aktualität Heideggers. Symposium der Alexander von Humboldt-Stiftung vom 24.–28. April 1989 in Bonn-Bad Godesberg,* vol. 1: *Philosophie und Politik.* Frankfurt am Main: Klostermann, 1991, pp. 118–40). This essay thinks through and presents in a new and thorough manner the illuminating

and fruitful contributions on the topic of the 'turn'. These are works, such as those by Walter Schulz ('Über den philosophiegeschichtlichen Ort Martin Heideggers', in *Philosophsiche Rundschau* 1 (1953/54): pp. 65–93, 211–32) and by Dieter Sinn ('Heideggers Spätphilosophie', in *Philosophische Rundschau* 14 (1967): 81–182), both of which at the time take some inspiration from my own understanding of Heidegger. There are also other contributions, which in the meantime had been made by the works of Otto Pöggeler and Friedrich-Wilhelm von Herrmann. I can fully agree with the specific result of Rosales's studies, although I do not consider it my own task to make this kind of differentiation in the concept of 'turn' in Heidegger.

On the Beginning of Thought (1986)

1   'Vom Anfang des Denkens' was presented as a lecture at the Heidegger Congress in Leiden in 1986. It has been published for the first time in *Gesammelte Werke*, vol. 3 n. 26, pp. 375–93.

2   'Die religiöse Dimension', in *Gesammelte Werke*, vol. 3, n. 22, pp. 308f.
    [Translators' note: English translation: 'The Religious Dimension', in Hans-Georg Gadamer, *Heidegger's Ways*, trans. John W. Stanley. Albany, NY: State University of New York Press, 1994, pp. 167–80.]
    The tenth anniversary of the death of Martin Heidegger in 1986, together with the progress of the complete edition of his works, has given us many opportunities to discuss his work. For my part I have repeatedly tried to contribute, not least as a surviving contemporary of his, to such a discussion: in Leiden, Oxford and London, Munich, Messkirch, Bochum, Trier and Perugia. I have made use of some parts from the proceedings under publication for the following three essays. These are: the present one, 'On the Way Back to the Beginning' (in this volume pp. 247–69), and 'Der eine Weg Martin Heideggers' (1986). [Translators' note: English translation: 'Martin Heidegger's One Path', in Theodore Kisiel and John van Buren (eds), *Reading Heidegger from the Start: Essays in His Earliest Thought*. Albany, NY: State University of New York Press, 1994, pp. 19–34.]

3   Watson and Watson-Franke have shown that ethnology on these grounds is right to be sceptical toward the survey method (see footnote 7 in *Gesammelte Werke*, vol. 2, p. 9). It is even in the name of science that we are compelled to be sceptical.

4   Translators' note: In English in the text.

5   Translators' note: The essay in question is 'The Question Concerning Technology'. Heidegger writes: 'The four ways of being responsible [Aristotelian causes] bring something into appearance. They let it come forth into presencing [*An-Wesen*]. They set it free to that place and so start it on its way, namely into its complete

arrival ... It is in the sense of such a starting something on its way into arrival that being responsible is an occasioning or an inducing to go forward [*Ver-an-lassen*]' ('The Question Concerning Technology', in *Basic Writings*, ed. David Farrell Krell. San Francisco: HarperSanFrancisco, 1993, p. 316).

6   Translators' note: Here is how Gadamer interprets Heidegger's three main terms *Anwesen, Anwesende*, and *Anwesenheit*: *Anwesen* is 'what allows presence'. Its opposite is *Verwesen*: what forecloses presence. Das *Anwesende* is the entity that is allowed presence or granted presence. *Anwesenheit* is the event of entering into presence through which 'what allows presence' is enacted, as it were. As Gadamer says, commenting on the Heraclitus quotation on the lintel of Heidegger's hut in Todnauberg – 'The thunderbolt steers all things' – this 'enactment' is a happening or an event and occurs in an instant as a thunderbolt that illuminates what allows presence, revealing it or disclosing it. Gadamer writes: 'This sentence in fact brings together the fundamental vision of Heidegger, namely that what is granted presence in entering into presence [*das Anwesende in seiner Anwesenheit*] emerges in a flash of lightning. For a moment everything is clear as day only to fall as instantaneously into the darkest of nights. Heidegger surmised that this suddenness, in which 'what allows presence' [*Anwesen*] is there only for an instantaneous flash of a moment, was the Greek experience of being' (pp. 243–4). What allows presence (*das Anwesen*) works by letting entities enter into presence, which is what the verb *anwesen* means, as used by Gadamer, interpreting Heidegger.

7   This happened probably in the middle of the 1920s when he was preparing *Being and Time*. The word is not to be found in the Marburg lecture courses of 1924/25 (GA 20).

   [Translators' note: Volume 20 is about the *Prolegomena zur Geschichte des Zeitbegriffs*. It was given in the summer of 1925, not during the winter semester 1924/25. The lecture of 1924/25 (GA 19) is *Platon: Sophistes*. The *Heidegger Concordance* (ed. François Jaran and Christophe Perrin. London: Bloomsbury, 2013) lists seven occurrences of *Vorhandenheit* in volume 20. Heidegger writes, for example, that in Descartes 'substantiality means presence-at-hand [*Substanzialität meint Vorhandenheit*]' (Martin Heidegger, *Prolegomena zur Geschichte des Zeitbegriffs*, Marburger Vorlesung Sommersemester 1925, Gesamtausgabe 20. Frankfurt am Main: Klostermann, 1979, p. 232). No occurrence is listed for GA 19, but there are several for GA 18, *Aristotles: Rhetoric* of the summer semester 1924.]

8   [Translators' note: 'Verbs of perception'.] See Ernst Heitsch in *Hermes* 97 (1969): pp. 292–6 and *Philosophisches Jahrbuch* (1968) 76: 23–6.

9   Translators' note: Here is the quotation: 'All of modern philosophy is based on something which both ethics and Christianity would consider a frivolity. Instead of deterring people and calling them to order by speaking of despair

and exasperation, it has winked at people and invited them to pride themselves on doubting and on having doubted. For the rest, philosophy, as abstract, floats in indeterminateness of the metaphysical. Instead of admitting this to itself and then pointing people (individuals) to the ethical, the religious, and the existential, philosophy has given rise to the pretence that humans could, as is said prosaically, speculate themselves out of their own skin and into pure appearance' (Søren Kierkegaard, *Einübung im Christentum* [Exercises in Christianity] (Diederichs IX, 1912), p. 70, n. 1, in Martin Heidegger, *Phenomenological Interpretations of Aristotle: Initiation into Phenomenological Research*. Bloomington, IN: Indiana University Press, 2001, p. 137.

10   Translators' note: See footnote 17 on *im Vollzug* p. 296.

11   Translators' note: the act exercised (as a performance).

12   Translators' note: the signate act (considered according to the content expressed by the words).

13   Translators' note: Here is Aristotle's text: 'And why man is a political animal in a greater measure than any bee or any gregarious animal is clear. For nature, as we declare, does nothing without purpose; and man alone of the animals possesses speech [*logos*]. The mere voice, it is true, can indicate pain and pleasure, and therefore is possessed by the other animals as well (for their nature has been developed so far as to have sensations of what is painful and pleasant and to signify those sensations to one another), but speech is designed to indicate the advantageous and the harmful, and therefore also the right and the wrong; for it is the special property of man in distinction from the other animals that he alone has perception of good and bad and right and wrong and the other moral qualities, and it is partnership in these things that makes a household and a city-state' (*Politics* 1253a, trans. H. Rackham. Cambridge, MA: Harvard University Press; London, William Heinemann Ltd. 1944). Gadamer quotes this passage in his essay 'Culture and the Word' [in *Praise of Theory*, trans. Chris Dawson. New Haven and London: Yale University Press. 1998. p. 5] when again discussing the standard translation of *zōon logon echon* as *animal rationale*. On that occasion he undertakes a close textual analysis of this passage.

14   Translators' note: The text reads *lesende Lege*. We assume that it is *legende Lese*.

15   Translators' note: This is the verb *anwesen*, entering into presence, different from *das Anwesen*: that which allows presence or grants presence.

On the Way Back to the Beginning (1986)

1   'Auf dem Rückgang zum Anfang' was first published under the title 'Heideggers Rückgang auf die Griechen', in Konrad Cramer, Hans Friedrich Fulda, Rolf-Peter Horstmann (eds.), *Theorie der Subjektivität. Festschrift für D. Heinrich*. Frankfurt

am Main: Suhrkamp, 1986, pp. 397–424. It is now in *Gesammelte Werke*, vol. 3, n. 27, pp. 394–416.

2   Translators' note: Leibniz describes this walk in Rosenthal in the letter to Nicolas Remond, written on January 10, 1716: 'I discovered Aristotle as a youth, and even the scholastics did not repel me; even now I do not regret this. But then Plato too, and Plotinus, gave me satisfaction, not to mention the other thinkers whom I consulted later. After finishing the schools of the trivium, I fell upon the moderns, and I recall walking in a grove on the outskirts of Leipzig called the Rosenthal, at the age of fifteen, and deliberating whether to preserve substantial forms or not. Mechanism finally prevailed and led me to apply myself to mathematics. It is true that I did not penetrate its depths until after some conversations with Huygens in Paris' (cited in Roger Ariew, 'G. W. Leibniz, Life and Works', in *The Cambridge Companion to Leibniz*, ed. Nicholas Jolley. Cambridge, Melbourne: Cambridge University Press, 1994, p. 25).

3   Translators' note: This is an idiom attributed to Napoleon Bonaparte, which means someone on his way to great things. The saying is supposed to have been: 'Every French soldier carries in his knapsack the baton of a Marshal of France.' According to Albert Montefiore Hymason, it was in fact an utterance of Louis XVIII to the students at the Collège de Saint Cyr in 1819 (*A Dictionary of English Phrases*. London: Routledge, 1922, p. 142).

4   Translators' note: Martin Heidegger, *Phänomenologische Interpretationen zu Aristoteles. Einführung in die phänomenologische Forschung*, GA 61, ed. Walter Bröcker and Käte Bröcker-Oltmanns. Frankfurt am Main: Klostermann, 1985, pp. 48–51. English Translation: *Phenomenological Interpretations of Aristotle: Initiation into Phenomenological Research*, trans. Richard Rojcewicz. Bloomington, IN: Indiana University Press, pp. 37–40.

5   *Sophist* 244 a. [Translators' note: *Theaetetus – Sophist*, trans. Harold N. Fowler. The Loeb Classical Library. Cambridge, MA: Harvard University Press, The Loeb Library. 1921, p. 363.]

6   Translators' note: 'The master's words'.

7   *Sophist* 248 af. [Translators' note: Plato writes: 'Stranger: You distinguish in your speech between generation and being, do you not? Theaetetus: Yes, we do. Str. And you say that with the body, by means of perception, we participate in generation, and with the soul, by means of thought, we participate in real being, which last is always unchanged and the same, whereas generation is different at different times' (*Theaetetus – Sophist*, pp. 379–81).]

8   See *Sophist* 250 c, p. 389. [Translation modified by translators]. On what follows, see 'Plato', in *Gesammelte Werke*, vol. 3, n. 16, pp. 138–48.

9   Translators' note: This text is *Die Kunst und der Raum*, a presentation Heidegger made at the Gallerie St. Gallen, which was published by Erker under the title *Die Kunst und der Raum – L' art et l' espace*, trans. Jean Beaufret and François Fédier.

St. Gallen: Erker-Verlag, 1969. English translation: 'Art and Space', trans. Charles Siebert, in *Man and World* 6 (1973): pp. 3–8.

10 *Sophist* 252 bf, pp. 397–8.

11 See the edition by Clemens Baeumker, *Eine lateinische Rechtfertigungsschrift des Meister Eckhart: Mit einem Geleitwort von Clemens Baeumker*. Münster i. W: Aschendorff, 1923.

12 Translators' note: 'Being is God'. Grammatically, it can also mean 'God is being'. In the English translation of Eckhart's work, Armand Maurer translates this by 'existence is God' (Master Eckhart, *Parisian Questions and Prologues*, trans. Armand Maurer. Toronto: Pontifical Institute of Mediaeval Studies, 1981, p. 31).

13 Translators' note: 'The Belgian Philosophers'.

14 246 de. [Translators' note: Plato writes: 'Our first duty would be to make them really better, if it were in any way possible; but if this cannot be done, let us pretend that they are better, by assuming that they would be willing to answer more in accordance with the rules of dialectic than they actually are. For the acknowledgement of anything by better men is more valid than if made by worse men. But it is not these men that we care about; we merely seek the truth.' 'Quite right' (*Theaetetus - Sophist*, p. 75).]

15 M. Heidegger, *Platons Lehre von der Wahrheit: Mit einem Brief [an Jean Beaufret, Paris] über den 'Humanismus'*. Bern: Francke, 1947. [Translators' note: English translation: *Plato's Doctrine of Truth,* trans. Thomas Sheehan, in Martin Heidegger, *Pathmarks,* ed. William McNeill. Cambridge, UK: Cambridge University Press, 1998, pp. 155–82.]

16 Translators' note: Gadamer speaks of 'the fact of science' in analogy with Kant's 'fact of reason', of which human freedom is an example.

17 Martin Heidegger, *Nietzsche*, 2 vols, Pfüllingen: Neske, 1961, vol. 2, pp. 399ff.

18 Aristotle, *Categories* 5, 2a 11–16. [Translators' note: Aristotle writes: 'Substance in the truest and strictest, the primary sense of that term, is that which is neither asserted of nor can be found in a subject. We take as examples of this a particular man or a horse. But we *do* speak of secondary substances – those within which, being species, the primary or first are included, and those within which, being genera, the species themselves are contained' (*The Categories; On Interpretation,* trans. Harold P. Cooke and Hugh Tredennick. The Loeb Classical Library. Cambridge, MA: Harvard University Press, 1938, p. 19).]

19 Plotinus, *Ennead* III, 8 *peri theorias*. [Translators' note: English translation: Arthur H. Armstrong. The Loeb Classical Library. Cambridge, MA: Harvard University Press, 1993.]

20 See in this regard my essay published by the Heidelberg Academy, 'Dialektik und Sophistik im VII. platonischen Brief', now in *Gesammelte Werke*, vol. 6, pp. 90–115. [Translators' note: English translation: 'Dialectic and Sophism in

Plato's Seventh Letter', in Hans-Georg Gadamer, *Dialogue and Dialectic: Eight Hermeneutical Studies on Plato*, ed. and trans. P. Christopher Smith. New Haven, CT: Yale University Press, 1980, pp. 93–123.]

21   See my explanations in the treatise mentioned above, pp. 96f.

22   Translators' note: In English in the text.

23   *Parmenides* 142 b 3f. [Translators' note: This passage is about the one: 'If one is, can it be and not partake of being?' (trans. Harold N. Fowler. The Loeb Classical Library. Cambridge, MA: Harvard University Press, 1996, p. 253).]

24   'Platos ungeschriebene Dialektik (1968)', in *Gesammelte Werke*, vol. 6, n. 8, pp. 129–53. [Translators' note: English translation: 'Plato's Unwritten Dialectic', in *Dialogue and Dialectic*, pp. 124–55.]

25   Translators' note: On the translation of *im Vollzug*, see note 17 p. 296.

26   Translators' note: 'Division'.

27   *Phaedrus* 242 d ff. [Translators' note: Plato writes: 'Phaedrus, a dreadful speech it was, a dreadful speech, the one you brought with you, and the one you made me speak.' 'How so?' 'It was foolish, and somewhat impious. What could be more dreadful than that?' 'Nothing, if you are right about it.' 'Well, do you not believe that Love is the son of Aphrodite and is a god?' 'So it is said.' 'Yes, but not by Lysias, nor by your speech which was spoken by you through my mouth that you bewitched. If Love is, as indeed he is, a god or something divine, he can be nothing evil; but the two speeches just now said that he was evil' (trans. Harold N. Fowler. The Loeb Classical Library. Cambridge, MA: Harvard University Press, 1914, p. 461).]

28   Translators' note: 'A lecture course in logic.' It is an allusion to Goethe's *Faust* in which Mephistopheles tells Faust:

'Use well your time! It flies so swiftly from us;

But time through order may be won, I promise.

So, Friend (my views to briefly sum),

First, the *collegium logicum*.

There will your mind be drilled and braced,

As if in Spanish boots 'twere laced,

And thus, to graver paces brought,

'Twill plod along the path of thought,

Instead of shooting here and there,

A will-o'-the-wisp in murky air.

Days will be spent to bid you know,

What once you did at a single blow,

Like eating and drinking, free and strong, –

That one, two, three! thereto belong'

(Johann Wolfgang von Goethe, *Faust*, trans. Bayard Taylor. *An Electronic Classics Series Publication*, ed. Jim Manis, Pennsylvania State University Hazleton,

2005–14, p. 65. http://www-220hn.psu.edu/faculty/jmanis/goethe/goethe-faust. pdf).

29   *Phaedrus* 237 a and 243 a. [Translators' note: Plato writes: 'I'm going to keep my head wrapped up while I talk, that I may get through my discourse as quickly as possible and that I may not look at you and become embarrassed' (p. 443). In the next passage Plato writes: 'For when he was stricken with blindness for speaking ill of Helen, he was not, like Homer, ignorant of the reason, but since he was educated, he knew it and straightway he writes the poem:

'That saying is not true; thou didst not go within the well-oared ships, nor didst thou come to the walls of Troy';

and when he had written all the poem, which is called the recantation, he saw again at once. Now I will be wiser than they in just this point: before suffering any punishment for speaking ill of Love, I will try to atone by my recantation, with my head bare this time, not, as before, covered through shame' (pp. 461–3).]

30   *Sophist* 264 df. [Translators' note: Plato writes: 'Let us try again; let us divide in two the class we have taken up for discussion, and proceed always by way of the right-hand part of the thing divided, clinging close to the company to which the sophist belongs, until, having stripped him of all common properties and left him only his own peculiar nature, we shall show him plainly first to ourselves and secondly to those who are most closely akin to the dialectical method' (p. 445).]

31   *Meno* 82 b–85 b. [Translators' note: Socrates asks: 'Do you observe, Meno, that I am not teaching the boy anything, but merely asking him each time?' Socrates concludes at the end of the demonstration: 'Without anyone having taught him, and only through questions put to him, he will understand, recovering the knowledge out of himself? … And must he not have either once acquired or always had the knowledge he now has?' (*Laches, Protagoras, Meno, Euthydemus*, trans. W. R. M. Lamb. The Loeb Classical Library. London: William Heinemann, 1924, p. 307).]

32   Translators' note: Gadamer is alluding to Nietzsche's portrayal in *Beyond Good and Evil* of Plato as someone who was corrupted by Socrates. Here are Nietzsche's words: 'It must certainly be conceded that the most dangerous of all errors so far was the dogmatist's error – namely, Plato's invention of the pure spirit and the good as such. But now that it is overcome, now that Europe is breathing freely again after this nightmare and at least can enjoy a healthier – sleep, we, *whose task is wakefulness itself*, are the heirs of all that strength which has been fostered by the fight against this error. To be sure, it meant standing truth on her head and denying *perspective*, the basic condition of all life, when one spoke of spirit and the good as Plato did. Indeed, a physician might ask: 'How could the most beautiful growth of antiquity, Plato contract such a disease? Did the wicked Socrates corrupt him after all? Could Socrates have been the corrupter of youth

after all? And did he deserve his hemlock?" (Friedrich Nietzsche, 'Beyond Good and Evil', in *Basic Writings of Nietzsche*, trans. Walter Kaufmann, New York: The Modern Library, 2000, p. 193).

33 See my essay 'Antike Atomtheorie', now in *Gesammelte Werke*, vol. 5, n. 7, pp. 263–79 [Translators' note: English translation: 'Ancient Atomic Theory', in Hans-Georg Gadamer, *The Beginning of Knowledge,* trans. Rod Coltman, New York: Continuum, 2001, pp. 82–101] and my talk in Leiden 'On the Beginning of Thought', in this volume pp. 227–45.

Works cited by Gadamer

Note: When Gadamer cites a work and gives the references in his essay, the work is listed below, followed by the English translation if available. When Gadamer only mentions the title, we provide the references of the English translation.

Aeschylus. *The Prometheus Trilogy,* trans. Ruth F. Birnbaum and Harold F. Birnbaum. Lawrence, KS: Coronado Press, 1978.

Aristotle. *The 'Art' of Rhetoric,* trans. John H. Freese. The Loeb Classical Library. Cambridge, MA: Harvard University Press, 1926.

Aristotle. *Categories; On Interpretation,* trans. Harold P. Cooke and Hugh Tredennick. The Loeb Classical Library. Cambridge, MA: Harvard University Press, 1938.

Aristotle. *Metaphysics,* trans. Hugh Tredennick. The Loeb Classical Library. Cambridge, MA: Harvard University Press, 1961.

Aristotle. *Nicomachean Ethics,* trans. H. Rackham. The Loeb Classical Library. Cambridge, MA: Harvard University Press, 1934.

Aristotle. *On the Soul; Parva Naturalia; On Breath.* trans. W. S. Hett. The Loeb Classical Library. Cambridge, MA: Harvard University Press, 1957.

Aristotle. *Physics,* trans. Philip H. Wicksteed and Francis M. Cornford. The Loeb Classical Library. Cambridge, MA: Harvard University Press, 1957.

Aristotle. *Poetics, 'Longinus' on the Sublime, Demetrius on Style,* trans. Hamilton Fyfe. The Loeb Classical Library. London: William Heinemann, 1927.

Aristotle. *Posterior Analytics; Topica,* trans. Edward S. Forster and Hugh Tredennick. The Loeb Classical Library. Cambridge, MA: Harvard University Press, 1960.

Arnim, Hans Friedrich August von. *Stoicorum Veterum Fragmenta,* vol. 2. Leipzig: Teubner, 1903.

Bachelard, Suzanne. 'Logique husserlienne et sémantique', in *Vérité et vérification – Wahrheit und Verifikation,* ed. Herman van Breda. The Hague: Martinus Nijhoff, 1974, 117–131.

Barth, Karl. *The Epistle to the Romans.* London: Oxford University Press, 1968.

Becker, Oskar. *Dasein und Dawesen: Gesammelte Philosophische Aufsätze.* Pfüllingen: Neske, 1963.

Becker, Oskar. 'Von der Hinfälligkeit des Schönen und der Abenteuerlichkeit des Künstlers', in *Jahrbuch für Philosophie und phänomenologische Forschung* (1929): 27–52.

Becking, Gustav. 'Die Musikgeschichte in Spenglers 'Untergang des Abendlandes,'' *Logos. Internationale Zeitschrift für Philosophie der Kultur* 9 (1920/21): 284–95.

Behler, Ernst. *Derrida-Nietzsche, Nietzsche-Derrida*. Paderbom/Munich: Ferdinand Schöningh, 1988. [English translation: *Confrontations: Derrida/Heidegger/Nietzsche*, trans. and ed. Steven Taubneck. Stanford, CA: Stanford University Press, 1991.]

Bergson, Henri. *Matter and Memory*, trans. Nancy M. Paul and William S. Palmer. London: G. Allen & Co., 1912.

Biemel, Walter. 'The Exchange of Letters Between Dilthey and Husserl', *Man and World* 1 (1968): 428–446.

Bollnow, Otto Friedrich. 'Der Ausdruck und das Verstehen', in *Materialien zur Philosophie Wilhelm Diltheys*, ed. Frithjof Rodi and Hans-Ulrich Lessing. Frankfurt am Main: Suhrkamp, 1984, 236–71.

Bollnow, Otto Friedrich. *Dilthey: Eine Einführung in seine Philosophie*. Leipzig and Berlin: B. G. Teubner, 1936.

Bollnow, Otto Friedrich. *Studien zur Hermeneutik*, vol. 2: *Zur hermeneutischen Logik von Georg Misch und Hans Lipps*. Freiburg/Munich: Karl Alber, 1983.

Bourdieu, Pierre. *L'ontologie politique de Martin Heidegger*. Paris: Les Editions de Minuit, 1988. [English translation: *The Political Ontology of Martin Heidegger*, trans. Peter Collier. Cambridge: Polity Press, 1990. German translation: *Die politische Ontologie Martin Heideggers*, trans. Bernd Schwibs. Frankfurt am Main: Suhrkamp, 1988.]

Bourdieu, Pierre. *Outline of a Theory of Practice*, trans. Richard Nice. Cambridge: Cambridge University Press, 1977.

Brentano, Franz. *On the Several Senses of Being in Aristotle*, trans. Rolf George. Berkeley, CA: University of California Press, 1975.

Brentano, Franz. *Psychology from an Empirical Standpoint*, trans. Antos C. Rancurello, D. B. Terrell and Linda L. McAlister. London: Routledge and Kegan Paul, 1973.

Burckhardt, Jacob. *Wissenschafliche Betrachtungen*, ed. Rudolf Stadelman. Pfüllingen: Neske, 1949. [English translation: *Reflections on History*, trans. M. D. Hottinger. Indianapolis: Liberty Classics, 1979.]

Cassirer, Ernst. *The Problem of Knowledge: Philosophy, Science, and History since Hegel*, trans. William H. Woglom and Charles W. Hendel. New Haven, CT: Yale University Press, 1978.

Celan, Paul. *"Tenebrae"*, in *Gesammelte Werke*, vol. 1, ed. Beda Alleman, Stefan Reichert, and Rolf Bücher. Frankfurt am Main: Suhrkamp, 1983, 163 [English Translation: "Tenebrae," in *Harper's Magazine*, trans. Scott Horton. 2008 online: http://harpers.org/archive/2008/03/hbc-90002696]

Cicero, *On the Orator: Books 1–2*, trans. E. W. Sutton and H. Rackham. Cambridge, MA: Harvard University Press, 1942.

Curtius, Ludwig. 'Morphologie der antiken Kunst', *Logos. Internationale Zeitschrift für Philosophie der Kultur* 9 (1920/21): 195–221.

Derrida, Jacques. 'Ousia and Grammē', in *Margins of Philosophy*, trans. Alan Bass. Chicago: University of Chicago Press, 1982, 29–67.

Derrida, Jacques. *Voice and Phenomenon. Introduction to the Problem of the Sign in Husserl's Phenomenology*, trans. Leonard Lawlor. Evanston, IL: Northwestern University Press, 2010.

Derrida, Jacques. *Writing and Difference,* trans. Alan Bass. Chicago: University of Chicago Press, 1978.

Descartes, René. *Discourse on Method and Meditations on First Philosophy*, trans. Donald A. Cress. Indianapolis, IN: Hackett, 1998.

Descartes, René. *Rules for the Direction of the Mind*, trans. Laurence J. Lafleur. Indianapolis, IN: Liberal Arts Press, 1961.

Die Kreatur: Eine Zeitschrift, ed. Martin Buber and Viktor von Weizsäcker. Berlin, 1926–30.

Dilthey, Willhelm. 'Epistle 29th June 1911 to Edmund Husserl', in *Materialien zur Philosophie Wilhelm Diltheys*, ed. Frithjof Rodi and Hans-Ulrich Lessing. Frankfurt am Main: Suhrkamp, 1984.

Dilthey, Willhelm. 'The Formation of the Historical World in the Human Sciences', in *Wilhelm Dilthey: Selected Works*, vol. III, eds Rudolf Makkreel and Frithjof Rodi. Princeton, NJ: Princeton University Press, 2010.

Dilthey, Willhelm. 'Friedrich Daniel Ernst Schleiermacher', in *Gesammelte Schriften,* vol. 4. Göttingen: Vandenhoeck & Ruprecht, 1990, 354–402.

Dilthey, Willhelm. *Gesammelte Schriften*, vol. 4, *Die Jugendgeschichte Hegels und andere Abhandlungen zur Geschichte des deutschen Idealismus,* ed. Hermam Nohl. Leipzig: B. G. Teubner, 1925.

Dilthey, Willhelm. *Gesammelte Schriften*, vol. 5. *Die geistige Welt: Einleitung in die Philosophie des Lebens.* First part: *Abhandlungen zur Grundlegung der Geisteswissenschaften*, ed. Georg Misch. Leipzig/Berlin: Teubner, 1924.

Dilthey, Willhelm. *Gesammelte Schriften*, vol. 6 *Die Geistige Welt. Einleitung in die Philosophie des Lebens.* Second Part, *Abhandlungen zur Poetik, Ethik und Pädagogik,* ed. Georg Misch. Leipzig/Berlin: Teubner, 1924.

Dilthey, Willhelm. *Gesammelte Schriften,* vol. 7 *Der Aufbau der geschichtlichen Welt in die Geisteswissenschaften,* ed. Bernhard Groethuysen, Helmut Johach and Martin Redeker. Berlin/Leipzig: Teubner, 1927.

Dilthey, Willhelm. *Gesammelte Schriften,* vol. 8, *Weltanschaungslehre. Abhandlungen zur Philosophie der Philosophie,* ed. Bernhard Groethuysen. Leipzig/Berlin: Teubner, 1931.

Dilthey, Willhelm. *Gesammelten Schriften*, vols 13–14, *Leben Schleiermachers,* ed. Martin Redeker. Berlin: de Gruyter, 1966.

Dilthey, Willhelm. *Gesammelte Schriften*, vol. 18, *Die Wissenschaften vom Menschen, der Gesellschaft und der Geschichte. Vorarbeiten zur Einleitung in die Geisteswissenschaften (1865–1880),* ed. Helmut Johach and Frithjof Rodi. Göttingen: Vandenhoeck & Ruprecht, 1977.

Dilthey, Willhelm. *Gesammelte Schriften*, vol. 19, *Grundlegung der Wissenschaften vom Menschen, der Gesellschaft und der Geschichte. Ausarbeitungen und Entwürfe zum zweiten Band der Einleitung in die Geisteswissenschaften (ca. 1870–1895),* ed. Helmut Johach and Frithjof Rodi. Göttingen: Vandenhoeck & Ruprecht, 1982.

Dilthey, Willhelm. *Gesammelte Schriften,* vol. 20, *Logik und System der philosophischen Wissenschaften. Vorlesung zur erkenntnistheoretischen Logik und Methodologie (1864–1903),* ed. Hans-Ulrich Lessing and Frithjof Rodi. Göttingen: Vandenhoeck and Ruprecht, 1990.

Dilthey, Willhelm. 'Ideas about a Descriptive and Analytic Psychology', in *W. Dilthey, Selected Writings,* trans. H P. Rickman. Cambridge: Cambridge University Press, 1979, 87–97.

Dilthey, Willhelm. 'Leben und Erkennen. Ein Entwurf zur erkenntnistheoretischen Logik und Kategorienlehre', in *Gesammelte Schriften,* vol. 19, ed. Helmut Johach and Frithjof Rodi. Göttingen: Vandenhoeck & Ruprecht, 1982, 333–88. [English translation: 'Life and Cognition', in *Selected Works,* vol. II: *Understanding the Human World,* ed. Rudolf A. Makkreel and Frithjof Rodi. Princeton, NJ: Princeton University Press, 2010, p. 58–114.]

Dilthey, Willhelm. *Leben Schleiermachers,* 2 vol. Leipzig: W. de Gruyter & Co., 1922.

Dilthey, Willhelm. *Selected Works,* vol. I, *Introduction to the Human Sciences,* ed. Rudolf A. Makkreel and Frithjof Rodi. Princeton, NJ: Princeton University Press, 1991.

Dilthey, Willhelm. *Selected Works,* vol. II, *Poetry and Experience.* Princeton, ed. Rudolf A. Makkreel and Frithjof Rodi. NJ: Princeton University Press, 1997.

Dilthey, Wilhelm and Paul Yorck von Wartenburg. *Briefwechsel zwischen Wilhelm Dilthey und dem Grafen Paul Yorck v. Wartenburg, 1877–1897,* ed. Erich Rothacker. Halle (Saale): Max Niemeyer, 1923.

Ebeling, Gerhard. *Evangelische Evangelienauslegung: eine Untersuchung zu Luthers Hermeneutik.* Darmstadt: Wissenschaftliche Buchgesellschaft, 1962 [1942].

Eckhart, Meister. *Eine lateinische Rechtfertigungsschrift des Meister Eckhart: Mit einem Geleitwort von Clemens Baeumker,* trans. Clemens Baeumker. Münster: Aschendorff, 1923.

Eckhart, Meister. *Prologi in Opus Tripartitum et expositio libri genesis (recensio L),* ed. Loris Sturlese. Stuttgart: Kohlhammer, 1987. [English translation: Master Eckhart, *Parisian Questions and Prologues,* trans. Armand Maurer. Toronto: Pontifical institute of Mediaeval Studies, 1981.]

Fichte, Johann G. *Fichte-Schelling-Briefwechsel (Auswahl),* ed. Walter Schulz. Frankfurt am Main: Suhrkamp, 1968.

Frank, Erich. 'Mathematik und Musik und der griechische Geist', *Logos. Internationale Zeitschrift für Philosophie der Kultur* 9 (1920/21): 222–59.

Freud, Sigmund. *The Interpretation of Dreams,* trans. A. A. Brill. New York: Macmillan, 1913.

Funke, Gerhard. 'Bewusstseinswissenschaft', in *Vérité et vérification – Wahrheit und Verifikation,* ed. Herman Van Breda. The Hague: Martinus Nijhoff, 1974, 3–58.

Gadamer, Hans-Georg. 'Antike Atomtheorie', in *Gesammelte Werke,* vol. 5, n. 7.

Tübingen: Mohr, 1985, 263–79.]English translation: 'Ancient Atomic Theory', in Hans-Georg Gadamer, *The Beginning of Knowledge,* trans. Rod Coltman, New York: Continuum, 2001, 82–101.]

Gadamer, Hans-Georg. 'Dekonstruktion und Hermeneutik', in *Gesammelte Werke,* vol. 10, n. 12. Tübingen: Mohr, 1995, 138–47. [English translation: 'Letter to Dallmayr', in *Dialogue and Deconstruction: The Gadamer-Derrida Encounter,* ed. and trans. Diane P. Michelfelder and Richard E. Palmer. Albany, NY: State University of New York Press, 1989, 93–101.]

Gadamer, Hans-Georg. 'Destruktion und Dekonstruktion', in *Gesammelte Werke,* vol. 2, n. 25. Tübingen: Mohr, 1986, 361–72. [English translation: 'Destruction and Deconstruction', in *Dialogue and Deconstruction: The Gadamer-Derrida Encounter,* ed. and trans. Diane P. Michelfelder and Richard E. Palmer. Albany, NY: State University of New York Press, 1989, 102–13.]

Gadamer, Hans-Georg. 'Die Dialektik des Selbstbewusstseins', in *Gesammelte Werke,* vol. 3, n. 3. Tübingen: Mohr, 1987, 47–64. [English translation: 'Hegel's Dialectic of Self-consciousness', in *Hegel's Dialectic: Five Hermeneutical Studies,* trans. P. Christopher Smith. New Haven, CT: Yale University Press, 1976, 54–72.]

Gadamer, Hans-Georg. 'Dialektik und Sophistik im siebenten platonischen Brief', in *Gesammelte Werke,* vol. 6, n. 6. Tübingen: Mohr, 1985, 90–115. [English translation: 'Dialectic and Sophism in Plato's Seventh Letter', in Hans-Georg Gadamer, *Dialogue and Dialectic: Eight Hermeneutical Studies on Plato,* ed. P. Christopher Smith. New Haven, CT: Yale University Press, 1980, 93–123.]

Gadamer, Hans-Georg. 'Eduard Zeller. Der Weg eines Liberalen von der Theologie zur Philosophie', in *Semper Apertus: Sechshundert Jahre Ruprecht-Karls-Universität Heidelberg, 1386-1986: Festschrift in Sechs Bänden,* vol. 2, ed. Wilhelm Doerr and Otto Haxel. Berlin: Springer, 1985, 406–12.

Gadamer, Hans-Georg. 'Der eine Weg Martin Heideggers', in *Gesammelte Werke,* vol. 3, n. 28. Tübingen: Mohr, 1987, 417–30. [English translation: 'Martin Heidegger's One Path', in *Reading Heidegger from the Start: Essays in His Earliest Thought,* ed. Theodore Kisiel and John van Buren. Albany, NY: State University of New York Press, 1994, 19–34.]

Gadamer, Hans-Georg. 'Der 'eminente' Text und seine Wahrheit', in *Gesammelte Werke,* vol. 8, n. 25. Tübingen: Mohr, 1999, 286–95. [English translation: 'The Eminent Text and Its Truth' by Geoffrey Waite, in *The Horizon of Literature,* ed. Paul Hernadi. Lincoln, NE: University of Nebraska Press, 1982, 337–47.]

Gadamer, Hans-Georg. 'Fruhromantik, Hermeneutic, Dekonstruktivismus', in *Gesammelte Werke,* vol. 10, n. 11. Tübingen: Mohr, 1995, 125–37. [English translation: 'Hermeneutics and Logocentrism', in *Dialogue and Deconstruction: The Gadamer-Derrida Encounter,* ed. and trans. Diane P. Michelfelder and Richard E. Palmer. Albany, NY: State University of New York Press, 1989, 114–25.]

Gadamer, Hans-Georg. 'Heideggers 'theologische' Jugendschrift', in *Dilthey-Jahrbuch für Philosophie und Geschichte der Geisteswissenschaften*, vol. 6. Göttingen: Vandenhoeck & Ruprecht, 1989, 228–34.

Gadamer, Hans-Georg. 'Hermeneutik und Historismus', in *Gesammelte Werke*, vol. 2, n. 27, 387–424. [English translation: 'Hermeneutics and Historicism Supplement I', in *Truth and Method*, 2nd rev. edn., trans. Joel Weinsheimer and Donald G. Marshall. New York: Continuum, 1998, 505–41.]

Gadamer, Hans-Georg. 'Hilde Domin, Dichterin der Rückkehr', in *Gesammelte Werke*, vol. 9, n. 28. Tübingen: Mohr, 1993, 323–8. [English translation: 'Hilde Domin, Poet of Return', trans. Margaret Korzus and Hilde Domin, *The Denver Quarterly* 6 (4) (1972): 7-17.]

Gadamer, Hans-Georg. 'Hören—Sehen—Lesen', in *Gesammelte Werke*, vol. 8, n. 23. Tübingen: Mohr, 1999, 271–8.

Gadamer, Hans-Georg. 'Idee und Wirklichkeit in Platos "Timaios"', in *Gesammelte Werke*, vol. 6, n. 15. Tübingen: Mohr, 1985, 242–70. [English translation: 'Idea and Reality in Plato's "Timaeus"', in *Dialogue and Dialectic: Eight Hermeneutical Studies on Plato*, trans. P. Christopher Smith. New Haven, CT: Yale University Press, 1980, 156–93.]

Gadamer, Hans-Georg. 'Lesen ist wie Übersetzen', in *Gesammelte Werke*, vol. 8, n. 24. Tübingen: Mohr, 1999, 279–85.

Gadamer, Hans-Georg. 'Lob der theorie', in *Gesammelte Werke*, vol. 4, n. 3. Tübingen: Mohr, 1987, 37–51. [English translation: 'Praise of Theory', in *Praise of Theory: Speeches and Essays*, trans. Chris Dawson. New Haven, CT: Yale University Press, 1998, 16–36.]

Gadamer, Hans-Georg. 'Die phänomenologische Bewegung', in *Gesammelte Werke*, vol. 3, n. 6. Tübingen: Mohr, 1987, 105–46. [English translation: 'The Phenomenological Movement (1963)', in *Philosophical Hermeneutics*, trans. David E. Linge. Berkeley, CA: University of California Press, 1976, 130–81.]

Gadamer, Hans-Georg. 'Plato', in *Gesammelte Werke*, vol. 3, n. 16. Tübingen: Mohr, 1987, 238–48. [English translation: 'Plato and Heidegger', in *The Question of Being: East-west Perspectives*, ed. Meryn Sprung. University Park, PA: Pennsylvania State University Press, 1978, 45–53.]

Gadamer, Hans-Georg. 'Der platonische *Parmenides* and seine Nachwirkung', in *Gesammelte Werke*, vol. 7, n. 11. Tübingen: Mohr, 1991, 313–27. [English translation: 'Plato's Parmenides and its Influence', trans. Margaret Kirby, *Dionysius* 7 (1983): 3–16.]

Gadamer, Hans-Georg. 'Platos Denken in Utopien', in *Gesammelte Werke*, vol. 7, n. 9. Tübingen: Mohr, 1991, 313–27.

Gadamer, Hans-Georg. 'Platos ungeschriebene Dialektik', in *Gesammelte Werke*, vol. 6, n. 8. Tübingen: Mohr, 1985, 129–53. [English translation: 'Plato's Unwritten Dialectic', in Hans-Georg Gadamer, *Dialogue and Dialectic: Eight Hermeneutical Studies on Plato*, ed. and trans. P. Christopher Smith. New Haven, CT: Yale University Press, 1980, 124–55.]

Gadamer, Hans-Georg. 'Das Problem der Geschichte in der neueren deutschen Philosophie', in *Gesammelte Werke*, vol. 2, n. 2. Tübingen: Mohr, 1986, 27–36.

Gadamer, Hans-Georg. 'Die religiöse Dimension', in *Gesammelte Werke*, vol. 3, n. 22. Tübingen: Mohr, 1987, 308–19. [English translation: 'The Religious Dimension', in Hans-Georg, Gadamer, *Heidegger's Ways,* trans. John W. Stanley. Albany, NY: State University of New York Press, 1994, 167–80.]

Gadamer, Hans-Georg. 'Stimme und Sprache', in *Gesammelte Werke*, vol. 8, n. 22. Tübingen: Mohr, 1999, 258–70.

Gadamer, Hans-Georg. 'Text und Interpretation', in *Gesammelte Werke*, vol. 2, n. 24 Tübingen: Mohr, 1986, 330–60. [English translation: 'Text and Interpretation', in *Hermeneutics and Modern Philosophy,* ed. Brice R. Wachterhauser. Albany, NY: State University of New York Press, 1986, 377–96.]

Gadamer, Hans-Georg. *Truth and Method,* 2nd rev. edn., trans. Joel Weinsheimer and Donald G. Marshall. New York: Continuum, 1998.

Gadamer, Hans-Georg. 'Über das Göttliche im frühen Denken der Griechen', in *Gesammelte Werke,* vol. 6, n. 9. Tübingen: Mohr, 1985, 154–70 (*Kleine Schriften,* vol. 3, n. 5, 64–79). [English translation: 'On the Divine in Early Greek Thought', in Hans-Georg Gadamer, *Hermeneutics, Religion, and Ethics,* trans. Joel Weinsheimer. New Haven, CT: Yale University Press, 1999, 37–57.]

Gadamer, Hans-Georg. 'Die Universität Heidelberg und die Geburt der modernen Wissenschaft', in *Gesammelte Werke,* vol. 10, n. 29. Tübingen: Mohr, 1995, 336–45. [English translation: 'The University of Heidelberg and the Birth of Modern Science', in *Hans-Georg Gadamer on Education, Poetry, and History: Applied Hermeneutics,* trans. Graeme Nicholson, ed. Dieter Misgeld. Albany, NY: State University of New York Press, 1992, 37–46.]

Gadamer, Hans-Georg. 'Vom Zirkel des Verstehens', in *Gesammelte Werke*, vol. 2, n. 5. Tübingen: Mohr, 1986, 57–65. [English translation: 'On the Circle of Understanding', in Hans-Georg Gadamer, Ernst Konrad Specht, and Wolfgang Stegmüller, *Hermeneutics Versus Science?: Three German Views: Essays,* ed. and trans. John M. Connolly and Thomas Keutner. Notre Dame, IN: University of Notre Dame Press, 1988, 68–78.]

Gadamer, Hans-Georg. 'Was muss der Leser Wissen?', in 'Wer bin Ich und wer bist Du?: Kommentar zu Celans Gedichtfolge 'Atemkristall', *Gesammelte Werke*, vol. 9, n. 36. Tübingen: Mohr, 1993, 436–9. [English translation: 'Who Am I and Who Are You?' in *Gadamer on Celan: 'Who Am I and Who Are You?' and Other Essays,* trans. Richard Heinemann and Bruce Krajewski. Albany, NY: State University of New York Press, 1997, 67–126.]

Gadamer, Hans-Georg. 'Der Weg in die Kehre', in *Gesammelte Werke*, vol. 3, n. 19. Tübingen: Mohr, 1987, 271–84. [English translation: 'Heidegger's Paths', trans. C. Kayser and G. Stack, *Philosophic Exchange: The Annual Proceedings of the Center for Philosophic Exchange* 2 (1979): 80-91.]

Gadamer, Hans-Georg. 'Zwischen Phänomenologie und Dialektik: Versuch einer Selbstkritik', in *Gesammelte Werke*, vol. 2, n. 1. Tübingen: Mohr, 1986, 3–23.

Galilei, Galileo. *Dialogue Concerning the Two Chief World Systems, Ptolemaic & Copernican*, trans. Stillman Drake. Berkeley, CA: University of California Press, 1953.

Goethe, Johann W. 'Ecstatic Longing', in *Selected Poetry*, trans. David Luke. London: Penguin, 1999, 183.

The Gospel According to St. John: Authorized (King James) Version. Champaign, IL: Project Gutenberg, 1990.

Habermas, Jürgen. *Erkenntnis und Interesse*. Frankfurt am Main: Suhrkamp, 1968. [English translation: *Knowledge and Human Interests*, trans. Jeremy J. Shapiro. Boston: Beacon Press, 1971.]

Habermas, Jürgen. *Der philosophische Diskurs der Moderne: Zwölf Vorlesungen.* Frankfurt am Main: Suhrkamp, 1985. [English translation: *Philosophical Discourse of Modernity: Twelve Lectures,* trans. Frederick Lawrence. Cambridge, MA: MIT Press, 1987.]

Hegel, Georg W. F. *Encyclopaedia of the Philosophical Sciences in Basic Outline: Volume 1*, trans. Klaus Brinkmann and Daniel O. Dahlstrom. Cambridge: Cambridge University Press, 2010.

Hegel, Georg W. F. *Hegel's Philosophy of Right,* trans. T M. Knox. London: Oxford University Press, 1967.

Hegel, Georg W. F. *Phenomenology of Spirit*, trans. Arnold V. Miller and J N. Findlay. Oxford, UK: Clarendon Press, 1977.

Hegel, Georg W. F. *The Science of Logic,* trans. George Di Giovanni. Cambridge: Cambridge University Press, 2010.

Heidegger, Martin. 'The Age of the World Picture', in *The Question Concerning Technology, and Other Essays*, trans. William Lovitt. New York: Harper & Row, 1977, 115–54.

Heidegger, Martin. 'Aus der Erfahrung des Denkens', in *Gesamtausgabe*, vol. 13, ed. Hermann Heidegger. Frankfurt am Main: Klostermann, 2002, 75–86. [English translation: 'The Thinker as Poet', in *Poetry, Language, Thought*, trans. Albert Hofstadter. New York: Harper & Row, 2013, 1–14.]

Heidegger, Martin. *Basic Concepts of Ancient Philosophy,* trans. Richard Rojcewicz. Bloomington, IN: Indiana University Press, 2008.

Heidegger, Martin. *Being and Time*, trans. John Macquarrie and Edward Robinson. New York: HarperPerennial/Modern Thought, 2008.

Heidegger, Martin. *Bremen and Freiburg Lectures: Insight into That Which Is, and Basic Principles of Thinking*, trans. Andrew J. Mitchell. Bloomington, IN: Indiana University Press, 2012.

Heidegger, Martin. 'The End of Philosophy', *in Basic Writings: From Being and Time (1927) to the Task of Thinking (1964)*, ed. David F. Krell. New York: Harper Perennial Modern Thought, 2008, 427–49.

Heidegger, Martin. *Kant and the Problem of Metaphysics*, trans. James S. Churchill. Bloomington, IN: Indiana University Press, 1962.

Heidegger, Martin. 'Die Kategorien- und Bedeutungslehre des Duns Scotus (1915)', in *Frühe Schriften*, ed. Friedrich-Wilhelm von Herrmann, Gesamsausgabe 1. Frankfurt am Main: Klostermann, 1978, 189–412. [English translation: *Duns Scotus' Theory of the Categories and of Meaning*, trans. Harold Robbins. De Paul University doctoral dissertation, 1978.]

Heidegger, Martin. *Die Kunst und der Raum – L'art et l'espace*, trans. Jean Beaufret and François Fédier. St. Gallen: Erker-Verlag, 1969. [English translation: 'Art and Space', trans. Charles Siebert, *L'art et l'espace Man and World* 6 (1973): 3–8.]

Heidegger, Martin. *Nietzsche*, vol. 2. Pfüllingen: Neske, 1961. [English translation: *Nietzsche*, vol. 2, trans. David F. Krell. San Francisco: Harper & Row, 1984.]

Heidegger, Martin. 'On the Essence of Truth', in *Being and Truth,* trans. Gregory Fried and Richard Polt. Bloomington, IN: Indiana University Press, 2010, 67–201.

Heidegger, Martin. *On Time and Being*, trans. Joan Stambaugh. New York, NY: Harper & Row, 1972.

Heidegger, Martin. *Ontology: The Hermeneutics of Facticity,* trans. John van Buren. Bloomington, IN: Indiana University Press, 1999.

Heidegger, Martin. *Parmenides*, trans. André Schuwer and Richard Rojcewicz. Bloomington, IN: Indiana University Press, 1992.

Heidegger, Martin. *Phänomenologische Interpretationen zu Aristoteles. Einführung in die phänomenologische Forschung,* Gesamtausgabe vol. 61, ed. Walter Bröcker und Käte Bröcker-Oltmanns. Frankfurt am Main: Vittorio Klostermann, 1985. [English translation: *Phenomenological Interpretations of Aristotle: Initiation into Phenomenological Research,* trans. Richard Rojcewicz. Bloomington, IN: Indiana University Press, 2001.]

Heidegger, Martin. *The Phenomenology of Religious Life: 1. Introduction to the Phenomenology of Religion, 2. Augustine and Neo-Platonism, 3. The Philosophical Foundations of Medieval Mysticism,* trans. Matthias Fritsch and Jennifer Anna Gosetti. Bloomington, IN: Indiana University Press, 2010.

Heidegger, Martin. *Platons Lehre von der Wahrheit: Mit Einem Brief [an Jean Beaufret, Paris] über den Humanismus.* Bern: Francke, 1947. [English translation: 'Plato's Doctrine of Truth,' trans. Thomas Sheehan, in *Pathmarks*, ed., William McNeill. Cambridge: Cambridge University Press, 1998, 155–82.]

Heidegger, Martin. 'The Question Concerning Technology' in *Basic Writings: From Being and Time (1927) to the Task of Thinking (1964),* 307–42.

Heidegger, Martin. *Unterwegs zur Sprache*. Pfüllingen: Neske, 1959. [English translation: *On the Way to Language,* trans. Peter D. Hertz. New York: Harper & Row, 1971.]

Heidegger, Martin. *What Is Called Thinking?* trans. J. Glenn Gray. New York: Harper & Row, 1968.

Heidegger, Martin. 'What Is Metaphysics?', in *Basic Writings: From Being and Time (1927) to the Task of Thinking,* 1964, 89–110.

Heidegger, Martin. 'Wilhelm Dilthey's Research and the Struggle for a Historical Worldview (1925)', in *Supplements: From the Earliest Essays to Being and Time and Beyond*, trans. John van Buren. Albany, NY: State University of New York Press, 2002, 147–76.

Heitsch, Ernst. 'Ein Buchtitel des Protagoras', *Hermes* 97 (1969): 292–6.

Heitsch, Ernst. 'Erscheinung und Meinung. Platons Kritik an Protagoras als Selbstkritik', *Philosophisches Jahrbuch* 76 (1968): 23–6.

Hildesheimer, Wolfgang. *Mozart*, Frankfurt am Main: Suhrkamp Verlag, 1977. [English translation: *Mozart*, trans. Marion Faber. New York: Farrar, Straus and Giroux, 1982.]

Homer. *The Iliad [of] Homer*, trans. A. T. Murray. The Loeb Classical Library. Cambridge, MA: Harvard University Press, 1924.

Huppert, Hugo. '"Spirituell". Ein Gespräch mit Paul Celan', in *Paul Celan*, ed. Werner Hamacher and Winfried Menninghaus. Frankfurt am Main: Suhrkamp, 1988.

Husserl, Edmund. *The Crisis of European Sciences and Transcendental Phenomenology: An Introduction to Phenomenological Philosophy*, trans. David Carr. Evanston, IL: Northwestern University Press, 1970.

Husserl, Edmund. *Formal and Transcendental Logic*, trans. Dorion Cairns. The Hague: Martinus Nijhoff, 2010.

Husserl, Edmund. *The Idea of Phenomenology*, trans. William P. Alston and George Nakhnikian. The Hague: Martinus Nijhoff, 1973.

Husserl, Edmund. *Ideas Pertaining to a Pure Phenomenology and to a Phenomenological Philosophy: Second Book, Studies in the Phenomenology of Constitution*, trans. Richard Rojcewicz and André Schuwer. Dordrecht: Kluwer Academic, 1989.

Husserl, Edmund. *Ideen zu einer reinen Phänomenologie und phänomenologischen Philosophie*, I. Buch: *Allgemeine Einführung in die reine Phänomenologie*. Husserliana vol. 3, ed. Karl Schumann. The Hague: Martinus Nijhoff, 1976. [English translation: *Ideas Pertaining to a Pure Phenomenology and to a Phenomenological Philosophy: First Book*, trans. Fred Kersten. The Hague: Martinus Nijhoff, 1983.]

Husserl, Edmund. *Logical Investigations*, 2 vols, trans. J. N. Findlay, ed. Dermot Moran. London: Routledge, 2001.

Husserl, Edmund. 'Philosophy as Rigorous Science', in *Phenomenology and the Crisis of Philosophy*, trans. Quentin Lauer. New York: Harper 1965, 71–148.

Husserl, Edmund. *Zur Phänomenologie der Intersubjektivität. Texte aus dem Nachlass. Erster Teil: 1905–1920*, Hua 13, ed. Iso Kern. The Hague: Martinus Nijhoff, 1973.

Husserl, Edmund. *Zur Phänomenologie der Intersubjektivität. Texte aus dem Nachlass. Zweiter Teil: 1921–1928*, Hua 14, ed. Iso Kern. The Hague: Martinus Nijhoff, 1973.

Husserl, Edmund. *Zur Phänomenologie der Intersubjektivität. Texte aus dem Nachlass. Dritter Teil: 1929-1935*, Hua 15, ed. Iso Kern. The Hague: Martinus Nijhoff, 1973.

Jaspers, Karl. 'Referat Kierkegaards', in *Psychologie der Weltanschauungen*. Berlin: Springer, 1919, 370–80.

Joël, Karl. 'Die Philosophie in Spenglers "Untergangs des Abendlandes"', *Logos. Internationale Zeitschrift für Philosophie der Kultur* 9 (1920/11): 135–70.

Kant, Immanuel. *Critique of the Power of Judgment*, trans. Paul Guyer. Cambridge: Cambridge University Press, 2007.

Kant, Immanuel. *Critique of Pure Reason*, trans. Paul Guyer and Allen W. Wood. Cambridge: Cambridge University Press, 1998.

Kant, Immanuel. 'On the Form and Principles of the Sensible and the Intelligible World', in *Theoretical Philosophy, 1755–1770*, trans. and ed. David Walford and Ralf Meerbote Cambridge: Cambridge University Press, 2003, 373–416.

Kant, Immanuel. *Prolegomena to Any Future Metaphysics That Will Be Able to Come Forward As Science: With Selections from the Critique of Pure Reason*, trans. Gary C. Hatfield. Cambridge: Cambridge University Press, 2004.

Kaufmann, Fritz. 'Die Philosophie des Grafen Paul Yorck von Wartenburg', *Jahrbuch für Phänomenologie und phänomenologische Forschung* 9 (1928): 1–235.

Kierkegaard, Søren. *The Concept of Dread,* trans. Walter Lowrie. Princeton, NJ: Princeton University Press, 1957.

Kierkegaard, Søren. *Einübung im Christentum*. Jena: Diederich, 1912. [English translation: *Practice in Christianity,* ed. and trans. Howard V. Hong and Edna H. Hong. Princeton, NJ: Princeton University Press, 1991.]

Kierkegaard, Søren. *Gesammelte Werke*, trans. Christoff Schrempf, Wolfgang Pfleiderer, Heinrich Cornelius Ketels, and Hermann Gottsched. Jena: Eugen Diedrich, 1910–38.

Köhnke, Klaus Christian. 'Über den Ursprung des Wortes Erkenntnistheorie— und dessen vermeintliche Synonyme', *Archiv für Begriffsgeschichte* 25 (1981): 185–210.

Landgrebe, Ludwig. 'Husserls Abschied von Cartesianismus', *Philosophische Rundschau* 9 (1962): 133–77. [English translation: 'Husserl's Departure from Cartesianism', in Ludwig Landgrebe, *The Phenomenology of Edmund Husserl: Six Essays,* ed. Donn Welton, trans. R. O. Elveton. Ithaca, NY: Cornell University Press, 1981, 66–21.]

Landgrebe, Ludwig. 'Wilhelm Diltheys Theorie der Geisteswissenschaften (Analyse ihrer Grundbegriffe)', *Jahrbuch für Phänomenologie und phänomenologische Forschung* 9 (1928): 237–366.

Leibniz, Gottfried W. *Leibniz's 'new System' and Associated Contemporary Texts*, trans. R. S. Woolhouse and Richard Francks. Oxford: Clarendon Press, 1997.

Lipps, Hans. 'Untersuchungen zu einer hermeneutischen Logik', in *Werke*, vol. 2. Frankfurt: Vittorio Klostermann, 1977.

Lipps, Hans. *Untersuchungen zu einer hermeneutischen Logik*. Frankfurt: Vittorio Klostermann, 1938.

Mandonnet, Pierre. *Siger de Brabant et l'averroisme latin au XIIIème Siècle*. Series "Les philosophes belges." Louvain: Institut supérieur de philosophie, 1908.

Meyer, Eduard. 'Spenglers Untergang des Abendlandes', *Deutsche Literaturzeitung* 25 (1924): 1759–80.

Mezger, Edmund, 'Oswald Spenglers "Untergang des Abendlandes"', *Logos. Internationale Zeitschrift für Philosophie der Kultur* 9 (1920/21): 260–83.

Misch, Georg. 'Der Aufbau der Logik auf dem Boden der Philosophie des Lebens', in *Philosophische Hermeneutik*, ed. Hans-Ulrich Lessing. Freiburg: Karl Alber, 1999.

Misch, Georg. *Der Aufbau der Logik auf dem Boden der Philosophie des Lebens. Göttinger Vorlesungen über Logik und Einleitung in die Theorie des Wissens*, ed. Gudrun Kühne-Bertram and Frithjof Rodi. Freiburg/ Munich: Karl Alber, 1994.

Misch, Georg. *Lebensphilosophie und Phänomenologie. Eine Auseinandersetzung der Dilthe'schen Richtung mit Heidegger und Husserl*. Leipzig: Teubner, 1930.

Mosse, George. *The Crisis of German Ideology: Intellectual Origins of the Third Reich*. New York: Grosset & Dunlap, 1964.

Muralt, André de. *La métaphysique du phénomène*. Paris: Vrin, 1990.

Natorp, Paul. *Allgemeine Psychologie nach kritischer Methode*. Tübingen: J. C. B. Mohr (P. Siebeck), 1912.

Natorp, Paul. *Einleitung in die Psychologie nach kritischer Methode*. Freiburg i.B: Mohr, 1888.

Newton, Isaac. *The Principia: Mathematical Principles of Natural Philosophy*, trans. I. B. Cohen and Anne M. Whitman. Berkeley, CA: University of California Press, 1999.

Nietzsche, Friedrich. 'Beyond Good and Evil', in *Selected Writings of Nietzsche*, trans. Walter Kaufmann. New York: The Modern Library, 2000.

Nietzsche, Friedrich. *The Gay Science: With a Prelude in Rhymes and an Appendix of Songs*, trans. Walter A. Kaufmann. New York: Vintage Books, 1974.

Nietzsche, Friedrich. *Jenseits von Gut und Böse*. Stuttgart: Reclam, 1988.

Novalis. *Hymns to the Night and Other Selected Writings*, trans. Charles Passage. New York: Liberal Arts Press, 1960.

Ortega y Gasset, José. 'Kant, reflexiones de centenario 1724–1924', *Revista de Occidente, April-May, 1924* [*Obras Completas*, vol. 4. Madrid: Revista de Occidente, 1947, 23–59].

Paci, Enzo. 'Vérification empirique et transcendance de la vérité', in *Vérité et vérification – Wahrheit und Verifikation*, ed. Herman van Breda. The Hague: Martinus Nijhoff, 1974, 59–70.

'Paul's First Epistle to Thessalonians', in *The New Testament: A Critical Introduction*, ed. Edwin D. Freed. Belmont, CA: Wadsworth/Thomson Learning, 2001.

Pažanin, Ante. 'Bewusstseinswissenschaft', in *Vérité et vérification – Wahrheit und Verifikation*, ed. Herman van Breda. The Hague: Martinus Nijhoff, 1974, 3–58.

Plato. *Cratylus; Parmenides; Greater Hippias; Lesser Hippias*, trans. Harold N. Fowler. The Loeb Classical Library. Cambridge, MA: Harvard University Press, 1996.

Plato. *Euthyphro; Apology; Crito; Phaedo; Phaedrus*, trans. Harold N. Fowler and W. R. M. Lamb. The Loeb Classical Library. Cambridge, MA: Harvard University Press, 1914.

Plato. *Laches; Protagoras; Meno; Euthydemus*, trans. W. R. M. Lamb. The Loeb Classical Library. Cambridge, MA: Harvard University Press, 1924.

Plato. *The Republic*, trans. Paul Shorey. The Loeb Classical Library. Cambridge, MA: Harvard University Press, 1930.

Plato. *Seventh & Eighth Letters*, trans. R. S. Bluck. The Loeb Classical Library. Cambridge: Cambridge University Press, 1947.

Plato. *The Statesman; Philebus*, trans. Harold N. Fowler and W. R. M. Lamb. The Loeb Classical Library. Cambridge, MA: Harvard University Press, 1925.

Plato. *Theaetetus; Sophist*, trans. Harold N. Fowler. The Loeb Classical Library. Cambridge, MA: Harvard University Press, 1921.

Plato. *Timaeus; Critias; Cleitophon; Menexenus; Epistles*, trans. Robert G. Bury. The Loeb Classical Library. Cambridge, MA: Harvard University Press, 1929.

Plotinus. *Ennead III*, trans. Arthur H. Armstrong. The Loeb Classical Library. Cambridge, MA: Harvard University Press, 1993.

Ranke, Leopold von, *Weltgeschichte*, 16 vols. Leipzig: Duncker & Humblot, 1881–8.

Ricoeur, Paul. 'Conclusions', in *Vérité et vérification – Wahrheit und Verifikation*, ed. Herman Van Breda. The Hague: Martinus Nijhoff, 1974, 190–209.

Riedel, Manfred. 'Diltheys Kritik der begründenden Vernunft', in *Dilthey und die Philosophie der Gegenwart: Beiträge*, ed. Karl-Otto Apel and Ernst Wolfgang Orth. Freiburg: Karl Alber, 1985, 185–210.

Rilke, Rainer Maria. *Duineser Elegien*. Leipzig: Insel-Verlag, 1923. [English translation: *Duino Elegies*, trans. J. B. Leishman and Stephen Spender. Columbia, SC: Camden House, 1993.]

Rilke, Rainer Maria. 'XIX' in *Sonnets to Orpheus*, trans. Leslie Norris and Alan Keele. Columbia, SC: Camden House, 1989.

Ringer, Fritz. *The Decline of the German Mandarins: The German Academic Community, 1890–1933*. Cambridge, MA: Harvard University Press, 1969.

Rodi, Frithjof. *Die Erkenntnis des Erkannten. Zur Hermeneutik des 19. and 20. Jahrhunderts*. Frankfurt am Main: Suhrkamp, 1990.

Rosales, Alberto. 'Heideggers Kehre im Lichte ihrer Interpretationen', in *Zur philosophischen Aktualität Heideggers. Symposium der Alexander von Humboldt-Stiftung vom 24.–28. April 1989 in Bonn-Bad Godesberg*, vol. 1: *Philosophie und Politik*, ed. Dietrich Papenfuss and Otto Pöggeler. Frankfurt am Main: Vittorio Klostermann, 1991, 118–40.

Erich Rothacker, *Einleitung in die Geisteswissenschaft*. Tübingen: Mohr, 1920.

Sartre, Jean-Paul. *L'Être et le néant: Essai d'ontologie phénoménologique*. Paris: Gallimard, 1937. [English translation: *Being and Nothingness: A Phenomenological Essay on Ontology*, trans. Hazel E. Barnes. New York: Pocket Books, 1972.]

Sartre, Jean-Paul. *Les Jeux sont faits*. Paris: Les Editions Nagel, 1947. [English translation: *The Chips Are Down = Les jeux sont faits*, trans. Louis Varèse. New York: Lear, 1948.]

Sartre, Jean-Paul. *Les jeux sont faits*. Les Films Gibé, 1947. Film.

Sartre, Jean-Paul. *La Nausée*. Paris: Gallimard, 1938. [English translation: *Nausea*, trans. Lloyd Alexander. New York: New Direction, 2007.]

Scheler, Max. 'Der Formalismus in der Ethik und die materiale Wertethik' in *Gesammelte Werke*, vol. 2 *Neuer Versuch der Grundlegung eines ethischen Personalismus*, ed. Maria Scheler. Bern/ Munich: Francke, 1966. [English translation: *Formalism in Ethics and Non-Formal Ethics of Values: A New Attempt Toward the Foundation of an Ethical Personalism*, trans. Manfred S. Frings and Roger L. Funk. Evanston, IL: Northwestern University Press, 1973.]

Scheler, Max. *Gesammelte Werke*, vol. 8. *Die Wissensformen und die Gesellschaft*, ed. Maria Scheler. Bern/Munich: Francke, 1960.

Scheler, Max. 'Das Problem der Seinsrelativität', in *Gesammelte Werke*, vol. 9. *Späte Schriften*, ed. Manfred S. Frings. Bern/Munich: Francke, 1976.

Schleiermacher, Friedrich. *Über die Religion. Reden an die Gebildeten unter ihren Verächtern*. Berlin: de Gruyter, 1995 [English translation *On Religion: Speeches to its Cultured Despisers*. Cambridge: Cambridge University Press, 1996.]

Schulz, Walter. 'Über den philosophiegeschichtlichen Ort Martin Heideggers', *Philosophsiche Rundschau* 1 (1953/54): 65–93, 211–32.

Schwartz, Eduard. 'Über das Verhältnis der Hellenen zur Geschichte', *Logos. Internationale Zeitschrift für Philosophie der Kultur* 9 (1920/21): 171–87.

Sinn, Dieter. 'Heideggers Spätphilosophie', *Philosophische Rundschau* 14 (1967): 81–182.

Spengler, Oswald, *The Decline of the West*, trans. Charles F. Atkinson. New York: Knopf, 1957.

Spiegelberg, Wilhelm. 'Aegyptologische Kritik an Spenglers Untergang des Abendlandes' *Logos. Internationale Zeitschrift für Philosophie der Kultur* 9 (1920/21): 188–94.

Strasser, Stefan. 'Logique husserlienne et sémantique', in *Vérité et vérification – Wahrheit und Verifikation*, ed. Herman Van Breda. The Hague: Martinus Nijhoff, 1974, 132–89.

Strauss, Leo and Hans-Georg Gadamer. 'Correspondence concerning *Wahrheit und Methode*', *Independent Journal of Philosophy* 2 (1978): 5–12.

Theunissen, Michael. *The Other: Studies in the Social Ontology of Husserl, Heidegger, Sartre, and Buber*, trans. Christopher Macann. Cambridge, MA: MIT Press, 1984.

Zeller, Eduard. *Über Bedeutung und Aufgabe der Erkenntniss-Theorie: Ein akademischer Vortrag*, in *Vorträge und Abhandlungen*, vol. 2. Leipzig: Fues, 1877.

Index of Names

Aeschylus 65–6
Anaximander 22, 34, 217–18, 239
Aquinas, St Thomas 213, 251 *see*
    Thomism
Aristotle xxv, xxvi, xxviii, xxx, xxxiii–
    xxxiv, 8, 18, 22, 23, 31, 78, 80,
    84, 100, 121, 126, 128, 156–7,
    180, 182, 183, 185, 199, 201,
    204, 213–14, 222, 234, 237, 245,
    253, 256–7, 260–2, 264, 284n.,
    287n., 292n., 305n., 307n.,
    308n., 309n., 310n.
  and Arabic philosophy 60
  and cause 7
  and ethics (practical philosophy) 83,
    116, 212, 241
  and Heidegger 16, 112, 172–4, 181,
    210–12, 217, 222–3, 235,
    238–42, 249–53, 255 *see*
    Heidegger
  and *Metaphysics* 16, 156, 181, 182, 205,
    212, 257
  and nature xxxi, 8
  and *Physics* xxx, 16, 33, 128, 182, 202,
    203
  and Plato viii, xii, xviii, xx, 17, 19, 45,
    118, 169, 189, 201, 232, 248,
    249, 255, 260, 262–3 *see* Plato
  and *Rhetoric* 222, 252
  tradition of 18
Augustine 131, 210, 232, 241, 249

Bachelard, Suzanne 146, 299n.
Behler, Ernst 117, 295n.
Bergson, Henri 22, 97, 151
Biel, Gabriel 210, 249
Biemel, Walter 154
Bloch, Ernst 174, 216
Boeckh, August 59, 105, 108, 110
Boethius 136
Bollnow, Otto Friedrich 74, 103, 106,
    294n.

Bourdieu, Pierre ix, xi, 284n., 298n.,
    300n., 301n.
  and activity of research 168
  and Dasein 172
  and Germany (fascism) 170–1
  and Heidegger 171–4, 177–8
  and Plato 169
  and sociology 167, 169, 171
  and solicitude 135, 171–2
Brentano, Franz 78–9, 128, 156, 157, 256
Bröcker, Walter 14, 209, 217, 227, 247,
    305n., 309n.
Bröcker-Oltmanns, Käte 247, 305n., 309n.
Buber, Martin 126, 133, 298n.
Burckhardt, Jacob 27, 286n., 288n.

Carnap, Rudolf xxxiii, 160, 228–9
Cassirer, Ernst 173, 216, 305n.
Celan, Paul 67, 176, 180, 190–1, 289n.,
    303n., 304n.
Char, René 176
Christ (Jesus) 67–8
Cicero, Marcus Tullius 49, 120, 237, 286n.,
    288n.
Cohen, Herman 92, 131, 173, 212–13,
    248, 261

Davidson, Donald xiii, xiv, 281n.
Democritus 7, 232, 286
Derrida, Jacques ix, xi, xviii, xxii, xxvi,
    174, 180–1, 183–6, 188–93, 196,
    199, 201–2, 205
  and deconstruction xviii, xxi, xxiii,
    117, 118, 179–81, 184, 188,
    287n.
  and dialogue (conversation) 117, 179
  and *différance* xx
  and Heidegger xxiii, 117, 175, 180, 186
  and logocentrism (phonocentrism)
    183
  and Plato 202
  and trace 190

Descartes, René xii, xviii, 20, 76, 97, 108,
    128, 129, 137, 156, 231, 233
Dilthey, Wilhelm x–xi, xiv, xvi–xvii, xx,
    xxix, xxxii, 14, 71–3, 89, 90–7,
    99–102, 106–7, 108, 110–13,
    117, 119, 214–15, 222, 241,
    295n.
  and Count Yorck xv, 103, 104, 109, 115,
    215
  Dilthey (Diltheyan) school ix, 13, 103,
    106, 108
  and explanation 78
  and Gadamer x, xi, xiii, xiv, xv, xvi–xvii,
    xx, xxix, xxxii
  and Heidegger 14, 15, 18, 94, 102,
    103–4, 105, 106, 110, 111, 113,
    115, 178, 214–15, 251
  and hermeneutics 93, 103, 105, 106, 110
  and the historical school 13, 75, 91
  and the human sciences 84–5, 88
  and Husserl 87–8, 93, 106, 111, 178
  and the inscrutability of life 94
  and lived experience 79–80, 85
  and neo-Kantianism 92
  and Nietzsche 95, 100
  and psychology 75, 93, 99
  and science 84, 96
  and understanding 78
Dionysius the Areopagite 202–3
Domin, Hilde 286n.
Droysen, Johann Gustav 78, 105, 108
Duns Scotus, John 14, 210, 241, 296n.

Ebbinghaus, Hermann 75
Ebbinghaus, Julius 210, 216
Ebeling, Gerhard 137, 298n.
Ebner, Ferdinand 126, 133
Empedocles 200

Falk, Johannes Daniel 67
Fetscher, Iring 152
Fichte, Johann Gottlieb 76, 97, 98, 112,
    126, 133, 143, 156, 162, 250,
    299n., 305n.
Fink, Eugen 140, 146, 154, 242, 296n.
Frank, Erich 301n.
Frank, Manfred 107, 159
Freud, Sigmund 95, 129, 168, 297n., 298n.
Freyer, Hans 107

Funke, Gerhard 139, 142, 148, 299n.

Galilei, Galileo xxv, 33, 231, 248
Geiger, Moritz 133, 209
Giacometti, Alberto 56, 176
Goethe, Johann Wolfgang von xxv–xxvi,
    17, 21, 33, 35, 64, 67, 95, 191,
    283n., 284n., 289n., 311n., 312n.
  and theory of colours 82
Gogarten, Friedrich 15, 133
Groethuysen, Bernhard 73, 74, 92, 106,
    290n., 291n., 292n.
Guardini, Romano 69, 290n.
Gurwitsch, Aron 125, 154

Habermas, Jürgen ix, xi, 167, 174–8,
    300n., 301n.
  and Bourdieu ix, xi, 177–8
  and Heidegger xi, xxvi, 174–8, 223
  and sociology 178
Haecker, Theodore 126, 133
Hartmann, Nicolai 15, 94, 176, 210, 213
Heidegger, Martin ix, xi–xvi, xviii–xxvi,
    xxxii–xxxv, 13–14, 18–19, 69,
    74, 88–9, 92–4, 102–3, 106,
    110–21, 130–1, 133–7, 140–3,
    147–9, 151–61, 163–5, 167, 169,
    171–8, 180–96, 207, 209–19,
    221–5, 227–45, 247–62, 264–8,
    287n., 295n., 296n., 300n.,
    305n., 306n., 307n., 310n.
  and Aristotle 16, 112, 213, 241, 242,
    249, 252, 257, 260, 261, 268
  and being 158, 164, 188, 212, 223
  and Derrida 117, 118, 181, 186, 189,
    202
  and 'destruction' 80, 120, 181, 187, 188
  and Dilthey 73, 100, 103–5, 110, 115,
    215, 251 *see* Dilthey
  and fundamental ontology 185
  and the Greeks 120, 245, 248, 249, 267
  and hermeneutics 115, 120, 131, 252
  and Husserl 130, 134, 149, 152, 153,
    154, 155, 177, 181, 184, 189,
    190, 212, 221, 250, 251, 255
  and language 120
  the late 22, 117, 178, 180, 186, 188, 219,
    229, 245
  and Nietzsche 117, 175, 186

and Plato 158, 257, 258, 259, 260, 261,
258
and politics 173
and Scheler 147, 211
and sociology 167, 171
and transcendental self-interpretation
142
and 'the Turn' *see* turn
the young 13–15, 21–2, 104, 173, 176,
178, 181, 209, 211, 213, 214,
217, 219, 227, 241, 249, 251
Heimsoeth, Heinz 92, 94
Heraclitus 63, 228, 307n.
and Heidegger 217–18, 239, 243–5
and *logos* 185
and Spengler 170
Herbart, Johann Friedrich 77, 93, 108,
303n.
Herder, Johann Gottfried 44–5, 155
Hermann, Friedrich-Wilhelm von 296n.,
306n.
Herodotus 20, 30–1, 287n.
Hesiod 34
Hildebrandt, Kurt 133
Homer 20, 28, 29, 31–3, 62, 262, 312n.
Homeric 32, 262
Humboldt, Wilhelm von 189, 238
Hume, David 6, 97
Husserl, Edmund xi–xii, xiv, xix, xxii,
xxiv–xxv, 14, 15, 73, 87, 89, 93,
111, 114, 120, 125, 130, 131,
133–4, 139–49, 151–9, 162, 163,
172, 180, 184, 186, 189, 242,
293n., 294n., 298n., 300n., 305n.
anti-psychologism 75
and Derrida 180, 183–4, 186, 189
and Dilthey 73, 87–8, 89, 103, 106, 111,
214–15, 251
and Heidegger xxii, xxiv, 73, 89, 106,
110, 112, 114, 130, 140, 149,
152–8, 161, 172–3, 177–8,
180–1, 183, 184, 186, 189, 190,
209, 211–12, 214–16, 221, 242,
250–1, 255, 259
and idealism 152
and intersubjectivity 119, 130–1, 132–3,
148, 162
and the life-world 140, 148, 214
and object 163

and phenomenology 14, 74, 89, 106,
111–12, 125, 130, 132–4,
139–49, 153, 159, 178, 189, 214,
216, 222, 250, 251
and psychologism 75, 184
and transcendental ego
(phenomenology, philosophy,
subjectivity, self-interpretation),
transcendentalism xxii, 112,
120, 125, 131, 133, 139, 142,
147, 148, 221, 222

Ingarden, Roman 144

Jaspers, Karl 93, 126, 295n.
Jonas, Hans 136
Jünger, Ernst 169, 171

Kant, Immanuel xix, xxiv, 36, 37, 74,
76–7, 86, 92–4, 98–100, 125,
127, 129, 137, 173, 188, 223,
232, 248, 249, 250
and causality 3
and ethics 116
and freedom 10, 11, 76, 310n.
and Hume 6, 97
Kant-book 18, 114, 147
Kantianism 133 *see* neo-Kantianism
and metaphysics 107, 188
and reason 10, 188, 233, 256
and religion 210, 213
and the third critique 98, 176
Kaufmann, Fritz 74, 104, 290n.
Kepler, Johannes 203
Kierkegaard, Søren 213, 215–16, 219, 222,
241–2, 249, 251–3, 297n., 308n.
Klee, Paul 176
Kojève, Alexandre 152–3, 157
Kroner, Richard 216
Krüger, Gerhard 216

Landgrebe, Ludwig 74, 104, 140, 146, 154,
290n., 300n.
Lange, Friedrich Albert 74
Lask, Emil 173, 211
Leibniz, Gottfried Wilhelm 76, 78, 129,
132, 137, 212, 248, 309n.
Lipps, Hans 74, 88, 106, 294n.
Lipps, Theodore 130, 133

Litt, Theodor 93
Lotze, Rudolf Hermann 108
Löwith, Karl 209
Lukács, György 211, 216
Luther, Martin 19, 104, 137, 210, 235, 249
    and Heidegger 114, 213, 222, 241
    and Yorck von Wartenburg 104

Mann, Thomas 95
Marc, Franz 176
Marx, Karl xxxiv–xxxv, 129, 132, 153, 162,
    282n.
    Marxist 152
McDowell, John xiii–xiv, 281n.
Meister Eckhart 21, 235, 259, 310n.
Mendelsohn, Moses 36
Merleau-Ponty, Maurice 151
Meyer, Eduard 169, 301n.
Mill, John Stuart 74, 76, 84
Milojcic, Vladimir 29
Misch, Georg 73, 89, 103, 106–13, 115–17,
    119, 214, 290n., 293n., 294n.,
    295n.
Mosse, George 170
Mozart, Wolfgang Amadeus 81, 290n.

Natorp, Paul 15, 92, 97, 103, 119, 154,
    158, 172, 189, 210, 213, 221,
    248, 249, 251, 294n.
Newton, Isaac 33, 35, 44, 82
Nicholas of Cusa 21
Nietzsche, Friedrich 129–30, 132, 296n.,
    297n., 298n., 310n., 312n., 313n.
    and consciousness 97, 120
    and Derrida 117, 174–5, 180–1
    and Dilthey 89, 95–7, 99, 100–2
    and Habermas 175
    and Heidegger 102, 117, 120, 175,
        177–8, 180–1, 185–6, 209, 211,
        219, 242, 244, 261
    and modernity 174,
    and Ortega 101–2
    and phenomenology 209
    and tragic (tragedy) 101
Nohl, Herman 106
Novalis 63–4

Ortega y Gasset, José xiii, xx, 73, 91–2,
    94–7, 99, 101–2, 290n., 293n.

Paci, Enzo 145, 299n.
Parmenides 114, 158–9, 189, 217–18, 239,
    259, 260, 265
    Platonic dialogue 21–2, 183, 201, 264,
        265, 285n., 311n.
Paul *see* Saint Paul
Pažanin, Ante 299n.
Pfänder, Alexander 130, 133
Plato xxiii, xxx, 11, 13, 62, 105, 118–19,
    149, 158–9, 182, 185, 189, 205,
    222, 232, 243, 248, 257, 262–4,
    267, 268, 309n.
    and Aristotle viii, xii, xviii, xx, 17,
        19–20, 23, 45, 84, 118, 127, 149,
        169, 181–2, 203–4, 212, 248–9,
        255, 260–2
    and the *Meno* 267
    and Nietzsche 312–13n.
    and the *Parmenides* 21–2, 159, 285n.
    and the *Phaedo* 34, 63, 289n.
    and the *Phaedrus* 114–15, 119, 169,
        252, 262, 302n., 309–10n.
    and the *Republic* 182–3, 202–3
    and the *Sophist* 258–9, 264–6, 309n.,
        311n.
    and the *Theaetetus* 310n.
    and the *Timaeus* 199–202
Pöggeler, Otto 222, 227, 305n., 306n.
Pythagoras 62

Ranke, Leopold von, 4, 104, 282n.
Rembrandt, Harmenszoon van Rijn 198,
    303n., 304n.
Rickert, Heinrich 75, 172, 221
Ricoeur, Paul xviii, xxxv, 139, 147,
    299n.
Rilke, Rainer Maria 21, 59, 177
Ringer, Fritz 170
Rodi, Frithjof 103, 105, 106, 108–10, 116,
    291n., 292n., 293n., 294n.
    on Heidegger 110–11, 295n.
Rosales, Alberto 305n.
Rosenzweig, Franz 133
Rothacker, Erich 75, 107, 291n., 294n.
Rousseau, Jean-Jacques 86

Saint Paul 210
Sartre, Jean-Paul ix, xi, xiv–xv, 151–65,
    298n., 299n., 300n.

Scheler, Max 14–15, 93, 128, 130, 133, 147, 157, 176, 211–12, 292n.
and critique of Husserl 143, 148
and existence 82
and personalism 137
Schelling, Friedrich Wilhelm Joseph 22, 33, 36, 73, 98, 161, 219, 250, 299n., 305n.
and philosophy of nature 129, 143, 203
Schlegel, Friedrich 78, 105, 108, 117–18, 293n.
Schleiermacher, Friedrich x, 14, 105, 108, 137, 222
and Dilthey 75, 78, 95, 288n., 289n., 295n.
Schliemann, Heinrich 31
Schopenhauer, Arthur xv, 10, 33, 95, 305n.
Schulz, Walter 143, 299n., 306n.
Schütz, Alfred 125
Schwibs, Bernd 168
Sextus Empiricus 33
Sheehan, Thomas 209, 227
Simmel, Georg 66, 115, 173, 215
Socrates 83, 85, 245, 265, 267, 304n., 312n., 313n.
in the *Apology* 61
in the *Meno* 267, 310n.
in the *Phaedo* 34, 289n.
in the *Phaedrus* 206, 266
in the *Protagoras*, 48
Socratic 119, 206, 233, 266
ignorance 185
pre- xii, 22, 217, 239

question 17, 83, 116, 118, 268
Spengler, Oswald 28, 169–71, 301n.
Spranger, Eduard 93, 107
Stein, Heinrich von 95
Strasser, Stefan 147, 299n.
Strauss, Leo x, 16–17, 284n.

Theunissen, Michael 133, 298n.
Thucydides 12, 30, 33
Troeltsch, Ernst 13, 107, 214
Tugendhat, Ernst 209, 227

Unamuno, Miguel de 126

Wagner, Richard 95–6
Weber, Max 5, 13, 214
Weiss, Helene 209, 227
Weizsäcker, Viktor von 126, 298n.
Whitehead, Alfred North 119
Wieland, Christoph Martin 67
Wilamowitz-Moellendorf, Ulrich von 32
Windelband, Wilhelm 26, 75, 216, 248
Wittgenstein, Ludwig xxiv, 121, 133, 180, 187
Wolff, Christian 176
Wundt, Max 94

Yorck von Wartenburg, Count Hans Ludwig Paul xv, 86, 103–4, 109, 115, 214–15, 290n., 294n.

Zeller, Eduard 77, 100, 291n.
Zeno 159

Index of Subjects

action 4, 7, 8–10, 12, 40, 81, 213, 287n.
  collective (social) xxx, 3
  as *praxis* xxx
aesthetics viii, 176, 197
agreement xxx, xxxv, 78, 88, 110,
        140, 179, 202, 245, 264 *see*
        understanding
alchemy (Bourdieu) 168, 171–2, 178
alētheia 114, 181, 217–18, 238–40, 264,
        265, 303n.
  alēthes 217, 257
  lēthē 339
alienation 51, 163, 248 *see* estrangement
aporia (*aporiai*) 65, 66, 131, 188, 264
appearance 8, 116, 132, 191, 201, 203,
        262–3, 265, 306n., 308n.
  mode of 200
  as phenomenon 158
  sensuous (sensible) 78, 263
  world of 158

Beautiful, the 119, 182, 203, 269
becoming 8, 9, 17, 52
  being and 21, 200–1, 219 *see* being
  history and 84 *see* history
  -other 8
beginning ix, xii, xxxii, xxxiii, xxxv, 4, 8,
        120, 126, 152, 155, 201, 218,
        231, 233, 268
  first 268
  Greek (of Greek thought, of Greek
        thinking) 114, 159, 232, 235,
        240, 245, 249, 260, 264
  Heidegger's 207, 209, 224, 227, 247–8,
        294
  historical (of history) 29, 231 *see*
        history
  of metaphysics 231
  new 200, 224
  of philosophy 228, 229, 245
  of the universe 25–6
  Western 33, 268

being xii, xvi, xxii, xxxii, 3, 8, 18, 20,
        21, 59, 64, 67, 76, 78, 79, 87,
        98, 101, 111–12, 114–15, 118,
        128, 130, 131–2, 136, 142, 148,
        157–9, 161, 164, 174–6, 178,
        180, 181, 183, 203, 211, 212,
        216–19, 223–4, 229–30, 232,
        236, 239–40, 244, 253, 255–66
  and becoming 200, 201
  and beings 216, 217, 223, 239, 266
  beyond 181–2, 183, 202–3, 261
  and concealment 223–4, 238 *see*
        concealment
  divine 114
  event of (as event, as happening) 218,
        239, 261
  and existence xvi
  for-itself (in itself) 161–3
  for others 51
  for the other 162–3
  highest 16, 19, 128, 180–1, 223
  history of xii, xx, xxiii, xxxv, 224 *see*
        history
  ideal 189
  in-itself 158, 159, 161
  in movement 21
  in-the-world 33–4, 100
  non-being (not being) 61, 63, 264
  and *ousia* 237
  and presence (presencing) 158, 188
        see presence
  the question of (about, concerning)
        xxxiv, 7, 16, 21–2, 110,
        112–14, 117, 119, 134–5,
        157, 158, 181, 184, 185, 222–3,
        256–60, 262
  sense of 16, 180, 238
  temporality of 186, 218 *see*
        temporality, time
  – there (being the there, of Dasein, of
        the 'Da') xxiii, 18, 23, 113–14
  toward death 15

truth of (and truth) 158, 177 *see* truth
understanding of 180, 181, 185, 187,
    238, 261 *see* understanding
– with (together, with one another)
    134, 163–4,196
beingness (*Seiendheit*) 232–33
bios 62 *see* life
bourgeoisie 176

category xxii, 6, 80, 89, 100–1, 111, 130,
    185, 213, 254, 256
  categorial xxii
  categorial intuition xxii *see* intuition
  of history (of historical thinking) 80, 89
    see history
  of life 80, 100, 217, 296n. *see* life
  of science 97 *see* science
causality ix, xiv, xvii, xxx, xxxi, 3, 5–7, 9,
    10–11, 12, 236
  and freedom 7, 10
cause 7–8, 10–12, 236
  Aristotle's four causes 7, 9
  causa efficiens 7–9, 12
  causal explanation 12
  and effect 3, 4, 10
  efficient (moving) xxxi, 9, 10
  final xxxi
  formal xxx
  formative 200
  material xxx
  moving 9
chōra 199–203
Christianity 15, 28, 36, 63, 66, 75, 86, 189,
    245, 251, 308n.
  and Greece (Greek) 28, 59
  and tradition (culture, heritage) 17,
    101, 104
Church 176, 182
  Catholic 176, 252
  Christian 221, 252
city (as *polis*) 203
cogito xxxv, 88, 127, 165
  cogito me cogitare 127, 156
  pre-reflective 156
concealment (*Verbergen, Verbergung*) 61,
    114, 218, 223–34, 239–40, 243,
    265 *see* being
  concealing 239, 244–5
  self-concealing 217, 239

unconcealment 114, 238, 240, 260 *see*
    alētheia; truth
concept xxii, xxiv–xxvii, xxx, xxxiii, 6, 34,
    62, 88, 114, 158, 185, 187–8,
    204–5, 218, 223, 232–5, 242,
    251, 254–5, 258, 260, 262, 268,
    287n.
  conceptual xiii, xxii, xxiv, 36, 64, 86,
    120, 126–7, 185, 187, 210, 216,
    218, 223, 234–5, 239, 242, 254,
    260, 265, 287n.
  fundamental 234, 257
  genesis of (history of) xvii, 126, 132
  and history xvii
  and mediation xxi, 287n.
  operative xvii, 242, 296n.
  and words (language, speech) xix, xxi,
    xxiv–xxvi, xxx, xxxiii, 118–19,
    127, 140, 185, 204, 234–5,
    254–5
  conceptuality xxvi, xxxii, xxxiii, 9, 113,
    115, 120, 165, 177, 178, 218,
    234, 241, 254, 256
  of Christian theology 241
  Greek 218
  conceptualization 200
connection
  of a life, (life-) (*Lebenszusammenhang*)
    79, 82
  of lived experience 79
  of mental life (Husserl) 87
  of the world 88 *see* world
conscience 5, 15, 40, 137, 213, 253
consciousness 19, 21, 43–4, 46–8, 51–2,
    62–3, 80–2, 87, 94, 97, 100, 118,
    121, 131–2, 147–8, 152, 156–7,
    161, 164–5, 176, 181, 190, 227,
    229, 232, 247, 248, 250, 257,
    263, 269, 303n.
  cultural 89, 102
  facts of 76–8, 88, 93, 96
  and finitude 19
  and freedom 5, 7, 11
  in general 92
  historical 13, 16, 31, 43, 44, 86, 107 *see*
    history
  historically affected (exposed to the
    effects of history) x, xiii, 80, 186
  and horizon 53

inner 3
and intentionality 157
life (living, and life) 46, 53, 67, 97, 162
modern 45
philosophy of 157, 252
public (social) 43, 47
and representation xix
self- 22, 51, 59, 64, 69, 76, 96–9, 101,
    118, 120, 128–31, 137, 156, 162,
    211, 251, 257
time- (-and time) 53, 130–1, 154, 156,
    189
transcendental 92
contingency 17, 20
construction 76, 81, 93, 100, 129, 133,
    183, 187, 199, 202, 203
anthropomorphic 9
conceptual (of concept) 108, 132, 254
historical 75
mathematical 82, 203
metaphysical 117
sociological 172
theoretical 130
conversation xxvi, xxx, 115–17, 122, 187,
    206,
copy 191, 210
and original 199–201
culture 40, 41, 44–5, 52, 55–6, 57, 59, 77,
    109, 122, 144, 184, 203, 204,
    230, 245, 268
academic (scholarly) 177, 234, 299n.
Asian 61
Christian 17
European 108
Greek 29, 63, 262
and life 92
literary 49
and nature 38
philosophy of 102
scientific (advanced) 28, 33, 89, 103,
    229 see science
Western 29, 35

Dasein xii, xxv, 88, 130, 131, 134–5, 164,
    172, 180, 189, 224, 234, 256,
    259, 287n., 300n.
analytic of 223
and authenticity (inauthenticity) 114,
    132, 135–6, 164, 172, 177

Da-sein xxiii, 18, 113, 223
and existence 18, 131, 135, 212
fall of (and fallenness) 113, 132, 217
hermeneutics of 111, 115
structure of xxxiv, 112, 118, 120, 135,
    137
death 17, 59, 61–70, 134, 244–5, 285n.,
    289n.
athanizein, athanasia 19, 60
being toward *see* being
birth and 52
deathlessness 60
and immortality 60
paradox of (mystery of, puzzle of,
    riddle of, unintelligibility of) x,
    21, 69, 245, 260
thanatos 19, 60
deconstruction 52, 117–18, 133, 185–8,
    205, 300n. *see* destruction
Derrida and ix, xviii, xxi, xxiii, 118,
    179–81, 184, 188, 285n.
hermeneutics and xi, 302n.
demiurge 199–200, 203
demiurgical 201
destruction
Derrida and 118, 180, 181 *see*
    deconstruction
Heidegger and 80, 113, 178, 181, 187,
    188, 254
of metaphysics (Greek ontology) xxiii,
    157, 234
dialectic xxxv, 10, 55, 56, 75, 97, 105, 129,
    183, 188, 219, 240
and Hegel 17, 18, 107, 162, 216, 240
and Kant 188, 233
and Plato xxx, 21, 115, 119, 181–3, 185,
    204, 264, 267, 310n., 312n.
of question and answer xxx, 186–7 *see*
    dialogue
and Sartre 163
dialogue ix, x, xiv, xviii–xix, xxiii, xxvi,
    xxx, xxxiv–xxxv, 105, 115–19,
    121, 137, 140, 155, 159, 163,
    179, 180, 182–3, 186–7, 189,
    193–6, 204–6, 219, 259, 263–5,
    267
and communication xxvi
with Derrida xi, xviii, 179, 189
and dissemination xix

and Galileo 33
with the Greeks 19
and history xvi, xxi
and language xvi, xx, 19
and Plato xxx, xxxiii, 20, 21, 34, 114,
        182, 183, 203, 205, 258, 265–6
and science 26
Socratic 119
and truth 22
différance (Derrida), xx, 183–6 *see* Derrida
difference xx, 113, 117, 146, 155, 213, 238
    between explanation and
        understanding xi
    and deconstruction xi, xxiii
    and hermeneutics xi, 109
    identity and 265
    ontological 172, 174, 185, 216
disclosure (*Entbergen*) 218, 238, 239, 240,
        265
discourse xxxv, 168, 176, 187, 223, 236,
        238, 243–4, 265, 266, 301n.,
        312n.
    discursive 113
    discursivity 119
    mediating xvi, xxiv, xxvi, xxvii, xxxii,
        xxxiii, 205
    of modernity (Habermas) 174–6, 177
    philosophical xxii, 228, 236
    poetic 228, 236,
    public 169
    as *Rede* (Heidegger) 115
dismantling, as *Abbau* 189
disposition 259
    and affects (*pathē*) 252
    as Aristotle's *hexis* 83
dissemination xiv, xviii, xxii–xxiii, 107,
        180, 185
    dissémination 118, 180, 186, 196

ego 51, 127, 141, 142, 145–6
    cogito xxxv, 88
    egoity (*Ichheit*) 126
    empirical 234
    transcendental xii, xxii, 73, 87, 120,
        131, 133, 140–1, 145–6, 154,
        215 *see* transcendental
Eleatism 161
    Eleatic 18, 158–9, 259, 265
empathy 96, 133

transcendental 133 *see* transcendental
empiricism xxiii, 74–6, 88, 213, 215
    British xxix, 75, 76, 93
    empirical
        ego 234
        experience xxix
        fact (data) 36, 77
        method xxix, 38
        science *see* science
        standpoint 74, 76, 93
energeia 181, 257, 303n.
enlightenment 15, 20, 23, 31–3, 83, 109,
        186, 231, 232, 252, 284n.
    German 15
    Greek 20, 268
    modern 13, 85–6, 176
epistemē xxviii–xxix, 45
epistemology 100, 139, 215, 221
    epistemological 26, 74, 93, 94–5, 100,
        214
essence xvii, 6, 21, 31, 98, 147, 158, 181,
        194, 200, 205, 237, 263, 265,
        266, 303n.
    and art (poetry) 240
    concept of 100, 112, 119
    and *eidos* 212
    of the human being 121
    intuition of 251
    and language 19
    and life 66, 217
    science of xxii, 247
    of self-consciousness (reflexivity) 98,
        131
    and substance xxv
    of technology 176
    of time-consciousness 131
estrangement 163, 189
ethics viii, 40, 83–4, 108, 116, 235, 252,
        306n.
    and Aristotle 86, 182, 210, 212, 222,
        242, 252–3
    ethical 308n.
    of intention (Weber) 5
    and Kant 116
    philosophical 86
    of responsibility 5
    Stoic 9
ethos xxix, 23, 40, 84, 86, 116, 118, 253
Euclid, Euclidean 31–2, 201–2

event xvi, 5, 12, 18, 26, 44, 82, 193, 199
  and being 218, 239
  as *Ereignis* 114, 182, 188, 218, 224
existence xvi, xxvi, xxviii, xxix, xxxiv,
        18–19, 45, 52–3, 69, 70, 82, 131,
        135, 160, 181, 212, 219, 244,
        249, 251–2, 286n., 288n., 292n.,
        302n., 303n., 310n.
  communal (social) xxx, 47, 51
  as Dasein xxv, 18, 135
  fallen 164
  and freedom 165
  and Heidegger xxii
  and history (historicity) 17, 73, 89, 214
        see history
  meaning of 77
  paradox of (puzzle of) x, 165
  pathos of 213
  science of 88 *see* science
  understanding of 15 *see* understanding
        existential
experience
  of death *see* death
  historical (of history) 4, 5, 6, 11, 27, 84,
        93, 129
  inner xxix, 76–9, 87, 99
  lived (life, of life) xxiii, 39, 52, 64, 77,
        79–83, 87, 92, 93, 94, 96, 242,
        254 *see* life
explanation 11, 78, 148, 167
  causal 12
  and history 77, 167
  and understanding *see* understanding

fact
  of consciousness (mental) 76, 77, 78,
        88, 93, 96
  empirical (of experience) xxix, 36, 37,
        77
  and history 30, 31 *see* history
  inner (of inner experience) 76–9, 82,
        83, 85, 87, 99
  of reason 36, 76, 310n. *see* reason
  science of 37, 92, 261, 310n.
facticity 17–18, 131, 189, 222, 249, 251,
        261
  hermeneutics of xxii, 212, 241
forest path (*Holzweg*) 112, 185, 223–4,
        232

freedom xxviii, xxxi, 7, 9, 10, 37, 45, 49,
        69, 85, 86, 104, 115, 137, 165,
        181, 204, 221, 222, 223, 282n.,
        283n.
  consciousness of 7, 11
  of experimentation 56
  as a fact of reason 36, 76, 188–9, 310n.
  and history 7 *see* history
  intellectual (of thinking) 6, 69
  and nature 10–12 *see* nature
  and responsibility 5
futuralness (*Zukünftigkeit*) 189
  futural 131

givenness 130, 134, 148
  and consciousness 147, 148
  and lived-experience 79
  self- 255
  of things (of objects) 128, 130, 133
Greece 9, 28–9, 31, 33, 60–1

hermeneutics xxvii, xxxii, 39, 99, 105, 108,
        110, 114, 116, 119, 137, 179,
        207, 295n., 302n.
  of Dasein *see* Dasein
  and deconstruction *see* deconstruction
  Dilthey and, *see* Dilthey
  of facticity xxii, 131, 212, 241
  hermeneutic
        circle 115, 120, 147
        dimension 111
        horizon 88
        phenomenology 74, 94
        philosophy 106, 117, 118, 122, 179,
              180
        situation xi, 249, 251, 252
        turn 18, 79, 103, 106
  and history xvi, xxxiii, xxxv *see* history
  and method x–xi, 179
  ontohermeneutics 117
  and phenomenology 111 *see*
        phenomenology
  philosophical ix–x, xii–xiii, xvi, 89, 105,
        107, 109, 116–17
  and psychology 74–5, 93, 106
  romantic (Schleiermacher, Schlegel)
        78, 117
  traditional 105, 107, 109
  universal 109

history viii–ix, xiii, xvi–xxiv, xxvii, xxxv,
        1, 3–7, 11–14, 21, 26–8, 31, 33,
        43–4, 46, 48–9, 51–2, 73, 86, 93,
        97, 101, 118, 120, 203, 216, 231,
        233, 241, 286n., 287n., 288n.
    and being xii, xxxv, 224 *see* being
    and cause (causality) 5–6, 11 *see*
        causality
    as a complex of events 4
    and concept (conceptual) 126, 132, 136
    and consciousness *see* consciousness
    critical 33
    of the earth 25
    of Europe (European) 28, 44, 102
    and experience ix, x, xxix, 4, 6, 11, 92
        see experience
    and freedom 7 *see* freedom
    happening of 7
    and hermeneutics, xxxiii *see*
        hermeneutics
    historicism xiii, xxix, 13, 17, 22, 43–4,
        88, 114
    and historicity 26, 251
    of humanity 27, 29
    intellectual 43, 93, 94, 249
    knowledge of 7
    laws of 7
    and life 52, 57, 63, 80, 146 *see* life
    and metaphysics 175, 181, 232
    and philosophy ix, xvi, xvii, 22, 28, 44,
        86, 126
    of problems 14, 216, 248
    and progress 198
    of religion 32, 88,
    revolutionary xxxv
    of salvation 86
    and science 77 *see* science
    and the subject xiii *see* subject
    universal (of the universe) 25, 26–30,
        44,
    of the West (Western) 17, 28, 56, 159,
        228, 230, 232, 233, 268,
    of the world (world) 4, 25, 27–30, 80,
        86, 254, 268 *see* world
horizon xiii, 28, 29, 53, 99, 100, 120, 132,
        140, 186, 187, 205, 223, 250
    and consciousness 53 *see*
        consciousness
    fusion of xviii, xxv, 186

historical xix, 27 *see* history
interpretive (hermeneutic) xxx,
        6, 88 *see* hermeneutics;
        interpretation
    and the question 134 *see* dialectic,
        dialogue
    and time 119, 130, 256 *see* temporality;
        time
    world 32 *see* world
humanitas 89, 102
hupokeimenon xviii

idealism 97, 129, 133, 143, 162, 177, 215,
        254
    German 36, 76, 79, 82, 93, 97, 98, 107,
        112, 129, 132, 156, 162, 234,
        241, 248, 250, 253, 261
    idealist/idealistic 75, 76, 77, 92–4, 111,
        119, 129, 212, 261, 305n.
    transcendental 125, 128, 131, 143, 212,
        214, 242
ideality xxv
induction 88
    inductive 74, 76, 78, 88
inscription xxi, 32, 192, 243, 285n.
inscrutability 101
    inscrutable xxxii, 85, 109, 295n.
    of life (inscrutable nature of life,
        inscrutable visage of life)
        xxxii, 85, 94, 96, 101, 109, 113
        see life
intentionality 87, 147, 157 *see*
        consciousness
interpretation xvii, xxii–xxiv, 32, 59, 81,
        129, 130, 132, 175, 186, 197,
        205, 212, 218, 240, 304n. *see*
        understanding
    of Aristotle 60, 182, 210, 212, 240, 249,
        253, 257
    of being 131 *see* being
    and the Bible 67–8
    and Dilthey 79, 84
    and hermeneutics 148, 293n. *see*
        hermeneutics
    and horizon 140 *see* horizon
    of life 113 *see* life
    of metaphysics 142 *see* metaphysics
    moral (moralistic) 82, 114, 130, 296n.
    and the original xviii

of phenomenology (phenomenological)
111, 112, 120 *see*
phenomenology
and Schleiermacher 75
scientific 215 *see* science
self-interpretation 31, 44, 142, 212, 221,
253, 254, 305n.
and sociology xi
and the tradition xviii *see* tradition
transcendental 137, 176, 177, 185, 221,
224
and translation xiv
and understanding xiii *see*
understanding
of the world xiv *see* world
intersubjectivity xi, xx, 119, 125–7, 132,
134, 142, 162 *see* subject
intertextuality 196–8 *see* text, textuality
intuition 16, 210, 234–5, 262, 295n.
categorial xxii, 22
of essences 251

judgment xx, 34, 109, 111, 147, 160, 176,
195, 225, 253
logic of 111, 181
misjudgment 31, 117
pre-judgment 6
justice, order of 34, 83
system 55
injustice 65

language xix, xxi–xxvi, xxxii, 21, 44, 107,
113, 119, 120, 121, 126, 130,
136, 147, 178, 184, 185, 187–8,
197, 198, 204, 211, 213, 225,
228, 234, 236, 238, 240, 263,
264, 286n., 287n.
and art 118 *see* aesthetics
and concept (conceptual) xxi, xxx,
xxxiii, 17, 118, 188, 235, 240,
285n. *see* concept
and dialogue xx, xxi, xxxv, 19, 116, 137
see dialogue
dimension of (*Sprachlichkeit*) xxi, 29,
114, 120, 186, 191
and the Greeks 178
and Heidegger xx, 224
and history xvi, xxxv, 218
and logos 242, 255

of metaphysics 113, 114, 187, 188, 190,
199, 244
and philosophy 137, 189
and play 184
and poetry (poetic) 190, 197, 204, 205
and reason 242 *see* reason
and text 78
and understanding xiv *see*
understanding
and writing 190, 206, 285n.
law 7, 34, 41, 81, 83, 87, 136
and history 7, 11
and life 32 *see* life
and logic 228 *see* logic
and nature xxviii, 3, 7, 11, 34, 261 *see*
nature
and order 34 *see* order
of production xxviii, 47
and science 26, 267 *see* science
lēthē 213, 218, 239, 253 see *alētheia*
liberalism
cultural 215
liberal 104
consciousness 89, 102
democracy xxxv
Hegelianism 225
life
anxiety of 68, 69
category of *see* category
connection (connection of a, nexus of)
79, 82, 100
and consciousness (life-consciousness)
46, 53, 67, 97, 99
experience of (life experience) xxxiii,
39, 64, 92, 93–4, 96, 224, 242,
254
form of (life-forms) 52, 56, 100, 101
and history (historicity, historical, life
history) 30, 52, 54, 57, 63, 80,
89, 92, 101, 111, 146
inscrutability of *see* inscrutability
and knowledge xxxii
and language xxiv, 187, 254, 255
law of 32
life-situation 40, 252, 253
life-world xii, xxii, xxv, 119–20, 122,
125, 139–43, 147–9, 212–14,
250 *see* world
memory of 49

philosophy of 89, 97, 106–7, 110–11,
  113, 120, 251
political 4
practical life 40
praxis of 39, 149, 252
religious 32
situatedness in (*Sitz im Leben*) xxiv,
  187
and transcendence 66–7
visage of 85, 109, 295n
logic 76, 113, 115, 146, 158, 185, 186, 196,
  204, 211, 216, 228, 240, 255,
  260, 268, 311n.
  apophantic 111, 146–7, 160
  of definition 185, 233
  demonstrative 45, 204
  dialectical (and dialectic) 107, 183
  inductive 74, 76, 78, 88
  inferential 31, 33
  of implication 146,
  of judgment 111, 181
  of life 113
  modern 146–7, 228
  pre-predicative 111
  of proposition (propositional) 147, 185,
    191, 228, 233
  scholastic 160
  symbolic xxxiii, 228
  transcendental 145
  of truth 145, 146
logocentrism 181, 182, 183, 196, 204,
  302n.
logos (*logoi*) 63, 116, 118, 183, 191, 200,
  218–19, 239, 243, 245, 257, 264,
  266, 304n., 308n.
  as common to human beings 19, 22,
    245
  and disposition (*hexis*) 83
  and language xx, 118, 213, 255
  meaning of 191
  and myth 202
  and presence 181, 183, 184
  and reason (rationality) 83, 253
  and thinking 185, 189
  spermatikos 185

mandarin(s) (Bourdieu) 15, 169
Many, the 159, 262, 264
meaning xx, xxiv, xxvi, 81, 87, 111, 184,

  194, 196, 235, 236, 237, 243,
    258, 287n., 302n.
  and category 89, 100 *see* category
  of death 69 *see* death
  of existence 77 *see* existence
  of experience (what is experienced) 82
    see experience
  historical 111 *see* history
  ideal 87, 184
  of intersubjectivity 132
  and life 87 *see* life
  objective 82
  of philosophy 35, 44
  and text xiv, xviii, 195 *see* text
  theory of 189
memory 38, 39, 48, 51, 53, 82, 185, 192,
  197, 198, 288n.
  of the dead x *see* death
  historical 26, 30 *see* history
  of life 49, 286n. *see* life
metaphysics xxiii, xxxii, 23, 34, 36, 78,
  96, 117, 126, 135, 142, 148, 157,
  158, 172, 180, 182, 183, 184,
  186, 188, 212, 217, 219, 222,
  225, 231, 233, 235, 237, 239,
  241, 242, 250, 252, 255, 256,
  260, 267, 268
  destruction of xiii *see* destruction,
    deconstruction
  dogmatic 36, 107, 188
  end of 107
  of finitude 223
  Greek 16, 20, 120, 136, 233, 238
  language of 113–14, 187, 188, 199, 244
  metaphysical xxiii, 16, 19, 88, 94, 112,
    115, 117, 120, 180, 252, 263,
    308n.
    anti-metaphysical 202
    concept(s) 118, 191, 257
    origin 80
    pre-metaphysical 217
    problem 160
    question 135, 257
    realism 251
    thinking 179, 183, 185, 189, 260
    tradition 76, 80, 185, 234, 242
  and ontology 88
  and onto-theology (onto-theological)
    128, 158, 261

overcoming of 111, 180, 218
and science xxxii, 15, 230, 248
substance 127, 185
tradition of (history of) 13, 128, 157,
        175, 177, 181, 185, 213, 222,
        232, 261
transformation of 181, 186, 218
Western 81, 218
modernity 13, 20, 33, 35, 37, 47, 57, 98,
        101, 107–8, 128, 174–7, 189,
        204, 221, 231, 233, 238, 240,
        248, 249, 253
modern art 144
modern consciousness 45
modern enlightenment 13, 85–6, 176
modern science xxvii–xxxiii, 7, 9, 20,
        23, 29, 31, 33–5, 37–8, 44–5,
        76, 80, 84–6, 108–9, 115, 119,
        128, 134, 188–9, 215, 221,
        228, 231–2, 234, 238, 248, 261,
        267–8
modern subject (modern philosophy
        of the subject, modern
        subjectivism) xxxv, 99, 127, 137
        see subject
modern thought (thinking) 9, 97, 128,
        160, 178, 216, 221, 247–8
modernism 221
postmodernism xix
postmodernity 174
Querelle des anciens et des modernes
        16, 57
moment, the (*to exaiphnon*) 22, 244,
        307n.
monad 132, 212
monadological 132, 162
monologue 189, 233
mores 32, 40, 86
mover 127, 187
first (prime, the mover-god) 16, 20,
        182, 183, 203
self 257
unmoved 20
muthos 201
myth 31–3, 175
of the demiurge 199
mythical 66, 200, 258, 266
    essence of the 31
    past 20

recollection 32
tradition 20, 31, 61, 62
world 32, 186
in the *Phaedrus* 20, 262
of Prometheus 65
mythology 32, 229, 262

narrative 31, 199, 200
naturalism ix–x, 254
nature xvii, xxxi–xxxiii, xxxv, 3, 8–9, 13,
        25, 28, 33–5, 37–8, 59–60, 62–3,
        67, 82, 84, 126–7, 201, 231–2,
        245, 255
and cause (causality) xix, 4, 10 *see* cause
complex of 3, 9
course of xxviii, 4, 9, 10, 26, 34
and culture 38, 77
domination of (control of, mastery of)
        10, 36, 45, 47
and freedom 9, 10, 12
human 3, 38, 255
law of (natural laws) xxviii, 7, 11, 261
        see law
natural
    entities 10
    event 9, 11
    law 34
    necessity 10
    occurrence 8, 9–10, 35
    science *see* science
order of 35, 40
philosophy of 129, 143, 203
and science (sciences of), 98 *see*
        science
negativity 159
neo-Kantianism 13, 92, 112, 125–6, 188,
        261
and Dilthey 74, 77, 91–2, 97, 215
and Heidegger 14, 74, 172, 211, 221,
        241–2, 251
and Husserl 14, 73, 125, 172–3, 221,
        250
neo-Kantian 92, 104, 158, 173, 181,
        212, 214, 255
    epistemology 139
    movement 248
    philosophy 178, 251
and Ortega 91, 94
and Yorck von Wartenburg 215

nihilation 159
nominalism 189–90, 224

object xii–xiii, xvii, xxii–xxiii, 26, 37, 79,
        108, 156, 163, 167, 189, 250,
        302n. *see* subject, subject-object
        schema
    of consciousness 148
    intentional 211–12
    of knowledge 17, 23, 100, 158, 204
    of perception xxii, 130, 157, 250
    of science 26, 37, 84, 205
objectivity 23, 80, 84, 94, 96, 101–2,
        108–9, 165, 188
    of knowledge xxix, xxxii, 25, 101, 234
    of science (scientific) 83, 85–6, 93, 101,
        115, 120, 122 *see* science
    of thought 86, 94
One, the 159, 202–3, 218, 264, 311n.
ontology 88, 98, 131, 141, 148, 167, 210,
        241, 255, 257, 260, 267
    ancient 98
    existential ix, xi
    formal 157
    fundamental 185
    Greek 131, 134, 157, 176–7, 188, 260
    material 157
    ontological xi, xxi, 69–70, 78–82, 89,
        102, 117, 119, 134, 147–8, 172,
        176, 185, 189, 192 219, 244,
        255–6
        difference 172, 174, 216
        pre- 225
        pre-conception 98, 120
        prejudice 97, 131, 134
        question 159
    traditional 88
order xxi, 8–10, 20, 34, 37–8, 40–1, 47,
        53–4, 80, 83, 128, 199, 257,
        261–2, 267, 311n.
    as cosmos 34
    idea of 201
    mathematical 203
    of nature 35, 40 *see* nature
    spirit of 213
ordering 121, 230
origin xviii, 8, 64, 178, 282n.
    ancient 98,
    Christian 35

Greek 247, 254
historical 136 *see* history
    of metaphysics (metaphysical), xxxii, 80
        see metaphysics
original xxx, 6, 8, 238
    and the Big Bang 26
    experience (source of experience)
        xxxii, 39, 178, 189, 237, 239,
        244, 263
    foundation 93
    and Heidegger xxiii, 112, 114, 155,
        173, 178, 217, 234
    and life 100, 105
    meaning (linguistic sense) xxxii, 234,
        237
    originally 3, 7, 36, 232, 234
    presence, See '*Urpräsenz*'
    self-givenness 255
    testimonies 59
    understanding 7
    Urbild 199–201
    philosophical 172
    of reflection 142
originality 240
    of the experience of being 217

path xii, xxiv, xxvii, xxxii, 73, 94, 101,
        128–9, 159, 161, 185, 193–4,
        218, 232, 233, 235, 240, 242,
        255–6, 267, 309n.
    forest (*Holzweg*) *see* forest path
    of thinking 94, 177, 182, 221, 224–5
    and the trace 190, 192
    and the turn 221–2, 224–5
perception xxi–xxii, 22, 98, 130, 133, 147,
        305–7n.
    apperception 127
    inner 99
    object of xxii, 130, 157,
    sense 250
phenomenology xxii, 14–15, 18, 77, 93,
        103, 106, 110–11, 125, 141, 143,
        145, 147, 153, 155, 158, 183,
        187, 210, 212 *see* transcendental
    of Heidegger xii, 74, 94, 110–11, 120,
        130, 134, 157
    of Husserl xi–xii, xix, xxv, 74, 111, 125,
        130, 132–4, 139, 142, 144–5,
        147–8, 159, 221–2, 250

phenomenological xxiii, 15, 88, 93,
        103, 112, 125, 130, 132, 141–2,
        145, 147, 156–8, 173, 176, 178,
        186, 190, 210, 212, 214, 250–1,
        254–5, 288n.
    analysis 14, 88,189,
    movement 73, 133
    philosophy 126, 139, 144, 254
    questioning 140, 145
    school 74, 156, 211, 216
    of religion 15
Phenomenology of Religion 209, 227,
        296n.
Phenomenology of Spirit 93, 144, 157, 162,
        216
phonocentrism 183
phronēsis xxix, xxx, xxxiii, 116, 149, 213,
        222, 253
    and Heidegger 213, 253
phusis 239, 257, 260
physics 36–7, 188, 231
    and Aristotle xxx–xxxi, 16, 20, 33–4,
        126–8, 182–3, 202, 234, 252,
        257, 261–2, 267–8
    and Galileo 33, 149, 231, 248
    of mental life 77, 93
    modern 203
    and Newton 35
    and Plato 20, 262
    quantum 204
platonic xxx, 20–1, 113, 185, 194, 201,
        203, 249, 257–60, 264, 266–8
    bodies 201
    dialectic 204, 264, 267
    dialogue(s) xxxiii, 21, 182–3, 203, 258,
        266
    metaphysics 20, 267
    philosophy 18, 63
    neo-Platonic 64, 203
    Platonist 47–8, 113, 199
Platonism 23, 175, 201–2, 259, 261
poetry 20, 31, 64, 89, 144, 180, 204–5,
        228–30, 235, 240, 268
    and Aristotle 31, 287n
    and Hölderlin 223
    and Plato 204, 229
poiēsis 47, 257
polis 34
politics 84, 86, 213

Aristotle's *Politics* 242, 308n.
positivism xxix, 73, 76, 88–9, 108, 290n.
    scientific 94; *see* science
practical philosophy xxviii, xxix, xxxiii,
        40, 85–6, 253
    and Aristotle 83–4, 116, 241
pragmatism, American 211
praxis xxviii, xxix, xxx, xxxiii–xxxv, 39,
        85, 119, 142, 144, 149, 252
    in Aristotle 23, 45, 84, 253
    historical xvi, xxxii
presence xviii, 21, 39, 44, 62, 80, 184,
        301n.
    as *Anwesenheit* 158, 239
    -at-hand 111, 115, 130–1, 180, 238, 257,
        305n.
    entering/coming into (*Anwesenheit*)/
        presencing 185, 218, 238, 240,
        244, 257, 260, 305n., 306n.
    (*Gegenwärtigkeit*) 18, 260
    metaphysics of 241
    as *Präsenz* 181, 185
    presence to itself 20
    présence 181
    present xviii, xx, xxv, 21–2, 49, 53–6,
        61, 63, 80–81, 115, 121, 134,
        148, 156–7, 195–6, 219, 240,
        255, 263–4
        -at-hand 100, 111
        being (*anwesend*) 131, 257
        as *Gegenwart/gegenwärtig* 218, 237,
            239
        and that which nihilates 160
    self- 131, 219
    as *Urpräsenz* 145
    what forecloses presence (*Verwesen*)
        239, 305n.
    what grants/allows (*das Anwesen*)
        237–9, 244, 305–6n.
    what is granted presence (*das
        Anwesende*) 237, 240, 244
presencing (*Gegenwärtigkeit*) 260
presentness (*Gegenwärtigkeit*) 218
pre-Socratics *see* Socrates
proposition 88, 119, 121, 160, 217, 233–5,
        242, 257
    logic of 147, 233
    propositional 160
        act 308n.

content 296n.
   logic 185, 191, 228, 233
   truth 181, 186
psuchē 62, 63, 127, 257 *see* soul
psychoanalysis 83, 168
psychology 107, 145–6, 250 *see*
      transcendental
   depth 83
   and Dilthey xi, 74–8, 83, 87, 93, 95–6,
      99, 106
   gestalt 143
Psychology of Worldviews 126

rationality 84, 202, 253, 255
   and natural science xxvii
   practical 83
   technical 86
   and vitality 102
readiness-to-hand 130, 238
reading 48–9, 108, 115, 184, 193–4, 196,
      204–5
   and Heidegger 191
realism 86, 212, 238, 251, 254
reason 36, 76, 97–8, 102, 149, 189, 200,
      230, 233, 252, 255, 262, 290n.,
      294n.
   fact of 36, 76, 308n.
   and history 44, 74, 95
   of life 96
   practical 116, 121, 188, 213, 252
   scientific 147
reflection 40, 79, 83, 98, 127, 131, 137,
      143–4, 156, 160–1
   self- 82–5
   transcendental 142–3, 147
reflexivity 98, 126–8, 131, 161
Reformation 19, 76
   anti- 18, 251
relativism xxix, 81, 86, 101, 111, 141
   historical 23, 76, 214
religion 20, 40, 88, 101, 113, 183, 210, 213,
      228, 230, 232, 241, 268
   and Heidegger 15, 177
   history of 32, 88
   Homeric 62
   phenomenology of 15
   philosophy of 15
re-living (*Nacherleben*) 78, 82–5 *see* lived
      experience

representation xix, xx, 98, 127, 131, 157,
      159, 161, 164–5
   poetic 96
   scientific xxv
retention 156
return (*Rückkehr, Rückgang*) (Heidegger)
      ix, xii, 55, 155, 207, 216, 219,
      224, 233, 255, 268, 305n.
   to the Greeks 120, 157, 247–9, 255, 261,
      267
romanticism xxxix, 22, 44, 107, 109, 119,
      282n.
   and Yorck von Wartenberg 215
   and Dilthey 73, 89, 97, 108, 290n.
   and Schleiermacher 105
Rome 28, 54, 233
rupture xxxv, 35, 185–8

scepticism 61, 86–7, 111
scholastics 309n.
   scholastic xxxiii, 7, 17, 107, 127, 136,
      160, 176, 204, 235, 238, 242,
      250–1, 254, 256, 296n.
   scholasticism 136, 204, 248, 254
science(s) xxii, xxvii–xxxiii, xxxv, 6–7,
      15, 19, 22–3, 25–8, 31, 33–5,
      37–8, 40, 44–7, 74–8, 80, 82–8,
      92, 96–7, 104, 108–9, 113, 120,
      122, 139, 141, 143, 146–7, 149,
      165, 168, 170–1, 179, 189, 194,
      204–5, 214, 228–33, 247–79,
      251–2, 255, 261, 267–9, 304n.,
      306n 310n. *see* modern science
   empirical xvii, xxix, 36–7, 44, 74–6, 93,
      108–9, 148, 229, 238
   Greek 32
   Hellenistic 31
   hermeneutic 119
   historical 26, 33, 85, 107, 215
   human xvii, xxvii–xxix, 22, 25, 27, 30,
      37–8, 40–1, 74, 82–5, 88, 92–3,
      95, 99, 104, 106–7, 119–20,
      127–8, 215
   ideographic 26
   natural ix, xi, xvii, xxvii–xxix, 3, 25–6,
      30, 37, 39, 46, 74, 77–8, 97–8,
      107, 119, 179, 202, 229, 231–2,
      238, 248
   natural scientist 26, 27, 39

nomothetic 26
social xi, 46, 85, 125, 174, 229, 231
self-referentiality 98–9
semantics 147
    semantic xxiv, 62, 114, 119, 135, 160,
        176, 187, 218, 235, 237, 239,
        249, 254
    field xxxvi, 135, 218, 237, 240, 243
    formation 238
sense 81, 100, 118–20, 132, 184–5, 190,
        193, 195–6, 236
    of being 16, 180, 238, 259
    conceptual 234, 237
    existential x
    formation 120
    linguistic 234
    ontological (*Seinsinn*) 189
    of the performance or operative
        (*Vollzugsinn*) 118, 120, 242
    phenomenological 176
sheltering
    Bergen 239, 243, 245, 264
    Bergung 114, 218
sign 188, 190–6, 198, 242, 245
    significability (*Bedeutsamkeit*) 287n.
    theory of 188, 190
significance (*Bedeutsamkeit* in Dilthey)
        79–82, 111
situatedness xi, xiii, 252 (*Befindlichkeit*)
    in life (*Sitz im Leben*) xxiv, 187
sociology 167, 169, 175
solicitude (*Fürsorge*) 134–5, 171–2
    liberating 135, 172
soul 20–1, 35, 40, 62, 136 *see psuchē*
    and Aristotle 60, 213, 295n.
    and the Greeks 34, 62
    and Plato 63, 182, 202, 257, 262, 266,
        309n.
speech xxiii, xxvi, 168, 180, 205, 235, 303n.
    as *logos* in Aristotle 308n.
    and Plato 48, 258, 266, 309n., 311n.
spirit 97, 107, 219, 244, 312, 313n.
    absolute 219, 257
    and Hegel 99, 128–9, 241, 257
    Holy 136
    objective 132, 164
    and Scheler 143, 147
    spiritual 199, 202
Stoics 185

structuralism 183, 186, 190
    hyper xix
subject xii, xviii–xx, xxiii, xxvi, 98, 126–7,
        181, 187, 216, 224, 234, 245,
        255, 297n., 303n.
    and Aristotle 127, 234, 310n.
    and history xiii, xvii, xix
    and Kant 137
    and modern thought xxxv, 97, 99, 127,
        216
    subject-object schema 215
    subjectivsm 216
subjectivity x, xviii–xx, xxxi, 97–8,
        125, 126, 128, 131–3 *see*
        transcendence, transcendental
        subjectivity
    and Descartes 127, 137
    and Heidegger 80, 134, 137, 221–2,
        257
    and Kant 127, 137
    problem of 130
substance xvii, xviii, xxv, 97–8, 181, 183,
        187, 234, 256, 259, 298n., 303n.
    and Aristotle 127, 185, 212, 308n.
    and Cartesianism 97, 127, 137
    and Plato 199
substratum 98
system 35–6, 49, 76, 126, 128–9, 230–1,
        248, 250
    of arguments xxxiii
    and Aristotle 18, 255–6
    information 38
    of philosophy 35, 86, 126, 186
    of signs xix–xx
    solar 25
    systematic xvii
    systematicians 251
    systematics 18, 118
    University 169, 171

technē 45, 213, 253
temporality xvii, 17, 18, 22–3, 52, 131,
        146, 161, 260
    of being 18, 218
    problem of 18
Testament
    New 20, 185
    Old 29, 210, 249
text xiv, xvii, xviii, xxv, 29, 59, 110, 116,

186, 195–8, 200, 205, 236–7,
   243 *see* intertextuality; textuality
eminent 195, 205
and trace 190, 193–5
textuality 286–7n.
Thomism 112, 176, 222
   Thomist 20
   Thomistic 137, 235
time xiii, xix, xxvii, 22, 26–7, 51–5, 70, 82,
   91, 119, 130, 154, 232, 240, 256,
   259, 283n., (*le temps*) 300n.,
   311n.
   Aristotelian concept of 23
   -consciousness 131, 154, 156, 189
   problem of 15, 18, 21–2, 161, 209, 227
   span 70
to en 218
to on 218
trace xxiii, 30, 52, 60, 69, 198, 203–4,
   300n.
   and dialogue 193–4
   and Levinas 192
   and sign 190–2, 195
   and *Timaeus* 202
tradition xii–xiv, xviii, 27, 29–31, 33, 35,
   39, 44, 48–9, 54, 56–7, 59–60,
   62, 76, 79–80, 84–5, 89, 92, 96,
   134, 136–7, 172, 234–5, 239,
   242, 249, 253, 255, 268
   Anglo–American viii
   Aristotelian 84, 127, 248
   Biblical 27
   Christian 18, 61, 104, 186
   Greco–Roman 30
   Greek 45, 63, 233
   Greek–Christian 59
   and history 102
   intellectual 103
   of metaphysics 13, 128, 157, 177, 185,
      211–13, 218, 222, 261
   mythical 20, 31–2, 34, 61–2
   Platonic 18, 249
   of romanticism 119, 155
   traditional hermeneutics 105, 107, 109
   Western 249
tragedy 100–1, 205
transcendence x, 85, 183, 223
   of life 66–7
   transcendental xix, xxii, 77, 93, 127,

137, 139, 141–7, 148, 155, 173,
   176–7, 185–6, 188, 221–4,
   234, 251, 255, 305n., *see* ego;
   empathy; turn; reflection
consciousness 92
idealism 125, 128, 131, 143, 212
phenomenology 104, 111, 125,
   139–42, 145, 147–8, 222
philosophy 76–7, 92, 120, 125–6,
   178, 222
psychology 97, 145
reduction 146
subjectivity xix, 88, 111, 125,
   131–3, 141
transcendentally xii
transcendentalism 92, 112
transcendentality 146, 181, 301n.
transformation xviii, 156, 231, 254
   of consciousness 44, 46
   and death 64
   and history 57
   of metaphysics 175, 181, 186, 218
   into structure (*Verwandlung ins*
      Gebilde) 197
   and substance 98
translation xiv, xxv, xxvi, 154
   and *alētheia* 238
   and *eidos* 262
   and *hupokeimenon* 126, 234
   and *ousia* 237
   and *zōon logon echon* 308n.
truth x, xxvii, 13, 22–3, 32, 36, 43–4, 86, 96,
   118, 128–9, 161, 167, 169, 177,
   188, 223, 233, 260, 285n., 308n.
   a priori 36
   of being 158, 260
   logic of 145–6
   mathematical 201
   and Method viii–xi, xiii, xxvii–xxix,
      107, 116, 119, 137, 225, 281n.,
      282–3n., 284n., 292n., 294n.,
      295n.
   propositional 181, 186
   rational 76
   as unconcealment 260
turn (*Kehre*) xii, 80, 112, 118, 137, 155,
   175–6, 216, 221–5, 240, 244,
   305n., 306n.; *see* hermeneutics;
   return

Copernican 129
linguistic 121
romantic 107
transcendental 142, 212, 214
turn around (*Umkehr*) 224
turning (*Umwendung*) xii, 141, 144–5

understanding x–xiv, xvi–xvii, xxvii, xxx,
   xxxiv–xxxv, 3, 5–6, 17, 41, 51,
   78–9, 84, 105, 110, 118, 120,
   131–2, 135, 137, 164, 179–81,
   186, 188, 192–7, 204, 225, 243,
   253, 261, 303n.
of being 115, 180, 185, 187, 238, 261
   see being
from a distance (*Auf-Abstand-
   verstehen*) 252
musical 81
pre-148
religious 104
self- 31, 51, 78, 80, 83, 87, 109, 125,
   233, 252

virtue (*aretē*) 40, 61, 80, 116, 253

world xii–xiv, xix, xxvii, xxxiv, 6, 11, 17,
   32–3, 35–6, 41, 43, 46–9, 51,
   53, 56–7, 82, 84–6, 100, 111,
   113, 118, 120–2, 132, 134, 136,
   141–2, 149, 156, 158, 161, 165,
   176, 184, 188, 194, 198–203,
   217, 231, 238, 240, 245, 249,
   253, 261, 266–8, 286n., 287n.,
   see being, in-the-world;
   life-world
bodily (*Leibwelt*) 157
civilization 57

connection of the world
   (*Weltzusammenhang*) 88
consciousness 156
cultural 94, 184
Greek 32, 38, 47
and Heidegger 136,
and history xiii, 4, 25, 28–30, 49, 80,
   84, 86, 93–4, 96, 101, 145, 254,
   268, 290n.
Islamic 60
linguistic 178
modern 47, 267
mythical 32, 186
natural 49,
nether 158
-picture 33, 188
real xxviii, 176
response to the world (*Weltantwort*)
   121
semiotic 190
social 134
-sphere 201
surrounding (*Umwelt*) 210
terrestrial 199
two- theory 201–2
view 17, 34, 86, 88, 101, 324 *see also*
   Psychology of Worldviews
visible 63
Western 230, 268
worldless xix
worldliness 64
worldly 34,

zōē 62, 64
zōon
   as *logon echon* 121, 242, 255, 308n.
   as *politikon* 83